LIFE

OF

JOHN HENRY STILLING,

DOCTOR OF MEDICINE AND PHILOSOPHY, COURT-COUNSELLOR AND
PROFESSOR OF POLITICAL ECONOMY IN THE UNIVERS-
ITY OF MARBURG IN GERMANY

AND

Author of many religious Works,

TRANSLATED BY

E. L. HAZELIUS, D. D.

Professor of sacred Literature and Church-history in the Theological Seminary
of the General Synod of the Ev. Luth. Church in the U. St.
Gettysburg, Pennsylvania.

GETTYSBURG:

PRINTED AT THE PRESS OF THE THEOL. SEMINARY.

H. C. NEINSTEDT PRINTER
1831.

To

THE REVEREND DANIEL KURTZ, D. D.

Pastor of the German Evangelical Lutheran
Church in Baltimore

THIS TRANSLATION OF STILLING'S LIFE

IS INSCRIBED

BY THE TRANSLATOR

AS A MARK OF HIS FRIENDSHIP AND RESPECT.

TO THE READER.

BEFORE you commence the perusal of this work, permit the translator to say a few words by way of apology for offering you the Biography of a man, whose name has probably never reached your ear. You doubtless know, that Germany ranks among the most enlightened countries of Europe in the different branches of literature, and that it has produced great men in almost every art and science. But from the limited intercourse between the two countries and the difference in language it is impossible, you should be acquainted with the wonderful effect, the life of Stilling produced on its appearance not only in his own country but through the greater part of the continent of Europe. It was the means, during a season of the grossest infidelity, of turning many from darkness to the light of the gospel, and I trust it may produce the same happy effects in this country. Should I be too sanguine in my expectations, should I be disappointed in my hopes, yet if God sees fit to make it the means of saving one soul, I shall feel, I have not labored in vain.—

I remember well the sensation, which the publication of the two first books of Stilling's life created among the reading public in the days of my youth—for the different books of this work were published at long intervals—and though nearly fifty years have elapsed since that period, it is still read with the same interest by the friends of Evangelical religion, and new editions of it are published from time to time.

Should my hopes be realized, and I have the unspeakable happiness of being the humble instrument in the hand of my God and Savior of leading many souls by this means to the knowledge of him, whom to know aright, is life eternal, I shall consider the time and labor spent in this translation as the most pleasing and profitable of my life.

THE TRANSLATOR.

Gettysburg, Oct. 1st 1831.

LIFE

OF

HENRY STILLING.

FIRST BOOK.

Henry Stilling as a child.

—◦●◦—

CHAPTER I.

IN one of the most mountainous parts of Westphalia is a parish, from whose hills the eye enjoys an extensive prospect over a district of country, subdivided into a number of small Lordships and Principalities. The parish village is called Florendorf, but its inhabitants, though farmers in the strictest sense of the word, averse to bearing the simple name of villagers, have claimed an ascendance, from time immemorial, over the peasants of the hamlets in their neighborhood; and the latter have accused the former of pride, in substituting the title of Florenburg for the more humble appellation of Florendorf. Be this as it may, Florenburg enjoys the privilege of having a corporation; whose president in the days of my·childhood was Mr. Ioannes Henricus Scultetus. The rude and the ignorant used to call him Mr. Hannes, when not seated in the chair of office, stately Burghers honoured him with the title of Mr. Shulde.

At the distance of three miles in a south-easterly direction from this borough, is the hamlet of Tiefenbach, whose cottages are scattered along the banks of a brook, which, increased by rivulets from adjacent vallies to the North and South, gradually swells into a narrow, but deep river, rolling its tributary waters, in a westerly direction, towards the Rhine. From the Giller, the highest mountain to the east of Tiefenbach, whose steep sides and summit present to the eye an uninterrupted forest of birchwood,

A

the prospect extends over the valley, delightfully diversified by fields, houses, cottages and meadows, bounded by other high mountains, whose brows and sides are covered with forests of birch and oak, here and there interrupted by a narrow cowpath, or a winding wood-road. The most northerly of these mountains, the Geisenberg, towering to the clouds in the shape of a sugar-loaf, bears on its summit the ruins of an ancient castle, and overhangs the cottage, which pertained to the parents and forefathers of Stilling.

Eberhard Stilling, a venerable man, by occupation a farmer and collier, inhabited this cottage about sixty years ago. During the summer season he was engaged in burning coal in the mountain forests. He usually returned home on Saturdays, to look after his domestic affairs, and to supply himself with provisions for the ensuing week; and on Sunday he accompanied his family to church at Florenburg, where he was a member of the vestry. Such was his mode of living. He was blessed with six children, two sons and four daughters.

One day, as Eberhard was coming down the mountain, on his way homeward, viewing the setting sun, as a suitable emblem of his advanced period in life, and was whistling on a leaf the tune of an evening hymn, his neighbor Stahler, who had been walking faster than Stilling, no doubt unmindful of the setting sun, overtook him and commenced the following conversation:

"Good evening, Ebert!"

"Good evening, neighbor Stahler!" (continuing to whistle.)

"If the weather keeps fair, our wood, we will cut and prepare and I think we'll be able to finish our pit in about three weeks."

"T'is possible."

"I can do no longer, as I used to, neighbor! I am already sixty-eight years of age, and you cant be far from seventy?"

"True enough! Look neighbor! the sun is setting behind yonder mountain! The goodness & the love of God, which he has manifested towards me, fill my heart with joy and gladness. I was just contemplating that subject; t'is evening with us too, neighbor Stahler! the shadows of death rise daily upon us, they will cover us, before we are aware. I cannot but render thanks to divine Providence, for that preservation, protection, and long suffering, which I have experienced all the days of my life."

"That is very possible."

"And I am now waiting without fear for that important moment, when I shall be delivered from this heavy, old and stiff tenement of clay, and shall be enabled to converse, during an everlasting Sabbath, with the spirits of my forefathers, and other holy men. There I shall meet Luther, Oecolampadius, Melancthon, Calvin, Bucerus and many others, of whom our departed minister Winterberg used to say, that they had been the most pious men since the Apostolic age."

"May be!—But tell me Ebert, did you ever see and know all those men, whom you mentioned?"

"How you talk, Stabler, these men died more than two hundred years ago."

"Is it possible!!"

"Now all my children are grown up, they have learnt to read and write, they are able to make their own living, and won't miss me and my Margaret."

"Not miss you? did you say? yes, yes, how easily may children depart from the course of duty, and by marrying into some poor family, bring disgrace upon their relatives, when parents are no longer able to superintend them!"

"I fear none of these things. God be praised, that my superintendence is no longer necessary. By my instruction and example I have implanted such an abhorrence for vice within my children, that I need not be afraid!"

Stahler replied with a loud laugh, "Ebert! you place great confidence in your children, however I think, you'll put your whistle in your pocket, when I shall have told you all I know."

Stilling stopt short, at these words, turned about, and leaning upon his ax-handle, asked him with a smile: "What do you know, Stahler, that would wound my feelings so very much?"

"Have you heard, neighbor Stilling, that your William, the schoolmaster, is about marrying?"

"No, I've heard nothing of it."

"Then I'll tell you, that he means to marry Moritz's the deposed minister's daughter, and they are already engaged."

"It is not true, that they are engaged," replied he, as he turned from Stahler, and continued his way homeward; "but it's possible, he wishes to marry her!"

"Is possible? Ebert, will you give your consent? Will you permit your son to marry a girl so wretchedly poor, as Moritz's daughters are?"

"The children of the honest man never have begged their bread, and suppose, they had, what of that?—But, which daughter is it, Moritz has two, you know?"

"Dorothy."

"With Dorothy I am willing to spend the remainder of my life.—I shall never forget—how once of a Sunday afternoon, she came to my house, brought her father's compliments to me and Margaret, and sat down in silence. I plainly saw, she stood in need of something, but her modesty and bashfulness prevented her from disclosing her wishes, and when I asked her, she merely sighed deeply I gave her four rixdollars, with these words: "I'll lend you this money, till you can conveniently return it."

"You might as well have given her the money as a present at once, for she could never return it."

"That was my intention, but if I had said so, I would have wounded her feelings. "Oh! said she, dearest, best father Stilling," and while she spoke, a gush of tears flowed over her cheeks, "when I see, how my poor old father endeavours to chew his crust of stale bread, and is unable to do it, my very heart bleeds within me." Margaret immediately fetch'd a pot of sweet milk for him, and since that time she sends him milk several times through the week."

"And you will allow William to marry that girl?"

"With all my heart, if it is his wish. Young and healthy people can make their living, and rich folks may loose, what they have."

"You said before, you knew nothing of the matter, and yet you seem to know, that they are not yet engaged?"

"I know that, because William will surely ask me, ere he takes such a step."

"What? He ask you? No! If you expect that, you may wait till doomsday."

"Stahler! I know my William. I have always told my children, that they might marry as rich or as poor as they could or would, and to look in the choice of their wives or husbands only for piety and industry. My Margaret was poor too, and the estate was very much involved; yet God has blessed me, and I can give each of my children one hundred guilders in cash."

"I cannot be so indifferent about these matters, as you are, neighbor! I must know, what I am about, and my children shall marry as I please."

"Every one cuts the garment according to his cloth," replied Stilling, just as he entered his house.

Margaret Stilling had already ordered her daughters to bed. She had placed a piece of pancake in an earthen dish over the hot embers, for her husbands supper. A bowl of milk was ready for him on the kitchenbench, and she began to feel uneasy, about his unusual delay. Just then the door-latch was raised and father Stilling entered. She took the bag from his shoulders, laid the cloth, and brought his supper. "Dear me," said Margaret, "William is'nt here yet. I fear, he has met with some accident. Are there any wolves in the neighborhood?" Where should wolves come from," answered the father, with a laugh; for such was his custom, he often laughed loud, when he was quite alone.

Soon after, the schoolmaster William Stilling entered. Having inquired after the health of his parents, he seated himself on a bench, supporting his head with his hand in a deep reverie, and for some time did not open his lips. At length the mother began: "William, I was afraid, you had met with some misfortune, you stayed so late." William replied: "O mother, there is no danger. Father often observes that a man who follows his lawful calling, has nothing to fear." While he spoke, his face changed colour several times, and it was evident, something pressed heavily on his heart. After a pause he at length stam-

mered out : At Lichthausen lives an old deposed minister, I would
wish, to marry his youngest daughter. If you my parents have no
objection, there will be no other difficulty." "William," answered the father, "you are 23 years old, I have given you learning,
and you have made very good proficiency in it; but you are
lame, and therefore cannot help yourself as well as others in the
world, the girl is poor, and not used to hard labour, how will
you make a living ?" The schoolmaster replied, : "I think, I can
maintain myself by my trade, and for the rest, I trust to Providence, believing, that that God, who feeds the birds of the air,
will likewise provide for me and my Dorothy. "What do you say,
Margaret?" asked the old man.—"Ah, what shall I say, was her
answer," do you remember, what I told you in the days of our
courtship ?—Let us take William and his wife into our house, he
may follow his trade here. . Dorothy will help me and my daughters, as much as she can; she is young, and may yet learn a great
deal. They shall board with us, he will give us his earnings,
and we will provide for both families; and then matters will be
arranged pretty well, in my opinion.—If you think so, answered
the father, he may bring his Dorothy hither.—William ! William ! think of what you are doing, it is no trifling business. May
the God of your fathers bless you and your girl ! William's eyes
were bathed in tears, he pressed the hands of his father and mother, promising them industry and obedience. — Stilling, having
sung his evening hymn, bolted the door with the wooden bolt,
while Margaret looked after the cows, if all were well, after
that both retired.

William had also gone up to his chamber, the only window
of which was still open. He walked to it, looking over the night-
ly landscape. Every thing was then in deep silence, two wake-
ful nightingales excepted, which were alternately warbling their
melodious notes to the midnight air. Their delightful songs reminded William of prayer. He sunk upon his knees. "O God!"
said he, "I thank thee, for the precious gift of kind parents. O !
that I may always be their joy and satisfaction! May I never be
burdensome to them! I give thanks to thee that thou favourest me
with the gift of a virtuous wife! O God! bless me!" Here the sensa-

tion of his heart became too powerful for utterance, he burst into a flood of tears, and prayed in groanings, which are only intelligible to Him who seeth the heart.

Never did any body sleep sounder than the schoolmaster did that night. His joy however waked him in the morning earlier than usual. He left his bed, went out into the forest, and there renewed all the good resolutions, which he ever had formed. At 7 o'clock he returned to the house, to take breakfast with his parents and sisters. Afterwards father Stilling shaved himself, whose example the son followed; the mother in the meantime consulted with her daughters, which of them must stay at home, and who might go to church; this being arranged, those who were to go, dressed for the occasion. When all were ready, the family moved in procession from the cottage; the daughters formed the van, William followed, and father Stilling brought up the rear, supported by his stout haw-thorn cane. Whenever Stilling went out with his children, he made them walk before him, that he might observe their manners, as he used to say, and be able to correct them, if necessary.

After church William returned to Lichthausen, where he kept school and where his elder brother John, who was married, resided. In a house adjoining that of John Stilling Mr. Moritz had rented a couple of rooms, for himself and his two daughters. It was William's duty as schoolmaster, every Sunday in the afternoon to read a sermon in the chapel to the people of the village, and to conclude with the singing of a hymn; this he did likewise on that day, and then hastened as fast as his lameness would permit, to Mr. Moritz lodging. He found the old gentleman seated at his piano, playing and singing a hymn. His morning gown, though covered with patches, was extremely clean. By his side on a chest sat his daughter Dorothy, a girl about 22 years of age, likewise cleanly though poorly dressed, who accompanied her father with her melodious voice. When William entered, she invited him with a smile, to a seat by her side, which he accepted, and assisted them in singing. As soon as the hymn was ended, Mr. Moritz welcomed him and said: "Schoolmaster, I never feel more happy, than when I play and sing. When I was yet in the ministry, I often made the congregation sing a long hymn, because the heart rises as it were, during the singing of so many united voices, above all that is temporal and earthly.—But I must talk of something else with you.—My Dorothy gave me yesterday evening to understand, though with a good deal of stammering, that she loves you, you know, I am poor, what do your parents say?" "They are very well pleased with the match," answered William. Dorothy shed tears of joy on hearing this. The aged father then rose from his seat, took hold of his daughter's right hand, and gave it to William with these words: "I have nothing in the world, but two daughters, this one here I regard as the apple of my eye; take her, son, take her!—May the blessing of Jehovah accompany you, and may you be blessed before him and his saints! yea, may you be blessed before the world! May your children become pious christians, may your posterity be truly great! May they be written in the lamb's book of life!—My whole life has been dedicated to God; I have loved all men ; children! follow my example, and my body shall rest in peace!" Both William and Dorothy kissed his hand, his cheeks and his lips, afterwards each other, for the first time. When all were seated, Mr. Moritz resumed the conversation by asking his daughter: "Dorothy, have you not observed, that your bridegroom is lame?" "Yes, Papa," said she; "I've seen that, but his conversation is always so interesting, and so pious, that I very seldom mind his feet." "But, Dorothy, girls look for all a little after beauty?" "I do too, Papa," was her answer, but William pleases me just as he is. If he had not these crooked feet, he would not be William Stilling, how could I then love him?" The old gentleman smiled at this answer with great satisfaction and said: "Dorothy, you must now make some provision for supper, for your William ought to sup with us." "I have nothing," answered the innocent bride, "except some milk, cheese and bread, and I doubt, if William will be satisfied with such fare?" "Yes," replied William, "I will rather eat a piece of stale bread with you, than the richest milk, wheat hread and pancakes with others." While the two lovers were thus conversing, Mr. Moritz dressed himself in his old brown coat with black buttons, took his cane, which had once been varnished, and said: "I'll go to our nobleman's steward, ask him for the loan of his gun, and see if I can shoot something." This he was in the habit of doing; for when young, he was a great sportsman.

The young couple being now alone, William took Dorothy's hand, and they related what they had felt, said and done, since they loved each other. As soon as they had finished, they began again, by turns enlarging and abbreviating. Thus their conversation was new and interesting to themselves, though to all others it would have been dull and disgusting.

While they were thus engaged, Frederica, Mr. Moritz's eldest daughter interrupted them. As she entered, singing an old ballad, she looked at them with astonishment. "Do I disturb you?" was her first question. "You never disturb me," replied Dorothy, "for I do not mind either what you say or do." "Ah! you are pious," answered Frederica, "but for all that, you seem to be engaged in very interesting conversation with the schoolmaster; however he is pious too".—"And besides that, your brother in law," replied Dorothy, "to day we were betrothed." "O delightful!" "there will be a wedding for me," exclaimed Frederica, skipping back again, and leaving the lovers to themselves. While they were still sitting together, Frederica suddenly rushed again into the room, exclaiming: "yonder they bring father all bloody into the village. Jost the forester, still beats him, and three of the nobleman's servants drag him through the street; they'll surely kill him!" Dorothy gave a loud shriek, & flew out of the house. William hastened after her, but the poor fellow could not proceed as fast as the girls. He called his brother John, and both went together to the place of tumult. They found Moritz sitting in the barroom, his grey hair clotted with blood, the servants & Jost standing round him, cursing, swearing, making fists under his nose and laughing at him; a dead snipe lay on the table. The impartial tavernkeeper supplied them with whiskey. Frederica was engaged pleading with them, to pardon her father, while Dorothy was begging for some whiskey, to wash her father's head; but as she had no money to pay, the loss would have been too great for the tavernkeeper, if he had given her a small glass without remuneration. However as women are constitutionally merciful, the ta-

B

vernkeeper's wife at last gave her a broken dish, which had stood under the spile of the whiskey barrel, and with the whiskey contained in that, Dorothy washed her father's head. Moritz had told the men more than once, that the nobleman had given him permission, to shoot as often as he pleased, but that gentleman was unfortunately from home; Moritz was therefore silent, and made no more excuses. Thus matters stood, when John and William entered. The first thing they beheld, was the tavernkeeper, carefully carrying a glass of whiskey, lest one drop of the precious liquor should be spilt, though this caution was rather needless, the glass lacking one fourth from being full. John gave it a blow with so much force, that it flew out of the landlord's hand against the wall, and fell in fragments on the floor. William immediately took hold of his father's hand, and led him with as much authority out of the room, as though he had been the nobleman himself, but he spoke not a word to any of the people. Jost and the servants threatened, and endeavoured to stop him, pulling sometimes on one side, and sometimes on the other. William took no notice of them, merely intent upon freeing his father in law from their clutches, in which he at length succeeded. John Stilling in the mean time warned Jost and the servants, to beware of what they were doing, and his words failed not to make the desired impression, for all knew, how intimate John was with the nobleman. One circumstance was particularly in their favour on that occasion. The place before the tavern was filled with people from the village, smoking their pipes, intent upon the issue of the contest; Jost and his companions were aware, that a hundred strong arms would be ready for the rescue of Moritz, if any of the peasants should happen to take umbrage at his seizure and consider it as an infringement of their rights; and it must be allowed, that father Stilling and his sons had by their weight of character obtained such an ascendency over the inhabitants of the village, that few ventured a jest in the presence of one of that family. The end of the business was, that Jost lost his place as soon as the nobleman returned, and was sentenced to pay 20 rixdollars damages to Mr. Moritz. The old gentleman was in a few days restored to his usual health, and this disagreeable occcurrence was soon forgotten by the family, because the minds of all were engaged in preparations for the wedding, which father Stilling and his Margaret were determined to have in their own house. They had fattened several fowls for soup, and a fat calf was killed and prepared for roasting; rice for puddings, prunes, raisins and currants were bought in great abundance. Old Stilling informed some of his good friends in confidence, that the expenses for the wedding had cost him near on ten rix-dollars. Be this as it may, every one was in high spirits, and thought little of the expense. William had given holidays to his scholars: for in wedding times it is impossible, to attend to such drudgery as schoolkeeping, besides he had to make clothes for his bride and sisters, and to attend to several other necessary preparations.

At length the long wished for Thursday came. Every one in Stilling's house was wide awake long before sunrise, except the good old father of the family, who had returned the preceding evening late from the forest, and had slept very sound, until it was time to go to church with the wedding people. The family marched in the usual Stilling fashion to Florenburg, where the bride and her friends had already arrived. When the marriage ceremony was over, all returned to Tiefenbach for the wedding dinner. Two long boards supported by some cross-pieces of scantling, served for the table, over which Margaret had spread her finest table linen; the spoons were of maple-wood, worked with roses and other flowers. The handles of the carving knives were of a bright yellow, and the plates were made of the hardest white beech-wood, neatly turned. Handsome white stone-pitchers adorned with blue flowers contained the foaming beer and perry.

Dinner being over, the company indulged in pleasant and interesting conversation. But William and his bride rather preferred a private walk, and therefore left their joyous friends, to ramble along the pleasant banks of the brook. They would have been completely happy, had it not been necessary to make provision for housekeeping, if there had been no such things, as cold frost and wet. Father Stilling and Moritz were enjoying a social glass of beer together, which they spiced with interesting and religious conversation. Eberhard began : "Mr. Moritz,

I have always been of opinion, you would have done better in the world, had you not meddled with Alchimy.

"How do you mean? Mr. Stilling?"

"If you had attended to your business a as watchmaker, you would have been able to make a decent living, but as it now is, your alchimistical experiments have deprived you of your earnings, and what little property you possessed, is likewise lost."

You are right in one sense of the word, and wrong in another. If I had known, that thirty or forty years would pass over my head, ere I could find the philosopher's stone, I would have reflected, before I commenced these experiments. But as experience has given me a deep knowledge of nature, I should be sorry to have laboured so many years in vain.

"Yes, surely have you laboured a long time in vain, for you have hitherto lived on scanty fare. Suppose, you should become ever so rich, yet can you not transform the years of misery, which you have seen, into years of happiness, and more than this, I do not think, you will ever discover that stone, for to give my opinion freely, I do not believe, there is such a thing as the philosopher's stone."

"I can prove that the philosopher's stone is a reality. A certain Dr. Helvetius at the Hague has published a pamphlet, entitled, "the golden calf" in which he plainly demonstrates it to the satisfaction of the greatest sceptic. But it is still very problematical, whether I shall obtain it; that depends on God alone, as it is a free gift from him."

"If it were the will of God, that you should obtain the philosopher's stone, you would have found it long ago. For why should he have withheld it so long from you? And its possession is not necessary to our happiness; for the world has hitherto gone on very well without the philosopher's stone."

"That is very true, but we ought to make ourselves as happy as possible even in this world!"

"To endure a state of wretchedness and misery for thirty years as you have done, is surely no happiness, but—do not take the comparison ill—I have never suffered want, have enjoyed good health for seventy years, and have seen my children advance in knowledge and piety. I am perfectly contented, and therefore happy, I would thank no body for giving me the philosopher's stone. And now, Mr. Moritz, I'll make a proposition to you. You have a fine voice and write an elegant hand. Take the office of schoolmaster in the village, Frederica may go to service. I have yet an empty chamber in the house, where you may place your bed, and live with me and your children."

"Your offer, Mr. Stilling, is noble, and I shall with pleasure accept it, after I shall have made but one more experiment."

"O Mr. Moritz! make no more experiments, they will fail you, as all the former have.—But let us converse on some other subject—I am very fond of Astronomy, do you know the star Sirius in the constellation of the great Dog?"

"I have not studied that science, but I know the star, you mention."

"In the month of February it stands South in the evening. How far do you suppose that star is from the earth? I have heard people say, that it is farther distant from us than the Sun?"

"Yes, doubtless a thousand times farther."

"How is that possible? I am very fond of gazing at the stars. It appears to me, as if I were already there, when I look at them. Do you know the waggon and the plough?"

"Yes, they have been pointed out to me."

"O what a wonderful God!"

Margaret Stilling had been listening to this conversation, seated by the side of her husband; when the latter burst forth into the last mentioned exclamation, she observed: "When I look at the most simple flower, I can see, that God is wonderful. Let us endeavor to comprehend him in that portion of his works! We now live among the grass and the flowers, when we shall get to heaven, we will then admire the stars."

"That is a correct observation," said Moritz, there are many wonders in nature, if we only reflect on them, we shall learn, how wisely the creator has formed all things. But as the works of nature are so various, each one of us selects that part for his contemplation, which excites his attention most. While the old people were thus engaged, Stilling's daughters amused themselves with singing. Thus the wedding day was spent, and William Stilling and his wife commenced housekeeping.

——————

CHAPTER II.

A new era commenced in the family of Eberhard Stilling, when William and Dorothy became its inmates. The important question arose, where shall the new comers sit at table?—To avoid obscurity, I have briefly to mention the table regulations of father Stilling. At the upper end of the room was a stout oaken bench fastened to the wall, reaching behind the stove. Before the bench opposite the stove, was the table, likewise fastened to the wall, in the form of a falling board. Father Stilling had made it himself, from a stout oaken plank. At the upper end and before this table, with his left arm toward the wall, Eberhard had taken his place. On his right hand were seated his four daughters; Margaret's place was at the lower end of the table, opposite the stove, partly, because she liked a warm seat, and partly also, that she might be better able to observe, if any thing were wanting at the table. John's and William's had been behind the table; but the former being married out of the house, and the other absent, their places were now vacant, and after mature reflection were assigned to the new couple. The only interruption to their uniform mode of living, which had hitherto taken place, was, when John Stilling came to see his parents; his visits always brought bustle and joy into the family; for he was a man of a highly respectable character, beloved and esteemed by all the inhabitants of the village. In the early part of his youth he had transformed a wooden plate into an astrolabe, and a wooden butter box into a compass, for the purpose of making geometrical observations. At a time when an engineer was forming a map of the country, by orders of the Prince of Nassau, John Stilling had been an attentive spectator; by application and persevering industry, he had become an excellent surveyor, and was frequently employed by the nobility, in dividing their landed estates. It is the general fault of artists, to be fond of new inventions, and to neglect what they know. John Stilling was consequently poor, for he neglected the business, which would have given him a livelihood, in quest of new inventions. His good wife frequently gave it as her opinion, that her husband would fare better, if he should apply his ingenuity to the melioration of fields and meadows, than in following arts, which brought no bread. But we must pardon the ignorance of the good woman, she did not know better — such was at least John's opinion—for he answered her remonstrances only by a smile of superiority.

At that time he was deeply engaged in studying the quadrature of the circle, and in making experiments, for inventing the perpetual motion. Whenever he supposed to have made some valuable discovery, he would forthwith hasten to Tiefenbach, in order to bring the joyful news to his parents, brother and sisters. When they saw him coming up the village, all the inmates of the house prepared themselves to welcome him at the door. All laboured with redoubled diligence, to get the work out of the way, that after supper they might have leisure to listen. The family seated themselves round the table, in the attitude of the strictest attention. All were eager to add their mite to the discovery of the quadrature of the circle, Eberhard not excepted, and I would wrong the sound sense of that good man, were I to say, he had effected nothing by his meditation. Engaged in his collier business, he employed his leisure moments in reflections on that subject. He measured the circumference of the bottom of his cider barrel with a cord, sawed a piece of board exactly square, and shaved it, until the cord accurately fitted the square. It could not fail under these circumstances, that the square board must equal in size the circle, which formed the bottom of the cider barrel. Eberhard whirled round on one foot, heartily laughing at those learned heads, who make so much ado about so simple an affair, and cheerfully communicated his discovery to John at his next visit.—And we will own the truth—for though father Stilling was not of a satirical disposition, yet in the present case, he was somewhat ironical in his narrative. But the surveyor soon spoiled his joy, by saying: "Father, the question is not, if a joiner could make a square box containing as many bushels of oats, as a barrel, but the question is, first: What is the ratio of the diameter and the periphery of a circle; and then, what ought to be the length of the side of a square, equal to that circle. But in both cases the answer must not deviate the thousandth part of a barley corn from the truth, and you must be able, to prove the truth of your statement, theoretically, by submitting it to the sifting powers of algebraical calculations."

Father Stilling would have been vexed and sorely disappointed, if his joy at the erudition of his son had permitted him to feel any vexation. He therefore only observed, there was no disputing with learned men; smiled, shook his head, and busied himself with cutting splinters from a birch-log for kindling a fire, or lighting a pipe.

Stillings daughters were healthy girls, used to hard work. They took care of the land, which richly rewarded them for their labour in field and garden. But Dorothy had a delicate constitution; she was soon exhausted by bodily exertions, and then she would sigh and weep. Her sisters, though not void of sensibility, could not comprehend how a woman, apparently as stout as themselves, should not be as able to work as they were; however their good nature induced them, to keep it as much as possible from their parents, that Dorothy scarcely earned her living. William observing it, desired his wife to assist him in future at the needle; when this arrangement was made, business went on without interruption or jarring in the family.

One day Mr. Moritz paid a visit to his daughter. Dorothy wept with joy, when she saw him, and wished for once to have the management of the family, that she might treat him with the best, the house afforded. He spent the afternoon with his children, chiefly in religious conversation. He appeared to be much altered; formerly he had always been very cheerful, but now he was dull and melancholy. Towards evening he said: "Children, let us go to Geisenberg castle."—Having reached a beautiful grove of birch-trees, he observed, that he felt himself very much at home under the shade of those trees. "The higher I rise, the freer I breathe; — of late my feelings have been far from comfortable. This will doubtless be the last autumn which I enjoy in this world!" On arriving at the summit of the mountain whence the prospect extends over a large tract of country to the banks of the Rhine, they seated themselves on the green turf leaning against the ruins of the castle walls.

The sun was casting his parting rays over the blue mountains, in an oblique direction towards them. Moritz looked for some time steadfastly and in silence at the image of the sun, his companions likewise viewed the scene without uttering a word. At last he said: "Children! when I depart this life, I have nothing to leave you. You will not miss me. No human being will mourn for me. I have spent a troublesome and useless life, and have made no one happy. "Dorothy and myself will deeply lament your departure."—"Children!" said Moritz, "our propensities frequently lead us into ruin. How useful might I have been in the world, had I not engaged in alchimistical experiments, I might have made my children and myself happy." While he was speaking, he was several times interrupted by his emotion from proceeding.—After a long pause he continued: "Yet I know, that I have acknowledged my fault, repented of it, and am seriously resolved to reform. God is also the father of his erring children!—I think it necessary to impart to you one paternal advice, before I am taken from you; and I entreat you, not to disregard it: Whenever you are about to undertake any thing, reflect, if by so doing you will also benefit others. Should your reason convince you, that this would not be the case, take it for granted, that it is a work without reward; for God only rewards us, when we serve our neighbor.— I have lived poor and despised in the world, and after my death, I shall soon be forgotten; but I trust, I shall find mercy before the throne of God, and be happy."——Soon after, they returned home.—— Father Moritz continued in a melancholy state of mind. He was engaged in making and repairing watches, which business afforded him in his old age, not only the necessaries, but also some of the comforts of life. His leisure hours were spent in visiting the sick and the poor, to comfort them with the consolation of religion, and to pray with them. But his days on earth were numbered; in the course of the succeeding winter he lost him-

C

self in the snow, and his body was not found, till three days after.

Soon after this calamitous event, a discovery of great importance was made in Stilling's family, which gave much joy to all its members. Even father Stilling was rejoicing in the hope of seeing a grandchild, and expected, to sing once more his cradle hymns, and to show his friends, how well he understood the art of education. Henry Stilling was born September the 10th, in the year 1740. He was a fine healthy child, his mother likewise recovered, in spite of the evil omens and prognostications of the Sibyls of Tiefenbach.

The child received the ordinance of baptism in the church of Florenburg, and Father Stilling prepared a christening feast, to which parson Stolbine was invited. For this purpose John was sent to the Parsonage. In approaching the house, he remembered, that the minister was a great stickler for ceremonies, and therefore had his hat under his arm, as soon as he entered the court-yard, lest he should prove unsuccessful in his mission. But alas! how useless is frequently all human foresight! The large house dog attacked him, and John unluckily picked up a stone, and hit him in his side, so that he began to howl most pitiously. The parson, who had seen the whole transaction from the window, rushed out of the house in a violent passion, shook his fist at poor John, and exclaimed: "You rascal, I'll teach you, how to treat my dog!" John replied: "I beg your pardon, I did not know, that the dog belonged to your Reverence. I came, to ask your Reverence, in the name of my brother and parents, to go with me to Tiefenbach, to honor them with your presence at the christening feast."—The parson walked back into the house, without saying either yes or no. However, when he had reached the door, he turned half round, muttering: "Wait, I'll go along." John waited nearly an hour in the yard, endeavouring to pacify and coax the dog, in which he by far better succeeded, than in gaining the good will of the learned parson, who however at length made his appearance. He stepped forward, in the consciousness of his dignity, supported by his cane. John followed him trembling, his hat under his arm, having learned from sad experience, how dangerous it was to wear a hat in his worship's presence; for Mr. Stolbine had frequently given him in former years a box on his ear, when he had forgotten to pull off his hat as soon as he appeared in sight. But in walking along, John found it an unpleasant task, to be exposed for an hour, to the burning rays of the sun, on a warm September day, and he was thinking of some excuse to cover his head, without offense to Mr. Stolbine. While he was engaged in maturing his plan, the parson suddenly stumbled and fell so hard on the ground, that it shook. John was frightened. — He approached the minister with these words: "I hope, your Reverence has received no injury?" "What is that to you, scoundrel?" replied Stolbine, as he was endeavouring to rise. At this John's temper became likewise somewhat irritated, and he said in a sarcastic tone: "Well, then I am very glad, you did fall." "What! What!" exclaimed Stolbine. But John fearlessly covered his head, going on his way, without minding the roaring of the lion. The parson likewise stepped briskly forward, and thus they both soon arrived at Tiefenbach.

Father Stilling stood uncovered before his door, his venerable grey locks glistening in the rays of the moon. "I rejoice," said he, smiling, to the minister, as he cordially shook his hand, "that I shall have the satisfaction, of seeing your Reverence in my old age at my table; but scarcely would I have been so bold, as to give you the invitation, if my joy at the birth of a grand-son had not been so great." The Parson congratulated him on this happy event, adding however in a very serious tone, that he ought to educate his children better, than he had hitherto done, unless he wished, that the curse of Eli should fall upon his head. The old gentleman received this rebuke in silence, with a conscious smile, of having performed his duty in that respect. When Stolbine had entered the room, he looked at the guests and observed: "I hope, you do not wish me to eat among this crowd of peasants?" Father Stilling answered: "Nobody shall eat here, but myself and my children, do you take us for a crowd of peasants?" "For what else shall I take you?" replied the minister. "Then I must tell you," answered

Stilling, "you are no servant of Christ, but a Pharisee. The Redeemer sat down to meat with publicans and sinners; he was always humble and lowly minded. Your Reverence!—my grey hair is rising on my head, sit down or return home, as you please. "Here," laying his hand on his heart, here is a monitor, or else I might disregard your uniform, for which I always have entertained respect.—Sir! some time ago our prince rode past my house, as I was standing yonder before my door; he knew me, and said: Good morning, Stilling! I answered: Good morning, Your Highness! He dismounted, for he was tired with the chase. Fetch me a chair, said he, that I may rest a little while. I have an airy room, was my reply, if your highness pleases, let us walk in, you will be more comfortable there. "Very well, I will," said he. He and the officer who was in his company, entered; yonder he sat, where I have placed my best chair for you. Margaret brought him sweet milk, with white bread and butter. He desired us, to eat with him, and assured us, that he had never taken a meal with a better appetite, than this. In a neat and cleanly house any man may eat with satisfaction. Take your choice now, your Reverence, will you, or will you not eat?—We all are hungry."—Stolbine sat down, without speaking a word. Stilling then called his wife and children, but they would not come. Margaret filled an earthen dish with chicken broth for the minister, put some meat and sauce on a plate, and placed a mug of beer before him. Father Stilling waited upon him, Stolbine ate and drank without saying a word, and as soon as he had finished his meal, returned to Florenburg. When he had departed, the whole family surrounded the festive board. Margaret pronounced the benediction, Dorothy had taken her mother's place at the table, with her infant at the breast, and mother Margaret made the hostess for that day. She was dressed for the occasion in a short gown and petticoat of fine black cloth; from under the cap her honorable grey locks were visible, powdered with age. It may appear strange, but nevertheless it was so, that not a word was said about Mr. Stolbine; I suppose, the only reason was, because father Stilling did not lead the conversation to that subject. While they were at dinner, a poor woman with an infant tied in a cloth to her back, knocked at the door, asking for a piece of bread. She was dressed in ragged, dirty clothes, though fashionably made. Father Stilling ordered a portion of the christening dinner to be given her, and a piece of the rice pudding to her child. Having eaten heartily of what she had received, she prepared to depart. But father Stilling requested her, to state her circumstances to the family. She was very willing to do so, and having taken a seat near Mary Stilling, commenced with the following observation: "A few years ago, you folks would have thought it a great honor, had I accepted an invitation to dine with you!"

W. Stilling. "Is it possible!"

J. St. I have no doubt of it, if your disposition had been similar to that of Parson Stolbine.

Father Stilling. Hush, children! let the woman tell her story!

"My father is pastor at——

Mary. "Dear me! your father a minister?" (she moves nearer towards her.)

"Yes, to be sure a minister. He is a very learned and rich man."

J. Still. Where is he minister?

"At Goldingen."

J. Still. "I must look for that place on the map. It can't be far from the Muhler lake, towards Septentrio."

"O my dear young gentleman, I am not acquainted with any place near by, called Santander!"

Mary. "Our John did not say Santander. How did you say?

F. Still. Hush, children! Do you continue.

"I was at that time a handsome girl, and had many fair offers for marrying, (Mary viewed her from head to foot.) but no match pleased my father. One was not rich enough, another one of too low an extraction, and a third did not go to church."

Mary. "John, tell me, how those people are called, who do not go to church?"

J. Still. Be still Sis!—Separatists.—

"Well, I plainly perceived, I would never have a husband,

unless I endeavoured to get one myself. A young journeyman barber—"

Mary. "What is a journeyman barber?"

W. Still. "Be still, Sister! you may afterwards ask any question you please, only let the woman now go on.—Barbers are persons, who shave people."

"I beg your pardon, Sir! My husband performed cures like the best of Doctors; yes, many, many cures did he perform. In short, I ran away with him. We settled at Spelterburg, on the Spa river."

J. Still. "Yes, that is true, a couple of miles up the river, where the Milder falls into it."

"Yes, that is the place. O what an unhappy woman am I! For I soon perceived, my husband was connected with certain people, whom I did not like."

Mary. "Who had married you?"

"Why, who would have married us—we were not yet married." (At these words Mary removed her chair a little farther off from the woman.) "I would not allow, that my husband should have any connection with thieves, for though my father was but a cobler."— Here the woman flung her child on her back, and rushed out of the house, as fast as she could run.

Neither father Stilling nor the family could comprehend, for what cause the woman broke off in the midst of her narrative, and ran away. All gave their opinions on the case, and at length they agreed, it was likely, that the woman had become suddenly ill, from eating a hearty dinner, to which she was not accustomed. Father Stilling drew this inference from the narrative, agreable to his custom, that it was highly necessary, to implant a love for religion and virtue into the hearts of children, and afterwards, when they have attained a suitable age, to give them a free choice in the selection of a companion, provided they do not disgrace the family. He observed, that parents ought indeed to admonish their children on such occasions, but no compulsion ought to be used; when a person has reached the age of manhood, he thinks, he knows what is right, as well as his parents.

While father Stilling made these observations, William was

musing, his head resting on his hand. When he had ceased, William said: "Every thing the woman has mentioned, appears to me doubtful. In the beginning she said, her father had been minister at——at——"

Mary. "At Goldingen."

"Yes, that was it. And at last she said, he had been a cobler." All present clapt their hands together with astonishment, they now discovered the cause of her sudden flight, and it was resolved, carefully to close every door and opening in the house; and I suppose the reader will not blame Stilling's family for taking that precaution.

Dorothy had not spoken a word while this scene was passing. If the reader ask me the reason, I must acknowledge my ignorance. She had been wholly engrossed in nursing her Henry, whom she was regarding with the most tender affection; and indeed, he was a fine hearty child. The neighbor women, who pretended great skill in the discovery of likenesses, were unanimously of opinion, that he bore a striking resemblance to his father, and fancied, they discovered the traces of a wart on the upper eyelid of the left eye, exactly as his father was marked in the same place. But some inexplicable partiality must have deceived all these good women; for the boy posessed and retained the traits of his mother's countenance, and her tender feeling heart.

By and by Dorothy fell into a quiet, placid melancholy. She appeared to take no interest in any thing, which occurred in the family. She seemed to enjoy herself in her sadness, her heart was as if melted into tears, but tears void of grief and sorrow. When the sun rose in full splendor, she pensively viewed the king of day, tears rolled down her cheeks, and sometimes she would say: "What splendor must he posess, who has created thee!" When the sun departed, she again wept, and frequently burst forth in expressions like these: "Yonder departs that consoling friend again!" and longed to be far away in the woods, at the time of twilight. Nothing however excited her sensibility more, than the moon; her feelings were at such times ineffable, and she spent whole evenings, in walking about at the foot of the Geisenberg. William was generally her companion in these rambles, and endeavoured to sooth her mind. His character in some respects resembled hers; they would not have missed the world, provided they could have enjoyed each others company, but not withstanding this, they deeply felt for the woe and misery of their fellow creatures.

When Henry Stilling was about a year and a half old, Dorothy desired her husband, one Sunday afternoon, to take a walk with her to Geisenberg castle. William, who had never yet refused to comply with her requests, consented. Arm in arm they walked slowly up the mountain, through the forest, amidst the warbling of various birds, while Dorothy commenced the following conversation:

"Do you think, William, we shall know each other again in heaven?"

"Most assuredly, my dear Dorothy, for doth not Christ say of the rich man, that he recognized Lazarus in the bosom of Abraham, and yet this rich man was in hell, therefore I certainly believe, that we shall know each other in eternity."

"O my William! how doth my heart rejoice, when I reflect, that, if your opinion is correct, we shall be forever united without grief and sorrow, in the full enjoyment of every heavenly blessing. And it has always appeared to me, as if I could not be happy without you in heaven. Yes, dear William! we shall surely know each other in that place of happiness. Has not God created my soul, and given me that heart, which entertains these wishes, and would he have made it thus, were I to cherish wrong desires? Yes, I shall seek you, among the thousands of redeemed spirits, I shall recognize you, and then I shall be truly happy!"

"We will be buried side by side, there will then be no need of seeking long!"

"Ah! if we could but die in one and the same moment!— But, what would in that case become of my sweet little boy?"

"Your son would stay here, and receive a religious education, and at last meet us again in heaven."

"But in the mean time I should be much troubled, and entertain many doubts about his piety, which would destroy my happiness."

"My dear Dorothy! you have been exceedingly melancholy for a long time, and if I shall speak with candor, I must own, that by such conduct you afflict me as well as yourself. Why do you always shun the company of my sisters? The poor girls believe, you do not love them!"

"But I do love them dearly."

"You frequently shed tears, which seems to indicate, you are dissatisfied with something or other, and this thought greatly afflicts me. Is there any thing on your mind, my dear, that gives you pain? Speak freely. If there is a possibility, I will endeavor to remove the difficulty."

"O no! I am by no means dissatisfied; I am not discontented, my dear William! I love you, I love our parents and our sisters, and I wish well to the whole human family. But I'll endeavor to explain my feelings to you. In the spring, when I see every thing flourishing, when I see the unfolding of the leaves of the trees, the opening of the flowers, the growth of the grass, it appears to me, as though I had no share nor interest in all this, and as though I were alone in the world, and did not belong to it. But no sooner do I discover a faded leaf, a withered flower, or a dry blade of grass, I feel a pleasing melancholy, but cheerfulness seems to have departed from me. In former times all these things would have affected my mind very differently, I was then never more cheerful than in the spring."

"I for my part am unacquainted with such sensations, though I must say, that the description you give of your feelings, deeply excites my sympathy."

During this conversation they arrived at the ruins of the castle, and observed, how the cool wind from the Rhine was playing with and whistling through the long dry grass-stalks and leaves of ivy, growing on and about its broken walls. This is my favourite place, said Dorothy, here I should like to dwell. Pray, tell me once more the story of John Hubner, who in times of yore lived in this castle. But let us take our seats yonder on the ramparts, opposite the walls. For the world I would not be within the ruins, when you tell the story; my blood runs cold, as I listen. William related as follows:

D

"In times of old, robbers lived in this castle. John Hubner was the last of them. He always wore a coat of mail, and was stronger in body, than any other fellow in the country. He had but one eye, and a thick frizzled beard. During the day he and his band, all of whom were stout men, generally drank beer in that part of the castle, where you see yonder broken window. Whenever they spied some person on horseback or in a vehicle, they pursued him, and if they caught him, they never spared his life. The horses and other property they sold at a great distance from this place."

"A certain prince of Nassau Dillenburg, named "the black Christian" hearing many complaints from the country people, of the murders and robberies which Hubner had committed, sent one of his men Hannes Flick, into this part of the country, to watch him. The prince was lying in ambuscade behind the Giller, which you see yonder. Flick had never seen Hubner, but was riding through the country, with a view of obtaining intelligence concerning him. One day he came to a blacksmith shop, where they were shoeing horses. A number of waggon wheels were set up against the shop, on which a man was leaning, who answered the description of Hubner. Flick stopt and asked him: Are you John Hubner of Geisenberg? The man replied: John Hubner of Geisenberg lies on the wheel. Flick, supposed the man meant to intimate, that Hubner had been executed, and therefore asked, did that happen lately? Yes, said the man, this very day. Flick not being altogether satisfied, continued to watch the fellow, who remained in the same position. When he perceived, that Flick would not go away, he whispered in the blacksmith's ears, to turn the shoes of his horse the wrong way. When the smith had done it, the man mounted his horse and rode off. Flick followed, with an intention of tracking him, but this was almost impossible, because all the tracks went backwards. However at last he discovered him in the forest, guarding several horses, that were browsing among the bushes. The moon shone bright. Flick hastened to prince Christian with the report, that he had found the robber. Before the Prince and his men went in quest of Hubner, he ordered them to tie grass about the feet of the

horses, so that the clatter of their hoofs might not betray their
approach. By this means they were enabled to come so close
to Hubner and his men, that they were unable to escape. John
fought for some time most desperately, but at length fell under the battle-ax of the prince. They buried him in yonder
corner: Geissenberg was taken. Prince Christian ordered the
foundation of the tower to be undermined. It fell at evening tide,
and the shock was so great, that the ground trembled in the hamlet of Tiefenbach. There down this mountain you see a heap of
rubbish, which is a remnant of the stones and lime, with which the
turret was built. Hubner, they say, shows himself frequently between eleven and twelve o'clock at night; our neighbor Neuser
believes, he has seen him often riding round the rampart."

While William was telling the story, Dorothy was starting
at the rustling of every bird among the bushes. When he had
finished, she said: "I am so fond of such stories, that I never tire
with the repetition. While they were walking round the ramparts, and Dorothy was singing an old ballad, the sun was setting, and William and his wife had in full measure tasted the
sweets of melancholy. As they were descending the mountain,
Dorothy was attacked by a violent paroxysm of fever, and was
scarcely able to reach Stilling's dwelling. It turned out to be an
inflamatory fever.

William nursed her day and night. One day, about a fortnight from the commencement of her illness, towards twelve
o'clock at night, she said to William: "Wo'nt you lie down a
while?" He undressed, and lay by her side. She embraced him with
her right arm, while his head was leaning against her bosom. All
at once he perceived, that her pulse was intermitting. With a heart
full of anguish he called for his sister. Soon the whole family came into William's chamber. But she was gone—she had
departed! — William's feelings were blunted for the moment,
and he wished, never to recover them so as to be fully sensible of
his loss; but at length he left the bed, mourned and lamented.
Father Stilling and mother Margaret were likewise deeply affected. It was a sad sight, to see the old couple looking at the
departed saint, while tears of grief were rolling down their aged

cheeks. The girls too were weeping, at the recollection of the last affectionate expressions of their departed sister.

CHAPTER III.

William Stilling had lived with his Dorothy in a very populous part of the country quite secluded; after she was dead and buried, he found himself, as it were, alone in the world. Though in the same house with his parents and sisters, he hardly noticed them. He was constantly tracing Dorothy's lineaments, in the face of his motherless child, and when he went to rest at night, his chamber appeared to him deserted and lonesome. He frequently fancied, he heard the sound of Dorothy's footstep, as though she were coming to bed. He often reflected on the time, which he had spent with her, from the day of his marriage to the moment of her death, every portion of which seemed to him, to have been spent in unalloyed happiness, and he wondered, that in the fulness of his enjoyment, he had not broken out in ecstatic exclamations of joy. In such moments he would clasp his Henry to his heart, bedew him with his tears, and fall asleep with him in his arms. While slumbering, he frequently dreamt of walking in the forest, adjoining to Geissenberg castle, accompanied by Dorothy, rejoiced at having found her again. During his dreams he was afraid of having his illusory happiness dispelled, by awaking from his sleep, and when he awoke, being disappointed, he shed a torrent of tears, and the state of his mind was truly deplorable. Father Stilling observed all this, without making a single effort to comfort William. Margaret and the girls attempted it frequently, though without the desired effect. For he was offended at every effort made to dispel his gloom. Mother and daughters often conversed on that subject, wondering, that father Stilling made no attempt to console him, and they resolved, to speak with father on the subject, as soon as William should again fall into one of his violent paroxysms of melancholy, wandering about in the Geissenberg forest, in search for some spot, where Dorothy had either stood or sat, with the view of indulging his gloom. They had not to watch long for such an opportunity. Margaret had taken it upon herself, to open the conversation, immediately after the removal of the cloth, when William was gone, and father Stilling was engaged in picking his teeth, and in meditation, according to his usual custom after dinner. "Eberhart!" said she, "why do you suffer our boy to wander about in this fashion? You seem not to care for him at all, you speak not one friendly word with him, but act, as if he were a total stranger to you. The poor fellow will surely fall into a consumption at this rate." Father Stilling answered with a smile: "Margaret! what do you suppose, I could say, that would comfort him? If I say, he should be resigned; Dorothy is in heaven, she is happy; that would be, as if somebody had taken your all in the world, and I should tell you: Be not uneasy, your treasure is in excellent hands, in about sixty or seventy years you shall have it all back again. Would you not be very angry with me, would you not say : but how shall I live these sixty or seventy years to come? Or do you suppose, I shall mention all Dorothy's faults, and endeavour to persuade him, that his loss has not been so irretrievable? In that case I would do injustice to her memory ; my conscience would reprove me, and after all, the only effect I could produce, would be, that William would ever afterwards entertain hostile feelings towards me; he would on his part recount all Dorothy's virtues, and I would fall short in my account. Or shall I search for another Dorothy? No — for even, if such a one could be found, he would not believe it. But alas! there is no Dorothy any more!" While he spoke these last words, his lips quivered, and his eyes were suffused with tears. The whole family shed tears also, but principally, because they saw father Stilling weep.

Under these circumstances William was unable to make a living for himself, much less take care of his child. Margaret therefore took her grandson under her own charge. The girls taught him to walk, to pray, and devoutly to recite hymns ; and when father Stilling returned from the mountain on Saturday evenings, and had taken his seat near the stove, little Henry would totter up to him, and attempt climbing on his grand father's knees. Sometimes the old man would give him a piece of bread and butter, a remnant of his last provisions, or Henry would himself examine the wallet, and search for the remaining crumbs, which, stale and air-dried as they were, tasted better to him, than the most delicious rice pudding would to other children. While he was thus occupied on his grandfather's lap, the latter would sing a little song for his Henry, for instance: "Gerberly was called my chicken dear" &c. or: "As riders and horsemen we trot now along:" &c. imitating at the same time with his knees the motion of a trotting horse. In short, Stilling was so complete a master in the art of education, that he always found some new diversion for Henry, adapted to his age, and of such a character, that every thing, which ought to be venerable to man, was also represented to him, as great and excellent. Such treatment could not fail of making a deep and lasting impression upon Henry; and his love for his Grandfather formed the most prominent feature in his character, and therefore, whatever the old man wished to teach him, Henry gladly received, learnt and retained ; for he believed without hesitation, all that grandfather said.

The deep though silent grief of William, which we have noticed before, was now gradually changing into a communicative and talkative sadness. He became willing to see company, spoke friendly with his housemates, conversed with them about Dorothy, sung with them her songs and ballads, and looked at her clothes. It was his heart's delight, to call Dorothy to his remembrance; and when he reflected, that in a few fleeting years, he likewise should be called out of this world, and become an inhabitant of those blissful regions, which now contained his beloved Dorothy; and that in her society he would enjoy happiness without fear of diminution; his bosom felt an inward peace, which transported him far beyond the troubles of this sublinary world, and produced a total change in his views and actions: though the acquaintance of a singular and extraordinary man, which he made about that time, contributed its share, in effecting the change, we have alluded to. This man, named Niclas belonged to a society of pious people, who had rented a castle from a certain count, six or eight miles distant from Tiefenbach, and had established a manufactory of silk stuffs, by which means they made their living. Neither the wise men of the world, nor the fashionable, liked the institutions of the society. Because it is unfashionable in the great world, publicly to profess the intention of following the Lord Jesus Christ, or to hold conversations for the avowed purpose, of encouraging one another in the obedience to his doctrines, and in following his example, the members of this society, were despised by the world, and there were men, who pretended to have been eye witnesses of every kind of wickedness and abomination, committed by these people; rumors, which being but too readily believed, had a tendency to increase the scorn, they had to bear. But what vexed people most, was, that the members of this society were rejoicing in the shame, cast upon them, and that they said, their Lord and Master had fared no better. Niclas, as we have mentioned, belonged to that society. In the days of his youth he had studied Theology; but having discovered defects in all the professed systems of religion, and publicly spoken and written against them, he had been cast into prison, and after liberation from confinement, had travelled with a certain gentleman through several countries of Europe. After his return he had joined the above mentioned society, and having no knowledge of the business, in which they were engaged, pedled their goods through the country. He had frequently been at Stilling's house, but knowing how rigidly that family adhered to the system and the principles of the reformed religion, had never entered into conversation on disputed subjects; but about the time, when William Stilling began to shake off his dark and gloomy melancholy, he found an opportunity of conversing with him. This conversation is important, and therefore I shall give it, as Niclas himself has reported it to me. After he had taken a seat, he said:

"How do you do to day, Mr. Stilling! has the grief, you experienced at the loss of your wife, subsided in some measure?"

"I am still very low spirited; my heart still bleeds with the wound, though I am rather more comfortable, than I have been."

"We all will feel a similar depression of spirits, if we attach ourselves too much to any temporal object. I acknowledge we are happier, if we have a good wife, than if we have none. But it is often beneficial, to deny ourselves this satisfaction, and we are then not exposed to so severe a loss."

"That is easier said, than performed, Mr. Niclas!"

Niclas answered with a smile: "I allow it to be difficult, especially if a man has been so highly blessed, as you have been; but if we are only seriously determined on it, it may be effected; and if we believe, that the doctrine of Jesus Christ directs us to the attainment of the highest happiness, we will form that determination, and find, that the execution of our resolution is not so very difficult, as we otherwise would imagine. Permit me, to explain this briefly to you. Christ has left us a doctrine, which is so completely adapted to the nature of our souls, that it cannot fail in making us happy, provided we follow and obey it. If we examine the doctrines of the wise men of this world, we will observe a variety of rules, which are as consistent with each other, as the system, from which they are derived, is consistent with itself. Sometimes they go lame, at another time they run, and then again stand stock still. The religion of Jesus Christ alone, drawn from the deepest mysteries of human nature, is wanting in no point, it irrevocably proves to all, who rightly understand it, that its author is no other, but the creator of man, because he alone has a perfect knowledge of man. All human beings have an insatiable desire for such pleasures, as are capable of satisfying their minds, and prove a never failing spring of fresh delights. In the visible creation we find nothing of this kind. If by a change of circumstances, we loose those pleasures, which this world can give, we experience a painful sensation, such, as for instance, you have felt, at the loss of your Dorothy. The divine lawgiver knew, that the principle of every human action is genuine self love. Far from condemning this principle, which is capable of doing much injury, if wrongfully applied, he merely gives us rules to refine and ennoble it. He commands us, to do unto others, as we wish, that others should do unto us. If we act in conformity to this precept, we are sure of the good will of our fellow men, provided, they do not belong to that class, which even the world calls malignant and wicked. He commands us, to love our enemies; if we live in conformity to this precept, and act kindly toward those, who entertain hostile feelings against us, they can have no peace, until they become reconciled to us, while we enjoy an inward peace in the exercise of these duties, which far surpasses every sensual & earthly pleasure. Further, if we search for the true source of what are called social vices, for instance, of envy, malice and disturbance of peace in society, we shall find it in the pride of man. The laws of Jesus Christ are the surest remedy against this root of all evil. At present I do not wish to explain myself more fully on this subject, I merely purpose showing you, that it is worth our while, to use all diligence, in following the doctrines of Christ, which offer us a real satisfaction and durable pleasures, the enjoyment of which will solace us in the loss of others."

"Friend Niclas! will you please to repeat what you now have said, that I may put it down in writing; for, I believe, what you say, is true?"

Niclas was very willing to comply with the wishes of William Stilling, who carefully noted, what the former dictated.

"But," continued William, "if we are made happy by obeying the doctrines of Christ, what benefit can we derive from his life and death? Do not the ministers teach us, we are unable to keep the commandments, and can obtain salvation only through faith in Christ, and through his merits, justification before God.

Niclas replied with a smile: "On that subject we may converse another time. For the present it is sufficient, to make this remark: as Christ has shewn us by his pure and holy life, what our lives ought to be, so that we obtain confidence by a look of faith towards him, and trust the grace, which watches over us, for obtaining that simplicity of heart, and childlike disposition, which may enable us to overcome every difficulty, so has he likewise planted his cross into the night of death, where the sun is set, and where the moon looses her light, that we may look up to it, and exclaim in humble hope: Lord! Remember me!

E

Thus we are saved by his merits, for he has merited the deliverance of his people from eternal death by the severest sufferings, and thus we are likewise saved by faith; for faith is salvation. However at present do not trouble your mind about any of these things, only be faithful in small things, for should you disregard the day of small things, you will effect nothing in weightier matters. I shall leave a tract with you translated from the French of the Archbishop Fenelon; it treats of the faithfulness in small things; the next time I come, I'll bring you Thomas a Kempis' "Imitation of Jesus Christ," and from that book you will receive farther instruction."

It would be difficult to determine, whether William adopted these doctrines, because he was convinced of their truth, or whether the condition of his mind was such, that their plausibility made a deep impression upon it, without more fully examining their truth. For my part I must acknowledge, that by calmly reflecting on the doctrines of Niclas, I observe some things, which are rather obscure, but on the whole, they are correct.

William bought several ells of cloth from 'Niclas, without needing it; and the good preacher went away with devout feelings of gratitude to God, for the conversion of William, and on departing, gladly promised soon to return. About that time, a change had taken place in the family; aunt Elisabeth had married a taylor by the name of Simon; and as William was strongly inclined to avoid the noise and bustle of the world as much as possible, he moved with Henry to a chamber in the upper loft of the house, where he lived for many years, maintaining himself by his trade, and spending his leisure moments in reading those practical works, which Niclas had recommended to him; but Simon took his place in the family. In this solitary mode of living, he endeavored to suppress every inclination of his heart, which had not eternity in view, and to educate his son in those principles, which he believed to be correct and scriptural. He was accustomed to rise early at four o'clock in the morning, worked at his trade till seven; then awoke Henry, reminding him in a feeling manner of the goodness of the

Lord, and of the protecting care he exercises over us by the ministry of his holy angels. "Return your thanks unto him, for all his mercies, my child!" said William, while he was dressing him. This being done, Henry was sent down to wash himself, and after his return, the father would bolt the door of the chamber, kneel down with him, and often pray to God with such fervor, that the tears of devotion became visible on the floor. After prayers, he breakfasted, and Henry was taught to take this as well as every other meal, with as much order and regularity, as if in the presence of a person, to whom he owed the highest respect. Breakfast being over, he had to memorize a portion of his catechism; when this was accomplished, he was permitted to enjoy himself in the reading of some book, which he could understand, and the contents of which were adapted to the capacity of boys of his age, for instance: "the Emperor Octavianus with his wife and children;" "the story of the four Haymon's children;" "the beautiful Melusina;" and such like books. His father never permitted him to play with other children, but kept him so secluded from all company, that at the age of seven years, he was unacquainted with any of the village boys, but had read a number of good books. Hence his whole soul was living in an ideal world, and the powers of his imagination were greatly enlarged. The heroes of old romances, whose virtues were drawn in strong and lively colours, were imperceptibly engraven on his heart, as the only objects worthy of imitation, and he held vice of every description in the greatest aversion; but as his father frequently conversed with him about God and pious men, his views of the piety and virtue of others as well as of their contrary vices, were regulated by the sentiments, they entertained of God and of Christ. Therefore he could scarcely cease reading, after he had obtained the loan of "Godfrey Arnold's lives of the fathers;" this work, and "Ritze's history of the regenerated" were his favorite authors, until he was ten years old; and the characters of those persons, whose lives he read at that time, remained so indelibly engraven on his mind, and idealized in his imagination, that he has never forgotten them. In the afternoon from two to three o'clock and sometimes a little later, William permitted Henry to take a walk in the orchard and the Geisenberg forest, in which he had marked out a district for him, within which he was permitted to ramble, and beyond which he was not allowed to go, unaccompanied by his father. Henry's range extended as far into the woods, as his father could see from his window, when the hour was past, or if another child approached him, William's whistle immediately recalled him to the house.

This district was therefore visited by Henry, as often as the state of the weather would permit; and he had formed the whole into an ideal landscape. In one place he had imagined an Egyptian desert, in which he transformed a bush into a cave, with a view to represent St. Anthony, and in his paroxysms of enthusiasm, he would often pray with great fervor. In another part was the well of Melusina; here was Turkey, where the Sultan and his daughter, the beautiful Marcebilla lived; on yonder rock was the castle of Montalban, where Rinold dwelt; &c. These places were visited by him, as often as he had permission to ramble through the forest, with pleasure indescribable, but unintelligible to all, whose powers of imagination are not equally lively on similar subjects. When he was engaged in these mental sports, his Spirit was overflowing, he would stammer rhymes, which sometimes contained really poetic ideas. Such was his education, until he entered into his tenth year. One circumstance in regard to Henry Stilling deserves particularly the attention of the reader. William was not an indulgent father, and the slightest transgression of his orders, was most severely punished. Hence an artificial reserve was added to his naturally timid disposition, so that he attempted to conceal his failings from fear of punishment, and was gradually led into a confirmed habit of lying, which afterwards cost him many severe struggles before he could overcome it. William's intention was, to train his son to obedience, and to make him tractable, and capable of keeping the divine and human laws, and he believed, severity to be the surest method of attaining so desirable an end; he could therefore not comprehend, how it was possible, that the happiness, he enjoyed in the good qualities of his son, should be marred by the vice of lying. He therefore increased his severity, especially, when he had detected him in an untruth, but all he effected by this mode of proceeding, was, to make Henry more artful, to invent plausible stories, and poor William was deceived after all; and as soon as Henry perceived, that his cunning had saved him from punishment, he was rejoiced, and became determined to try the same method again.

CHAPTER IV.

Father Stilling was a quiet spectator of these proceedings. He did not pronounce judgment against the austere way of living, which his son had adopted, and merely smiled, with a shake of his grey locks, when he saw William seize the rod, whenever Henry had eaten or done any thing contrary to his orders. Sometimes, when the child was absent, he would say to William: "If we do not wish, to see our regulations frequently neglected and disobeyed, we ought rather to be sparing in giving orders, for all men love liberty."—"True," was generally William's answer, "but then he will become obstinate." Father Stilling replied: "Warn him against errors, when you find, he is on the point of doing a wrong thing, and tell him your reason, why you disapprove of one action or another; but if you publish as it were, a whole code of laws before hand, the child will forget them, be always in fault, and you must be as good as your word, and thus whippings will become the order of the day." William acknowledged the correctness of this observation, suffered the many laws to fall gradually into oblivion, and did no more reign so much by rule and line, but rather as a patriarch issuing his orders, whenever he found it necessary; the child of course received fewer chastisements, breathed much freer, and enjoyed himself by far better.

Such was the education of Henry Stilling; he grew up without having any intercourse with other children, knew therefore nothing of the world, nothing of vices, if we except a pernicious disposition of telling falsehoods, that he might screen himself from punishment, otherwise he was communicative, and free from that volatile disposition so generally observed in children. His daily occupations were, to pray, to read and write; the stock of his mind was therefore not extensive, but what he posessed, was so distinct, so clear, so refined and ennobled, that his expressions, phraseology and actions were altogether uncommon for his age. The whole family were amazed, and father Stilling often said: "This boy's feathers grow larger than those of any body else in our connection, he will fly above us, we ought to pray, that God may direct him by his good Spirit." All the neighbors, that saw the boy, were lost in wonder, for they comprehended nothing of all he said, though he spoke the German language correctly. One day Stahler came into the house for the ostensible purpose of having a jacket made by William, but his chief aim appeared to be, to find a husband for his daughter Mary; for father Stilling was highly respected by all the inhabitants of the village, and William was known as a pious and industrious man. Henry was at that time about eight years of age ; and when Stahler entered, was seated in a chair, deeply engaged in reading. Stahler looked at him with astonishment, and asked him : "Henry what are you doing there ?"

"I read."

"What ! can you read already?"

Henry looked at him with surprise and replied: "That is a foolish question, for what human being cannot read, or do you suppose, I do not belong to the class of human beings ?" Having said this, he read loud, distinctly, very fluently, and with proper accentuation; upon which Stahler burst out into this exclamation : "The d——l take it, I never saw such a thing before in my life."

At this oath Henry started up all in a tremor, cautiously looking round the room, to see, if the devil was coming. When nothing appeared, he exclaimed; "O God, how merciful art thou !" and stepping up to Stahler, said: "Man, have you ever seen Satan ?" When Stahler answered, "No——" Henry replied: "Then don't call him again——" and walked into another room.

Henry's fame spread far and wide, every body talked about him with amazement. Pastor Stolbine himself felt some curiosity to see the boy. Henry had hitherto never been in a church, and had therefore never seen a man, in a large white powdered whig, and dressed in a fine black coat. The rumor of the pastor's arrival in Tiefenbach, soon reached Stilling's house. William therefore gave his son a few hasty instructions, in regard to his behavior before the minister. When he arrived, father Stilling was in his company; Henry had placed himself straight against the wall, in the position of a soldier presenting arms; his cap made of pieces of blue and grey cloth, he held in his folded hands, and kept his eyes fixed upon the minister. After Mr. Stolbine had seated himself, and spoken a few words with William, he turned towards the wall and said: "Good morning, Henry!"

"The general custom is, to say good morning on entering into the room."

Stolbine perceiving, that he had rather an uncommon child before him, turned his chair towards Henry and asked: "Do you know your catechism?"

"Not perfect as yet."

"What? not perfect as yet? the catechism is the first thing, children ought to learn."

"I beg your pardon, your Reverence! the catechism is not the first thing; children ought in the first place learn to pray, that God may open their understanding, to comprehend the catechism.

Stolbine's wrath had been rising previous to this answer, and a severe lecture had awaited William, but Henry's answer assuaged it. He asked: "How do you pray?

"Good God! open my understanding, that I may comprehend what I read!"

"That is very right, my son! continue thus to pray!"

"You are not my father!"

"I am your spiritual father."

"No, sir! God is my spiritual father; you are a human being, you cannot be a spirit."

"How is that? have you no Spirit, no Soul?"

"Yes, to be sure! how can you ask so silly a question?—But I know my father."

"Do you likewise know God, your spiritual father?"

With a smile Henry replied: "Is there a rational being on earth, and not know God?"

"But you cannot see him!"

Henry, without answering a word, fetched his Bible, and opened at Rom. 1. 19, 20. showing that passage to the minister.

This completely satisfied Mr. Stolbine; having ordered the boy to leave the room, he observed to his father, that his son would excel all his forefathers, he should therefore continue to keep him under the rod, for he was an uncommon boy, and would make a great man, if well brought up.

William's heart was still bleeding with the wound it had received, when he lost his beloved Dorothy—he continued to visit Geisenberg castle, and those spots, which had been her favourite haunts. Sometimes he would take Henry with him in these excursions. He would then point out to him, where his mother had been seated, what places she had most frequented, and what she had either said or done in this or that particular spot. Henry was so much taken with every thing which concerned his mother, that he endeavored to copy her as far as he was able, which gave great satisfaction to his father.

Once, on a fine evening in autumn, the two lovers of Dorothy were walking, according to their custom, among the ruins of the castle, picking up snail-shells, which lay scattered about in great profusion; an occupation, in which Dorothy had frequently indulged. While thus engaged, Henry found a small pocket knife, with a green handle and brass rivets. Having lain in a sheltered situation against the wall, and in a measure protected by it from the influence of the weather, the rust had not injured it in the least. Full of joy at the treasure he had discovered, he ran and shewed it to his father. William, in seeing it, was affected to tears. Henry was frightened, tears started ed likewise into his eyes, without knowing the cause of his father's emotion, neither dared he to inquire. In turning the knife, he discovered these words etched on the handle : *"Johanna Dorothea Stilling."* He gave a loud shriek, and fainted. William had heard him pronounce the name and give the shriek ; he seated himself by his side, and shook him, that he might recover. While he was thus engaged, all grief forsook him, peace and joy filled his breast, he folded his son in his arms, and pressed him to his bosom with indescribable sensations. He felt, that he could call God his friend, his ecstatic joy raised him, as it were, to the sanctuary of heaven; he almost imagined, he beheld his beloved Dorothy among the angels of God. Meanwhile Henry recovered, and found himself locked in his father's embrace. Sensations, never felt before, filled his heart at this discovery, for he could not remember, that his father had ever before taken him in his arms. "Father ! do you love me ?" was the first question, his lips were able to utter. Hitherto he had known his father only as an austere man, whom he ought to reverence and fear.— Seeing himself now unexpectedly in his embrace, and his countenance beaming with paternal affection, he began to believe, that his severe father also loved him. When therefore William replied, while his head rested on the bossom of his son, "Yes, my child, I love you !" Henry was nigh fainting a second time, being overcome by his feelings ; but his father suddenly arose, and placed him on his feet. "Come," said William, "let us take a walk." They looked for the knife, but it was not to be found, it had probably fallen among the ruins. After a long but vain search, which grieved Henry more than his father, William conducted him from the place, and addressed him as follows :

"My son ! you are now almost nearly nine years of age. I have instructed and educated you in the best manner I was able, and you have now sense enough, for me to reason with you. You will have to pass through various trials in this world, and I also am yet young. We cannot expect to spend our days in our chamber, we ought to hold again converse with the world ; I shall keep school, as I formerly did, and you shall accompany me as my scholar. Be diligent in all the branches, which you feel an inclination to learn; the necessary books shall be furnished you, but in order that you may be sure of gaining a livelihood, I shall teach you my trade. If God should place you in another and a higher sphere of action, you will have reason to be thankful to him; you will not be despised for being my son, should you rise ever so high in the world."—Henry was in raptures at this display of parental confidence; he became sensible for the first time, that *he too* was something in the world. He looked at his father with pleasure, and said: "I will do all you desire me to do." William replied with a smile: "If you do so, you will be happy, provided you forget not God, but continue to regard him as your almighty heavenly Father, who can and will always protect and guard you against every evil." During conversations of this nature, they again reached their chamber. From that day, William was an altered man, his heart was enlarged, and his piety no longer prevented him from being social and communicative. All, even the rudest, felt something of a reverential awe in his presence, for his character had assumed an irresistible though mild seriousness, through which a soul without guile was apparent. Frequently, when he went from home, he permitted Henry to accompany him, to whom he was drawn with new parental affection, since the occurrence with Dorothy's knife, on which occasion he had discovered her character in his son, and in consequence of this discovery, his affections henceforth centered in him.

A few Sundays after, William for the first time took his son to church. He was surprised at every thing he saw; but when the organist commenced playing, his sensibility overpowered him, so that he almost fainted; every soft harmony melted his heart, the flat notes brought tears into his eyes, and the quick Allegro made him start on his feet. Unskilful as the organist was, Henry believed him to be a perfect master of his art, and he teased his father, till he permitted him after church, to go into the gallery, to see the artist and his instrument. His wishes were gratified, and the virtuoso played an Andante, to please him, which was probably the first time, that a peasant boy was so highly honored in the church of Florenburg. On the same occasion, Henry saw his mothers' grave for the first time. He felt a great desire to look at her remains, but as this was impossible, he seated himself on the grave, gathered a few fall-flowers and other herbs, which grew on it, fastened them in his buttonhole, and left the spot. His sensibility was not so much excited, as on finding the knife; though he and his father shed tears in abundance. The former incident had taken them by surprise, but the latter was an act of his own volition; moreover, the effect of the church-music had not yet passed off.

Father Stilling perceived with much satisfaction the favorable change, which had taken place in his son; William's affection for Henry, and his grand-son's rapid improvements, filled his soul with delight, and it seemed almost as if he had renewed his age. One Monday morning, in the spring of the year, as he was about to go into the forest, to follow his usual occupation, he desired William, to permit his son, to accompany him. Henry was overjoyed, when he obtained his father's consent. As they were walking up the Giller, his grandfather requested him, to relate the tale of the beautiful Melusina. "I like to hear such stories," said he, "time passes away more pleasantly in attending to them, than it otherwise would." Henry related it, with indescribable delight, in all its details. Father Stilling appeared to be as much interested as Henry, and to believe it true in all its circumstances. But this was indeed necessary, if he would not offend his grandson, who believed all these tales as firmly, as he did his Bible. The spot, where Stilling was burning coals, was about nine miles from Tiefenbach, the road passing through one continued forest. To Henry, who idealized every thing, the whole and every part of it, appeared to be a paradise. Having arrived at the spot, which was situated on a high mountain, the collier's hut, covered with green sods, immediately caught his eye; he entered, and was delighted with the couch of moss, and the fireplace between two rough stones.—— While his grandfather was at work, Henry roved about in the woods, taking a view of the beauties of nature; every thing was new to him, and inexpressibly charming. One evening, as they were sitting before the hut, at sun set, Henry said: "Grandfather! when I read in books, that the heroes of the tales were able to count their ancestors so far back, a desire arises in me likewise, to know, what my ancestors have been; who knows, but we derive our origin from some prince or great lord. My mothers' forefathers have all been ministers, but I am unacquainted with yours; I will write them all down, if you will communicate them to me." Father Stilling replied with a smile: "We do not derive our origin from any prince, but that is of little consequence, and you ought not to wish it. All your forefathers have been honest pious people; there are few princes, who can say as much for themselves. Let this be your greatest honor in the world, that your grandfather, great-grandfather and their fathers, have all been men, who, though without any command beyond the threshhold of their own house, have been beloved and honored by all, who were acquainted with them. None of them ever married dishonorably, or entered into an unlawful connection with any woman; none of them ever coveted his neighbor's property, and all died beloved and respected at a good old age." Here Henry interrupted his grandfather, "I may therefore hope," said he, "to find all my forefathers in heaven?" "Yes," replied father Stilling, "so you will; our family is flourishing there. My dear grandson, keep the occurrence of this evening indelibly fixed in your mind; in the world to come you will find our family ranked among the higher classes; do you not forfeit that claim to superiority. The blessing of our family shall rest upon you, as long as you are pious; should you become wicked, and despise your parents, we will deny you before the throne of God." Henry replied, with eyes bathed in tears: "Be not uneasy, grandfather, I will be pious, and I rejoice, that my name is Stilling. But please, tell me, what you know of my forefathers." Father Stilling related: "The name of my great-grandfather's father was Ulli Stilling, he was born about the year 1500. From old documents I have learned, that he came to Tiefenbach and married Hannes Stahler's daughter about 1530; he had emigrated from Switzerland, where he had been acquainted with Zwinglius. He was a pious man, and posessed of such extraordinary bodily strength, that he re-captured his cows from the hands of four robbers. His son, Rinehart Stilling, born in 1536, was my great-grandfather. He was a quiet, inoffensive man, taking delight in the performance of acts of neighborly kindness. In his fiftieth year, he married a young wife, by whom he had many children, among whom was a son, Henry, born to him in the sixtieth year of his life, who was my grandfather. He was born in 1596, reached the one hundred and first year of his age, hence I can just remember him. This Henry was an active man; he purchased horses, and followed teaming, to Brunswick, Brabant and Saxony. He had generally from twenty to thirty other teams in company, acting as their conductor and leader. In those days, robberies were frequently committed, and few public houses were in existence, therefore the carters were obliged, to carry arms and provisions with them. In the evening they placed the carts in a close circle, forming an enclosure around the men and horses. After foddering time, grandfather would call out: "To prayers, neighbors!" whereupon all assembled, and Henry Stilling offered up a prayer to the father of mercies. One of the men kept watch, while the others slept under their carts. At one time, when my grandfather himself was on guard, about eleven o'clock at night, he heard several horses approaching in full trot. They were then in the country of Hessia, encamped on a meadow to the number of twenty six strong men. He quietly alarmed them, and every one took post behind his cart, with gun loaded and cocked. Henry Stilling, after having commended himself and his company to the protection of God in a silent prayer, mounted his cart, to reconnoitre the enemy. There was just light enough to discern objects near him, as the moon was just setting. He saw about twenty men on horseback in the act of dismounting, and softly marching towards the carts. Having observed their movements, he hid himself again behind the cart, that the robbers might not discover him, while he attentively watched their proceedings. They went all round the inclosure, to look for an entrance, and when they found none

began to pull at the carts. When Stilling saw this, he gave the
order : "In the name of God! fire !" Six of the robbers fell, the
rest, being frightened, withdrew to some distance, and consulted
together. The carters all loaded for a second fire ; this being
done, Stilling said : "Attention ! if they approach a second time,
give fire—"however, they did not make another attempt, but gal-
loped off. At daybreak, the carters having harnessed their
horses, continued the journey, every one carrying his loaded
gun in the hand, and the sword under his arm—ready for self-
defence. Stilling drove his team in front of the line. In the forenoon a troop of horsemen came towards them, Stilling exclaimed :
"Every man behind his cart! Guns cocked !" The horsemen stopped; their captain rode alone and unarmed towards the carters, calling out : "Leader ! come forward !" My grandfather came from
behind the cart, equipped as mentioned before. "We come as
friends," said the man on horseback. Henry Stilling was still
suspicious, and ventured not to stir from the spot. The horse-
man dismounted, offered him his hand, in token of friendship,
and asked : "Were you not attacked last night by robbers ?"
"Yes," replied my grandfather, "not far from Hirshfeld, in a
meadow." "We have been in pursuit of them," said the stranger,
"and arrived at the meadow, when they made off, after you had
killed some of their number. You are a brave set of fellows !"
Stilling asked : "Who are you, sir ?" The stranger answered :
"I am count Witgenstein, I'll leave ten of my men with you for
a guard, for I have people enough with me in yonder forest."
Stilling accepted this offer, and agreed with the count, to pay
him yearly a stipulated sum, provided, he would always see him
and his company safe through Hessia. My grandfather married
at twenty-two years of age, and in his twenty-fourth, that
is, in the year 1620, had a son, Hannes Stilling, who was my
father. He led a secluded life, took care of his farm, and endeavored to serve his God. He lived through the whole of the
thirty years war, and was frequently almost reduced to beggary
by its ravages. He had ten children, of whom I am the youngest; I was born in 1680. By the grace of God, I have enjoyed
peace during my life, and have cleared my estate from all debts.

My father died in 1724, in the one hundred and fourth year of his age, and it fell to my lot, to nurse him. He was buried by the side of his forefathers, in the church-yard at Florenburg."

Henry Stilling had listened to this narrative with the closest attention. When the grandfather had finished, he said: "Praised be God, that I have been blessed with such forefathers! I shall carefully record all you have told me, lest I should forget it. Noblemen call their forefathers, their ancestors; so will I call mine." The old man replied to this observation of his grandson only by a significant smile.

Next day, after their return to Tiefenbach, Henry wrote all he had heard of his ancestors, on the blank leaves of a writing, book.

While I am writing these occurrences of my childhood, tears start into my eyes. Whither have you fled, ye happy moments? Why doth nothing but your recollection abide with man? If the soul is ennobled, there exists no meanness of birth! Let my tears, inform every pious heart, since my lips cannot pronounce it to all, how noble that man is, who is acquainted with God his Father, and enjoys his gifts in their fullness!

CHAPTER V.

Henry Stilling was the joy and hope of his family, for though John Stilling had a son, much older than Henry, who frequently visited his grandparents, yet no one entertained great expectations of him, and he was generally treated with indifference. This was strange indeed—for Eberhard Stilling was by no means a partial father.—But why do I detain the reader with these trifles. Who can avoid loving one more than another?"

Parson Stolbine knew, that something might be made of the boy, provided the proper means were used. He therefore proposed to William, and to grandfather Stilling, that they should send him to a latin school. We have a very good one at Florenburg, send him thither, he said, it will not cost much. While the parson made this proposition, Father Stilling was seated at the table chewing a splinter, as he was wont to do, when a subject of importance was to be considered. William had laid his thimble on the table and sat with folded arms in deep meditation. Margaret sat with clasped hands, twisting her thumbs, her eyes fixed upon the door, and likewise meditating. Henry was seated in a little chair, his flannel cap in his hand, he had no troubled thoughts, but his little heart was beating in joyous expectation of the issue of the conference. Stolbine was seated in an arm chair, one of his hands rested on the knob of his staff, the other placed a kimbo, waiting for an answer to his proposition. After a long silence father Stilling said:

"Well William, it is your child, what do you think of it ?"

"Father, I do not know, whether I can go through with the expense."

"Is that your greatest care, William ? Ought not the first question to be, whether it is likely, that your latin scholar will give you any satisfaction ?"

"What satisfaction ! !" said the pastor, "get away with your satisfaction ! The question is here, whether you want to have a clever [fellow made of the boy or not.   If you want him to be a clever fellow, he must learn latin, if he does not, he may remain a lubber as——"

"As his parents," said father Stilling.

" I believe, you want to jeer me," replied the minister.

"By no means," replied Eberhard, "for your own father was a woolen draper, and knew no latin, and yet people say, he was a fine man, though I never bought cloth of him.   My dear Mr. Stolbine, a christian loves God and his neighbor, he acts righteously, and is afraid of nobody, he is diligent, provides for himself and his family.   Tell me, Mr. Stolbine, for what purpose does he do all this ?——"

"I verily believe, you want to catechise me, Stilling ! Be respectful, and mind with whom you are talking.—He does it, because it is right and equitable, that he should do it."

"Be not angry if I contradict you; he does it, that he may have satisfaction both in time and in eternity."

"Nonsense! he may after all go to hell."

"What do you say? go to hell with love to God and his neighbor in his heart?"

"Yes, I say, if he has not true faith in Christ."

"To be sure, that is a matter of course, for no one can love God and his neighbor, who has not true faith in God and his word. But answer me, William! what do you think of the business?"

"My opinion is, if I knew, how to meet the expense, I would take good care, that the boy should not be spoiled by his latin; he should make buttons between times, and assist me in sowing, till we see, what God will make of him."

"I have nothing to say against it, William," said father Stilling, that is my opinion too. The boy has a fine head for learning, let him learn, what he can and will, give him sufficient time for it, but not too much, else he will become idle, and read not a great deal either; but if he is kept close at the trade, so that he fairly longs after his book, then give him an hour to himself for reading, and that's enough. Only take care, that he learns his trade well, that will always give him a living till he can use his latin, and become a gentleman."

"Yes, yes,—becomes a gentleman!" grumbled Stolbine, "he shall be no gentleman, he shall be a village schoolmaster, and for that, it is a good thing to know a little latin. Ye peasants suppose it to be an easy matter, to become a gentleman. You plant ambition and pride in the hearts of your children, though you know, these come from the evil one."

At these words father Stilling's eyes brightened, he rose like a little giant, shook his honorable grey head and said: What is ambition, Mr. Stolbine?

Stolbine jumped up, exclaiming: "Again a question? I need not answer you, but you ought to answer me. Be attentive in church, there you will hear, what pride and ambition are. I don't know how that is, churchwarden! you have become very proud of late, you used to be a modest man!"

"As you take it, proud or not proud. I am a human being; I have loved God, and have served him, I have given to

G

mankind their due, I have educated my children, I have been faithful; I know, that God has forgiven me my sins.—I am now old, my end is approaching, though I am perfectly well, I know, I must soon die, and I rejoice in the prospect of setting out on my great journey. Allow me to be proud, because I have the expectation of dying in the midst of grown up and pious children."

"One doth not ride booted and spurred into Heaven!" said the parson.

Ah! my Grandfather will pull them off ere he dies," said ittle Henry.

All burst out into a laugh, Stolbine not excepted.

Margaret put an end to the conference by proposing, to give Henry in the morning a hearty breakfast, put a piece of bread and butter in his pocket for his dinner, in the evening he might again have a good supper at home. The boy might therefore go early in the morning to Florenburg and return in the evening.—

This proposition was adopted and Stolbine started for home.

About that time a great change took place in Stilling's family; the elder daughter married and left home, and Eberhard with his Margaret, William, Mary and Henry remained its inmates. Eberhard resolved, to give up his collier business, and to confine himself to his farm. The village school at Tiefenbach was at that time vacant, and every inhabitant had his eye fixed on William as schoolmaster. He was offered the birth and accepted it, though with some uneasiness of conscience, because duty compelled him to quit his solitary life, and mingle again with the great world. The good man was not aware, that the grief for the loss of his Dorothy had been the only cause of his becoming an hermit, and that, as soon as it should become less poignant, he would again feel a desire, to hold converse with men, and enter into business. His views were very different on that subject. He feared, that he was about to lose the holy desire of serving God, and therefore accepted the office with trembling. He filled it however with zeal and faithfulness, and gradually began to think, that it could not be displeasing to God, if he improved his talents, by endeavouring to serve his neighbor.

Henry, in the meantime, attended the latin school. The reader may easily imagine from what has been said, that his whole conduct differed much from that of other scholars. Hitherto he had known nothing of any part of the world, beyond father Stilling's house and orchard, neither had he been accustomed to see much company ; his language was therefore uncommon, and few understood him ; he found no recreation in juvenile plays, in which other boys take great delight ; he saw his school-companions engaged in them, without taking the least notice of their sports. The teacher, whose name was Weiland, perceived his genius and great application, and when he observed, that memorizing was a task too difficult for Henry, he suffered him to choose his own method of learning Latin, which he found very advantageous to himself. He would take, for instance, a latin sentence, look for the words in the Lexicon, and having found, what part of speech each was, he would turn to his grammar, observing, under what rules, or exceptions to rules, the words belonged, &c. In this manner, his mind found nourishment at that early stage of his progress in the best latin authors, and he soon learned to read, understand and write that language with tolerable accuracy. But the library of Mr. Weiland was the greatest source of satisfaction to him ; he had received permission, to take out any of the books and read them. This library consisted of a considerable number of authors, among whom were the following : "Reineke Fox," with very neat cuts; "the Emperor Octavianus, with his wife and children." "the delightful story of the four Haymon's children ;" "Peter and Magelone;" "the beautiful Melusina," and finally, the excellent tale of Hannes Clavert. When school was over in the afternoon, Henry went home to Tiefenbach, reading one or the other of these tales by the way. His road led him through green meadows, woods and groves, up and down hill, and the beautiful landscapes, by which he was continually surrounded, made a deep and solemn impression upon his susceptible heart. In the evening, the five housemates, so much endeared to each other, met, and communicated to each other their mutual feelings, and Henry related his tales, in which all became much interested, Margaret not excepted. William, strict as he was in religious observances, used to read them, when he was performing his pilgrimages to the old castle. Whenever Henry accompanied him, he would watch his father with his eyes, as he was reading, and when he observed, that he had come to a favorite part of the narrative, he was enraptured, when he saw, that his father's sentiments sympathized with his own.

In the mean time, Henry made satisfactory progress in the latin school, at least so far, as being able to read and understand latin prose authors, to talk and write latin, are deserving of that name. But Pastor Stolbine demanded more. Henry having been about a year at latin school, parson Stolbine took it into his head, to examine him. From the window of his study, he saw Henry standing in front of the schoolhouse; he whistled, and Henry flew in haste to the parson.

"Are you a diligent scholar?"

"Yes, your Reverence."

"How many verba anomala are there?"

"That I don't know."

"What? clown! don't know it? Have a good mind to box you—Sum—possum,—well, go on!"

"I have not learnt that."

"Magdalene! call the schoolmaster."

The schoolmaster came, and stood in the door, with his hat under the arm.

"Pray, sir! what does this boy learn?"

The schoolmaster humbly replied: "Latin, your Reverence."

"What kind of Latin is that? you good for nothing fellow! he don't know, how many Verba anomala there are!"

"Don't you know that, Henry?"

"No," replied the boy, "I don't know it."

The schoolmaster asked him: "Henry, what species of verbs are *Volo* and *Malo?*"

"They are Verba anomala."

"What are *For* and *Volo* ?"

"Verba anomala."

"Your Reverence," said the schoolmaster to Stolbine, "in this way, the boy knows all the verbs."

Stolbine replied : "But he shall also commit all the rules—that's what I want—go home now."

Both. "Yes, your Reverence."

From that time, Henry committed with little trouble all these rules, but he very soon forgot them again. However, enough has been said of Stilling's learning the latin language.

About this time, father Stilling remitted much of his austere parental authority, and became more kind in the treatment of his family; he kept Henry, who was now eleven years of age, frequently from school, being fond of the child's company, while he attended to his farming business; spoke often with him how necessary it is for every man, to preserve integrity and rectitude through life; recommended to him the reading of good books, especially of the Bible, and likewise the writings of Luther, Calvin, Oecolampadius and Bucerus. One morning early, father Stilling, Mary and Henry, went together in the forest to prepare firewood. Margaret had put up some thickened milk, bread and butter in a basket, which Mary carried, leading the way; Henry followed, relating with great delight the story of the four Haymon's children, while father Stilling slowly came after them, according to his custom, supported by his axehandle, listening with great attention to the story, the child was relating. At length they arrived at a green plain, in a remote part of the forest, with an excellent well at one end of it. "Let us tarry here," said father Stilling, seating himself on the green turf. Mary took the basket from her head, and seated herself by the side of her father. But Henry again saw in his imagination the Egyptian desert, in which he would fain have made an Antonius; soon after he discovered the well of Melusina, and wished, he were Raymond; then again both ideas united in one pious romantic fiction, which gave him an opportunity perfectly to enjoy the beauty and excellency of this solitary landscape. After a while father Stilling rose and said : "Children, remain here, while I walk about in the forest, to look for some dry wood. I shall call from time to time, and you must answer me, that I may not lose my way."—Henry and Mary enjoyed themselves in the mean time by relating stories of night-errantry to each other.

While they were thus engaged, Father Stilling whistled. Mary and Henry answered with: Heigh! Holla! After a little while he came to them, his countenance was beaming with cheerfulness, as if he had found some great treasure; now and then he would smile, stand still and shake his head, looking at one spot, then he would fold his hands and smile again. Mary and Henry looked with astonishment at him, but ventured not to ask, what was the matter, for he was in the habit of laughing to himself. But Stilling's heart was overflowing, he could not refrain from telling, what he had heard and seen; he therefore took a seat: as he was commencing his narrative, his eyes filled with tears; Mary and Henry observed it, and were forthwith sympathetically affected.

"After I had left you," said he, "I went deeper into the forest, and was amazed, to see all at once a light before me, as bright, as when the sun rises in the morning. I thought, what can this mean? There stands the sun in the heavens, can this light yonder be another Sun? This is something very curious, I must go and see it. As I approached, I beheld an extensive plain before me, extending as far as my eye could reach. I never saw a light equally charming, the air was filled with fragrance, a refreshing coolness was wafted across it, and the whole scene baffled all description. The light, which shone over the plain, was so bright, that the light of the sun would be a comparative night. Thousands of splendid castles were glittering in its rays, the one close to the other. Castles——O I can't describe them to you, as bright as if they had been constructed of polished silver. Gardens, groves and brooks were visible, scattered through the plain—O God! how delightful! Not far from me was an extensive splendid building. From its principal gate, a beautiful female came towards me; and at her nearer approach I found, it was Dorothy!—At these words of Father Stilling, his listeners as well as himself began to sob, and for some time he was unable to proceed. Henry mean while burst forth, in this exclamation! "O my mother! my dear mother!"—After the emotion had somewhat subsided, the grandfather continued: "She addressed me in the same friendly accents, which so frequently had stolen my heart in former times: "Father, yonder is our everlasting habitation, you will soon be among us"!—I looked, and behold! all was forest round about me, the splendid vision had fled. Children! I shall soon die, and I rejoice at the prospect of my approaching departure from this world!" Henry could not cease making inquiries about the appearance of his mother, how she was dressed and so forth.—During the day they finished their work, all the while conversing about this occurrence. But Father Stilling appeared from that time to be no more at home any where.

An old family custom, which, as many others I have not mentioned, was, that father Stilling as head of the family, yearly thatched part of the roof of the cottage anew; a custom, which he had observed for forty-eight years; and the time was approaching, that this labor should again be performed. Michelmas was that appointed time, and it was so near, that father Stilling commenced making the necessary preparations. Henry was destined to assist his grandfather in that business; the latin school was in consequence put off for a week. Margaret and Mary held daily consultations together in the kitchen, in what manner they might prevent their father from performing this dangerous business. Finally they resolved, to represent the matter seriously to him, and entreat him to employ some one else to perform that labor, "I don't know, how it happens, Ebert," said Margaret, as she laid her left hand upon his shoulder, you begin to fail very much! Do you feel any change?

"Why we get older every day, Margaret!"

"Law, yes, old and stiff."

"Yes, to be sure," said Mary, fetching a deep sigh.

"Grandfather is quite strong yet for his age," observed Henry.

"Yes, my boy," replied father Stilling, "I think, I could still beat you in running up the ladder."

Henry laughed, and Margaret, seeing she could not effect her purpose in that way, attempted another method. "Yes, yes," said she, "it is a peculiar providential favor, that you are so well at such an advanced age; I believe, you never have been sick all your life time, Ebert?"

"Never in my life—I do not know, what sickness is, for with the small pox and measels I was not sick at all."

"But I think, father," observed Mary, "You have had several heavy falls; if I remember right, you told us so your-self."

"Yes, I came three times very near losing my life from falls."

"And the fourth time," interrupted Margaret, "you'll kill yourself, I know it. You have lately had a vision, and one of our neighbor women has earnestly requested me, not to let you go on the roof, for she had heard a falling noise and groaning in the road, close to our house, as she was milking her cows in the evening. I beg you, Ebert, let somebody else thatch the roof, there is no necessity, that you should do it."

"Margaret, may not I or some one else have a misfortune in the street? It is true, I have seen a vision, and our neighbor may have heard such a noise; but can men escape from what God has ordered respecting them? If he has decreed, that I shall end my life here in the street, how can I, shortsighted creature, avoid it? Or if I shall fall dead from the roof, can I preserve myself? Suppose, I stay away from it, may I not to day or to morrow, stumble, fall and break my neck in the street, at unloading wood?—Margaret, leave me in peace; I shall continue to pursue my business in the manner, I have hitherto done; wherever my hour overtakes me, there I shall bid it welcome."

Margaret and Mary spoke yet one thing and another, but he did not regard what they said; talked with Henry about the manner of thatching, and the good women, seeing that all their attempts were vain, dropt the subject. The next morning the whole family rose very early; father Stilling mounted the roof, and while he sang his usual morning hymn, loosened the old straw, and threw it down; which work he finished that day, and the next put on the new thatch; in one word, the work of thatching was almost completed without any accident. One thing remained yet to be done, which was, to place fresh sods of turf on the ridge of the roof; but this part of the business required no haste; and a week elapsed, before he thought of putting the last finishing hand to the work. The next Wednesday morning, Eberhard rose unusually early, and went from one chamber of the house to the other, as if he were in quest of something. The family watched him with much uneasiness. To their question, what he wanted, he replied: "I want nothing. I feel perfectly well; but at the same time I am uneasy, and, as it were, a stranger in my own house. Margaret proposed, that he and Henry should visit John Stilling at Lichtenhausen. This he consented to do, as soon as he should have placed the sods on the ridge of the roof. Margaret and Mary were not at all pleased with this idea. During dinner, they begged him once more, to hire some one else to finish the work. But the good old man gave a sovereign smile, and replied: "I think of getting on the cherry tree, and once more enjoy the sweet fruit of the labor of my younger years." His wife and daughter were surprised, and feared the consequences, for he had not climbed a tree these ten years; but he walked into the yard, and Henry followed him as a faithful companion. He reached the top of the tree without difficulty, seated himself on one of its branches, and ate heartily of the cherries, throwing now and then a small bunch to Henry. After a while Margaret and Mary came likewise. "Mary," said the honest woman, "lift me up a little, that I can lay hold of one of the lower limbs, I must try, whether I am yet able to climb." She was successful in her attempt. Stilling looked down with a hearty laugh, and said: "This I call being renewed as the eagle." It was a pleasing sight, to behold grandfather and grandmother seated on the cherry tree, eating in their old age once more the fruit of their

H

youthful labor; and father Stilling seemed to enjoy it, for he was peculiarly cheerful. After some time, Margaret and Mary came down, and went into the garden, which was a considerable distance from the house, below the hamlet. When they had been absent about one hour, Eberhard likewise left the tree, fetch'd an iron hook for the purpose of pealing sods, and went with it to the upper end of the yard near the forest, while Henry remained seated under the cherry tree. After a while grandfather returned with a large piece of sod hanging about his head; as he passed Henry, he stooped down to him, and said in a very serious tone: "Look, what a sleepy head!" These words startled Henry, so that he trembled; he remained, however, where he was, cutting a small piece of wood with the penknife. In the mean time, father Stilling mounted the roof with the sods. While Henry's eyes are fixed on his piece of wood, he hears a noise— looks up—all becomes black as night before his eyes.—There lay the dearly beloved man stretched out at full length under a load of ladders, the hands were folded over his breast, the eyes fixed, the teeth shattering, and all the limbs shaking as those of a person in a violent paroxysm of ague. Henry threw in haste the ladders from his body, and ran down the hamlet without hardly knowing what he did, holding his arms stretched out for help, and filling the whole valley with his plaintive cries. When Mary heard the first sounds of the well known voice of her beloved boy, she gave a loud shriek, and wrung her hands, while she hastened up the valley. Margaret followed her as fast as she could; with her hands stretched forward, her eyes gazing wildly about; and a convulsive shriek uttered from time to time, gave some ease to her compressed heart. Mary and Henry arrived first at the mournful scene; father Stilling lay still in his former position, with his mouth and eyes closed, his hands folded over the breast, his respiration strong and slow, as that of a sound person in a deep sleep, and no bruises were perceptible. Mary, in a flood of tears, exclaimed: "My father! o my dear father!" Henry sat down at his feet, sobbed and cried. In this state of affairs, Margaret arrived, knelt by his side, lifted his head from the ground, calling him by name, with her mouth close to his ear, but there was no sign of recognition; she wept not, nor had she in the least lost her presence of mind. Meanwhile, some neighbors had arrived to lend their aid; for father Stilling was universally beloved. Margaret entered the house, prepared a low bed, on which the neighbors laid him: she then undressed and covered him. Henry was sent to Florenburg after a surgeon, who arrived in the evening, examined the patient and bled him, but declared, that, though no bones were broken, there was not the least hope of recovery, and that death must ensue within three days, because his brain was injured and very much shattered.

Stilling's children were now sent for, and the next morning all six arrived, mourning at the expected loss of their father.— On Friday morning, Catharine observed, that her father's respiration was intermitting. She exclaimed in a plaintive voice: "My father is dying!" All the children leaned their faces down upon the bed, weeping and sobbing. Father Stilling every minute gave a deep groan; not a limb of his body stirred, except the lower jaw, which seemed to move a little forward at every groan. Now the last moment approached; the body stretched itself, a shriek was heard, and father Stilling had departed. Margaret took hold of her departed husband's right hand, pressed it and said: "Farewell, Eberhard, in heaven we shall see each other again." At these words, her fortitude forsook her; she sunk down by his bedside, giving vent to her grief by tears and lamentations. After some time the neighbors came in, washed and dressed the corpse, after the relations had left the room. He lay on the bier till next Monday, and was then carried to the churchyard at Florenburg. From what has hitherto been related concernig pastor Stolbine, he must have appeared to the reader only as an eccentric and headstrong man; but excepting his irritability, he had a tender feeling heart.— When Stilling was lowered into the grave, he burst into a flood of tears, and in the pulpit he repeatedly broke out into this exclamation: *"I am sorry for thee, my brother Jo-*

nathan, would to God, I had died for thee! The text for his funeral sermon was: *"Well, thou good servant, because thou hast been faithful over a few things, I will make thee ruler over many things, enter thou into the joy of thy Lord."*—

Should ever any of my readers come to Florenburg, father Stilling sleeps opposite the churchdoor, in the most elevated part of the grave-yard.

LIFE

OF

HENRY STILLING.

SECOND BOOK.

Henry Stilling as a Youth.

—◦●◦—

CHAPTER I.

Father Stilling had departed to the peaceful habitations of his ancestors, and a deathlike silence prevailed in his house. For better than one hundred years, every axe, every milk pail, as well as every other piece of furniture, had been kept in its destined place, which had become smooth and polished from long usage. Neighbors and friends always found every thing in the customary order, a circumstance, which creates confidence. As soon as you entered the door, you felt yourself at home. But now all was deathlike silence, song and mirth had ceased, grandfather's place at the table was vacant; and no one ventured to take it, till at length Henry seated himself in it, though he hardly half filled it. Margaret mourned, without making any loud complaints, but Henry frequently conversed with her about his grandfather. He represented heaven to himself as a charming country of forests, meadows and fields, as they blossom and flourish in the month of May, when the Zephirs blow, and the warm rays of the sun bring animation and growth into every being. His imagination represented father Stilling to his mind in the midst of that delightful scenery, his brow encircled with a halo, and clad in garments of the purest whiteness. All the allusions which he made, as to the present state and situation of his grandfather, were in conformity to that idea. When Margaret for instance asked him; "Henry, what do you think, your grandfather is doing?" he answered, "he is no doubt travelling to Orion, to Sirius, to the Plough and the Seven Stars, viewing all the wonders of creation, and then he will say as he often did when yet in our midst: "O! what a wonderful God!" "But I shall have no delight in these things, what shall I do there?" replied Margaret. "You'll do, as Mary did," said Henry, "who sat at Jesus' feet." In such conversation, they often renewed the remembrance of their departed friend and father.

Family affairs could not remain for any length of time in the state they then were; therefore the aged mother requested, that her son-in-law Simon might move in the house, who had for some time previous to the death of grandfather lived on a rented farm, some distance from home. He arrived with his family and furniture, and took possession of the paternal estate; forthwith every thing was changed, and the house enlarged. Simon had not room enough, he was no Stilling,—and the oaken table full of blessing and hospitality, the good old table, was exchanged for one of yellow maple, full of drawers, provided with strong locks; the old table was thrown in the garret, behind the chimney. Henry visited it sometimes, lay down by its side and wept. "Simon found him one day in that position, and asked him, what he was doing there? who answered: "I weep for the table!" His uncle laughing replied: "You have indeed reason, to weep for an old oak board!" Henry answered rather hastily: "This joint, that foot, and these ornaments about the joint my grandfather made; any person, who loved him, would not break them." Simon replied in an angry tone: "It was not large enough for me, and where should I have left my own?" "Uncle," said Henry, "you ought to have put yours here, till grandmother were dead, and her children should have left the house.

But, all this was of no avail, the mild breathing of Stilling's spirit was exchanged for a noisy desire after wealth. Margaret felt it, and so did her children; she therefore withdrew into a corner behind the stove, where she spent her remaining years; she became blind, which however did not prevent her from spinning flax by way of pastime.

Father Stilling has departed, and I shall now follow his grandson, the young Henry, step by step: of other things, pertaining to the family, I shall only mention, that John Stilling was assessor and surveyor; William schoolmaster; Mary had hired herself as a servant to her sister Elisabeth, the other daughters were married and had left the house.

CHAPTER II.

William had reserved a chamber in his father's house, where he and Henry slept. Under the window was a table with his tools; for when school was over, he worked at his trade. Early, every morning, Henry took his school bag, immediately after breakfast, in which he kept the history of the four Haymon's children, or some other similar book, and a shepherd's flute, and started for Florenburg; as soon as he had reached the open fields, he either took his book out, to read while he was walking, or he played some old romances or other tunes on his flute. It was not difficult for him, to learn the latin language, and he had sufcient leisure to read those tales, in which he so much delighted. During summer, he came home every evening, but during winter, he saw his paternal chamber only once a week, on every Saturday evening, returning Monday morning to school. Four years passed away in this manner; however during the last summer he was much at home, assisting his father in his trade. The road to Florenburg, and the school itself, afforded him many happy hours. The teacher was a mild and reasonable man, who understood, how to maintain his authority, without harshness. After they had dined, Stilling generally collected a number of children round him, and went with them in the fields or to some brook, relating to them sentimental tales, & when he had finished, others would take their turn in narrating. One day when a number of children were collected in a meadow, one of the boys began: "Children, to day I can tell you a very interesting story. Next door to our house lives old Fruhling; you know how he trembles, as he walks supported by his cane; his sight and hearing are almost gone, nor has he any teeth to chew his victuals. When he sat at the table, shaking and trembling, he would spill a great deal and soil the table-cloth. His son and daughter-in-law became disgusted with it, and sent old grandfather in a corner behind the stove to eat his victuals; they gave him something or other in an earthen dish, and that not sufficient; I myself have seen him eat, he looked so wishful at the table, and his eyes filled with tears. The day before yesterday he broke his dish. The young wife scolded him severely, he made no reply, merely gave a deep sigh. They bought him a small wooden dish for a few farthings, and yesterday noon he had to eat for the first time out of it. While the family were eating their dinner, Peter, young Fruhling's little son, about four and a half years of age, brought some ends of boards into the room. His father asked him: "Peter! what are you about there?" "O," answered the child, "I'm only fixing a trough for father and mother to eat out of, when I shall be grown up. The young couple looked at each other for a while, but soon burst into tears, arose from the table, led their grandfather to a seat, and invited him, to eat with them. All the children expressed their satisfaction, with the story, by a general rise from their seats, by clapping of hands, by laughing and exclaiming: "that was well done!" "Did little Peter do so?" "Yes," replied the relater, "I stood by, when he did it." But Stilling could not laugh, he stood looking on the ground; the story had pierced his very soul, at length he said, "that should have happened to my grandfather! I verily believe, he would have risen from his seat, would have gone into one corner of the room, and exclaimed: O Lord God! strengthen me I pray thee, that I may be avenged of these Philistines! and then would have taken hold of the corner post with all his might, and crushed the house to pieces!" "Softly, Softly, Stilling!" said one of the larger boys, "that would have been rather too rash of your grandfather." "True" said Henry, "but only think of the treatment, old Fruhling had received; reflect, how often he doubtless had his son when a child; on his knees and given him the best he had; it would not

ful, if under these circumstances a severe judgment of God had befallen the young couple.

Thus time passed away, until it was necessary, he should leave the school, and assist his father at his trade. This was a severe trial for him; his mind was wholly engaged in books, he imagined always, he had not sufficient time for reading, therefore he entertained a strong desire of becoming a schoolmaster, which in his opinion was the highest place of honor, he ever expected to attain. The idea of becoming a minister, was quite beyond his hope. But when he sometimes raised his thoughts to the pulpit, and represented to himself, how happy a man must be, who can spend his whole life among books, his heart was elated with joy, and he thought: "God has surely given me this desire for some good purpose, he will guide me, and I will follow him." This enthusiastic love for the profession, induced him frequently to play the parson; he would gather the neighbor's children round him, hang an apron about his shoulders, put a paper collar round his neck, mount a chair with the back before him, and commence preaching in a style, which amazed his little auditors; and this sport was the only one, in which he ever indulged. Once it happened, as he was declaiming with all his might, and pourtraying hell to his hearers in the most glowing colours, that parson Stolbine unexpectedly entered the exhibition room: it was not often he smiled, but at that sight he could not altogether suppress it. Henry felt no inclination for laughing, he stood on his chair like a statue, as pale as the wall; his hearers placed themselves with folded hands against the wall, at the sight of the formidable Mr. Stolbine. Henry now and then gave a timid glance at him, fearing, he would raise his cane and strike him, for this was his practice, when he saw children at play. However he did not do it then, and after having enjoyed the scene for a moment, only said: "Get down there, and stand yonder, and throw that foolish dress away!" Henry willingly obeyed, and Stolbine said: "I believe you have the parson in your head?"

"I have no money, to attend the university."

"You shall be no parson but a schoolmaster."

"I am willing to obey your Reverence! but if God should

I

desire me to be a minister, or some other learned man, shall I say, No! I will remain schoolmaster, because Mr. Stolbine will have it so?"

"Hold your tongue, you good for nothing fellow, do'nt you know, to whom you speak?"

He then catechised all the children, in which he was peculiar gifted. At his next visit, he endeavored to persuade William, to let his son study, and promised, to assist him; but this mountain was too steep to ascend. Henry in the meantime was doomed to pass through a severe trial on account of his situation; he had a great desire to keep school, for this one reason, that he might get rid of the tailors trade, and be enabled to read as much as he wished; for he believed himself, that the routine of teaching children, would be an unpleasant task; mean while he endeavored, to make his present mode of living as comfortable as possible. The study of the mathematical sciences was his favorite occupation, and in leisure moments, he amused himself by reading old tales and stories of knighterrantry. He was particularly pleased with the art of making sun-dials; the corner of the room in which he was sowing, was comically adorned according to his own taste; every pane of glass in the window was a sun-dial; a square piece of wood in the form of a cube, covered with paper, was placed against the window; on five sides of the cube he had drawn sun-dials, the hands of which were broken needles; the ceiling was likewise adorned with a sun-dial, which received its light from a piece of looking glass in the window; an astronomical ring of whalebone was suspended by a thread before the window, which served him for a watch, when he went abroad. He likewise understood the principles of plain Geometry, was a good penman and so well acquainted with common Arithmetic, as to pass a rigid examination in these branches, though he was but twelve years old, and an apprentice to the tailor's trade.

CHAPTER III.

Henry was now attending the catechetical instructions of Mr. Stolbine, a task easy in itself, though connected with some difficulties in his particular situation: for the parson, who always had his eye upon him, generally discovered something about his person, which he did not like; for instance: when he came into church or the catechisation room, in company with the other boys, he was always the first, and likewise kept the first place, which Mr. Stolbine did not like, for he was a great admirer of humility in others. At one time he addressed him thus: "Why are you always the first ?"

Stilling answered: "If learning is in question, I do not like to be the last.

"Why, you good for nothing fellow, don't you know how to hold a middle course between last and first?"

Stilling would fain have given him a suitable answer, but was afraid to excite the parson's ire.—Stolbine took a turn up and down the room, and when he came again to Henry, said with a smile: "Siilling ! what means this ? medium tenuere beati ?"

"That means: Whoever holds a middle course in every respect, is happy," but I think it would be more suitable to say: plerique medium tenentes, sunt damnati. (*Most people who hold a middle course, are unhappy.*)

Mr. Stolbine was startled, looked at him and said: "My lad ! I tell you, you shall have the right to stand a-head, for you have answered well indeed." But from that time Stilling never went a-head, lest he should excite the ill will of the other boys, and I cannot say, whether this conduct proceeded from cowardice, or from true humility. Mr. Stolbine asked him again; "Why don't you take your place ?" Henry replied: "Whosoever humbleth himself, shall be exalted; and—"Hold your tongue," exclaimed the parson, "you are an impertinent fellow."

Matters proceeded in this way till Easter in the year 1755, when Henry Stilling was fourteen and a half years of age; a fortnight before that time, parson Stolbine called Stilling into his study and said: "Stilling! I would like to make a good, honest fellow of you, but you must be pious, and obedient to me your superior; at Easter I shall confirm you with some others, who are older than you, and afterwards I will see, if I cannot obtain a schoolmaster's birth for you." Stilling was overcome with joy; he thanked Mr. Stolbine and promised obedience, which pleased the old man very much, who dismissed him in peace, and faithfully kept his word: for on Easterday Stilling was confirmed, and immediately afterwards was appointed schoolmaster at Zellberg, which office he was to assume by the first of May. The inhabitants of Zellberg had been very anxious to obtain him for their schoolmaster, for his good name had spread far and wide. Stilling's satisfaction was great on this occasion, seeing he had reached the acme of his wishes; scarcely could he wait for the day, appointed for entering upon the duties of his office.

Zellberg is situated nearly on the highest point of the Giller, the road from Tiefenbach to Zellberg passes through the forest, straight up the mountain. When the traveller has reached the summit, he beholds an extensive plain before him; at his right hand a forest of aged oak and beech trees, extending towards the East, whose venerable tops tower towards heaven; at the termination of the forest rises a bushy hill, called the Hangesberg, the highest land of all Westphalia. The distance from Tiefenbach to the summit of that height, is two miles and a half all the way up hill. On your left you have a fertile tract of land, which toward the north rises up into a well cultivated hill called St. Anthony's church. At the foot of this hill is a farm house with its barns, stables and other out-buildings. Towards the north-east, the plain descends into a delightful meadow, which winds along among bushes and hills; between the meadow and the Hangesberg, an old wood-road passes through the bushes, along the side of the mountain, losing itself finally in the sombre shades of the forest. Having passed the highest part of the mountain, the hamlet of Zellberg presents itself to view: it is situated at the head of a brook, which as it winds its way through meadows, increases to a river, and falls into the Fulda not far from Cassel. The situation of that hamlet is delightful, especially are the lat-

ter part of spring, summer, and the commencement of autumn
charming seasons at Zellberg; but the howling of the storm,
the snowbanks drifted in and about the village in winter, change
this paradise into a Norwegian landscape. Such was the
situation of the place, where Stilling was to make the first trial
of his abilities.

In the small villages and hamlets of that part of the country,
school is only kept on Fridays and Saturdays, from the first of
May until the tenth of November; *(Martinmas)* and this was likewise the custom at Zellberg. Stilling arrived there usually at
sunrise on Friday morning, and returned home on Sunday
evening. This walk was indescribably delightful to him——
especially, when he had reached the height of ground before sunrise, with the extensive plain before him; and beheld the glorious orb rising in majesty at a distance from between the
bushy hills, a light breeze, preceding the approach of the
king of day, played with his locks, his heart melted into tender
feelings, he thought himself transplanted into the spiritual world,
enjoying a vision of angels as Jacob did at Mahanaim; turning round in this ecstacy of joy, he beheld Tiefenbach low in the
valley, still wrapt in the shades of night. At his left a high pro-
jecting rock called "the heated stone" lay stretched along the
declivities of the Giller; at his right hand, close by, were the
ruins of Geisenberg castle. All the scenes, which had occurred
there between his father and departed mother, and between his
father and himself, passed as so many beautiful pictures before
his mind, he stood gazing, lost in rapturous sensation. Then he
would cast his eye upon the distant prospect; forty-eight miles towards the South he spied the Faunus or Feldberg near Frankfort;
thirty-two or thirty-six miles to the West, he beheld the Seven
mountains near the Rhine and a long row of hills of minor dimen-
sions; towards the northwest a high mountain, whose towering
top was almost even with the Giller, shut the prospect into the
theatre of his future activity from Stilling's eyes. This was the
spot, on which he frequently lingered for an hour, scarcely
knowing where he was, his mind was wholly engaged in prayer,

and his heart was filled with peace, and love towards that Almighty Being, who had formed all these beauties of nature.

Sometimes he wished he were a prince, to be able to build a city in these delightful regions; and forthwith his imagination had created it; at St. Anthony's church was his residence, on the Hangesberg his imagination presented to him the fort built for the protection of the city, its name was Heinrichsberg, but he could not exactly agree with himself as to the name of the city, yet he thought "Stillingen" sounded best in his ear. When, full of these princely projects, he had reached the height of Hangesberg, he beheld Zellberg, and found he was pro tempore nothing but schoolmaster in that hamlet, and well satisfied with his calling, because it afforded him leisure to gratify his insatiable thirst for reading.

There lived at Zellberg at that time a Mr. Creger, a forester by profession, a man of an open and honorable character, who had two sons, whom he wished to give a good education. He had been an intimate friend of Eberhard Stilling, and therefore loved likewise his children. He was particularly pleased with Henry as schoolmaster in his village, and offered to board him. Stilling accepted this offer with the greatest pleasure, for Mr. Creger possessed a fine library; and having been a customer of his father, he was better acquainted with his family, than with any other in Zellberg. As soon as he was settled in some measure, he examined Mr. Creger's library. Having opened a large folio volume, he found it to contain a translation of Homer into German verse. He jumped for joy, kissed the book, pressed it to his heart and asked Mr. Creger's permission to peruse it, which being granted, he took it into the schoolhouse, locked it up in a drawer, and read in it, as often as he enjoyed a leisure moment. His latin teacher had frequently spoken about Homer, when Stilling read Virgil at school, and he would have been exceeding glad at that time, could he have found an opportunity to read that work, now it presented itself, and he was determined to profit by it as much as possible.

Scarcely ever since its existence, has this poem been read with deeper interest and with greater rapture. Hector was his favorite hero; he did not like Achilles, and Agamemnon still less; in short, he favored the Trojans, though he despised Paris and Helen, principally, because he always stayed at home, though he was the sole cause of the war. None shared his pity more than aged Priam. The imagery and delineations of characters and things, drawn by Homer, were so much in harmony with his own taste, that he could scarcely refrain from shouting aloud at the discovery of their complete adaptation and fitness, and that would have been the most suitable time for him to read Ossian.

This high wrought sensibility was however not the effect of the poem alone; the beautiful scenery of the country, in which he read it for the first time, exercised its full share in producing these sensations. Let the reader represent to himself a young man, enthusiastically sentimental, whose taste had been formed by nature, not by fashion, living without care or trouble, satisfied with his situation, and susceptible of pleasures of that kind—such a mind reads Homer in the midst of one of the most delightful landscapes in the world, and that early in the morning. Let the reader represent to himself Stilling seated before one of the eastern windows of his schoolhouse, built along the southern declivity of the Hangesberg; a grove of birch trees, planted in olden times on the green turf, surrounded the house, whose snow white trunks formed a pleasing contrast, both with the green color of the grass, and the still darker leaves of the trees, continually agitated by the wind. In front of his window was an extensive meadow, terminated by hills and mountains overgrown with bushes and forests. Towards the south, somewhat lower down, was the village of Zellberg, on its southern extremity a meadow, from which fertile fields were gradually rising, terminated at a distance by a forest. Towards west, close by, was the lofty Giller, with its thousands of venerable oaks. Among this scenery, Stilling read Homer in the months of May and June, when the whole northern hemisphere is arrayed in its most beaute-

ous garb, and exults in the power and goodness of its Creator
and Preserver.

The inhabitants of Zellberg were a good-hearted people,
children of nature, who had always tales of knighterrantry at
hand, so that their schoolmaster found himself in that respect
likewise transferred into his very element.

CHAPTER IV.

Henry's method of teaching was peculiar, and so regulated,
as to give him leisure for his own studies. In the morning he
had prayers with the children, and afterwards catechised them
in the principles of christianity, without any text-book, according to his own system ; then he made each of them read a piece ;
that being done, he exhorted them to learn the catechism, promising to relate interesting stories, provided they knew their lessons ; during that time he set copies for the scholars, made them
read once more, and then related, till he had exhausted all the
stories he ever had read, either in the Emperor Octavianus, the
beautiful Melusina, or other books ; even the destruction of the
royal city of Troy was not passed by. Such was the method he
invariably pursued. The children applied themselves with uncommon zeal to their lessons, because they wished to hear some
new story as soon as possible. Whenever they were disobedient
or negligent, the schoolmaster related nothing, but read for himself. By this method of teaching, the a-b-c-scholars and the
spelling-class were the only losers ; that portion of the duties of
his office was too irksome for Stilling. On Sunday mornings,
the children gathered around their teacher, who marched with
them to Florenburg, in order to attend preaching, relating stories
all the way, and after sermon they went home in the same order.
The inhabitants of the village were pleased with Stilling ; they
observed, that their children were learning, without being frequently punished, several also were fond of hearing the tales,
which the children again related at home. Mr. Creger was particularly attached to him, for he could talk with him about Pa-

racelsus, of whose works he possessed a German translation, being a great admirer of all men, whom he imagined to have been in possession of the philosopher's stone.

However, this paradisical life was but of short duration.—Pastor Stolbine and Mr. Creger were bitter enemies. When Stilling had been several weeks at Zellberg, Mr. Stolbine came to visit his new schoolmaster. He arrived about nine o'clock in the morning; fortunately Stilling was neither reading nor relating. But the parson had heard already, that Stilling was boarding with Creger, and looked quite angry when he entered.

"What are you doing with these slates here?" was his first question.

"The children receive instruction in Arithmetic," was Stilling's reply.

"I suppose," said Stolbine, "that is the case; but who ordered you, to give that instruction?"

Henry did not know, what he should say; with an air of astonishment he looked the parson full in the face, and replied with a smile: "He, who ordered me, to teach the children reading, writing and the catechism, has likewise ordered me to instruct them in Arithmetic."

"You—I had almost spoken a hard word!—Teach them first the necessary branches, and when they understand them, it will be time enough, to teach them Arithmetic."

Stilling was on the point of bursting into tears, according to his custom, while others give vent to their feelings by harsh and angry expressions; however, there is a case, in which he too can become very angry—either when he is ridiculed, or when any thing serious or important is placed in a ridiculous light: "Mr. Stolbine!" was his reply, "what shall I do? The people here wish me to instruct their children in Arithmetic, and your Reverence forbids it! Whom shall I obey?" "I have to give orders in school affairs, and not your peasants!" said Stolbine, and with these words he left the room.

Stilling immediately ordered all the slates to be taken down, and to be laid in a heap under the bench, behind the stove. After school, he related the affair to one of the elders of the church,

K

and asked his advice. The man replied with a smile: "The parson has undoubtedly been in an ill humor, put your slates away, so that he doth not see them, should he come again; but continue to instruct the children as you have done heretofore." He also told the circumstance to Creger, who said, he believed, the evil one had taken possession of Stolbine, and according to his opinion, the girls should now receive instruction in Arithmetic too, at least *his* children should learn it before all other things, and his two boys should receive instruction in Geometry.

Thus affairs stood during the summer, but no one suspected, what would happen in autumn. A fortnight before Martinsday, one of the elders came into the schoolhouse, and announced to Stilling in the name of the minister, that he was to leave the school on Martins-day, and return to his father. This was quite unexpected, both by teacher and scholars, who were mutually attached to each other. Creger, and the rest of the Zellbergers, were enraged, and almost swore, the parson should not take their schoolmaster away. But William Stilling, though he was by no means pleased, thought it advisable, to take his son home, lest opposition to Mr. Stolbine's wishes, might be an obstacle to Henry's future promotion. On Sunday afternoon before Martinsday, the good schoolmaster put his clothes and books in a bag, slung it over his shoulders, and left Zellberg, accompanied by all his scholars. Many tears were shed on both sides, for Stilling was grieved, that the pleasant season, which he had spent at Zellberg, should so soon have ended. The whole western sky seemed to bear a gloomy aspect; an immense black cloud covered the sun, while he walked through the dark forest down the Giller. On Monday morning his father again set him to work. But the tailor's trade was now the more annoying to him, since he had tasted the sweets of another mode of life. His only enjoyment was, to arrange his sun-dials, and relate the siege and taking of Troy to his grandmother, who was much pleased with it, because she recollected, that her deceased husband had been very fond of such narratives.

CHAPTER V.

Troubles and sufferings were the daily companions of Henry Stilling in his present situation. He firmly believed, that he was not destined for this trade, and felt a sort of shame, whenever a person of distinction entered the room, and found him engaged at the needle. After he had been a few weeks with his father, parson Stolbine met Uncle Simon in the road : "Well," exclaimed Stolbine, "what is William Stilling's son doing?" "He works at his trade." "That's the very thing I wanted," said Stolbine, and went his way. When Simon came home, he told William what the minister had said. Though Henry felt unpleasant at this declaration of Mr. Stolbine, yet it was some comfort to him, to observe, that his father was highly displeased with the minister's interference in this business. "And it is my will," said he, vehemently throwing down the needle, "that he shall keep school, as soon as I can find an opportunity for him." Simon replied : "I would have left him at Zellberg, the minister might have been put down, I suppose." "It might have been done, I acknowledge," said William, "but then he would have been always my enemy, and I would have seen no peaceable day in all my lifetime—it is better to bear things with patience, than to live always in contention." "For my part," continued Simon, "I care nothing at all for the parson, should he trouble himself much about my concerns, I would teach him manners!" William was silent—but thought it easier to threaten, than to perform.

An opportunity of being released from the drudgery of the trade soon presented itself; for a fortnight before christmas, a letter arrived from Mr. Steifman at Dorlingen, in the county of Mark, inviting Stilling, to engage himself as private tutor to his children. The conditions were, to instruct Mr. Steifman's children from New-year till Easter, for which he would board Stilling and pay him five rix-dollars wages, but he should be obliged also to give instruction to as many children of the neighboring farmers, as might be sent, and whose tuition-money Mr. Steifman was to draw. Stilling's family held a consultation on the contents of this letter, and though Margaret and Mary were decidedly against accepting the proposition, yet William's opinion in favor of the measure, finally prevailed. Henry being asked, if he were willing to go, answered: "Yes, I am, and I wish I were there already!" His father therefore returned an answer to the letter, and the conditions were accepted. Dorlingen is twenty-seven miles from Tiefenbach. The last morning came—the whole family was deeply affected, and though William appeared at first indifferent towards Henry, yet, at the moment of separation, his parental heart could not suppress its emotion. Henry too felt much at parting with his friends. In passing through Lichthausen, he paid his uncle John a visit, who gave him much good advice. The country, through which he had to pass, bore a melancholy aspect at that season of the year, and left no agreeable impression on his mind. If the situation of Dorlingen, thought he, be similar to this landscape, I can never like it. He travelled in company with some teamsters, who came from that place. They had not proceeded far, when he perceived, that they were making repeated remarks respecting him; for as he did not converse much with them, and appeared reserved, they looked upon him as a blockhead, whom they might make the butt of their coarse wit with impunity. But Henry soon gave them to understand, that he was the new schoolmaster of their place, and for their children's sake, they left him in peace. At nine o'clock in the morning, they arrived at Dorlingen. Steifman viewed him from head to foot, and so did his wife and the whole family. Steifman was a very rich man; he owned several farms, a large stock of cattle, a steel manufactory, which was very profitable, besides a large sum of money at interest. Mrs. Steifman was his second wife; she appeared to be a good-natured woman, whom her husband frequently entertained with the enumeration of the excellent qualities of his former wife. His temper was not very irritable; he never said a great deal, but what he said was sarcastic, and generally calculated, to offend some one present. In the beginning, he conversed occasionally with his new schoolmaster, but was not pleased with him. Mr. Steifman understood nothing of what was interesting to Stilling;

and on the other hand, Stilling did not comprehend Mr. Steifman. Therefore both were silent in each others presence.

The next Monday morning school commenced. Steifman's three
boys came first—by and by eighteen other strapping fellows made
their appearance, who, when compared with Stilling, were as so
many Patagonians to one Frenchman. Ten or a dozen girls of
the same calibre, found their way likewise to the school-room,
and seated themselves behind the table. Stilling did not exactly
know, how to deal with this kind of people; he was afraid of
their savage looks; however, he attempted the usual school-me-
thod, prayed and sung with them, and made them read, and learn
the catechism. This course he regularly pursued for about a
fortnight, but then he came to a complete stand. One or the
other of his Cosack-like scholars attempted to vex his teacher.
Stilling was not sparing of the rod, but with so little success,
that after he was tired with beating the broad and strong back,
the scholar burst into a loud laugh, and the teacher wept.
This was fine fun for Mr. Steifman; whenever he heard a noise,
he stept in the door, in order to enjoy the confusion.

This behavior completely destroyed the usefulness of Stilling in that place. The school resembled a polish Diet, every
one acted as he pleased. While the poor schoolmaster was
thus experiencing every kind of vexation during school-hours, he
likewise had not a moment of enjoyment, when school was out.
There were scarcely any books in the house; at last he found
a large folio Bible with many cuts, which he careful examined, though he had perused the Bible before. In the family no
one liked him—all looked upon him as a simple, foolish boy;
for he did not understand their low, ironical and ambiguous
speeches; his answers were always in conformity with the
plain sense of the words, he thought they bore, and he endeavored to gain the good will of others by an obliging manner,
which was in this place the right way to become the butt
of all.

Once a circumstance happened, which nearly had cost him
his life, if the bountiful father of men had not in mercy preserved him. It was his duty to make every morning fire in the

school-room. One day, not finding fuel in the usual place, he went into the smoke-house, where the dry wood was kept.— The thrashing-floor was adjoining the kitchen, and a stair-way went from the floor to the smoke-house. Six men were employed in thrashing. Henry ran up stairs, opened the door. from which a cloud of smoke issued. He left the door open, and quickly laid hold of a few pieces of wood ; in the mean time the thrashers bolted the door on the outside. Poor Stilling was now in utter darkness ; the smoke was so suffocating, that he lost all presence of mind. and could not find the door. In his agony he jumped against the wall, and lukily hit the door ; it burst open, and he fell headlong down stairs on the floor, where he lay senseless for some time. When he recovered, the thrashers with Mr. Steifman were standing around him, immoderately laughing. "The d—l himself would laugh at this." said Steifman. "Yes," replied Stilling, "he doth laugh, because he has found his equals." With this answer Mr. Steifman was quite delighted, and he afterwards used to say, it had been the first and last witty word, he had heard from his schoolmaster.

- Henry's father was meanwhile more agreeably engaged at home. The wound of his heart, which the death of Dorothy had occasioned, was healed; he still remembered her with tender affection, but no longer mourned; fourteen years had elapsed since her death; he had become less rigid in his mysticism, and conversed freely with his neighbors, quite in the manner of father Stilling. He wished to keep house again, and to carry on farming in connection with his trade; he therefore sought a wife, who, besides the necessary good qualities of health and an amiable disposition, possessed also some property; and he soon found what he desired. There was a young widow. a pleasant, agreeable woman, with two children in Linedorf, about six miles from Tiefenbach towards the West. She consented to marry him, though he was lame. The marriage contract was made, the wedding day appointed, and Henry received a letter from his father, announcing his intended marriage and inviting him to the wedding in very affectionate terms. Henry read the letter, and so fluctuating were the feelings of his heart, that it was necessary for him to reflect on its contents, before he was able to discover his real sentiments on the occasion. Having taken a few turns up and down the room, he came to the following conclusion : "My own mother is in heaven, let the new one take her place, while I remain in this vale of tears; when I depart hence, I shall leave her, and seek the other. My father acts right—I will endeavor to love and please her, thus she will return my affection, and I shall be happy. Henry immediately informed Mr. Steifman of the invitation, and having obtained some money from him, set out for Tiefenbach. His reception was highly gratifying; his father was delighted to see him arrive with a smiling countenance, having entertained some fear, lest he should be dissatisfied with the step he had taken; he therefore embraced him, and bid him welcome with paternal affection.

"How do you do, dear father !" said Henry, "I congratulate you with all my heart on your marriage, and rejoice in the prospect of comfort for your old age."

William sunk upon a chair, held both his hands before his face and wept. At length he said : "You know, I have saved about five hundred rix-dollars since your mother's death, I am now forty years old, and I might doubtless have saved a great deal more, which you now will lose, you would have been my only heir, had I remained a widower."

"Father ! I may die, and so may you, or we both may live a long while, you may become feeble, and have not money enough for your own support.—But father ! Doth my new mother resemble my departed mother ?"

William again covered his eyes with his hands, and said: "No! but she is a very fine woman."—"Very well," replied Henry, as he walked to the window to enjoy once more the romantic scenery, which thence presented itself to the eye.— There was no snow on the ground, and the prospect into the forest appeared to him so inviting, that he resolved, though it was in the last days of February, to take a walk thither. After he had gone a considerable distance from the village, he felt so comfortable, that he forgot the whole world, and without knowing it, arrived at the west-side of Geisenberg castle. Already were its ruins visible between the trunks of the trees, when he heard a noise among the brush-wood, and looking towards that spot, saw a girl, standing before him, with pale but very pleasant features, dressed in linsey, after the fashion of the country. Stilling's heart began to beat, but as it was still full daylight, he was not frightened, but asked her: "Whence do you come?" She answered: "From Tiefenbach." This appeared singular, as she was a total stranger to him.—"What is your name?"— "Dorothy!"—At this word Stilling gave a loud shriek and fainted away. The good girl did not know, what she should do, the young man was likewise a stranger to her; for she had come to Tiefenbach since New-year. She ran to him, knelt by his side and wept. She was wondering, who he could be, especially because his face and hands were more tender and his clothes better and neater made than those of the other young men in the village. The stranger pleased her. In the mean time Stilling gradually recovered, he saw the girl close by his side, rose up, and inquired in an affectionate tone: "What are you doing here?" She answered in a similar manner: "I am gathering dry wood. Where do you live?" "I am William Stilling's son from Tiefenbach." Then she told him, that she had come to Tiefenbach since New-year, and had hired out as maid in the village; Stilling on the other hand made her acquainted with his circumstances, and both were sorry, when they had to part from each other. Stilling walked towards the castle, and she continued gathering wood; bnt so strong was the impression, which the girl had made on his mind, that two years elapsed, before he completely forgot her. When the sun was about setting, he returned home, but said nothing of what had occurred; not so much from a propensity to secrecy, as from other causes.

The next day he went with his father and other friends to Linedorf to the wedding. His step-mother received him very affectionately; he began to like her, and thought, she liked him also, which William observed with pleasure. Henry informed his parents, how unpleasantly he was situated at Dorlingen. The mother advised, he should not return thither; but William said: "we have always kept our word, you ought not to fail this time;

if others do not as they ought, they have to answer for it, but you must stay out your time." Henry was willing to adopt his father's advice, and started the next day for Dorlingen. But his scholars did not return, spring came on, and every one went to work in the field. Mr. Steifman employed Stilling in the meanest services about the house, so that he really earned his living by the sweat of his brow. On the second Easter-day, Stilling took leave of Dorlingen, and in the evening arrived at Linedorf, the new residence of his parents.

CHAPTER VI.

Stilling was now again in his element, because he was able to obtain books, though he had to work hard at his trade. The first leisure moments after his return, he improved to fetch Homer from Zellberg; and wherever else he heard of a book, which he thought would be useful or interesting to him, he would spare no pains in obtaining, so that the shelf over the windows, where house-hold-goods had been stored, was soon completely filled with books. William liked to see it, but the books were sometimes in the way of his mother, who frequently asked him: "Henry what will you do with all these books?" He often read during meal-times; his mother therefore shook her head and said: "This is a strange boy!" Upon which William answered, smiling in Stilling's fashion: "Margaret, let him go his own way!"

A few weeks afterwards the heavy farming work came on. William was under the necessity, either of employing his son, or hiring a man in his place, which would not have pleased his wife; this period therefore was the commencement of Stilling's severest sufferings, for though he was tall, and apparently strong, yet being unaccustomed from his youth, to this kind of work, he frequently thought, he must sink down with weariness and pain, as often as he handled the hoe or sythe; but there was no alternative, William was afraid of unpleasant

L

consequences in the family, and his wife believed, Henry would gradually accustom himself to such work. This mode of life became insupportable to him, he was glad, if on a rainy day he could sit down to his needle and refresh his weary limbs, he often sighed under this yoke, and frequently went to solitary places, praying to his heavenly Father for relief from this terrible situation. William suffered with him. When he returned from the field in the evening with swollen hands full of blisters, and trembling with weariness, his father sighed, and both longed for a change of circumstances, and particularly for a school service. At length such an opportunity offered, after a fatiguing and painful summer. At Michaelmas in the year 1756 he received a call as schoolmaster at Linedorf, where his father lived, and Stilling readily accepted it. He boarded among his employers, but had to assist his father in his business before and after school. In that way he gained no time, to prosecute his own studies, except during school-hours. William perceived it, and severely reprimanded his son for making use of that time for himself, which ought to have been devoted to the instruction of others. Stilling told him with a heavy heart: "Father, my inclination is bent on studying, I cannot overcome it, give me some time for reading before and after school, and I promise you, I will take no book to school for self information." William replied: "It is a pity! all you learn, is not calculated to make you a living, and you are unfit for any thing else, which might maintain you." Stilling was grieved at his situation, for he did not like to keep school, unless he could gain time for studying; he therefore wished to leave his father, to try his fortune elsewhere.

The people at Linedorf were tolerably well satisfied with him, though they believed, their children might learn a little more, but his treatment of them, and his conversations gave universal satisfaction. Pastor Dahlhime, to whose parish Linedorf belonged, loved him. He was a man, who reflected honor on his office. Stilling was filled with surprise and admiration, when he for the first time entered his Study. Dahlhime was at that time eighty years of age: when Stilling arrived, he lay on his sofa, but immediately arose, as he entered, offered him his hand and said: "Excuse my lying on the sofa, schoolmaster, I am old, and my strength begins to fail me." Stilling respectfully replied, "Mr. Dahlhime, I am glad to keep school under your superintendence. May God bless you in your old age." "I thank you, schoolmaster," replied the aged minister of God: "The Lord be praised, that I am near the end of my pilgrimage, and I am rejoiced to know, that my great Sabbath is approaching." When Stilling returned home, he could not refrain from making this observation in his own mind: Mr. Dahlhime is either a real Apostle, or Mr. Stolbine is a priest of Baal. Mr. Dahlhime sometimes visited the school at Linedorf, and though he did not always find every thing in the best order, he did not scold like Mr. Stolbine had done, but admonished Stilling in the most affectionate terms, to make suitable alterations; a mode of proceeding, which always had the desired effect upon a mind like Stilling's. Mr. Dahlhime's mild and affectionate behavior will appear the more surprising, if the reader is informed, that he was naturally very irritable; which however manifested itself only, when he had to contend with vice. In order to give the reader a specimen of his character, I shall relate a circumstance, which occurred, when he was chaplain to the Prince of R———. The lady of that prince was an excellent woman, and the mother of several children; but notwithstanding this, he fell in love with a citizen's daughter in his residence, with whom he spent a considerable part of his time, to the great grief of his lady. Mr. Dahlhime's conscience would not permit him, to suffer such conduct to pass unnoticed, he therfore preached against vices of that description; the prince soon perceived the intentions of his chaplain, came no more to church, but took every Sunday a ride to his country seat, or into his park. One Lord's day Mr. Dahlhime was crossing the castle square, on his way to the chapel, just as the prince was stepping into the coach: he approached, and boldly asked him: "Whither does your Highness think of going?" "What business have you to ask me that question?" was the reply. "I am deeply interested in it, answered Dahlhime, as he proceeded on to the chapel. Here he preached in the plainest terms against the vices and excesses of the great of this world, and pronounced one woe after the other against them. The lady of the prince was in church: after sermon she invited him to dine with her: and expressed her concern at his liberty of speech, fearful of evil consequences. In the meantime the prince returned, but went immediately to his mistress in town, who unfortunately had been in church that day. Mr. Dahlhime as well as the princess had seen her, and could therefore prognosticate, that a heavy storm was gathering over Dahlhime's head; but he informed the princess, that unconcerned for his own fate he intended to see the prince, and tell him the truth to his face. When he entered, the prince cast an angry look at him, and asked him : "What is your business here?" "I come to lay before your Highness the blessing and the curse; if you will not depart from your vicious life, the curse will fall upon yourself and your family, and your land strangers shall inherit." The next day, he was deposed from his office, and sent into exile. However the prince had no peace of conscience; two years afterwards he recalled him with honor, and presented him with the best parish in his gift. But Dahlhime's prophecy was accomplished; and it is now better than forty years, since every branch of this princely family has been cut off. But I return again to the narration of Stilling's life.

With all the good nature Stilling possessed, he could not prevent people from finding fault with his private studies during school-hours; this dissatisfaction gradually became general throughout the village, because they believed, their children were neglected. It is true, the people had some reason for their suspicions, though upon the whole, he was not inattentive to the interests of his scholars. The peasants were amazed, at seeing so many strange figures in the school-windows, as his sun-dials appeared to be. They frequently stopt in the street, when they saw him looking through a piece of glass towards the sun. One would say : "This fellow is out of his senses;" another guessed, he was viewing the courses of the heavenly bodies; both were mistaken in their conjectures, for Stilling merely made use of a broken piece of a wineglass to observe the beautiful colors, which the refracted rays of the sun exhibited by means of it.—Thus keeping school, working at the trade, and stolen reading-hours, made the round of Stilling's occupations throughout the greater part of that year, until a short time before Michaelmas he received a letter from parson Goldman, offering him the large school at Prysingen. This village is situated six miles to the South of Linedorf, in an extensive and charming valley. Stilling rejoiced at the receipt of this letter, and his father and mother were likewise gratified to see Henry's prospects brighten. He expressed his thanks to Mr. Goldman, for his kind recommendation, and promised to be faithful in the discharge of his duties.

Mr. Goldman was a distant relative of Stilling's deceased mother, which circumstance, together with the general report of his abilities for such an office, had induced him, to propose Stilling as schoolmaster to the congregation at Prysingen. Immediately after Michaelmas he commenced his labors; and sincerely resolved to fulfill the duties of his station with zeal and diligence, and to pursue his own studies only in leisure moments. He boarded in the house of a rich widow-lady, by the name of Smoll, who had two handsome and modest daughters, whose names were Maria and Anna. The former was twenty, the latter eighteen years of age. The members of that family were much attached to each other, and favored with every earthly blessing, they could desire. Being wealthy, they attended to no particular business, except the usual family work, and spent their time in singing, playing on some musical instrument, and in other innocent amusements. Stilling, though himself fond of recreation at suitable times, was of opinion, that the continual round of pleasures, in which these ladies indulged, without any active employment of the mind, must necessarily create an incurable ennui; yet he was fond of their society, whenever he sought relaxation from studies. He had never yet seriously felt the passion of love, and being of opinion, that neither of the Miss Smolls' would marry him, since he was but a tailor and schoolmaster, he carefully suppressed every germ of love, which arose in his heart, especially towards Maria. Yet, what do I say of

suppressing ! No one can do it in his own strength or power !—
Stilling's angel, who led him, turned off every arrow, that was
shot at him. But the two sisters thought very different on that
subject; they liked the schoolmaster, who was in the bloom of
youth, full of vivacity, and very sentimental ; for though in general he was calm and sedate, there were moments, when life and
sentimentality shone forth from every corner of his heart, and all
were pleased and gratified in his company. On such occasions
Mrs. Smoll generally sat playing with her snuff-box, reflecting
to what class of people the schoolmaster belonged. He appeared to her to be a clever and pious young man'; but as he seemed
to take only delight in objects not well qualified to procure him
a living, she often said, when he had left the room : "Poor fellow ! what will become of him !" "We do not know," Maria replied, "but I believe, he'll yet become a great man in the world."
Her mother answered with a smile : "May the Lord prosper
him, he is a very good lad ;" which evidently pleased her
daughters.

We have already mentioned, that Stilling was resolved to
do his duty as instructor of youth, but it was a pity, that this
resolution proceeded not from any inclination of keeping school ;
for had it been optional with him, either to spend eight hours
of the day at the needle, or in keeping school, he would have
preferred the former, because it laid him under no responsibility, and was an easier task. With a view, to make his present
occupation less burdensome, he invented various methods to
induce the children to be diligent with less attention on his part ;
for instance : he introduced degrees of rank, which were conferred agreeable to the diligence or application of the scholars ;
he also invented several plays and games, calculated to promote
a spirit of emulation in the different classes ; and as he was very
fond of music, he made himself acquainted with the notes, and
introduced the singing in parts into his school. By this means
he filled Prysingen with mirth and song. When the moon shone
solemn and bright through the boughs of the trees, and the stars
were twinkling in the blue canopy of heaven, he went with his
choir of singers on a rising ground before the village, and sung,

that it sounded over hill and dale, while the people, old and young, stood listening before the doors of their houses. Frequently he went with his scholars into the orchard behind Mrs. Smoll's house, and sung evening hymns with taste and harmony. The two girls would on such occasions seat themselves in a chamber up stairs, and listen with deep attention. He generally found them in this situation on his return; and sometimes he would take Maria by the hand, and ask her: "How do you feel, Maria?" She would then sigh heavily, press his hands and say: "Your singing has left a pleasing impression on my mind." "Let us be pious, girls," was his reply, "in heaven we shall sing in more harmonious strains;" and then he left them—and though his heart frequently was strongly affected on such occasions, yet the cause of such affection was almost hidden to his own breast.

In his leisure-hours he studied Geography and Wolf's principles of the Mathematics; he likewise found an opportunity to improve himself in the art of making sun-dials. He painted one with dark colors on the ceiling of his school-room, as large as the space would permit; and as one window looked to the South, he fastened a round looking-glass before it, over which he had drawn a cross-line with oil-colors, by which the rays of the sun were so reflected against the dial, in which he had placed the twelve signs of the Zodiac with accuracy, and divided each into its thirty degrees, that it not only pointed out the hour of the day, but likewise the place of the sun in the zodiac. Above the window was written in large Roman characters: "*The heavens declare the glory of God.*"

History, as yet, had occupied but little of his time; his knowledge in that branch extended merely to church history, the history of the martyrs, the biographies of pious men, and the history of the thirty years war. In poetry he had only read some antiquated German works; he had frequently perused them, and related the stories they contained, as frequently unto others; he was now desirous of reading later productions, in order to become acquainted with the poets of his native country; and he soon found, what he sought. A son-in-law of parson

Goldman, a surgeon and apothecary by profession, owned a large number of poetical productions, especially of novels, and very kindly offered to lend them to Stilling.

The impression which the reading of these productions of the imagination left on his mind, was astonishing; he fancied, he would experience similar incidents in *his* life; he longed for their developement, but placed his confidence in his heavenly Father, and resolved implicitly to follow the direction of an all-wise Providence. At the same time they left a strong desire to act as nobly and as disinterestedly in his own life, as the heroes in the works of fiction were represented to have acted. With a heart thus rendered susceptible, he again read the Bible and the religious experience of pious men; as for instance: "Godfrey Arnold's lives of the Patriarchs," his history of the christian church, and of the heresies, which have arisen in it," and other works of a similar nature. Such promiscuous reading gave an uncommon cast to his mind, which I can neither describe nor compare with any other disposition, with which I am acquainted. He idealized every landscape into a paradise; every thing in nature appeared beautiful to him, and the whole world almost a heaven. Vicious men he ranked with the brutes, and wherever he could discover the least trace of goodness in any man, he felt disposed to think well of him. But he utterly despised lips, whose expressions he found at variance with the sentiments of the heart; but was willing to palliate and excuse almost every other human infirmity.

CHAPTER VII.

As Mrs. Smoll became better acquainted with Stilling, and felt a greater affection for him. she was very sorry, that his prospects were of so unpromising a character. Her judgment was in that respect correct enough, and Stilling knew it as well as she did; but his studies during leisure-hours were as little satisfactory to her, as his other occupations were; and she sometimes observed with a smile : "I shall either see the schoolmaster come as a beggar to my door, or as a great gentleman in a splendid equipage." Then she would present her snuffbox to him, and with a slap on his shoulder say : "Take a pinch, schoolmaster, we shall yet live to see strange occurrences." Stilling's reply generally was : The Lord will provide."

Having lived in this manner for better than a year, the girls began to be more unreserved in their attachment for him. Maria had moral courage enough to declare herself, and to reason obstacles away. Stilling knew, he could love her, but was afraid to enter into an engagement—reflecting on his own destitute and dependent situation ; he therefore continued to resist the idea of marrying, though in the family he persevered in his affectionate treatment of Maria. Anna perceiving, that he treated her sister more affectionately than herself, despaired of gaining his heart; however she disclosed her sentiments to no living soul, but bore her grief in silence.—Stilling suspected nothing of her disposition towards him, otherwise he would have been prudent enough, to pay likewise some attention to her. The family however observed with surprise, that Anna became very sedate and melancholy, though no one suspected the cause of the change. Attempts were made, to cheer her, but without effect. One day she expressed a desire to visit an aunt, who lived about three miles from Prysingen near Salen. Her mother gladly gave her consent, and despatched a servant girl with her, who on her return in the evening reported to her mistress, that Anna had become quite cheerful, when she arrived at her aunts. A few days afterwards, the family began to look for her return, but in vain ; neither was any message received from her. Mrs. Smoll became very uneasy ; she trembled as often as the house-door opened, especially in the evening, from fear of hearing bad news.—— To put an end to this state of uncertainty, she asked Stilling to go on Saturday for Anna. It was late in October; the sun stood low in the South ; here and there a green leaf was still visible, and a rough east-wind was whistling through the leafless birch trees. He had to cross a long heath ; and the gloomy state of nature tuned his soul to sad forebodings. On his arrival, Anna met him, skipping about and dancing, and at the same time exclaiming aloud : "You are my dear lad ! though you do not love me ! But you shall have no nosegay of flowers !—such a nosegay—of flowers, which grow on rocks and cliffs—a nosegay of wild cumin and moss—that's for you !"— Stilling stood aghast, without being able to speak one word. Her aunt burst into tears on seeing Stilling, but Anna continued dancing about, singing as she danced :

On rocky hills a lamb was seen ;
No blade of grass could find it—
And felt with anguish sharp and keen,
The shepherd did not mind it.

On inquiry he learnt, that two days before his arrival, Anna had gone to bed in perfect health, but in the morning had acted in the manner, she now did ; no one, however, conjectured the cause of this misfortune, and he only suspected it from the tenor of her talk. The aunt would not permit them to start that day, but desired Stilling, to stay over night, and return with her poor niece in the morning. During supper, Anna was very quiet, and ate very little, until Stilling asked her : "Have you no appetite, Anna ?" when she immediately replied : "I have been eating, but it does not agree with me—I have the heart-ache!" "You must be quiet," said Stilling, "you have always been a good and peaceable child, what has happened, that could effect this sad change? see how aunt is grieved on your account ! are you not sorry for it ? Your strange behavior has caused me to shed tears too. Ah ! formerly you were not as you are now—I entreat you, rouse yourself, and behave as you formerly did !" She replied : "Mind ! I'll tell you a fine story ! There was once an old woman,"—she took a cane in her hand, bent her back, and walked the room, very naturally mimiking an old woman. "I suppose you have seen an old woman go begging ere now ? This old woman went begging too, and whenever she received any gift, she used to say : 'God reward you !' Not so ? Beggars generally say so, if you give them any thing ? That beggar-woman came to a door—to a door—there stood a friendly lad before the fire, warming himself ; it was a lad as"——here she pointed towards Stilling.—"This lad invited the poor old woman, to come to the fire, as she stood trembling in the door, saying : 'mother come, and warm yourself.' She came ;"—now she walked quite smart, and stood all bent up by Stilling's side,—"but she approached too close to the fire ; her rags began to burn, and she did not observe it. The lad saw it—he ought to have quenched the flame, shouldn't he, schoolmaster?—shouldn't he have quenched it?"—Stilling returned no answer, for his suspicions about the cause of her derangement becoming now confirmed, he did not know, what to do, nor how to act. However, she insisted on an answer, and therefore repeated the question : "He ought to have quenched it, ought he not? Give me an answer, and I'll say *too ;* God reward you! "Yes:" replied he, "he ought to have quenched it ; but if he had no water, how could he quench it ?" Stilling rose, deeply affected in his mind, but endeavored to hide his agitation as much as possible from the company. "Yes," continued Anna weeping : "In that case he ought to have shed tears, until he could have quenched the fire with that flood."— Having said this, she again approached him, looked keenly into his face, and when she observed, that tears had started into his eyes, she continued : "Well, these I'll wipe off;" took her handkerchief, wiped his face, and again sat down in silence at the table. All were deeply grieved, and soon rose from the table, and each retired to his bed-room. No sleep came into Stilling's eyes ; he pitied the situation, in which he had found Anna, but saw no remedy. He reflected, what in this case would be his duty to do. His heart spoke for mercy, but his conscience demanded the strictest reserve. He examined with which of these demands he ought to comply. The heart said : you can make her happy ; but conscience replied : This happiness will be of short duration, and years of misery will follow in the train. The heart hoped : God would grant a happy turn to future events ; but conscience judged, it was wrong to tempt God, and that we could not expect, he should alter or break a whole chain of future occurrences, in which so many others were interested, in order to gratify the passion of two poor worms. "This is true," said Stilling, as he jumped out of bed, and walked the floor: "my conduct towards her shall be affectionate, but at the same time distant and reserved." On Sunday morning, he went home with the poor girl. She insisted on leaning on his arm; at first he did not like to permit it, for fear, people might take offense at it. However, he overcame this prejudice, and offered her his arm. On reaching the heath, she left him, gathered wilted and dry herbs, all the while singing her shepherd's song, so that Stilling could scarcely refrain from sobbing aloud. At length she again took his arm, and asked him: "Henry, have you ever been in hell?"—"God preserve us from hell!" replied he. She then seized his right hand, placed it under her left breast, and said: "How it beats here!—There is hell—thither you belong!"—She gnashed with her teeth, and looked wildly around her. "Yes," continued she, "you are already in it!—but like an evil spirit!"—Here again her tears stifled her voice. After a while she said: "Not so—not so!" During conversations of this kind, which were as so many daggers to Stilling's heart, they arrived at her mother's dwelling.— When they entered the house, Maria came out of the kitchen, and the mother from the family-room. Anna ran to embrace her mother, kissed her and said: "Ah, dear mother! I have become very pious—as pious as an angel! and you, Maria, may say what you please"—shaking her finger at her—"you have stolen my shepherd; but do you know the song: 'On rocky hills a lamb was seen?'"—She then skipped into the room, kissing all she met. Both, Mrs. Smoll and Maria, sobbed aloud. "Ah! have I lived to see this!" said the good mother, wringing her hands. Stilling related, what he had heard from her aunt; his soul was overwhelmed with grief; for he now saw plainly the cause of the misfortune, and yet durst not speak of it to any living soul. Maria too became aware of it, took warning from her sister's fate, gradually withdrew her affections from Stilling, and accepted the attentions of other young men. Poor Anna was placed in an upper room of the house, and an old woman was hired, to take care of her. Sometimes she raved, tearing every thing within her reach. When she was in that situation, they usually called Stilling, who generally succeeded in quieting her. Happily, this unfortunate state of poor Anna was not of long duration; in a couple of weeks, she again recovered; and regretted, that she had given way to the passion of love, so as to have been deprived for a time of reason; she became more prudent than formerly, and Stilling rejoiced at this happy change, chiefly, because he had escaped the dangerous cliffs, against which he might have suffered a dreadful shipwreck. But of the rest of the family no one ever discovered the true cause of Anna's misfortune.

CHAPTER VIII.

Though Stilling continued to manage his school with unremitting attention and zeal, there were still many among his employers unfriendly to him. The reason of this he could never discover. At length he committed himself in a manner, which deprived him of the school, though his conscience exonerated him from any improper intention. He had never approved of the old method of keeping school, and had endeavored, as I have mentioned in another place, to invent new plans, by which he might excite his scholars to emulation, and make learning rather an amusement, than a burden. Among the novelties, which he had introduced in his school at Prysingen, was the following : he cut pieces of white paper to the size of cards, which he numbered according to the questions of the Heidleberg catechism; with these cards, if you will call them by that name, the children played, and he who attained the highest number, had only to learn that question, which his number indicated; and if he knew it before, had no lesson for that day ; but the others had to learn those numbers, which their cards pointed out ; and their fortune consisted in knowing either few or many of those questions, which had fallen to their share. Stilling had sometimes seen people play at cards, and the idea of *his* play was taken from that. This circumstance gave rise to great agitation in the vil-

lage, and it was represented in the worst possible light to pastor
Goldman, who loved Stilling from his heart, but was grieved at
his imprudence, and therefore gave Stilling a severe reprimand.

Stilling related the whole proceeding to him, as it really
was, shewed him the play, and endeavored to convince him of the
advantage, which his scholars had derived from it. Mr. Goldman however, who knew the world better than Stilling, answered
him: "My dear cousin! we ought not only to look upon the advantage, which we may derive from the introduction of any new
plan, but we have likewise to reflect, if the means we use, meet
with the approbation of men : if we neglect this, we gain nothing at all, and often will be injured by it: this is at present your
case, for your employers are so enraged, that they will get rid of
you at Michaelmas; and if you do not take your dismission before that time, they purpose to enter a complaint against you before the General Inspector Minehold ; and you know, what sort
of a man he is. I should be sorry, if this affair were carried thus far ; because in that case you would deprive yourself
of every chance of obtaining another situation as teacher in
this country. I therefore advise you, to take your dismission,
and tell the congregation this very day, that for the present you
wish to keep school no longer ; and that they therefore might
choose another person in your place. By pursuing this course,
your honor will be preserved, and in a short time you will have
a better school than this ; I shall not forget you, but endeavor
to do all I can, to render you happy." This declaration of his
cousin made a deep impression upon Stilling, for he plainly saw,
that Mr. Goldman's reasoning was correct, and resolved, to act
in future in all things with the utmost circumspection. At the
same time it appeared enigmatical to him, that many of his brethren in office, though less gifted and fittted for it than he
was, enjoyed more ease and happiness than he did, and he
began to doubt in his mind, whether the instruction of children was the station, his heavenly Father had designed for
him. When he came home, he announced to the congregation,
that he wished to be dismissed from his present office. Many

were surprised at the annunciation, but the major part received the news with gladness, because they had already a person in view for the office, and believed, no one would now oppose their wishes.

Mrs. Smoll and her daughters did not like his removal at all; for he had initiated himself into the good graces of the old lady; and the love of her daughters had been changed into an intimate friendship. All three shed tears on hearing the news, and dreaded the day of his departure, which however came but too soon. Stilling was much affected on this occasion, and so were both mother and daughters; before he left the house, he had to promise, to visit them frequently. Having reached the highest elevation of the mountain on the road to Linedorf, he once more viewed with mingled emotions the village of Prysingen, which had been endeared to him in many respects. He thought: Mr. Lampe justly sings:

My life is but a pilgrim's state!

and exclaimed: "I return home now for the third time, to earn my bread with the needle; when! oh when! will it please God, to make me lastingly happy. He knows, that it is my heart's desire, to become a pious and a useful man." He then commended himself in prayer to God, and continued his way towards Linedorf, with his budget on his back. After a walk of about two hours, he arrived there; William cast a reproachful glance at him as he entered the room, but his mother did not even honor him with a look. Having sat a while in silence, his father began: "Have you returned again, you good for nothing boy? I once hoped to reap joy and satisfaction from my son— of what benefit are those foolish things, you are so eager to learn?—You are dissatisfied with the tailor's trade, you sit here sighing all the time, and when you keep school, you no where succeed! At Zellberg the people were indulgent toward you, because you were still a child; at Dorlingen you were every one's butt; you have no strength of mind at all; here at Linedorf you set the people against you, by paying attention to arts, which are neither profitable to yourself, nor others; and from Prysingen you had to make your escape, to save your honor! What will you now do here? You must mind your needle, and the work in the field, or I do'nt want you at all." Stilling gave a deep sigh and answered: "Father, I feel, I am innocent, but I cannot make my defense, God in heaven knows my heart! I ought to be resigned to every dispensation of his Providence. But——

> Once shall come the joyful year
> With tidings of full liberty!

For it would be a dreadful thought indeed, that God's Providence should refuse me the gratification of those desires and inclinations, which he has planted in my soul!" William made no reply, but laid a piece of work before him, which Stilling managed with so much skill and apparent ease, that his father thought, God had no doubt destined him for that trade; this idea however seemed insupportable to Stilling, and his soul revolted at it; whenever therefore William expressed himself to that effect, he generally replied: "I do not believe, that God could have condemned me in this life to a continued hell." It was now autumn, and the farm work partly over, so that he attended to the needle with little interruption, which he preferred, because it exhausted his strength less than the work in the field. Nevertheless his melancholy soon returned; it appeared to him, as if he were in a strange country and forsaken by all. When his father was in a good humor, he sometimes ventured to complain and to communicate to him the gloomy state of his mind. William would on such occasions observe with a smile: "This is something, which is unknown to us of the Stilling family, you have inherited it from your mother. We are always good friends with nature, whether it is green, variegated or white. But your mother was not so, she was skipping and dancing in the spring, calm and happy in summer, plaintive in autumn and winter, till Christmas; when hope seemed to kindle again in her heart." "Would to God, she were alive." was the reply of Henry, "she would understand me better than any one else." Sometimes he stole an hour or two for reading, and seemed to taste the sweets of better days, but alas! the enjoyment was but momentary! In the family, things were no more as they used to he; he saw and felt nothing, but a greedy desire after riches; the quiet and peaceable spirit of father Stilling had departed. He bewailed the days of his childhood, as a bridegroom laments his departed bride. But all was to no purpose; he durst not complain, if he wished to avoid reproaches. He had however one friend in Linedorf, who perfectly understood him. His name was Casper, by trade an ironsmelter; a noble soul, a friend to religion, and possessed of a feeling heart. In the month of November, the weather was still fair; which Casper and Stilling improved, by taking an occasional walk for the purpose of communicating their mutual feelings. Friend Casper endeavored to convince Stilling, that a gracious Providence had destined him for something else, than a tailor or a schoolmaster, which afforded great comfort to him, and he resolved, to be resigned to the dispensations of divine Providence. About Christmas fortune again smiled upon him. The church wardens of the parish of Clafeld, gave him a call as schoolmaster; this was the most profitable school in the principality of Salen, and Stilling accepted it with gratitude towards God for his gracious deliverance. On taking leave of his father, William gave him many paternal admonitions, and Stilling almost vowed to apply himself diligently to his profession as a teacher of youth, with the view, of obtaining a high standing therein. The wardens accompanied him to Salen, where his call was confirmed before the consistory, by Mr. Minehold the Inspector General.

In the commencement of the year 1760 he entered upon the duties of his office. The faithfulness and zeal he displayed in his calling, raised his name as a teacher in the estimation of the community; all his enemies were silenced, and his friends began to triumph. His private studies were attended to only in leisure - hours. The pianoforte and Mathematical sciences principally engaged his attention at Clafeld, though poetry and works of fiction were not totally neglected. Toward spring he became acquainted with another teacher by the name of Glaser, who lived in the village of Clinehofen, about two miles from Clafeld. He was one of those men, who are generally silent, with a significant look, and whose actions are always

N

performed under the cover of mystery. I have frequently thought of classifying our race; in such a classification I would call the division to which Glaser belonged, the humorous. In the first subdivision of that class, are the silent observers, who are not possessed of much sensibility; to the second belong the fawning sharpers, and in the last and worst are the spies and traitors. Glaser appeared always favorably disposed towards Stilling, without making a confident of him: Stilling on the contrary was both friendly and communicative to Glaser, which pleased the latter very much: for he took delight in observing others, while he remained unobserved. In order to gain Stilling's friendship and confidence, he spoke of great secrets he had discovered; pretended to understand magic and sympathetic arts, and at one time whispered to Stilling under the seal of secrecy, that he was well acquainted with the first principles of the philosopher's stone; and at the same time looked so wise and so mysterious, as though he really were in possession of the great secret itself. Stilling suspected he was; and Glaser denied it in such a manner, that he almost convinced him of his knowledge; and what confirmed him still more in this opinion, was, that Glaser had always more money, than his situation as village-schoolmaster would afford him. He was therefore delighted with his new acquaintance, and entertained the hope, of becoming an adept himself with the assistance of his friend. Glaser lent him the works of Basilius Valentinus. He read them with the utmost attention, and when at the close of the book, he came to the process with the Hungarian vitriol, he really believed himself able to fabricate the philosopher's stone. But reflecting a while on the subject, it occurred to him, that, if that work contained the discovery of the great mystery, every man in possession of that book would be acquainted with it. I can assure the reader, that Stilling's inclination for the study of alchimistical works proceeded not from an anxious desire of finding the philosopher's stone, he would have been glad, it is true, could he have found it, but it originated in an insatiable thirst after the knowledge of the primitive powers of nature. At that early period of life he was as yet unacquainted even with the name of that science. The term philosophy appeared to him inappropriate, he supposed that alchimy would guide him into the desired haven, and therefore he read all the authors on that subject, that came within his reach. But there was always a something in his mind, which demanded proofs for the assertions made in alchimistic books. He was acquainted with only three sources of truth : Experience, mathematical demonstration, and the Bible ; and these three fountains did not disclose to him the mysteries of alchimy, he therefore finally gave up this study as useless.

One Saturday afternoon he visited his friend Glaser, whom he found engaged in his schoolroom at something, which looked like a seal ; Stilling asked him : "At what labor are you engaged, Mr. Glaser ?"

"I am making a seal."

"Please to let me look at it, that is admirable workmanship!"

"It is destined for Mr. de R——. Gladly would I assist you, friend Stilling, in making a decent living without the drudgery of schoolkeeping or of working at your trade; but I must charge you before God, not to betray me !"

Stilling promised, to keep the secret buried in his breast. "Well then, I will tell you, I am in possession of the secret of changing copper into silver, I'll take you into partnership, and allow you half the gain ; you will have nothing else to do, but to undertake now and then a journey, for the purpose of secretly disposing of the silver."

This proposition did not please Stilling; his wish was not to acquire wealth, he only thirsted after knowledge, that he might become a useful instrument in the hand of God, to serve his neighbor ; and he began to suspect, notwithstanding his want of knowledge of the world, that all was not fair in the occupation of his friend; for the longer he looked at the seal, the more he became convinced, that it was an instrument for stamping money. Without committing himself therefore, he only told Glaser, that he would reflect further on his proposition. A few days afterwards an alarm was raised in the whole neighborhood, the police officers had been at Clinchofen to arrest Glaser, who however had made his escape, and was gone to America; and nothing was afterwards heard of him. But his accomplices were taken and punished. Had Glaser been caught, the gallows would doubtless have been his reward, as he had been the instigator of the others. Stilling continued to live very happy at Clafeld, supposing, that the time of his sufferings was past. In the whole congregation he knew no one, whom he believed to be his enemy; but a terrible storm succeeded this calm. He had been nearly nine months at Clafeld, when he received a summons, to appear before the consistory at Salen. This circumstance startled him in some measure, still he did not think, that he would have to answer an accusation preferred against him; he rather supposed, that some new school-regulations had been resolved upon, which were to be communicated to him and others; he therefore went to Salen, without feeling much anxiety about the business. Having reached the anti-chamber of the consistory, he observed, that two men of his congregation were there, of whom he had never entertained the most distant idea of their being his accusers. He asked them, what the matter was? but they replied, they likewise had been summoned, without knowing for what purpose. Soon after they were all three called before the consistory. At the upper end of the room was a table, at one side of which sat the President, a learned lawyer, a man of small stature with an oval face. Opposite to him was seated the Inspector General, the Rev. Mr. Minehold, a corpulent man; his double chin proudly rested on his well starched bands. He wore a large powdered whig, and a black silk gown, falling in graceful folds from his shoulders. He had high arched eyebrows, and whenever he looked at any person, he was accustomed to draw the lower eyelids upward, so that he continually appeared to blink with his eyes. When he pressed on the heels of his shoes, which he frequently did, they creeked. A secretary was seated behind a large table full of papers and writing implements. Such was the court. before which Stilling and his accusers appeared. He took his station at the lower end of the table, his accusers stood on the opposite side, leaning against the wall. The Inspector General, having cleared his throat, turned towards these men, and asked them in the low dialect of the country :

"Is that man yonder your schoolmaster?"

"Yes, your Reverence!" was the reply.

"Ah, so! you are the Schoolmaster of Clafeld?"

"Yes," answered Stilling.

"You're a fine fellow, worthy to be whipt out of the country."

"Gently, gently," interrupted the President; "audiatur et altera pars."

"Mr. President that belongs ad forum ecclesiasticum, you are not to interfere in this matter. The President was silent, but looked rather angry. The Inspector General said, pointing to Stilling with a contemptuous look: "How he stands there, the good for nothing fellow."

His accusers laughed sarcastically at him, and Stilling could scarcely refrain from saying: "As Christ before the High-Priest." But he restrained himself, approached nearer to the table and said: "What have I done? God is my witness, that I am innocent!"

The Inspector laughed ironically and replied: "As if he didn't know, what he has done! ask your conscience?"

"Mr. Inspector, my conscience doth not accuse me, and I believe, he who judgeth right, doth not condemn me either, but I do not know, what may be done in this place."

"Hold your tongue, you impudent fellow! Churchwarden, tell me, what is your complaint?"

"Reverend Sir, we had it registered in the minutes a fortnight ago."

"Ah! that's true."—"And these minutes," said Stilling, "I ought to have."

"What ought you to have?" "No—sha'nt have them!"

"That is flying in the face of all justice," said the President, and left the room.

The Inspector then dictated to the Secretary as follows: "This day appeared N. R. churchwarden at Clafeld, and N. N. inhabitant of the same place, against their schoolmaster Henry Stilling. Plaintifs referred to the minutes of last session; the schoolmaster desired a copy, but was refused for particular reasons."

The Inspector then creeked a few times with his heels, and with arms a kimbo said : "You may go home !"—

I appeal to God, that this relation of the proceedings of an ecclesiastical court is literally true. I would blame myself, were I (without sufficient cause) to accuse the Protestant church of fostering such a man in its bosom. May every youth, who devotes himself to the ministry take a warning example from this man, and think of that precept of the gospel : "whosoever will be chief among you, let him be your servant."— —

To Stilling the whole proceeding appeared like a dream, he returned to Clafeld scarcely knowing, how he got there. Immediately after his arrival, he rang the chapel-bell, as the signal agreed upon, when the congregation was to be called together on an extraordinary occasion. The green before the chapel was soon filled with the inhabitants of the village, and Stilling gave them a circumstantial account of what had occurred. An unconcerned spectator might have observed, how differently the same cause affects different characters; some were raving, some humorous, others grieved, and others again appeared quite calm on the occasion, some pushed their hats on one side, exclaiming : "No d...l shall take our schoolmaster !" During this noise and confusion a young fellow by the name of Rehkopf had gone to the tavern, to frame a petition to the consistory, and a power of attorney for himself. With these papers in his hand, he returned, and addressed the people, as follows : "Let every one, who loves truth and our schoolmaster, come hither and subscribe." Forthwith the whole troop of peasants to the number of one hundred, went into the house, to do as they had been requested. Rehkopf started the same day, accompanied by about twenty stout fellows for Salen, to see the Inspector. Without knocking at the door, or waiting to be announced, he entered the parsonage, followed by the whole troop; in the hall they were stopt by the butler : "What do you want here ? stop, I'll announce you!" Rehkopf replied : "go your way, fill your wine-bottle, we can announce ourselves." With these words the twenty-one men came stamping up stairs, and straight way into the room of the Inspector General, whom they found seated in his arm-chair, dressed in a damask morning gown, a white night cap on his head, sipping his dish of chocolate with great satisfaction. Frightened at the appearance of so many men, he placed his cup on the table and said :

"Good God ! — ye people — what do you want ?"

Rehkopf answered : "We come to inquire, whether our schoolmaster is a murderer, adulterer or a thief ?"

"God forbid ! who says so ?"

"Sir, whether you say it or not, you treat him as if he were either the one or the other. You shall now either prove, that he is a malefactor, and then we will dismiss him ourselves ; or you shall give us satisfaction for your ill treatment of him, and in that case we will keep him. Here is our power of attorney."

"Let me see it !" The Inspector seized it, as if he were about to tear it in pieces. Rehkopf snatched the paper from his hands, with these words : "Sir, let that alone, or you'll burn your fingers, and perhaps I will mine too."

"You insult me in my own house !"

"As you please, Sir, insult or no insult."—

The Inspector then put on a milder face, and said : "Dear people, you don't know, what a bad fellow your schoolmaster is; let me alone in this business."

"That very thing we want to know, whether he is a bad fellow or not ?"

"Terrible things, terrible things indeed I've heard of that fellow !"

"May be ! I too have heard, that your Reverence was drunk as a beast, the last time you kept chapel-visitation at Clafeld."

"What ! what !—who says so ? will you—Hush, hush, I have heard it ; your Reverence judges from hearsay, and so may I."

"What ? I'll teach you manners !"

"Sir, you'll teach me nothing, and respecting your getting drunk, Sir—I stood by, when they lifted you up on one side of the horse, and you fell down on the other. In the name of the

Clafeld congregation we declare to you, that we will keep the schoolmaster, till he is convicted of a crime,—now goodbye."—

On his return Rehkopf walked the whole evening up and down the streets, coughing and hemming, that it might be heard all over the village.

But Stilling found himself again involved in new perplexities, he knew that he would have to yield, and was aware of what he had to expect at home. Meanwhile he learnt the whole mystery of this persecution. The former schoolmaster, who had been generally beloved, had married a girl of the village, and endeavored to obtain an increase of wages, to maintain his family with more comfort. For this purpose he watched his time, and informed the congregation, when he received a call to another place, that he would leave them, unless they were willing to increase his wages; hoping, they would rather consent to do this, than let him go. But he was mistaken, they gave him liberty to depart, and Stilling was chosen. The reader will readily imagine, that the relatives of the girl would be disposed to dispossess Stilling of the office, that they might get the former teacher back again, and hoped to effect this to their satisfaction, by sending frequent presents to Mr. Minehold the Inspector, by which means they at length succeeded.

A few days after the above mentioned occurrence before the consistory, the President sent for Stilling. On his arrival he addressed him thus : "My friend Stilling, I pity you with all my heart, and I have sent for you, in order to give you such advice, as I suppose will be serviceable to you in your present situation. I have heard, that your employers have subscribed a petition to the consistory, to keep you, and have given Mr. Rehkopf a power of attorney for that purpose ; but that will be of no avail to you; for the business must finally be settled in the High-consistory, in which none but the friends and relatives of Mr. Minehold have seats and votes. You will only irritate him the more, and he will not rest, until he makes your country too narrow for you. Therefore ask for your dismission, when you again appear before the consistory." Stilling thanked him for this advice, but objected, that his honor would suffer, if he should act accordingly. The president answered: "I will take care of that." In consequence of this declaration Stilling promised to do, what he had requested.

At Stilling's next appearance before the consistory, Rehkopf was likewise there, without any summons. His affair was taken first in hand. The president gave him a hint, to declare his resolution, upon which he addressed Mr. Minehold in the following manner: "Reverend Sir, since I find, that my enemies wish to deprive me of my office, I yield for the sake of peace, and herewith ask for my dismission." Upon this the Inspector looked very smilingly at him, and said: "Very well, schoolmaster! you shall have it, and in addition you shall have a testimonial of your good conduct, as fair as ever a man has received from the consistory."

"No, Mr. Inspector, no testimonial. My testimony is deeply engraven on my heart, which neither death nor the fire of the judgment-day can obliterate; and this testimony shall once shine so bright into the face of my enemies, that they shall be dazzled by it." Stilling pronounced these words with great emotion. The President smiled, but Mr. Minehold took no notice of Stilling's reply, pretending to be engaged in the reading of some instrument of writing.

When Stilling had ended, the President addressed the Inspector in these words: "To pronounce sentence is your part of the business, but the execution of the judgment is mine. Therefore I order the Secretary to record as follows: "The schoolmaster Stilling of Clafeld appeared this day before the consistory, and asked for an honorable dismission for peace's sake; which was granted him, with this express condition, that, if he should receive another call as schoolmaster, or be employed in some other suitable business, we consider it his duty, not to deprive his country of his abilities and fine talents."

"That's right," observed the Inspector; "and now schoolmaster, that you may know, that I had a right to reprimand you, I'll tell you, you have committed a profanation of holy things; when you went the last time to the communion table, you gave a sarcastic laugh."

O

Stilling looked him in the face, and said : I do not know, whether I have laughed, but this I know, that I have not laughed sarcastically."

"One ought not to laugh at all, during the solemn performance of that holy institution."

Stilling [answered : "Man beholdeth, what is before the eye, but the Lord knoweth the heart. It is possible, I may have laughed, but I know very, well what profanation of holy things is and have known it long ago ; and therefore know, that I have not been guilty of it."

The President then ordered his accusers to come forward : on their appearance the Secretary was directed to read to them the minutes of the transactions in the case. They looked at each other, and felt ashamed. "Have you any objections to make ?" asked the President : they answered : "No."

"Well then," replied the good man, "I have an objection to make. It is the business of the Rev. Mr. Minehold, to confirm the election of your schoolmaster; my duty is, to see that peace and order is preserved; therefore I forbid you under the penalty of one hundred guilders, to choose the former schoolmaster, but to elect one, who has had nothing to do with this business, so that peace may be restored in the congregation."

The Inspector was startled at this declaration of the President, looked at him and said : "In this manner the people will never be satisfied."

"Mr. Inspector," replied the other, "that belongs ad forum politicum, and has nothing to do with your part of the business."

In the mean time Rehkopf had desired admittance; being admitted, he demanded in the name of the congregation, to see the minutes. The Secretary was ordered to read them. Rehkopf looked at Stilling, and asked, if these things were so ? Stilling replied : "we cannot always do as we like, but have to submit to circumstances ; however I thank you, my worthy friend, a thousand times for the trouble, you have taken in my behalf : God will reward you for it." Rehkopf said after a minute's reflection : "I protest against the election of the former schoolmaster, and demand, that this my protest be entered on the minutes." "Well," said the President, "that shall be done ; I likewise have forbidden such an election under a fine of one hundred guilders."

All parties were then sent home, and the business was concluded.

CHAPTER IX.

Stilling found himself again in a very critical situation ; he took leave of his dear Clafelders, with a heart deeply affected ; but instead of returning home, went to parson Goldman, and informed him of his unpleasant situation; who expressed commiseration for his calamity, and desired him to stay all night, that they might take counsel together, what could be done under existing circumstances. Mr. Goldman acknowledged, that Stilling could enjoy no happiness in the house of his father. After some consultations on the subject, Mr. Goldman proposed, to give Stilling recommendations to his son, Judge Goldman at Rothhagen, about three miles from Salen, and to Mr. Snaberg his cousin, chaplain to two princesses at Lahnburg, six miles further on ; and he hoped, that either the one or the other of these two gentlemen would be able to do something for Stilling. He himself began to hope, that every thing would turn out to his advantage ; and with these expectations and letters of recommendation, he started next morning for the above mentioned places. The weather was that day very cold and windy, and the travelling was very bad on account of the storm and bad roads. However Stilling continued his way more happy in the midst of the storm, than he should have felt, had he been on his return to his father. He enjoyed peace of mind, being enabled to look unto God as his kind and gracious father, which would not have been the case, if Minehold's accusation had been well founded.

In the evening at seven o'clock he arrived fatigued and drenched with rain at Rothhagen. Mr. Goldman received him very kindly. "Welcome cousin Stilling," "said he, welcome to my house;" with these words he led him up stairs and introduced him to Mrs. Goldman, who immediately procured him a change of garments, and made preparations for a good supper, during which Stilling related his history. Having finished, Goldman observed: "Cousin, there must be something in your character, which displeaseth the people, else it would not be possible for you to be so unfortunate. If you stay a few days with me, I shall perceive what it is, and as a true friend make you acquainted with it." Stilling answered with a smile: "I shall be glad, cousin Goldman, if you will tell me my faults; but I can tell you myself, where the difficulty lies." I do not follow the calling, for which I am born, I have no satisfaction in any thing I undertake; and therefore there is no blessing in it." Goldman shook his head and replied: "For what do you suppose you were born? It appears to me, you have impossibilities in your head, in consequence of your novel reading; the good fortune which the imagination of poets ascribes to their heroes, makes frequently a deep impression on both head and heart, and awakens a desire after similar changes." Stilling replied after a few moments of reflection, with great emphasis: "No, Sir!—It is true, when I read novels, my heart is affected; I feel, as if every thing I am reading, were happening to myself; but I have no desire for a similar fate. My mind is bent on study; if I had a calling, which would enable me to gain a living, and at the same time continue my studies, I should be happy." Goldman replied: "Cousin! examine this disposition impartially; is not a restless desire after honor and greatness connected with it? Do you not feed your imagination with the fond idea of being dressed in fine clothes, and having the command of an equipage? Do you not entertain an expectation, of once becoming the head and pride of your family?"

"Yes," replied Stilling, "I feel such a desire, and acknowledge, that it sweetens many a bitter moment." "Well," continued Goldman, "are you likewise firmly resolved, to live righteously and soberly in this world, to serve God and your neighbor, and are you really concerned for your everlasting welfare, the salvation of your immortal soul? Answer me this question with sincerity, is this your determination?" "Most assuredly," replied Stilling, "this is the true Polar star, towards which my spirit turns, after many vibrations to and fro." "Well then, cousin," said Goldman, "I will prognosticate your fate. God abhors nothing more, than vain pride, and the desire of the proud man, to behold his neighbor far below himself; this is corrupt human nature. But he loves that man, who in secret and without show labours for the welfare of his brethren. Such a man he raises in his own good time from the dust, and placeth him on an elevated situation. There the man of rectitude sits, without any danger of being cast down; and because the burden of his high station keeps him humble, he considers all men as his equals ; and this I call truly regenerated human nature. God will therefore discipline you by many severe trials, that you may lay aside every vain desire, and if you learn obedience, you will, after many probations, become a happy man, and an instrument in the hand of God for the happiness of many of your fellow creatures. But if you disobey, you will perhaps soon rise very high in the world, and then fall at once, so that it shall sound as a warning example to many." This declaration of his cousin made a deep impression on Stilling ; it appeared to him, as if Goldman had read his very soul. He therefore replied with great emotion : "Yes, you are right, cousin, I feel, this will be the course, Providence intends to take with me." Goldman smiled, and concluded the conversation in these words : "Now I begin to hope, you will be finally happy."

The next morning he took Stilling into his office, and gave him some writings to copy, which he performed with so much dexterity, that Mr. Goldman would have employed him as clerk, if his wife had not been rather too economical. A few days afterwards, Stilling went to Lahnburg. He met the chaplain, as he was taking a walk in the winding paths of a noble park, and immediately delivered the letter, with the compliments from both the Messrs. Goldman. Mr. Snaberg recognized Stilling as soon as he saw him, for they had met once before at Salen. When Mr. Snaberg had read the letter, he desired Stilling to walk with him till sunset, and in the mean time give him a narration of his life. Stilling did it with his usual frankness and vivacity, which frequently drew tears from the eyes of his companion. After supper Snaberg said to Stilling : "My friend, I have a station in view, which I think will suit you. The only question is, whether you can fill it with honor and faithfulness. The princesses have a valuable mine in the neighborhood. They want a man to superintend it, who is faithful and honest, and understands the business well. The present occupant will move away in the spring, and then the office will become vacant. You will have a house, orchard, garden and sufficient land to cultivate, free of rent, and three hundred guilders salary. Now I must ask you two questions. The first is : Have you the necessary knowledge of mineralogy and of the art of mining ? the second : Do you suppose yourself capable of undertaking an office with a fixed salary ?" Stilling, unable to conceal his joy at this proposition, answered : "The first question I can answer in the affirmative, for I have been brought up among colliers and miners ; and in regard to the second, my conscience permits me to say, that I hate every unfaithfulness from the bottom of my soul." The chaplain replied : "I believe, there is no question about your fitness for that office, as far as skill in business is concerned ; I have heard of that already in your own country. But you ought not to speak so positively as to faithfulness ; for you don't know yet all that belongs to it. I have no doubt, you abhor every wilful dishonesty, but here a peculiar prudent kind of faithfulness is required, with which you cannot be yet acquainted. For instance : Suppose, you had that office, and were in want of money—suppose, your family stood in need of something, and you could not get that article without cash, would you not take it from moneys entrusted to you, in consequence of your office ?" "No doubt," said Stilling, "I would do it, so long as I had any claims of salary." "I will admit that for argument's sake," observed Mr. Snaberg, "but this opportunity will make you perhaps venture farther, so that you fall in arrears ; the first year may be only twenty guilders ; the second probably forty ; the third eighty; the forth two hundred, and so forth—until you either must run away, or be arrested as a defaulter. Do not suppose, that there is no danger ! You are kind-hearted—people will soon perceive it—*one* bottle of wine per day will not be sufficient, and this article alone will cost you yearly not less than one hundred guilders, besides the other nick-nacks. Clothes for yourself and family cost another hundred!—Do you expect to satisfy all your other wants with the remaining hundred?"—Stilling replied: "We ought to be on our guard against such a state of things." "Yes," continued the chaplain, "so we ought; but how would you guard against it?" Stilling said: "I would frankly inform every one, who comes to see me: 'My circumstances will not admit of my presenting wine to you—with what else may I serve you?'" Snaberg laughed.—"Yes," said he, "that will do very well, but you may rest assured, you will find difficulties in the execution of your plan, of which you are not aware at present; and I will give you an advice on that subject, which may be advantageous to you through life: whatever or wherever you may be in the world. Let your external appearance in clothes, food and drink be moderate, and no one will demand from you more, than your appearance indicates. If I come into a well furnished house, to a man in fine clothes, I do not ask of what rank in life he is, but I expect a bottle of wine and some cake; on the other hand, if I come into a house, plainly furnished, I expect nothing but a glass of beer and a pipe of tobacco."

Stilling acknowledged the truth of his observation and answered with a smile: "This advice I shall never forget." "And yet," observed Snaberg, "you will find greater difficulties in the execution of this plan, than you imagine; man is very easily elated, if placed in an honorable situation, and it will be very difficult to remain Stilling; we desire to wear fashionable clothes, and this involves us in unexpected expenses, till our ruin is completed. And now my friend, a full stop to all advice, I shall assist you, as far as my influence extends, in obtaining this office. Hope and joy prevented Stilling that night from closing his eyes in sleep. He imagined himself already in his new house, one room of which was to be set apart for a library, and for all the various mathematical instruments, he thought he needed; in short, his imagination was wholly occupied with his future happy situation.

The next day he remained at Lahnburg, to await the issue of the chaplain's application. Success crowned his efforts, and Stilling returned with these glad tidings to cousin Goldman, who laughed heartily, as he listened to Stilling's enthusiastic relation of his good fortune. When he had finished his story, the judge exclaimed: "O cousin, how will it end with you?—This is a situation, which God gives you in his wrath, if you obtain it; it is the straight road to your ruin, and I will prove it to you. As soon as you shall have the place, all the courtiers will visit you, and will make themselves merry days at your expense. If you do not gratify their wishes, they will deprive you of the office, as soon as they can find an opportunity; and if you let them do in your house as they please, your salary wo'nt be sufficient." Stilling was alarmed, when he heard his cousin talk in this manner, and mentioned, what advice he had received from the chaplain. "Ministers can seldom give good practical advice in economy," said Mr. Goldman, "they reason very well in the abstract; and a preacher of a good moral character may likewise live as he reasons, because he is not exposed to many temptations, but we lay-men are in a different situation.—I must tell you too, cousin, all the moralizing preaching is not worth a straw, reason never determines our actions, if our passions are strongly interested; the heart has always an excuse prepared, and persuades us, that black is white.—Cousin, I must tell you a truth, worth more than friend Snaberg's advice! A man, who has not learnt to love God with his whole heart, derives no good from all moralizing preaching. The love of God alone fits us, to become morally good. Let this occurrence be a warning to you; and I beg you, dismiss the Gentleman overseer of the mines of their Highnesses, and welcome the poor needle again, till God shall open a door for you. As tailor you are still my dear cousin Stilling, and I shall put a stop to that business, as soon as I shall come to Lahnburg." Stilling replied with great emotion: "Ah! my dear cousin! all this is very true! Whence shall I derive strength, to resist that deep-rooted and indwelling pride!—The time of man is short on earth.—What benefit shall I derive from having been a gentle-

man ?—Yes, it is true—My heart is the most deceitful thing on
earth—It persuaded me to believe my views to be pure, and that
I intended to do all for the glory of God, and the good of my
neighbor ;—but alas! it is not so!—I merely desire to become
a great man, and to rise high in the world. O! whence shall I
obtain strength to overcome myself ?"

When Stilling had ceased speaking, Goldman embraced
him and said : "My noble cousin, be of good cheer—God will
not permit your faithful heart to fall ; he will be your father.—
We can obtain strength only by exercise in godliness ; the blacksmith in the forge wields a hundred weight of iron under the
forge-hammer, and that apparently with as much ease, as if
there were no weight at all in it, and yet it is impossible for us
to do so. In the same way, a man exercised in trials and probations, can overcome a great deal more, than a petted child,
which has undergone no trials. Be therefore of good courage,
rejoice even in hours of adversity— believe, that you are
in the school of Providence, and that God is educating you for
his own purpose."

Comforted and strengthened in spirit, Stilling returned the
next day to his own country. His severest trial at that moment
was to part from Mr. Goldman ; he judged him to be one of the
best men he had ever known, and I still believe, that his opinion
was correct. A man, such as *he* was, deserves the name of Goldman, or the *golden man*, because his words and actions were always in correspondence. On his way homeward, Stilling resolved to continue at his trade, to harbor no vain thoughts, and
to employ merely his leisure-hours for the prosecution of his
studies. But a deep gloom spread over his mind, when he approached Linedorf, being afraid of the reproaches of his father.
He found William and an apprentice engaged in sewing. Having inquired after the health of his father and mother, he sat
down in silence. William was likewise silent for some time,
but at length pulled off his timble, and with folded arms addressed him as follows :

"Henry, I have heard every thing, which has happened to
you at Clafeld ; I make you no reproaches, but I plainly see,

P

that God has not destined you for a schoolmaster. Stick now to your needle, and work with pleasure at the trade. You will still find many hours, during which you may pursue your studies."

Stilling felt quite angry at himself, for his distrust towards his father, and renewed the resolution, which he had taken on the road, to await God's own time. He therefore replied:

"Yes, father, you are right, and I will pray, that God may change my heart."

He then sat down to sew. This occurred a fortnight before Michaelmas, 1760, after he had just entered into his twenty-first year. If he could have remained at his trade, he would have been tolerably well satisfied; but his father put him likewise to thrashing. During the whole winter he was compelled to rise every morning by two o'clock, and go to work on the thrashing-floor. His hands became full of blisters—his body trembled with pain and weariness, but all this availed him nothing. His father would perhaps have taken pity on him, but his mother demanded, that every one in the family should earn his clothes and living. To all this ought to be added, that Stilling as schoolmaster could never live by his wages; for in those parts of the country, the salary is exceedingly small; twenty-five rix-dollars being the highest sum a schoolmaster receives, besides board, which the employers give him by turns. Therefore all the schoolmasters have a trade, which they carry on during leisure-hours, that they may get with honor through the world. Stilling however did not like this mode of living; he found more agreeable employment; besides, he wished now and then to purchase a book, which was suitable for his purpose—therefore his clothes were poor and worn out, so that he made but an indifferent appearance in the world.

William was very saving—his wife was still more so—they had several small children, and great prudence was requisite, to make a living for the family. The father believed, that his son was tall and strong enough, to earn his own living, and when he found himself disappointed in that hope, he was grieved, and frequently expressed a fear, that his son would become a vagabond. He therefore withdrew his love from him, treated him harshly, and compelled him to perform every kind of labor, in despite of his weakness. Stilling thus found himself sunk almost into the lowest abyss of wretchedness. He knew, that he was unable to endure this way of living for any length of time; he almost hated his father's house, and endeavored to obtain work with other masters, to which his father readily consented.

Sometimes, however, a ray of hope broke through this cloud of misery. John Stilling had been appointed president of the board of commerce, in consequence of his knowledge of Mathematics and Chemistry, his mechanical genius, and for the services, which he had rendered his country. Therefore he gave up his former business of surveying to his brother William. When the latter went into the county of Mark, to survey and divide estates, he generally took his son with him, who was delighted with this occupation, and his father was pleased to observe, that his son understood the art by far better, than himself. This gave frequent opportunities for forming projects, and for building airy castles, which at least amused them for a while, though in the end they amounted to nothing.

Sometimes men of business, desirous of engaging a surveyor, took notice of him, and admired his skill, but his dress, which indicated extreme poverty, created suspicion, and they judged him to be a worthless fellow. Stilling perceived it, and this perception increased his misery. And when he returned home, his wretched situation fell upon him with redoubled weight from its contrast with his former pleasing occupation.— He therefore left his father's house as often as he had an opportunity of obtaining work with other masters, but his earnings were by no means sufficient, to clothe himself decently. One day he came home. He had been working in a neighboring village, and intended to fetch several things from his father's house; thinking of no evil, he entered the room with a free and smiling countenance. When his father saw him, he jumped from his seat, laid hold of him, attempting to throw him; but Stilling seized both the arms of his father, holding him in a position, that he could not stir, and gave him a look, which might have moved a stone. William could not bear it—he attempted to liberate his arms, but could not; he was kept locked fast by the arms and hands of his son, which were convulsively closed.

"Father!" said he in a mild but penetrating tone: "father, your blood flows in my veins, and the blood—the blood of a now happy angel—do not provoke me to anger! I honor you—I love you—but"—

He let go his father, hastened towards the window, exclaiming:

"O! that my cry might reach the centre of the earth and the stars of heaven!"—

Then he again approached his father, addressing him mildly:

"Father, what have I done, that you wish to chastise me?"

William held both hands before his face, sobbing aloud, and Stilling went into a distant corner of the house, to give vent to *his* tears. Next morning he made up his bundle, and told his father, that he intended to travel as journeyman-tailor; and asked him to let him depart in peace.

"No," said William deeply affected, "I can't let you go now."—

Stilling observing his father's emotion, consented to stay. This happened in the autumn of 1761.

CHAPTER X.

A short time after this occurrence, a master tailor at Florenburg hired Stilling to work for him a couple of weeks.— On the first Sunday of his stay at that village, he paid a visit to his grandmother at Tiefenbach. He found her in the old place, behind the stove. She soon recognized his voice, though unable to see him.

"Come Henry," said she, "sit down by my side."
Stilling did so.

"I have heard," continued she, "that your father treats you harshly, is it perhaps the fault of your mother?"

"No," said Stilling, "I ascribe it to my grievous situation alone."

"Mind me!" said his grandmother, "it is dark round about me, but in my heart shines a bright light; I know, your case is similar to that of a woman in labor; with great pain you will become, what you ought to be. Your departed grandfather foresaw all this; I shall remember it as long as I live. One night we were lying in bed, and could not sleep. We conversed of our children, and likewise of you, for you are my son, and I have educated you. 'Yes, Margaret,' said he, 'I wish to know, what will become of that boy. I think William will get into trouble; he will not be able to persevere in the way he holds religion; I hope he will remain an honest, pious man, but he will have to undergo many trials, for he is very economical, and desirous to become wealthy. He will marry again, and then his lame feet wo'nt be able to follow his head. But his son cares nothing for money; his heart is bent on books, and in our situation as farmers, we can make no living that way. I cannot imagine, how father and son will agree; but the boy will without fail be finally happy. If I make an axe, it is, because I want to cut wood with it, therefore I conclude, that God deals in a similar way with man.'"

Stilling felt, as if he had been in the sanctuary, and had listened to an oracle. It seemed to him, as if his grandfather had spoken to him from the grave in his well known voice: "Be of good courage, Henry, the God of thy fathers will be with thee."

He then conversed on various subjects with his grandmother. She entreated him, to exercise patience and resignation, which he promised with many tears, and then left her. On his return to Florenburg, he took a farewell view of the beloved spot of his nativity, and recalled to mind all the occurrences of the years of his childhood.

During the few weeks, which he spent at Florenburg, his mind was in a peculiar situation. He found himself in a pleasing state of melancholy; but the cause of this singular state of mind he was not able to discover; though it is probable, that the family circumstances of the master, with whom he worked, contributed a great deal towards it. There was a perfect harmony in the family, the wish of one seemed to be the will of all the others. His master had likewise a well educated daughter, celebrated as one of the first beauties of the country, gifted with a fine talent for singing and in possession of a large store of good songs and hymns. Stilling sympathized with her and she with him, though without any inclination to marry. They could for hours sing and converse together, without feeling more than friendship for each other. But I cannot say, what might have taken place, if Stilling's stay in that family had been of longer continuance. In the mean time he enjoyed many happy hours during his abode in this family, which enjoyment would have been greater, if he had not been under the necessity of returning to Linedorf.

While he was at Florenburg, pastor Stolbine sent him word, that he should come to him. He found Stolbine seated in a armed-chair engaged in writing. Stilling stood before him, with the hat under his arm.

"How are you, Stilling?" asked the minister.

"I am but indifferent, your Reverence, I may compare my situation to that of Noah's dove, who found no place for the sole of her foot to rest upon."

"Then go into the ark!"

"I ca'nt find the door."

Stolbine laughed heartily and said: "It is very possible. Your father and yourself were angry at me, when I told your uncle Simon, that you should mind your trade; for you went soon after into the county of Mark, and meant to keep school in spite of parson Stolbine. I have heard, how matters have turned out. Now, having fluttered about long enough, without being able to find the door, it is my turn, to point it out to you."

"O pastor Stolbine, if you can assist me, I'll love you as an angel sent by God:" replied Stilling.

"Yes, Stilling, there is a place vacant, for which I have destined you from your infancy, for which reason I insisted on your learning latin, and that you should continue your trade, after you had fared ill at Zellberg; and I disliked your boarding with Creger, because he would doubtless have drawn you over to his party; but I durst not mention at that time, why I treated you harshly, though I meant it well. Had you remained at the trade, you would now have good clothes, and money besides. And what harm would have come of it, it is still time enough for you to become happy. The Latin school here is vacant, you shall be the Rector; you have ability enough to learn soon, what may perhaps be lacking yet in sciences and languages."

This proposition was in complete accordance with Stilling's inclination; he thought himself drawn from a dark dungeon and transferred into a paradise. He could not find words sufficient to express his gratitude to Mr. Stolbine, though he still entertained a secret dread of keeping school again.

Mr. Stolbine continued: "One difficulty is yet to overcome. The borough council must be gained over; I have already done something towards it. I have probed the people, and found them inclined to employ you. But you know the situation of things here. As soon as I attempt any thing, which I consider useful, they immediately oppose me, because I am the parson; we must therefore be careful and watch for a favorable opportunity. Do you keep to your trade, till I tell you, what is to be done." Stilling agreed to every thing and returned to his shop.

Before Christmas William had a great deal of work to finish, and therefore called upon his son for assistance. Scarcely had he been a few days at Linedorf, when Mr. Kilehof the assessor, one of the first men at Florenburg came to his father's house. He was a bitter enemy of Mr. Stolbine; he had heard of the report, that the Florenburger's intended to engage Stilling for their Rector, and this agreed perfectly with his own wishes. But supposing, that the parson would use all his influence to prevent his plan, he had taken measures, to carry his point in despite of him. He accordingly proposed to William and his son, that the latter should move into his house after New-Year, and give his children private instruction in the latin language. The other citizens of Florenburg would then likewise send their children and the business would be settled in such a manner as to carry the point even against Stolbine's will. This intention of Mr. Kilehof was very wrong, for Stolbine had by law the superintendence of the latin as well as of all other schools in the parish; and consequently the first vote at every election. Stilling knew well, how matters stood, and was glad to see affairs take a favorable turn, but durst not mention Mr. Stolbine's real sentiments from fear, that Kilehof should forthwith change his mind.

William and his son were of opinion, that the end of all troubles was at hand, for the situation was very respectable, and connected with a salary sufficient to make a living for a family. His stepmother likewise rejoiced at his favorable prospects, for she loved Stilling, but was fearful he would become burdensome to them; though he had never received the most necessary articles of clothing in his father's house. On New-years-day 1762 he moved to Kilehof's at Florenburg, and commenced his private Latin school. After a few days Mr. Stolbine gave him to understand, that he wished to have a private interview with him. Stilling went therefore one evening to him. The parson expressed his satisfaction, that affairs had taken the turn he desired. "Now," said he to Stilling, "when they have made up their minds about choosing you, they must after all come to me, to obtain my consent. And because they generally make blunders, I am opposed to them. How will they study upon pointed sarcasms!—And when they find, in the present case I am of their opinion, they will doubtless be sorry, for having elected you, but then it will be too late. Do you keep yourself quiet, be diligent in your business, and all will do well.

In the mean time the Florenburgers had frequent meetings at Mr. Kilehof's, to counsel together, how they might arm themselves against the parson. Stilling, being present at all these consultations, was often compelled to leave the room, to give vent to laughter. Among the men who usually met at Kilehof's of an evening, was a Frenchman by the name of Gayet. No one in the village knew the place of his birth, whether he was of the Reformed or of the Lutheran religion, or how it happened, that he was always flush of money. In cases of disputes in the borough, he always played his cards so dexterously, that it was difficult to find out to what party he belonged. Stilling had formed some acquaintance with him, when he attended the latin school at Florenburg. Gayet was fond of the company of intelligent people. Meeting with none of that description in the town, he delighted in exercising his wit at the expense of his fellow townsmen. Whenever the Florenburgers were assembled in council for the purpose of laying plans to take parson Stolbine by surprise, *he* likewise attended, with the view of enjoying a laugh at their expense.

One evening as six or eight of them were in earnest conversation about the election of their teacher, Gayet addressed them as follows: Neighbors! I will tell you a story. At the time when I was peddling hats, I took a notion to visit the kingdom of Siberia and its capital Emugia. The king of that country had died a short time before my arrival, and the States of the realm were assembled for the purpose of electing another king. But there was one difficulty to overcome: the kingdom of Crossgrainland bounds on Siberia, and both States had been from time immemorial at war with each other. The cause of this hostility was not unimportant. The ears of the Siberians were long and straight, such as asses have; the ears of the Crossgrainlanders were hanging down over their shoulders, like the ears of the Elephant. The bone of contention was the assertion of each nation, that the ears of Adam, the progenitor of the human family, had been such as they respectively possessed. It was therefore absolutely requisite, that in each country an orthodox king should be chosen. The most infallible criterion of his orthodoxy was the degree of hatred which he manifested towards the other nation. When I was there, the Siberians proposed a very clever man, as a candidate for the crown, not so much on account of his orthodoxy, as in consequence of his good sense and general knowledge. On the day of election it appeared that many were dissatisfied with him, and withheld their votes, because he was defective in orthodoxy, according to the fashionable definition of that term. But at length he was chosen, and the parliament resolved, that their king should forthwith declare war, and march with a well disciplined army of asses-ears against the king of Crossgrainland. This parliamentary decree was forthwith put in execution: and the new king gave orders for the assembling of a large army. When collected, he placed himself at its head, and marched against the king of the hostile country. But when the armies had met, the king of the Siberians demanded an interview with the king of the enemy, and—strange to tell—at this meeting embraced and called him brother. This so enraged the Siberians, that they immediately deposed their king, cut off his ears and sent him into exile.

When Gayet had finished his story, Scultetus the burgomaster observed: "Why, Mr. Gayet, you have been a great traveller!"

"Ah!" observed another, I suspect he means us by that story; he intends to tell us, that we are as stupid as asses."

But assessor Kilehof looked at Gayet with a smile and whispered in his ear: "The fools are not aware, that you mean the Parson and his consistory."

Gayet whispered back: "You have hit it in part."

When they thought they were sufficiently prepared, they sent a deputation to the parson.—This took place about the beginning of Lent. Kilehof was chosen speaker. Stilling waited with much impatience for the result. Kilehof addressed the minister as follows:

"Your Reverence, we have elected a latin teacher, and come to announce it to you."

"But you have not asked for my vote on that occasion?"

"That is of no importance, the children are our own, the school is our property, and the schoolmaster is our own."

"But government has appointed me to examine your Rector, and confirm your election. Do you understand me?"

"With this intention we have come."

"Well then, I likewise have a teacher in view, a real good one, and that is the well-known schoolmaster Stilling.

Kilehof and the other men looked at each other, but Stolbine smiled in triumph; thus both parties were silent for a while. At length Kilehof replied: "Well, we are then of one opinion!"

"Yes, Mr. Headstrong, we are for once of one opinion, send me your schoolmaster, I'll confirm him in his office."

"We are not quite so far yet, Mr. Stolbine, we must have a separate school-house, and disconnect the Latin and the German school." (For both the schools were united, each teacher receiving half the salary, and the latin teacher assisted the german, as much as possible.)

"God pardon my sin! Here the devil sows tares again after all! How shall your rector make a living?"

"That is our look out, not yours."

"Mr. Kilehof, you are really a very foolish fellow, a beast as big as ever trod upon the earth. Go your way."

"What?—You—You abuse me?"

"Go home you fools, you shall not have Stilling, as long as I am minister." And so he left them.

Before Mr. Kilehof reached home, Stilling received orders, to come to Stolbine. He thought he would now be confirmed in his office. But how great was his disappointment, when Stolbine addressed him as follows: "Stilling! this situation is not for you; unless you wish to run into utter ruin, meddle not at all with the Florenburgers!"

Then he related what had occurred. Stilling took leave of Mr. Stolbine with a very agitated mind. As he was leaving him, the minister gave him the following parting advice: "Be patient, God will yet bless you, and make you happy; keep to your trade, till I can find something better for you."

The Florenburgers were now angry with Stilling too, because they believed he had secretly played one game with the parson. They therefore forsook him and elected another teacher. Mr. Stolbine gratified their wishes this time; he confirmed the Rector they had chosen, and they gave him a separate house. But because they could not withdraw the salary from the old german school, they resolved to procure sixty latin scholars for him, and agreed to pay four rixdollars tuition per year for each scholar. But the man had sixty scholars only during the first quarter, forty the second, at the close of the year twenty, and after some time scarcely five, so that he died in misery and want, and his wife and children went a begging.

After this occurrence Mr. Stolbine withdrew from public business, and attended only to his ministerial and official duties. The causes which had most frequently led him into error, were, his great family pride; an extreme fondness of power; and an unyielding claim to personal attention. With these exceptions, he was a good hearted man, whom the poor never asked in vain, for he gave as long as he had any thing to bestow, and endeavored to relieve the distressed among his fellow beings, whenever he had it in his power. But if he saw a man from the lower walks of life rise in the world to an honorable station in society, his jealousy was kindled, so that he lost every charitable feeling towards him. For this reason he had also disliked John Stilling, and frequently given him to understand, that he did not believe him capable of filling the office, he held ; and if John had not been prudent enough, to give way to the old man, their disagreement would have been the cause of many quarrels.

But Stolbine's example shews, that, where the fruits of religion, goodness of heart and honesty, exist, they will finally prevail over all imperfections. The board of commerce, to which Stolbine and several other Florenburgers belonged, met at the house of their President, John Stilling. When Mr. Stolbine arrived, John Stilling arose to meet him, and led him to a chair on his right hand. The minister was on that day uncommonly friendly. After dinner he addressed the company in the following manner:

"Gentlemen and friends! I am an old man, and feel my strength failing every day; this is probably the last time, that I'll meet you in this body ; if there is any one here, who has not yet forgiven me, in whatsoever I may have offended him, I ask his pardon from all my heart."

All persons present looked at each other in silence, till president Stilling answered:

"Reverend Sir, this declaration penetrates my heart. We

are all weak, imperfect men, I am under infinite obligations to you, for having instructed me in the truths of our holy religion ; and I have frequently given you cause of offense, I am therefore the first, who asks your pardon from the bottom of my heart for every thing wherein I may have offended you."

Mr. Stolbine was so affected by this address, that he was compelled to give free course to his tears. He arose, embraced Stilling and said: "I have frequently offended you, I am very sorry for it, henceforth we are brethren."

"No," answered Stilling, "you are my father, give me your blessing."

Stolbine holding him still in his embrace replied: "You are blessed, you and your family, and that for the sake of that man who so often was my pride and my joy.",

This scene was so affecting, that most of the gentlemen present could not refrain from shedding tears. The minister then went to Mr. Kilehof and the other Florenburgers, and asked with a smiling countenance:

"Shall we not likewise balance accounts to day ?"

Kilehof answered: "We are not angry with you!"

"I do not speak of that now," said the minister, "I for my part most solemnly beg your pardon for every thing, wherein I may have offended you !"

"We forgive you," replied Kilehof, "but you ought to ask pardon from the pulpit."

Stolbine felt his whole fire again, but said nothing, and sat down by the side of Stilling, whose zeal kindled ; he arose and said :

"Mr. Kilehof, you cannot expect, that God will forgive your sins. Mr. Stolbine has performed his duty. Christ commands us, to love one another, and to entertain a desire after reconciliation. He will reward your obstinacy upon your own head." Mr. Stolbine concluded this moving scene in the following words :

"I will likewise do, what Mr. Kilehof has demanded, and from the pulpit ask the pardon of my congregation, and I will prophesy to them, that one will come after me, who shall recompense them for all the evil, they have done to me." Which prophecy was afterwards more than fulfilled.

Soon after this occurrence, Mr. Stolbine departed in peace, and was buried in the church at Florenburg by the side of his wife. He had been hated while living, but after his death he was lamented and honored. Henry Stilling at least shall hold him in grateful remembrance all the days of his life.

Stilling stayed till Easter in the house of Mr. Kilehof, where he with grief observed, that they were tired of him, which caused him frequently to sigh for a change. One morning, lying sleepless in his bed, he reflected seriously on his present situation.— To return to his father, was an idea, he could not endure, for the work in the field would have ruined his constitution; besides, his father gave him nothing but his board, and whatever he earned besides, was deducted from the loan, which he had received, when his salary as schoolmaster was insufficient for his maintenance. He could therefore not think of getting any new clothes, and his old ones would be completely worn out in a year's time. To work out from home as journeyman with other masters, was likewise disagreeable to him, and his wages of half a guilder per week, would not have been sufficient, to procure him even the most necessary clothing. These reflections had so powerful an effect upon his mind, that he left his bed and exclaimed: "Almighty God! what is to become of me!"

In that moment the following scripture passage occurred to his mind: "Go out of thy country, from thy kindred and thy father's house, into a land, which I shall shew thee."— This passage at once allayed the storm in his mind, and he resolved to follow the example of Abraham. This happened on Tuesday before Easter. The same day his father came to see him, who had heard of his critical situation. Both, father and son, went into a private room, and William began:

"Henry, I come to consult with you. I see, that you are not the author of your misfortunes; God has not destined you to be a teacher—you are an excellent tailor, but your circumstances are such, that your trade will not procure you the necessaries, of life; you dislike to live in my house, at which I do not wonder, because I am unable to provide a living for you, unless you could do the work, which I have to do; for it falls hard upon me, to maintain my wife and children. Have you considered, what you ought to do?"

"Father! I have reflected on it for years, but only since this morning I have a clear view of what I ought to do.—I must leave my country, and watch the ways of Providence."

"This is my opinion too, my son! If we take past occurrences into consideration, it is plain, that the course, which Providence has led you hitherto, directs us to take that step. And besides, what can you expect here? Your uncle has his own children to provide for, and, as father he ought to do so, before he thinks of you; in the mean time you advance in years without any prospects for the future. But—when I think of your first years—and the satisfaction—which I promised myself—and you will now be gone—Stilling's joy will be gone too,—the very picture of the honest, old father."—

Here tears stifled his voice; he held his hand before his eyes and wept aloud. Henry's feelings were overpowered by this scene.—he fainted away. When he had recovered, his father rose from his seat, took him by the hand, and said:

"Henry, take leave of no one; but set out, whenever your heavenly Father directs you to go. His holy angels will accompany you, whither-soever you may travel—write me frequently, how you are!"—

With these words he left the room.

Stilling commended himself to God; he felt, that the bonds were broken, which had bound him to his relatives and friends. He waited with some impatience for the second Easter-day, on which he was determined to depart. He spoke with no one of his intention, nor visited any body. In the interval he paid one more parting-visit to the graves of his grandfather and mother. It was on the evening before Easter; the full-moon shone in all her brightness; he sat a while on each grave, reflecting how much happier he would be, if these two persons were still living; he then took a solemn farewell of the resting-places of these two dear departed friends, and went his way.

On the morning of the second Easter-day, which was the 12th of April, 1762, he settled accounts with Mr. Kilehof, received about four dollars in cash, packed three old shirts, one pair of stockings, a nightcap, his thimble and scissors into a valise, dressed himself in his best suit, which consisted in a pair of tolerably decent shoes, black woolen stockings, leather small-clothes, a black broadcloth waistcoat, a half-worn coat of coarse brown broadcloth, and a large brimmed hat, according to the fashion of the times; he took his long haw-thorn cane in his hand, and went to Salen, to procure a passport.

From Salen he started in a northwesterly direction, till he came to a post-road, which he followed without knowing, whither it was leading, and arrived in the evening at a village on the confines of the principality of Salen. At the tavern he addressed a farewell-line to his father, promising to write again, so soon as he should have found a place of rest. Among the guests were several carters, of whom he inquired, to what place the post-road was leading, and was informed it led to Shonenthal. He had frequently heard of that celebrated commercial city, and therefore resolved to go thither, and for that purpose inquired after all the towns and villages along the road, and their respective distances from each other; and having carefully made a memorandum of all this, went to bed.

The next morning, after breakfast, having commended himself to God, he continued his journey; but the weather was so foggy, that he could see but a short distance before him. He soon reached an extensive heath, which was crossed by roads in almost every direction, of which he followed the one, which appeared to him the plainest. Between ten and eleven o'clock the fog dispersed, the sun made his appearance, and to his astonishment he found, that the road he had taken, was leading in an easterly direction. He continued it however, till he came to a rising ground, whence he saw the town again, where he had stayed the preceding night. He again turned, and, because the sky was clear, soon found the post-road, which in about one hour's time brought him to the top of a very high hill. Here he seated himself on the green sod, and looked towards the South-East.—

At a considerable distance, he beheld the Geissenberg castle, the Giller and other well known mountains and countries. A deep sigh stole from his heart, tears started into his eyes, he pulled out his pocket-book, and wrote the following lines :

> With throbbing heart, and deeply mourning,
> Once more I these dear hills descry ;
>   Yet, while my longing tears are flowing,
> For yonder hills, where Luna's eye
>   With cool refreshing shade me bless'd,
>   And nought but joy did fill my breast.
>
>   I feel, as if in sweetest dreaming,
> The purest Zephyrs waft me air,
>   And at life's fount, through Eden streaming,
> I see our father Adam there.
>   While draughts of life I'm freely drinking,
>   And faint with joy in rapture sinking.
>
>   Well then ! I turn my looks for ever,
> To unknown mountains, brooks and fields,
>   To see my much lov'd country never,
> Till life its due to nature yields.
>   O gracious God ! direct with blessing,
>   My dark and unknown paths unceasing !

Having written these lines he arose, wiped away his tears, seized his cane, swung his valise over his shoulders, and walked down into the valley.

R

LIFE

OF

HENRY STILLING.

THIRD BOOK.

Henry Stilling's Peregrinations.

CHAPTER I.

When Henry Stilling had descended the mountain, and lost sight of his native country, he began to breathe more freely; every connection and relation, in which he had hitherto stood, seemed to cease, and he felt perfectly happy and satisfied. The weather was very fine; at noon he stopt at a tavern, and having taken some refreshment, pursued his way, which about sunset brought him to a miserable looking village, situated between swamps and bushes, in a narrow, lonely valley. It had been his intention, to spend the night at a village six miles farther on, but having missed the road in the morning, he could not reach it. At the first house he inquired after a place of entertainment for strangers. This being pointed out to him, he entered, and laid down his valise. Soon after the landlord came in, accompanied by several small children, and hung a lamp in the middle of the room. Every thing had such a miserable and suspicious appearance, that Stilling became very uneasy, though he possessed nothing, which would have been worth stealing. They gave him his supper, which he ate with a good appetite, and afterwards lay down on a bed of straw prepared for him. But fear prevented him from closing his eyes in sleep till midnight. Towards twelve o'clock he heard the woman call her husband :

"Arnold! are you asleep?"

"No," replied he, "I am not."

Stilling listened, but kept himself very quiet, that they might suppose him asleep.

"What kind of a fellow may that be ?" said the woman.

Arnold replied: "God only knows—I have been studying the whole evening about it—he did not say much—perhaps he is a bad fellow."

"Do not always think ill of folks," replied Catharine, "that young man has a very honest look, but I fear, he has been unfortunate. I do pity him ! he had such a melancholy appearance, when he entered our door. I believe he is in some trouble or other ; may God assist him !"

"You are right, Cate," replied Arnold, "may God pardon my suspicion—I was just thinking of the schoolmaster from the country of Salen, who stayed all night here, a few years ago; he was dressed just so, and we afterwards heard that he had been forging money."

"Arnold," said Cate, "can you not distinguish people from their looks ? That other fellow had a gloomy and dark appearance, and durst not look any body in the face, but this one seems very friendly and pious ; I'm sure, he has a good conscience."

"Yes, yes," concluded Arnold, "we will commend him to God, he will be his helper in every time of need, if he walks in his ways."

The good people afterwards fell asleep, and Stilling thanked God on his bed of straw, that a Stilling's spirit was ruling in this family, and slept as soundly till morning, as if he had lain on a bed of down. When he awoke, the people of the house were dressing ; he looked at them with a smile, as he bade them good morning. They asked him, how he had slept?

He replied : "After midnight very well."

"I suppose, you were tired yesterday evening," said Cate, "you looked rather melancholy and low-spirited."

Stilling answered : "My dear friends, I was not so very tired, but I have passed through many trials in my life, though I am young, and I therefore appear to be more gloomy, than I really am. Besides, I have to acknowledge, I entertained some fear, that I was not among good people."

"Yes," said Arnold, "you are among people, who fear the Lord, and desire to have an interest in Jesus; if you had ever so much money, it would be secure with us."

Stilling took him by the hand, and said : "May God bless you ! You and I have the same desire !"

"Cate,' continued Arnold, "make us a good dish of tea, and fetch some of your best cream, we will breakfast together, perhaps we may never meet again."

Cate performed the desire of her husband with alacrity.— Stilling was sorry, that he had to part from these people ; tears filled the eyes of all, when he bade them farewell. Comforted and encouraged, he continued his journey. After five hours travelling, he came to a handsome borough, situated in a charming part of the country. On inquiry, a tavern was pointed out to him, which he entered. An old man was seated near the stove, the make of whose clothes indicated, that he had once been in better circumstances than now, but their present condition proved, that he had been reduced to poverty. Besides him, there were two young men and a girl in the room, dressed in deep mourning. The girl seemed to have the management of the kitchen. Stilling took his seat opposite the old man, who seemed disposed, to enter into conversation with him. They soon became very communicative, and Stilling gave him the whole history of his life, in which the old man appeared to take great interest.

Conrad Brower—such was the name of the old man—commenced now a narrative of the occurrences of *his* life.

"I am the oldest of three brothers," said he, "the youngest was the father of these children, whose mother died several years ago, but the father within a few weeks. My second brother is a wealthy merchant in this place. I have been a woolen-draper, and as our parents had left us no property, I instructed my two brothers in the same business ; but the youngest brother married a rich wife, left the trade and kept a public house. I and my second brother continued the business so successfully, that I obtained wealth and honor. My brother, who had shared my good fortune with me, began to think of marrying. There was an old maid living in our neighborhood, who had passed her sixtieth year, and had become proverbial on account of her deformity and want of cleanliness. Her money, however, had sufficient attraction for my brother, to overlook every thing else. She was as stingy as she was rich, so that she satisfied the cravings of hunger and thirst with scarcely any thing but the coarsest food and drink. Rumor said, that she kept her money secreted in some hiding-place, unknown to all but herself. My brother was successful in his courtship, and they were married. For some time he was unable to discover her mammon, but at last he found it, and secured it to himself. His wife was so grieved at the loss of her treasure, that she became consumptive, and died to the great satisfaction of my brother. The fashionable mourning-time having elapsed, he married a young woman, who was about as rich, as he had chanced to become. He now began to use his wealth to the best advantage, and that too at my expense. For he traded in woolen cloth, which he was enabled to sell much lower, than I was, and by this means I lost my customers; my affairs became disordered, and I was involved.

When he saw, his plan had fully succeeded, he pretended all at once great friendship for me; offered to loan me as much money, as I wanted, and I was foolish enough, to enter into the trap. When he thought it was time, he seized upon every thing, I possessed; my wife grieved herself to death, and I live now here in misery and want. After he had ruined *me*, he played the same game with my brother."

Stilling had listened with horror to this story. When Brower had finished, he observed :

"This man must be one of the worst characters in existence; he will have a long account to settle before the tribunal of God."

"True enough," replied Brower, "but persons of this description do not think of that now."

After dinner, Stilling played on a piano-forte the tune: Commit thou all thy griefs and ways into his hands, &c. Mr. Brower folded his hands, and accompanied him with his voice. The young people also joined them. Stilling then paid his bill, shook hands with all and bade them farewell. They followed him to the door, commending him to the protection of God. He continued his way to Shonenthal, delighted to have hitherto met with so many kind-hearted and religious people. I shall call the borough, where Stilling had dined, Holzhime, as I have to conduct the reader once more to that spot in the sequel.

Shonenthal is but fifteen miles from Holzhime, yet having stayed a good while at the latter place, he could not reach the former that evening. He therefore stopt for the night at a place called Rasenhime, about three miles from Shonenthal. The people with whom he lodged, did not suit his taste, he was therefore silent and reserved. The next morning he went to Shonenthal. When he had ascended the hill, whence a full view of that beautiful city burst upon his sight, it being situated in a paradisical valley, he sat down on the green turf, to enjoy the prospect. He wished, it might be his lot, to spend his life in that place. He reflected, what he should do? His dislike to the tailor's trade induced him, to think of a situation as clerk in a store; but having no acquaintances in Shonenthal, who would be likely to interest themselves in his behalf, he resolved to go to Dornfeld, a village a few miles East of the city, where the son of his friend Dahlhime was minister. He found him at home, gave him an account of his present circumstances, and made his wishes known. If Stilling had been better acquainted with the world, he would have been aware, that Dahlhime could do very little for him, he being a total stranger in that place. Mr. Dahlhime, though a countryman of his, was unacquainted with Stilling and his family, and therefore could not recommend him. He therefore returned to Shonenthal, without having effected any thing, and intended to look for a place as journeyman-tailor. But perceiving, in passing through the streets, that the tailors were seated cross-legged on the table, whereas he had been accustomed, to work in a sitting posture before the table, he rejected the idea of following his trade.

As he was walking through the town, uncertain what he should do, he observed a well dressed man engaged in fastening two large baskets to the saddle of a horse. Stilling inquired of him, if he intended to leave town that evening? The man informed him, that he was the penny-post from Schauberg, and was on the point of starting for that place. Stilling recollecting, that a son of parson Stolbine was minister there, and that several of his countrymen were tailors in that village, resolved, to take that opportunity to go thither. Schauberg lies about nine miles in a southerly direction from Shonenthal. Having arrived there, Stilling went forthwith to Mr. Stolbine, who was glad to see him, as he had been acquainted with Stilling's grandfather, mother and father, and had been Henry's school-mate at Florenburg. He advised him to follow his trade, until he could find some more suitable occupation for him. He immediately sent for a journeyman-tailor, to inquire, if Stilling could obtain work in the village, and being informed that a certain Mr. Nagle was in want of a journeyman, ordered his hired girl to point out the house to Stilling, where he was gladly received.

When he went to bed and reflected on the occurrences of the last days, grateful acknowledgments arose from his heart for the faithful Providence of his heavenly father. Stilling had left his native country, without knowing whither to direct his course, and Providence had graciously led him at the close of the third day to a place, where he was enabled to earn his living.

He convinced himself now of the truth of his father's declaration, that a trade was an excellent gift of God, and would always maintain the man who understood it well. He was angry with himself, for having been so unwilling to follow it; he addressed himself in prayer to God, that he would in future direct him by his divine spirit, expressed his gratitude for God's gracious guidance and protection, which he had vouchsafed him hitherto, and then lay down to sleep. The next morning he commenced his work. Mr. Nagle had no other journeyman; his wife, her two daughters and two sons assisted him in his business. Stilling's skill at the trade soon gained him the good will of the master who employed him, and his communicativeness and desire to please, secured to him kind treatment from the woman and the children. He had scarcely been three days in the house, when he felt quite at home: and fearing neither reproaches nor persnation, he was for the present perfectly happy. The first Sunday of his stay at Shauberg, in the afternoon he wrote letters to his father, uncle and other relatives and friends, to inform them of his present situation and circumstances. He soon received cheering answers ; his friends admonished him to an humble and pious life, and warned him against connecting himself with persons of a doubtful character. He soon became known through town ; for on Sundays at church he always took his place before the organ, and as the organist was very unskilful in his business, Stilling attracted the attention of the people by his superior skill in music. They generally stopt at the church-door, until he came down from the organ, inquiring of one another, who the stranger was ? until it became universally known, that he was working as journeyman with Mr. Nagle; who with his whole family treated him in the kindest manner. Pastor Stolbine was pleased to see his countryman beloved and respected in the village. Thus thirteen weeks passed on very pleasantly; Stilling was not ashamed of his trade, nor did he feel a strong desire of changing his present condition.

One Sunday afternoon he took a walk through the streets of the town, the sun shone bright, detatched white clouds were floating in the air ; he was not engaged in any peculiarly serious reflections, when of a sudden an unknown power pervaded his soul, he began to tremble in all his limbs, and could scarcely refrain from sinking to the ground, and from that time he felt a strong desire to live wholly to the glory of God, and for the welfare of his fellow men ; yea, so great was in that moment his love to God and the divine Redeemer, as well as to all mankind, that he would willingly have sacrificed his life to serve them, had it been required. At the same time he was determined, to watch in future over his thoughts, words and deeds, that they might all be acceptable unto God and useful to his fellow-creatures. On that spot he covenanted with God, to give himself up to his guidance and direction, and to entertain no longer vain wishes, but gladly to remain what he was, if it should be the will and direction of God. He immediately returned home, but said nothing to any person concerning this occurrence.

S

CHAPTER II.

Three weeks after this as Stilling was returning from church, the thought occurred to him, that he had never visited the town-schoolmaster, and forthwith went to see him. He knew Stilling already, expressed his satisfaction at seeing him, and asked him, if he were willing to accept a place as private teacher in a good family. "I have received a letter from Mr. Hochberg a rich merchant," said he, "desiring me to procure him a teacher for his children, I did not think of you until you entered the room; it is my opinion, you will be the most suitable man for him that I know. Stilling was elated with joy, believing the hour had come, in which he should forever be liberated from the tailor's trade. He therefore gladly assented, telling his friend at the same time, that it had always been his intention, to serve God and his neighbor with the talents he had received, and he was the more willing to accept the office, because he looked upon it as the means of promoting his own happiness. "I have no doubt of that," replied the schoolmaster; "it will altogether depend on your conduct, whether this situation shall prove a means of promoting your own happiness; I shall write to Mr. Hochberg by next mail, and I expect, he will soon send for you. When Stilling came home, he communicated his new prospects to Mr. Stolbine, Mr. Nagle and his family. The minister was glad, but Mr. Nagle and his family were not in favor of Stilling's leaving them, he was however determined to go ; for he had the greatest aversion to the tailor's trade, and lived in anxious expectation of the time, when he should be called to his destined place. Still he felt something in his breast, which resisted this call ; this unknown something was continually endeavoring to convince him, that the strong desire for changing his situation proceeded from his corrupted heart; this new conscience, if I dare say so, had never troubled him before the Sunday, on which he had made that covenant with God. This conviction grieved him, he knew, what his conscience said was true, but his inclination for accepting the office, was too strong to be resisted : and besides the old serpent represented it

to him as impossible, that God should wish him to remain forever a tailor, and bury the talents, which he had received for improvement, and that therefore the resistance of his conscience was
nothing but a hyprocondrical idea. But conscience objected: how frequently hast thou desired to improve thy talents,
in the instruction of youth and how hast thou fared! The serpent on the other hand replied: that all these difficulties had
been so many probations to prepare and fit him for a station of
greater consequence., And Stilling believed the serpent, and conscience was silent. The next Sunday a messenger came from Mr.
Hochberg, to take Stilling to his house, Mr. Nagle's family were
much affected at his leaving them, but he departed with pleasure.
Mr. Hochberg's house was situated in a pleasant valley near a
considerable creek, and not far from the post-road, which Stilling
had travelled on leaving his native country. He had hardly entered the house, when Mrs. Hochberg made her appearance. She
was a lady of fashion, and of uncommon beauty. She welcomed
Stilling and conducted him into a handsome and well furnished
parlor. Two fine little boys dressed in a scarlet uniform, and a
little girl in fashionable clothes, entered, to make their obeisance
to their new teacher; the bows and courtesies, were all in the
latest fashion. When they came to kiss his hands—a new thing
for Stilling—he did not know how to act, or what to say; he held
out the palm of his hand to them; and the little things were greatly at a loss how to turn it, so as to apply their kiss; which being done, the children hopped away, glad enough to have performed their duty. Mr. Hochberg and his father-in-law were gone to
church, when Stilling arrived, and Mrs. Hochberg was engaged
in the kitchen; Stilling was therefore left chiefly to his own reflections. He plainly saw that two things were essential for him
in order to fill the office of private tutor to Mr. Hochberg's children with credit to himself. The first was, to learn the art of living in fashionable circles, and the second to have fashionable
clothes. His manners were far from being coarse, though he was
utterly ignorant of the rules of politeness; this difficulty however
could be overcome by attention, but it was impossible for Stilling
to obtain fashionable clothes. He had indeed earned eight guil-

ders during his stay with Mr. Nagle, but that was a small
sum to enable him to purchase a new suit. For two guilders
he had bought a pair of new shoes, for two others a new hat, for
two a shirt, and two he had still in his pocket. The only method of extricating himself out of this difficulty, appeared
to be a close application to the duties of his office, whereby he
hoped, to gain the good will of Mr. Hochberg his patron, so
that he might be induced to assist him in obtaining what he wanted. At length Mr. Hochberg arrived. He united in his person
an exterior dignity with a mercantile spirit. After the first in-
troductory compliments were passed, Mr. Hochberg commenced
the following conversation:

"Are you resolved to enter into engagements with me as
teacher of my children?"

"Yes, Sir, I am."

"Have you any knowledge of languages?"

"I am tolerably well acquainted with the Latin."

"This is very well. You will not want it immediately, but
doubtless in the sequel. Do you understand Arithmetic?"

"I have studied Geometry in some measure, and Arithmetic
is absolutely requisite for that purpose, besides I have acquired
some knowledge in the art of making sun-dials and in other Mathematical branches."

"All this is very well, I shall pay you twenty-five guilders
per year, besides board."

Although Stilling supposed, the salary was too low, yet
he agreed to the proposition, and answered:

"I shall be satisfied with what you may add hereafter, and
I hope, you will give me what I earn."

"Your knowledge and application shall determine my actions."

Dinner was now ready. Stilling soon observed, that here
too there was much to learn, before he could eat and drink in a
fashionable manner. Yet, notwithstanding these difficulties he
rejoiced at seeing himself raised, as it were, from the dust, and
at having come into the atmosphere of people of fashion, which
to enjoy had been for a long time the ardent desire of his heart.

He became a close observer of every thing, which belonged to good breeding, he exercised himself in fashionable bows, when he was alone and unobserved. He looked upon his present situation as a school, in which he would be prepared for entering the higher circles of life. The next day he commenced school with his pupils, and was pleased to observe their polite and affectionate behavior towards their teacher. A few days afterwards Mr. Hochberg left home for the Frankfort fair. Stilling missed his company, for Mr. Hochberg was the only person, with whom he could converse, the conversation of the rest of the family generally turned on subjects, in which Stilling felt no interest. A few weeks passed away in an agreeable manner, and his wishes were confined to a suit of new clothes. He mentioned the change of his situation in a lettter to his father and received an approving answer. Mr. Hochberg returned about Michaelmas.

Stilling was glad to see him, but his joy was of short duration. Mr. and Mrs. Hochberg had believed, that the teacher of their children had not brought all his clothes with him from Schauberg. But when they found, he had no other clothes besides those he wore, they began to suspect him of pilfering; they became rererved, locked every thing from him, and threw out hints, that they regarded him as a vagabond and thief. Stilling could have borne more patiently almost any other suspicion, because he was convinced in his own mind, that he was incapable of defrauding any person, or of stealing the worth of a single penny; and he was astonished, that the family of Mr. Hochberg could seriously harbor thoughts of this description.— It is however probable, that some one of the servants had been unfaithful, and was but too successful in his endeavors, to cast suspicion on Stilling; and the worst of the whole affair was, that they never gave him an opportunity of defending himself.

From this time his office became very burdensome; as soon as he was dressed in the morning, he went into the family-room to breakfast, which was finished by seven o'clock; immediately afterwards he accompanied the children into the school-room—

a small chamber, four feet wide and ten feet long—which he did not leave, until he was called to dinner, between twelve and two o'clock. After dinner school was resumed till four o'clock, when the family drank tea; but as soon as that was over, the parents would call out to the children: "Go now to school, children!" in which he was engaged till nine o'clock, the usual time for supper, after which all went to bed.

In this manner he had no time for self-improvement, except on Sundays; and that day too was spent most wretchedly, because the want of suitable clothes prevented him from going to church. Had he stayed at Shauberg, Mr. Nagle would have provided him with every necessary article, for which preparations had already been made. Cerberus was now raging against poor Stilling with all his fury. Towards the middle of November, he began to feel all the misery of his situation, and the darkest gloom took possession of his mind.

He cried to God, but there was no comfort! He even could not think of God with satisfaction; a state of wretchedness, which he never had felt before. In the family, in which he resided, there was not an individual, to whom he could speak with confidence; and the state of his clothes made it impossible for him, to seek such a friend from home. The behavior of the family towards him, made his situation every day more insupportable; neither his patron, nor any other person of the family, took the least notice of him, though they appeared to be satisfied with his instruction. Towards Christmas his situation seemed to have attained the acme of wretchedness. During the day, Stilling was generally sullen and reserved, but when he came into his bedroom at night, his tears commenced to flow; he trembled and shook like a condemned criminal in the moment of execution, and so strongly sometimes did the anguish of his mind affect his body, that not only the bed, but likewise the panes of glass in the windows shook from his convulsive motions, till he fell asleep, which was a blessing; but when he awoke in the morning, sullenness and cold reserve again spread over his countenance.

The sun appeared to him as being the emblem of God's flaming wrath, which threatened to hurl thunder and lightening upon him. The sky always bore a red appearance in his eyes; he was startled at the sight of a human being, but it would have been a pleasing task to him, could he have watched in a lonesome cave, between corpses and other images of horror. During the holidays he found a little time, thoroughly to mend his worn-out clothes. He turned his coat, and as poverty is the mother of invention, he learnt to patch every part of them in such a way, as to enable him, to go, without a blush, a few times to church at Holzhime; his troubles, however, had reduced him so much, that he was unable to cover his teeth with his lips. All his features were distorted; his eye-brows drawn up; his forehead full of wrinkles; his eyes were sunk deep in their sockets; the upper-lip was drawn upwards; the corners of his mouth were sinking down, together with his skinny cheeks. All, who saw him, turned their faces away with looks of compassion.

The Sunday after New Year he went to church. No one of the congregation spoke with him, except pastor Bruck, who had observed him from the pulpit, and who after church searched him out among the crowd. He took hold of his arm, and invited him to dine and spend the afternoon with him. This friendly conduct of the minister made so powerful an impression upon his mind, that he could scarcely refrain from weeping and sobbing aloud. He was unable to give any coherent answers to Mr. Bruck's questions, who, on perceiving the state of his mind, said no more, but conducted him into the house, where his wife and children were terrified at the appearance of Stilling, and felt for him the deepest sympathy. When Mr. Bruck was unrobed, they sat down to dinner. During the repast the pastor spoke with Stilling of his present situation in such a manner, that he was compelled to give free vent to his tears, and all present were deeply affected. Mr. Bruck told him, that all his sufferings had been wise plans of probation, by which means God's providence and love intended to cure him of many infirmities, and prepare him for something extraordinary; and he hoped, that the Lord would soon extricate him from his present troubles. Such and other similar encouraging conversations refreshed the parched soul of Stilling, as the cooling morning-dew refreshes the grass of the field. But this comfort was of short duration, for towards night he had to return to his prison, when his grief became the more poignant in consequence of the temporary relief.

CHAPTER III.

These sufferings lasted from November till the 12th of April, 1763. That day was the joyful moment of his redemption. In the morning he rose with the same oppressive feelings, which he had unfortunately experienced for some length of time; he went down to breakfast as usual, and then into the school-room. At nine o'clock, while he was sitting at the table, under the pressure of his sufferings, he suddenly perceived a total change in his condition; the gloom of his mind had departed; he enjoyed perfect peace, and his happiness was unbounded; he reflected on the cause of this change, and found, that he was resolved to leave the house. He arose, went into his bed-room, to consult with himself; and those persons only, who have been in similar situations, can conceive the sensations of joy and gratitude, which pervaded Stilling's bosom. He packed his few rags together, tied his hat into the bundle, but left his cane. This budget he threw out of the window into the back-yard, went down, walked slowly out of the gate behind the house, took up his bundle, and marched with a quick step through the fields a considerable distance into the woods, where he put on his worn-out coat and his hat; his every-day-jacket he put into the bundle, cut himself a cane, and walked over hill and dale in a northerly direction, without following any road. Though his mind was at ease, and though he was tasting the sweets of recovered liberty in their fulness, yet he had lost all presence of mind, so much so, that he could not realize his present condition.— Having walked about three miles through desert places, he came to a post-road, leading to a small village, which he saw at the distance of a couple of miles before him. He went thither, without having any particular reason for doing so, and arrived about eleven o'clock before the gate.

He inquired after the name of the town, and was informed, it was Waldstat, a place, of which he had frequently heard.

He went in at one gate, straight through the town, and out at the other. There were two roads, which appeared to him equally well beaten. He took one of them, and followed it with a quick step. After a walk of a mile or two, he came to a forest, in which the road gradually lost itself, and no other could be found. He sat down, for he was much fatigued. His presence of mind returned in full force; he knew, he had not one penny in his pocket, for he had received no salary from Mr. Hochberg, and yet was very hungry. He was in a solitary place, where there was no human being near, with whom he was acquainted. He could not refrain from the following soliloquy:

"I am now about to drink the last dregs of wretchedness; I have no alternative, I must either beg or starve. This is the first noon of my life, in which no table is spread for me!—Yes, the hour is come, in which that great promise of the Redeemer is to be fulfilled in me: 'The hairs of your head are all numbered.' If this be true, help must soon appear, for I have to this moment trusted in him, and believed his word. I likewise am one of those eyes, which wait upon the Lord, that he may give them their meat in due season; I am his creature, as well as every bird, which sings here in the forest, and which receives its nourishment as often as it stands in need of it."—

Stilling's heart was during this soliloquy very much like that of a child, which has been cured of its obstinacy by severe discipline; the father turns away his face, to hide his tears.—O God! what precious moments are those, when we see the bowels of compassion of the Father of mercy yearning over his way-ward children!

While his mind was thus engaged, he felt as if somebody told him: "Go into the town, and seek work with a master-tailor." Immediately he returned, and searching his pockets, found his scissors

T

and thimble, without being conscious that he had taken them. As soon as he had entered the town, he inquired of the first citizen he met, where the best master-tailor resided? This man called a child, desiring it, to show the stranger to Mr. Isaac. The boy ran before Stilling into a narrow lane, towards a small house, and pointed it out to him as Mr. Isaac's habitation.— Stilling entered the room, where he found a pale and slender but cleanly dressed woman, who was preparing the dinner-table. He inquired, if he could obtain employment as journeyman-tailor? The woman, after having examined him from head to foot, said in a friendly tone :

"My husband wants a journeyman very much—from what place are you ?"

Stilling replied : "From the principality of Salen."

The woman was glad to hear it, and said :

"My husband is from the same country—I will send for him ; he is at work somewhere in town with a journeyman and an apprentice."

She sent one of the children to call him, and in a few minutes Mr. Isaac arrived, and after having made the necessary inquiries, observed, that he was willing to employ him.

The woman invited him to dine with them ; and thus Stilling's table was spread, while he was lost in the woods, and had doubted, if God would grant him the nourishment, necessary for the day. After dinner, Mr. Isaac took Stilling to the house of judge Showerhof, where he was at work.

When Mr. Isaac and his new journeyman had seated themselves to their work, the judge entered with his long pipe, and, being seated, recommenced the conversation with Mr. Isaac, where they had probably broken off in the forenoon.

"I represent to myself the spirit of Christ," said the judge, "as an omnipresent power, which strives every where with the hearts of men, in order to impart its own nature to every soul— the more estranged a person is from God, the more he is alienated from this spirit. What do you think of it, brother Isaac ?"

"I have pretty much the same idea of it," replied Mr.

Isaac, "it chiefly depends on the will of man; *that will* makes him capable—

Here Stilling could no longer contain himself; he perceived, that he was among pious people, and therefore burst out in the following exclamation: "O God! I am at home, I am at home!" All present were astonished; they did not know, what to make of it. Mr. Isaac looked at him and asked:

"What is the matter, Stilling?"

Stilling replied: "This kind of language I have not heard for a long time, but perceiving, that you love God, I must give vent to my joy."

Mr. Isaac continued: "Then you are likewise a friend of the religion of the heart and true piety?"

"Yes," answered Stilling, "I am."

Upon this, judge Showerhof and Mr. Isaac shook hands with him, and the former observed: "We have now one brother more."

In the evening, after supper, when the other journeyman and apprentice had departed, Isaac and Stilling remained a while, conversing on religious subjects, while they smoked a pipe and drank a glas of beer together.

Henry Stilling was very happy at Waldstat; peace and liberty had the greater charms for him, from the intensity of his late sufferings. He had never mentioned a word of his troubles in the letters to his father; but now, being again at his trade, he gave him an account of his trials. In his father's answer he found a confirmation of his own opinion, that he was not destined to be an instructor of children. When Stilling had been several days at Mr. Isaac's, the latter took an opportunity, to converse with him about his clothes, (the other journeyman and apprentice being absent) and inquired of him, what clothes he had? upon which he brought a piece of fine purple cloth for a coat; bought him a new hat, black cloth for a vest, stuff for an under-jacket and small clothes, a pair of fine stockings, and a pair of new shoes, and Mrs. Isaac made him six new shirts; all these different articles were finished in a fortnight. His employer gave him likewise one of his canes. Thus Sitlling saw himself better and more fashionably dressed, than he had ever been before, so that in point of dress he was fit for any company. The last enemy had thus been overcome. Stilling could not find words, to express his gratitude towards God and his benefactor; he wept for joy, and was perfectly satisfied and happy. But blessed be thy ashes!—thou friend of Stilling—where thou restest!—When once that voice shall sound over the orb: "I was naked, and ye clothed me," then shalt thou likewise lift up thy head, and thy immortal body will shine seven times brighter, than the sun in the morning of spring.—

Stilling's inclination to become a great man in the world, was subdued, at least for the present; he was resolved, to remain a tailor, till he should be convinced, that it was the will of God, to follow some other calling, and he solemnly renewed that covenant with God, into which he had entered with him the last summer in the street of Showberg. His employer was so well pleased with him, that he treated him like a brother; and Mrs. Isaac and her children likewise loved and esteemed him. He still felt a strong inclination for learning, but it was slumbering, as it were, under the embers; it was no longer a passion, and he suffered it to slumber.

Mr. Isaac had an extensive acquaintance among awakened and pious people, and Sunday was generally destined for visiting them. On the morning of the Lord's day, he usually went with Stilling to a place of that description, spent the day in religious conversation, and returned home in the evening. It was gratifying to Stilling, to become acquainted with so many pious persons, who were by no means fanatics, but endeavored to manifest their love to God and man by imitating their Savior Jesus Christ in their walk and conversation, which perfectly agreed with their religious system; and he could therefore unite in brotherly love and religious fellowship with these pious souls. This connection was likewise very beneficial to his spiritual advancement in christian piety. Isaac was unremitting in his admonitions to watch and to pray, and to walk circumspectly in word and deeds before God and man. About the middle of May, Mr. Isaac resolved to visit some religious friends in the county of Mark, about thirty miles from Waldstat. in a village, which I shall call Rothenbeck. The weather was delightful, and the road passed through picturesque landscapes. Isaac and Stilling stayed at the house of a retail merchant, by the name of Glockner, a man of an excellent character, possessing also a considerable share of wealth. He was married, but had no children. Mr. and Mrs. Glockner received them with great cordiality, though strangers to Stilling.

During supper Glockner related the remarkable conversion of his brother-in-law Mr. Freymuth. Mrs. Freymuth was an exemplary christian, and on Sunday afternoon she, Mrs. Glockner and several other christian friends would frequently meet for the purpose of conversing on the sermon they had heard in the forenoon, for reading the Bible and for singing hymns, which Mr. Freymuth did not like. He was indeed a good church-man, that is, he attended divine service very regularly, and went at stated times to the Lord's table, but farther his religion did not extend. He delighted in uttering the most horrid oaths, in drinking, revelling and gambling. When he came home in the evening and found his wife engaged in reading the Bible or some other edifying book, he would curse and swear at her, drag her about the room by the hair, and would strike her, until frequently the blood would gush both from her nose and mouth. She on her part said nothing, but, when he let her go, she would cling to him and intreat-him with many tears, that he should seek religion and change his life, this however made no impression on him, he would often kick her from him and declare with dreadful oaths, that he never would become a Pietist. He treated her in the same manner, when she had been in company with her pious friends. But a short time previous to Stilling's visit Mr. Freymuth became an altered man, and this had taken place in the following manner:

He was gone to Frankfort fair, during which time Mrs. Freymuth could do as she pleased in the house; she not only went to other friends, but likewise invited them to her house. At one time, when a goodly number of pious persons were assembled one Sunday evening, some of the towns people, opposed to

prayer-meetings, came before the house, and after having bro.
ken the windows within their reach, attempted to enter the
house, and finding the door locked, broke it open and forced their
way in. The persons assembled being frightened hid themselves as well as they could; Mrs. Freymuth alone remained in the
apartment and when she heard the door burst open, came out
with the candle in her hand. Several fellows had already
entered, whom she met in the hall. She addressed them in a
mild tone as follows:

"Neighbors! what do you want?" and these few words were
sufficient, to put them to flight, they looked at each other, felt
ashamed, and went home. The next morning Mrs. Freymuth
had all the damages repaired, and scarcely was this done, when
her husband returned from the fair.

He immediately observed the new windows, and questioned
his wife as to what had happened. She told him the whole truth,
praying at the same time in her mind to God for assistance, for
she expected nothing else, but he would beat her in a more cruel
manner than he had ever done before. But he became so raving
at the mob, that he forgot her, and only meditated, how he might
obtain revenge. He therefore commanded his wife with heavy
threatenings to give him the names of the perpetrators, for she
had seen and recognized them.

"Yes, said she," my dear husband, I will name them to you,
but I know a still greater sinner, than all these, for he has beaten me most cruelly for the same reason. Freymuth did not
understand her, he jumped up in a great fury, struck his breast
with his fist and roared out: "The D—— shall take him and
you too, if you do not name him this very instant!"

"Yes, replied Mrs. Freymuth," I will name him to you,
revenge yourself on him as much as you please,—you are the
man, who has done this, and who is of course a much greater
sinner, than the people who have broken the windows. Freymuth was unable to utter a word for some time, at length he
began:

"God in heaven!" this is true! I am a villain worse than

any other—I want to take revenge on people, better than my-self !—Yes, wife, I am the most impious wretch on the face of the earth !" With these words he jumped up, ran up stairs into his bed-room, prostrated himself, and remained in this position for three days and nights without eating a morsel, now and then only asking for a glass of water. His wife was with him as much as possible and joined him in prayer, that he might find mercy with God through the merits of the Saviour. On the morning of the fourth day he arose, praising God and say-ing : "Now I know, that my manifold sins are forgiven !" From this time he was an altered man, as humble, as he had been proud before, as mild as he had been insolent and overbear-ing, and as pious as he had been wicked before. This man would be a noble subject for my friend Lavater. His physiognomy is the most savage you can imagine, if any one passion, for in-stance anger should be excited and the muscles of his face should be strained, he would have the appearance of a complete madman. But now he is similar to a lion changed into a lamb. The peace of Christ is imprinted on his face, which has converted his savage countenance into that of the meek christian. After supper Glockner sent his hired girl to Freymuth's, to tell them, that christian friends had arrived, upon which they both came to welcome them. Stilling was engaged the whole evening in making observations on this singular couple; he did not know, whether the meekness of the lion or the heroism of the lamb deserved the greater admiration.

They stayed several days at Rothenbeck, visited and were visited. The Schoolmaster of the place, who was also a Stil-ling from the principality of Salen, belonged to the society of awakened people at Rothenbeck. Henry Stilling visited him, when they entered into an agreement of keeping up a correspon-dence as long as both should live ; and after an agreeable visit Mr. Isaac and Stilling returned home to their business.

About three miles from Wadstadt lived a merchant called Spanier, who had a family of seven children, three sons and four daughters, the eldest of whom was a girl sixteen years of age, and the youngest a child of one year old. He owned seven for-ges, of which four were near his house, but the others about three miles distant not far from Mr. Hochberg's house. Whenever Mr. Spanier had occasion to employ a tailor in his family, he called upon Mr. Isaac to do the work at his house. Stilling had been about twelve weeks at Mr. Isaac's, when it happened, that he was called to work for Mr. Spanier. They went thither one morning early. On their arrival they found him at his breakfast-table. When he saw Stilling he turned slowly towards him, and said:

"Good morning, Mr. Preceptor!" Stilling blushed a little, but after a moment's reflection replied:

"Your servant, Mr. Spanier," and then went to work. A few hours afterwards Mr. Spanier who had been walking up and down in the room without saying a word, suddenly stopped before Stilling, looked at him a while and said:

"You are as ready at that work, Stilling, as if you were born for the needle, which however you are not."

"How so?" inquired Stilling.

"Because I want you to become private tutor to my children." At these words Mr. Isaac looked at Stilling and smiled.

"No, Mr. Spanier," replied Stilling, "that won't do, I am irrevocably resolved to take no such charge again upon myself. I am now satisfied with my trade, which I shall not quit."

Mr. Spanier laughed, shook his head and said: "I will teach you something else, I have levelled many hills in the world, and shall I not be able to change your sentiments? indeed, I would be ashamed of myself!"

With these words he went away, and said that day no more about the business. Stilling plead with Mr. Isaac to let him go home in the evening, to get out of temptation's way, but Isaac would not permit it, and therefore Stilling armed himself in the best manner he could against Mr. Spanier's attacks.

Next day, as he was again walking up and down in the apartment, he addressed Stilling in these words:

"If you have made me a handsome coat, am I not a fool, if I hang it on a nail, without using it?"

"Yes," replied Stilling, "provided you need it, and it fits you. But if I make you a coat, without your needing, or without fitting you, what else would you do, but hang it on the nail and leave it where it is?"

"I will tell you, what I should do in that case," replied Mr. Spanier, "I would give it to some one else."

"But supposing, you had given it to seven, and each one had returned it, with the declaration, it does not fit me, what would you do in that case?"

"I would after all act a foolish part, if I should suffer it to hang against the wall where the moths would eat it; I would give it to the eighth, and tell him to alter it, till it did fit. And supposing, that the eighth man were willing to take the coat just as it was, would I not commit a great sin, were I to refuse it him?"

"You are right," replied Stilling, "but for God's sake, I beg you, Mr. Spanier, let me remain at my trade!"

"No," answered he, "I will not leave you, you shall and must be the instructor of my children, and this under the following conditions: You are unacquainted with the French language, a knowledge of which will be necessary for you in my service, therefore I desire you to apply to a teacher of that language, to instruct you; and stay with him, till you understand it, I shall pay all the expenses, and give you the privilege besides, of returning to Mr. Isaac, whenever you shall think proper. And finally, I will give you what you need in clothing, board and so forth, provided, you enter into no other engagement as long as I stand in need of you, unless you can obtain a permanent settlement.

Mr. Isaac was delighted with these conditions. "Well," said he to Stilling," you would commit a sin, if you were to refuse this offer, which doubtless comes from God; all your other engagements were creatures of your own creation." Stilling examined himself faithfully, and finding no desire for honor rising in his bosom, declared to Mr. Spanier, that he would once more undertake the office of teacher, though with fear and trembling. Spanier arose at these words and shook Stilling by the hand and said:

"God be praised! now I have levelled this hill also, but

now you ought to go to a linguist as soon as possible." Stilling
was pleased with this proposition, and Mr. Isaac said :

"The day after to morrow is Sunday, and then I will dismiss you with a blessing. Isaac felt pleased with the good fortune
of his friend, though he was sorry, to part with him so soon,
and Stilling was grieved, that he should leave the best friend, he
ever had, and the most upright man in the world, before he had
sufficient to pay for his clothes : he therefore conversed with Mr.
Spanier on this subject, who was not only willing to pay Isaac,
but observed with tears in his eyes : "this excellent man shall
never want, if I can avoid it ;" and forthwith handed Stilling
a sum of money to pay him and desired him, to keep the remainder for his own use; when that should be expended, he promised, to give him more, but stipulated at the same time, that
he should render him an exact account of the manner, in
which he spent the money. Stilling was rejoiced, for he had never before met with so generous a man. He paid Mr. Isaac,
who acknowledged to him, that he had taken the cloth for his
suit on trust. Stilling thought : "If ever a man has merited a
marble monument, it is Mr. Isaac, not, because he *has* made whole
nations happy, but because he *would have* done it, if his situation had permitted. Once more—blessed be thy ashes—my
friend ! chosen among thousands—where thou sleepest—these
tears shall be sacred to thy memory——thou true follower of
Christ !—

CHAPTER IV.

On the Sunday following. Stilling took leave of his friends
at Waldstadt, and went to Shonenthal in search of a good linguist.
When he approached the city, remembering, that a little better
than a year before he had traveled the same road for the first
time, and reviewing all his adventures during that short period
of time, and reflecting, how happy he now was, he fell upon his
knees, thanking God for all the severe but holy and wise dispensations of his divine providence, and prayed at the same
time, that his grace and favor might henceforth shine upon him.

He then hastened down the hill into the city, but soon learnt, that the French teachers there would not suit him, because they were too much engaged already, to pay him sufficient attention, which he particularly desired, as his time was precious, and he was in haste to acquire a knowledge of the language. At length he found the man he wanted at Dornfeld, where Mr. Dahlhime was minister. He arrived there in the afternoon, and soon discovered that Mr. Heesfeld the teacher, was a singular, original character. When Stilling saw him for the first time, he was seated in a small chamber, dressed in a dirty camlet morning gown, fastened round the waist by a sash of the same stuff; on his head he wore a netted cap, his lengthy visage was as pale, as though he had just risen from the grave; he had a fine forehead and from under his dark eyebrows peeped a pair of small black eyes, his nose was narrow and long, the mouth well formed, but his chin was sharp and pointed, he had black curly hair, his person was slender, tall, and well made. Stilling was somewhat disconcerted at the sight of so singular a face, however he soon collected himself and inquired, if Mr. Heesfeld would give him the desired instruction. He received him in a friendly manner and promised to do what lay in his power to gratify his wishes. Stilling's next care was, to find a boarding place, and then he applied himself to the study of the French language. Eccentric as Heesfeld was in his outward appearance, so original be likewise was in his walk and conversation. He belonged to the reserved class of men, for he was not at all communicative, no one knew, whence he came, or whether he was rich or poor. He probably never liked any man better than Stilling, and yet did he learn no particulars of his life, nor that he had been a rich man till after Heesfeld's death. He concealed his abilities. It was evident from his manner of teaching, that he was perfect master of the French language, but that he was also an eminent scholar in the latin language became only apparent, when he commenced the instruction of Stilling. He conducted it upon the plan of the latin Grammar, and in leisure moments gave noble specimens of latin versification. He possessed fine talents for drawing, and manifested an acquaintance with physiology, natural philosophy and chemistry. It happened two days before Stilling's departure that the latter was playing on a piano, while Heesfeld listened attentively. When Stilling had ceased, Heesfeld sat down, and at first appeared rather to be a stranger in the art, but in a few moments gave such specimens of his skill, that all persons present were delighted with him. He had formerly sustained a military character, his professional skill had introduced him to the notice of a certain celebrated general, who gave him every opportunity for improvement, and afterwards traveled with him through different parts of the world, and who had left him a handsome legacy. Heesfeld was forty years of age, when he returned from his travels, but gave no notice of his arrival either to his parents or brother's, though they lived not farther than six miles from Dornfeld where he had fixed his residence. On his death-bed however, he sent for his relatives, communicated his circumstances to them, and left them a a valuable property. You may call this disposition as you please, a fault or a virtue, so much is certain, that he possessed a noble heart, he was very humane, but all he did was done in secret, the persons themselves whom he benefitted, did not know their benefactor. Nothing pleased him better than when he heard, that people did not know, what to make of him. When he took a walk with Stilling, their conversation was generally on literary subjects. He preferred the most lonesome and solitary places. Sometimes Heesfeld would mount a tall sapling, seat himself in the top and swing himself with it down to the ground, lay down and rest a while among the branches. Stilling sometimes followed his example; when they were tired of this sport, they would rise, and the saplings would spring up, which afforded Heesfeld great amusement; sometimes he would say : "we have fine beds, when we rise, they ascend to heaven." At another time when a stranger happened to be with them, he would propose the enigma: "What kind of beds are those, which fly in the air when you rise?"

Stilling was very happy at Dornfeld. Mr. Spanier supplied him with sufficient resources, he studied diligently, and at the close of nine weeks had advanced so far, that he could translate a

French newspaper and read it from the sheet, as if it had been German, and was able to write a French letter without any grammatical faults; he therefore judged his progress in the knowledge of that language sufficient to give instruction to others, and returned to Mr. Spanier towards the end of September 1763, who was greatly rejoiced at seeing him so soon. He treated him from his first entrance into his house as an intimate friend, and the whole family endeavored to make his stay pleasant.

This gentleman demanded, that his children and their teacher should be continually in his own room, which afforded him an opportunity to watch their application and progress, as well as to converse with the teacher. But Mr. Spanier had not only intended Stilling for an instructor of his children, he likewise wished to employ him in mercantile affairs; he entrusted him with the superintendence of three forges, which were not far from Mr. Hochberg's house. Stilling went thither every third week, to send off the iron ware and to purchase raw materials. For the latter purpose he traveled every week several times to a place, about nine miles from Spanier's house, whither carters brought the raw iron. When he had returned, he found a few days rest very agreeable, and performed the duties of instructor with the greater alacrity and satisfaction to himself.— As Mr. Spanier was a complete agriculturist and merchant, his conversations with Stilling became highly instructive, and he considered that gentleman's house as the college, where he studied political economy, agriculture and commerce, in all their different branches.

CHAPTER V.

Thus four years of Stilling's life passed away without one intervening dark hour; I shall therefore say little of that time, except that he continued to improve in his knowledge of the world, his manners, and those different branches of sciences, which have been named before.

He instructed his scholars during this period in the Latin and French languages, in Arithmetic, Reading, Writing and the principles of the Reformed religion.

His private studies were chiefly confined to Philosophy; he read Wolf's and Gottshed's philosophical writings; Leibnitz's Theodicy; Baumeister's Logic and Metaphysics. Though he was pleased with the study of these sciences, yet he felt a certain distrust of those philosophical systems, because they were destructive to the religion of the heart; it may be, that they are a chain of truth, but we have not yet found the real philosophical chain, which unites every branch of human knowledge. Stilling fancied, he could find that chain, but hitherto all his attempts have proved abortive.

Mr. Spanier's parents had formerly lived in the principality of Salen, and he had frequently business to transact in that country; and as Stilling was well acquainted there, he was glad to employ him in that quarter. After he had been a year with his patron, and two and a half from home, he paid his first visit to his relations in his native country. The distance from Mr. Spanier's house to Lichthausen, the abode of John Stilling, was about thirty-six miles, and to his father's residence at Linedorf, three miles farther, which journey he intended to perform in one day. He therefore started one morning at day-break from Mr. Spanier's. In the afternoon at four o'clock he arrived on a rising ground, at the boundary line of the principality of Salen, whence all the mountains of his earliest recollections presented themselves to his view. Tears of gratitude for God's gracious and providential care started into his eyes; he reflected, how poor he had left his native country, and how abundantly he was now provided with every thing necessary for life. At five o'clock he arrived at his uncle's at Lichthausen. The whole family were rejoiced to see him in such prosperous circumstances. His uncle embraced him, while tears of joy trickled down his cheeks. His aunt Mary, who had married during his absence, and who was now living at Lichthausen, likewise came, and almost suffocated him with her kisses. Stilling stayed all night at his uncle's, and next morning went to Linedorf. When he entered his father's house, the good man arose in great haste from his seat, but immediately sunk back again. Henry Stilling however has-tened to embrace him. William held his hands before his face and wept; his son likewise shed many tears; the stepmother came also, shook hands with him, and was glad to see him so well and hearty.

Stilling related all his adventures to his parents, and how pleasantly he was now situated. In the mean time, the news of Stilling's arrival had spread through the village, and the house was soon filled with people, who came to see their former school-master. Towards evening William took a walk with his son, during which he conversed with him about his past and future life, quite in the tone of old Eberhard, so that Stilling was filled with love and respect for his father.

The next morning he went to Tiefenbach to visit his grandmother. Indescribable were his sensations, when he saw the old castle, the Giller and the village itself. He com-pared the scenes of his childhood with his present prosperous si-tuation, and found, that he would gladly make an exchange, if this had been possible. In a short time he reached the vil-lage—the people ran out of their houses, to accompany him to the residence of his forefathers. When he entered the house, a solemn tremor ran through his frame, as if he were entering a sanctuary. He met his aunt Elizabeth in the kitchen, who took him by the hand, and led him into the room. Here lay Marga-ret Stilling in a clean bed, between the wall of the room and the stove. Her breast and the joints of her fingers were swollen with rheumatic pain. Stilling took her by the hand and said:

"How are you, dear grandmother! I am glad to see you once more in this life."

She endeavored to raise herself in her bed, but her efforts were ineffectual.

"Come, my child," exclaimed she, "come, that I may feel and hear you once more before my death, come, that I may feel your face!"

Stilling bowed down to her; she felt over his forehead, eyes, nose, mouth, chin and cheeks. During this occupation, her stiff fingers came in contact with his hair; she felt, that it was powdered.

"Ah!" said she, "you are the first of our family, that uses powder, I hope you will not be the first, who neglects honesty and piety!"

"Now," continued she, "I have as good an idea of your person, as if I had seen you, tell me now how you have fared, and how you are?"

Stilling gave her a brief account of his peregrinations. When he had finished, she said:

"O my Henry! if you continue pious, you will always fare well in the world, and though you should rise ever so high, be not ashamed of your forefathers and your poor friends. A man in a low station in life, may become great by humility, and a man in a high station may be brought low by pride. After I shall have departed from this world, it will be indifferent, whether my station has been high or low, provided I have lived the life of a christian."

Stilling promised to follow her advice, and after he had conversed a while with her on various subjects, was on the point of taking leave of her, when she stopt him by taking hold of his hand, and said:

"You hasten away, my child! God be with you! I hope to meet you again before the throne of God!"

He pressed her hand and wept. She perceived it and continued:

"Do not weep for me, for I am very happy—I commend you to the paternal care of God—may he bless you, and preserve you from all evil; and now depart in the name of God!"

Stilling hastened out of the house, and has never been there since. A few days afterwards, Margaret Stilling departed this life, and was buried by the side of her husband in the grave-yard at Florenburg. Stilling found a longer stay in his native country unpleasant, and therefore prepared for his return to Mr. Spanier with all possible speed; and arrived after an absence of five days. I shall not detain the reader by a minute relation of Stilling's occupation and uniform mode of life, during the first four years of his residence with Mr. Spanier, but shall hasten to occurrences of greater importance. He was now advancing in years, and sometimes had some uneasy sensations respecting his future prospects. To work again at his trade was altogether out of the question; he had done nothing at it for several years. The instruction of youth was likewise burdensome to him, neither had he any inclination of entering into mercantile business, yet was he neither dissatisfied nor melancholy, but willing to wait with patience the issue, what God might have in view with him.

CHAPTER VI.

About this time, Stilling had an ardent desire of learning the Greek language, without knowing, if it would ever be of service to him. He made his wish known to Mr. Spanier, who after a short pause of reflection replied: "If you must learn that language, go and learn it."

Stilling made immediate application for that purpose to a friend of his, a candidate of Theology at Waldstat, who was much pleased with his intention, and encouraged him to study Theology. He furnished him with the necessary books, wishing him at the same time the blessing of God on his undertaking. One of the neighboring clergymen, a Mr. Seelburg, promised him likewise every assistance, which he was the more able to give, because he came regularly twice every week to Mr. Spanier's house.

Stilling commenced the study of the Greek language with all his usual zeal and enthusiasm, and Mr. Seelburg was delighted with the progress he made. He likewise undertook about the same time the study of the Hebrew language, and advanced in a short time so far, that he could read his Hebrew Bible with the assistance of a Lexicon. While he was occupied in these studies, Mr. Spanier permitted him to go on without interruption. No one knew, for what purpose he was learning these languages; Stilling himself had no particular object in

X

view, but most of his friends were of opinion, he would study Theology. But this Gordian knot was cut all at once. One afternoon Mr. Spanier was walking up and down the room, as he was wont to do, when he was reflecting on any thing of importance, while Stilling was giving instruction to his children, when his patron all of a sudden said to him:

"Stilling, I believe you ought to study medicine."

Stilling's sensation at this proposition cannot be described; he could scarcely keep his feet, and Mr. Spanier being frightened, took hold of his arm and asked him:

"What is the matter, Stilling?"

"O, Mr. Spanier! what shall I think, what shall I say? this is my real destiny. Yes, I feel it, this is the very object, I have been seeking so long, and have not been able to find. For this very station my heavenly Father has prepared me from my youth, by many severe trials. Praised be his name, that I know his will—with obedience will I follow the path, he points out to me."

Having said this, he hastened into his chamber, sunk upon his knees, praying to God, that he would lead him the straightest road to the destined end. Mr. Spanier gave him every evening several hours for his private use, and did not so often employ him in mercantile business, as he had before done. Stilling improved this opportunity with a view of continuing his attention to the classical languages, and of commencing the study of anatomy, as far as this branch of knowledge could be acquired from books. He also read Kreger's Physiology, and endeavored to form a plan, with the assistance of several eminent physicians, with whom he entered into correspondence, according to which he might regulate his studies.

Thus he went through the several branches pertaining to the science of medicine, so that he might have at least general ideas of every thing connected with it. He immediately informed his father and uncle by letter of this important resolution. His father's answer was, that he left him to the direction of God's providence, but told him at the same time, that he should not expect any help from him in the prosecution of his plan, and advised him to be cautious, lest he should be entangled in new difficulties, without any hope of being extricated from them. But his uncle was quite angry with him; he ascribed Henry's desire of studying medicine, to a foolish hankering after novelties, which would finally prove fatal.

Stilling however was not deterred from his plan by this discouraging advice, but continued his studies, and left it to Providence, to point out the means. In the spring of the next year, Mr. Spanier wished him to undertake another journey on business into his native country. Stilling was rejoiced at having this opportunity of convincing his friends of the correctness of his course more effectually by conversation, than he could have done by letter.

He started early one morning, and in the afternoon arrived at the house of his uncle. This good man immediately commenced a dispute with him concerning the study of medicine, and enforced his arguments chiefly by starting the difficulty, whence the money should come for the prosecution of these extensive and costly studies? But Stilling remained firm, answering this objection by his symbol: "The Lord will provide."

The next morning he started for Linedorf. His father likewise expressed many fears about his ultimate success, though he did not dispute with him, but said, that he left all these things to his own discretion. Having finished his patron's business, he took leave of his father, and returned to his uncle, who, to his utter astonishment, had completely altered his sentiments in regard to Henry's intention. He received him with these words: "Henry, you ought to study medicine, I am now convinced, it is the will of God."

In order to explain this change of sentiment, it will be necessary to make a digression concerning John Stilling. Before he became surveyor, he had formed an acquaintance with a Roman catholic priest, by the name of Molitor, who was also a skilful oculist. Molitor soon perceived, that John Stilling was a man of talents, and therefore encouraged him to study Geometry. His plan with John Stilling was, to employ him in the service of a certain rich Baron, who wished to obtain accurate maps of his landed estates, and with whom Molitor lived in the quality of steward, which situation he preferred to the ministerial office. He received permission from his patron, to employ John Stilling in that work, and as long as the Baron lived, he found sufficient employment in the survey of his land.

After the death of the Baron, Molitor accepted the office of Vicar in a parish, about twelve miles from Lichthausen.—Here he devoted much of his time to curing diseases of the eye, and was esteemed the most skilful oculist in the country. After Henry Stilling had left his uncle, the latter received a letter from Molitor, informing him, that he had written a work on the diseases of the eyes, and the manner of treating the different cases of such diseases—that, as he was drawing towards the close of his life, he was desirous of leaving it in suitable hands, and in consideration of the intimate friendship, which had subsisted between them, notwithstanding their difference in religious opinions, he wished to inquire of him, if there were a man of good character in his family, who had a mind to study medicine, in which case he would make him a present of the manuscript, on condition, he should cure the poor without reward. This letter had produced the above mentioned change in John's sentiments.

Molitor's writing the letter at the very time, when Henry Stilling was preparing for the study of medicine, appeared to him to carry a convincing proof along with it, that the hand of God was in this affair, and therefore on Henry's return from his father, he gave him the letter with these words: "Read, Henry, read; I have no more objections against your intentions; I see the finger of Providence in it."

He forthwith provided his nephew with a letter of recommendation to Molitor, and the next morning Henry Stilling sat out for Molitor's residence. Having on his arrival in the town inquired after this gentleman, he was shown a small but neat building as the place of his residence. Stilling pulled the bell, when an aged woman came to the door, desiring him to give his name and business. This being reported, the old gentleman came down, and invited him to enter the house. Stilling deliver-ad the letter, and when Molitor had read it, he embraced him, and kindly entered into a conversation about his circumstances and intentions. He stayed a whole day with the priest, who showed him his chemical laboratory and library; made him acquainted with his medicines, and promised, that he would will his whole apparatus to him.

The next morning he gave the manuscript to Stilling on condition, he should copy it, and return him the original, which he solemnly promised to give to no one else, but dispose of it in such a way, that it would not easily be found again. The good old gentleman had likewise laid aside several books, which he promised to send him by the first opportunity; Stilling however packed them into his port-manteau and carried them away with him. Molitor accompanied him as far as the gate, where he stopt, took Stilling by the hand and said:

"May the Lord, the holy One, the Omnipresent, make you by the operations of his holy Spirit. the best of men, the best of christians, and the best of physicians!" Having said this he once more embraced him and returned. Molitor's place of residence was thirty miles distant from that of Mr. Spanier's, which Stilling walked that day, though heavy laden with books. He told Mr. Spanier the circumstances, which had occurred during his journey, who admired with him the singular providence and direction of God. Stilling immediately copied Molitor's manuscript, which he finished in about four weeks. To fulfill the promise he had given his friend of returning the manuscript, he started one morning early, and arrived in the afternoon before his door. He pulled the bell, in hopes, that some one would open, but in vain. A woman, standing in the door on the opposite side of the street, asked him, whom he wished to see? When he told her, that he wished to see Mr. Molitor, she informed him, that he had died a week ago. Stilling struck with astonishment at these news, went into the tavern, where he learnt all the circumstances of his death; that he had died suddenly from a stroke of the palsy, without having made a will. He immediately returned to his patron, and the first work in which he engaged was to prepare Molitor's medicines, and then made his first attempt at a cure on a boy twelve years of age, the son of a hired man in Mr. Spanier's family, who had suffered for a long time from sore eyes, and this attempt was crowned with complete success. He obtained thereby a regular practice, and towards autumn the fame of his cures had already spread as far as Shonenthal. Mr. Isaac at Waldstat rejoiced in the good fortune of his friend, and the idea of seeing him established as a physician filled his soul with delight. However God had ordained otherwise; Mr. Isaac became sick, and Stilling saw with deep grief his approaching dissolution. The day before his departure Stilling was sitting near the bed of his friend; Isaac took hold of his hand and said:

"Friend Stilling, I shall die, I leave a wife and four children behind me, and I am not concerned about their support in life, for the Lord will provide for them; but I do not know, if they will continue to walk in the ways of the Lord, and therefore I desire you, to watch over them and assist them with good advice; the Lord will reward you for it."

Stilling promised to comply with the request of his friend, as long as circumstances would permit him so to do. Isaac desired him then, to keep his promise during his stay with Mr. Spanier, after which he could not expect it. "But," continued he, think always in love of me, and live so in this world, that we may be reunited in heaven without fear of separation." Stilling replied with tears:

"Assist me to pray for grace and strength!"

"Yes," said Isaac, "I will, when I shall have finished my course, at present I have enough to do with myself."

He did not expect, that his friend was in immediate danger, he therefore left him with the promise of returning next day; but that very night Isaac departed. Stilling walked at the funeral with the family, mourning his loss, as that of a beloved brother. Isaac's wife died soon after, but his children have all done well in the world.

After Stilling had been six years with Mr. Spanier, the latter conversed with him several times about plans for the prosecution of his studies. His propositions amounted to this, that he should stay yet a couple of years with him, and pursue his private studies, he would then give him two hundred Dollars, with which he might go to some university, be examined and obtain the Diploma as a graduated physician and afterwards return to his house and live with him. But Mr. Spanier would never positively say, what his intentions were in regard to him. Therefore his plan did not please him, whose desire was, to study the science of Medicine thoroughly at the university; he was likewise confident, that God, who had called him to that profession, would point out the ways and means for accomplishing his design. But Mr. Spanier desired, that Stilling should implicitly follow his direction, to which the latter could not consent, and therefore they finally conversed no more on this subject.

CHAPTER VII.

In the autumn of 1769 when he had entered his 30th year, he received a letter from a merchant by the name of Fredenberg at Rasenhime about three miles from Shonenthal, inviting him to visit a son of one of his neighbors as soon as possible, whose eyes had been very sore for several years, and was in danger of becoming totally blind. Stilling accepted the invitation at the particular desire of Mr. Spanier, and arrived at Mr. Fredenberg's after a walk of three hours. His house was a neat building, lately erected by its owner, and the country round about was very pleasant. As soon as he entered the house and observed every where cleanliness, order and neatness, unaccompanied by any vain parade, he thought, he would like to live there. But after he had become acquainted in some measure with Mr. and Mrs. Fredenberg, and their nine well educated children, when he saw, that all their faces bore the stamp of serenity, truth and rectitude, he was enraptured, and wished, never to be separated from them. Mr. Fredenberg invited him to stay to dinner, which offer Stilling gladly accepted. By his conversation with this family, he soon discovered, that the minds of all its members were in unison; they plainly shewed, that they liked him, and he on his part felt very soon a strong attachment to them. His conversation with Mr. and Mrs. Fredenberg was confined to religious subjects and vital piety. After dinner Mr. Fredenberg accompanied him to his patient, and on their return they took a cup of coffee together. Towards evening Stilling left them again for Mr. Spanier's house, but from that day felt a void in his breast, to which he had hitherto been a stranger.

His patient at Rasenhime gradually recovered, which circumstance increased his practice both in that neighborhood and at Shonenthal. He therefore resolved with the approbation of Mr. Spanier to go every other Saturday afternoon to Mr. Fredenberg's, to visit his patients, and to return on Monday morning. These frequent visits at Mr. Fredenberg's house increased his attachment to the family, and afforded him also opportunities to make very agreeable acquaintances with many pious persons in Shonenthal.

This continued until Feb. 1770; When Mrs. Fredenberg became the mother of a daughter. This news Mr. Fredenberg not only immediately communicated to his friend Stilling by letter, but also invited him to become god-father to his child, which honor he accepted with great pleasure. Mr. Spanier however thought, that Mr. Fredenberg as a merchant rather degraded himself by inviting the clerk of another merchant, to stand god-father to his child, but Stilling wondered not at it, for Mr. Fredenberg and he had lost sight of the distinctions of rank in regard to each other, for they were brethren in Christ. At the appointed time he went to Rasenhime, to attend this solemn rite.

The oldest of Mr. Fredenberg's children was a daughter by the name of Christina, at that time twenty years old. She had always been fond of retirement, being of a reserved disposition, and had likewise avoided Stilling as much as possible. Her education had been plain, but thorough as far as it went. She had been brought up in the principles of the christian religion, according to the system of the Evangelical Lutheran church, and her mother had instructed her in the art of housekeeping and the female work necessary in every family; in short, she was

he took an affectionate farewell of Christina, and at the same
time threw out a few hints concerning his doubts and fears on
the occasion; but she comforted him by saying: "I am sure,
this business comes from God, and he will finish it to our mutual satisfaction."

On his way home, he had time to pursue his own reflections. He was convinced, that Mr. Spanier would withdraw his
hand and dismiss him, when he should learn the step he had
taken, and thus he would again be placed in his former destitute
situation. Neither could Mr. Fredenberg be pleased with him,
for it was indeed a sorry piece of friendship, and a most
shocking abuse of that sacred name, to engage himself to his
daughter under circumstances, in which he was not able to
make a living for himself, far less maintain a family, and in
which he needed a considerable sum of money, to prosecute and
finish his studies.

These things made Stilling afraid, that his future situation
would be worse than any, in which he had hitherto been placed.
He compared it to that of a man, who has been climbing up a high
rock on the shore of the sea, and has no prospect of tracing
his way down again, except by jumping into the ocean, to save
himself by swimming. Stilling's only comfort in these trying
circumstances was, to cast himself and his Christina in
the almighty arms of his heavenly Father, and for the present
not to say a word of this occurrence to any one. Mr.
Fredenberg had given him permission, to send the medicines
destined for that part of the country, where *he* lived, to his house,
and promised that he would deliver them to the proper persons.

Nine days after the above mentioned occurrence, he sent a
small package of medicines to him, adding a letter to Mr. Fredenberg, in which he partly disclosed his views and intentions
in regard to Christina, and even ventured to send a sealed letter
to her, inclosed in that to her father. He did all this, without further reflection; but when the package was gone, he saw,
how inconsiderately he had acted, and his heart failed him for fear
of the possible consequences.

Stilling started for Rasenhime on the next Saturday; his sensations were indescribable. The nearer he approached the house, the more violent were the pulsations of his heart. On entering the family-room, Christina with her parents received him with the usual cordiality, and his courage revived in some measure, supposing that his friend either entertained no suspicion, or intended to make no objections to the match. He soon went into his own room to dress himself. When he came down stairs, Christina stood in the door of an apartment, opposite to the family-room, and invited him to enter. Being seated, she told him, that the letter had excited the suspicion of her father ; that her mother had questioned her about it, and she had been under the necessity of giving her an account of their engagement : "in this state," continued she, "matters now stand ; my father has not spoken a word with me on the subject. But I believe it is our duty to ask the consent of our parents this very evening ; my father told me, as you went up stairs : "go with Stilling intot he other room, I presume you have something to say to him."

Stilling's heart was elated with joy on perceiving his affairs had taken so favorable a turn. He conversed a while with his Christina ; they renewed their mutual promise of faithfulness towards each other, and resolved to walk in uprightness before God and man.

After supper, when all the children were gone to bed, he told her parents all the circumstances, under which he had entered into an engagement of marriage with their eldest daughter, and concluded in these words :

"I ask you now, if you will receive me among the number of your children ? By the grace of God, I will endeavor to fulfil the duties of a son towards you, and I do herewith solemnly protest against your giving me any assistance for the prosecution of my studies. I wish to marry your daughter, and I take God to witness, that I form this connection, without any ignoble views."

Mr. Fredenberg gave a deep sigh, and tears trickled down his cheeks, when he said :

"Mr. Stilling, I have no objection, and willingly receive you as a son, for I believe, the will of Providence directs us in this matter. Besides I know, you are too upright, to harbor any un-christian views; and I must add, that I am unable to advance the money, for your studies."

He then turned to Christina and said :

"Do you think, you will be strong enough, to bear the long absence of your bridegroom ?"

She answered : "I hope, God will give me the necessary strength."

Mr. Fredenberg then arose, embraced Stilling, and Mrs. Fredenberg followed his example. It would be as impossible, to express in language Stilling's sensations of joy, as it would be above the power of any pen, to describe the anguish of mind he had felt before the developement of the scene. He felt as if he had been translated into a paradise—no anxious thought, whence he should obtain money for the prosecution of his stu-dies,disturbed his breast; these words : "The Lord will provide," were so deeply engraven on his heart, that he could not fear.

Mr. Fredenberg advised him, to stay during the summer with Mr. Spanier, and to go the ensuing fall to some university. Stilling was the more willing to comply with these wishes of his father-in-law, because they perfectly coincided with his own in-tentions. Finally they agreed, to keep the engagement with Christina a secret for the present, in order to avoid the rash judg-ment of the world, and the family united in fervent prayer for the divine blessing in a matter of so great importance.

Towards the end of June, Stilling informed Mr Spanier of his intention to enter a university, and begged him not to think hard of him for taking this step, and to reflect, since he was now in his thirtieth year, that it was high time, he should look out for a permanent settlement. His patron made no reply, but from that time withdrew his friendship from him, so that the latter part of his stay in Mr. Spanier's house, was in many respects unpleasant. Four weeks before the Frankfort fair he took leave of his patron and his family. He shed tears without saying a word. One great difficulty was, that, having never agreed with Mr. Spanier for a stipulated salary, but having been always abundantly supplied with every thing he needed, and besides, having drawn considerable sums from his patron for books and other articles, he now received no money from him, and arrived pennyless at the house of his father-in-law. The latter however paid him one hundred rix-dollars, to procure the most necessary articles, and to defray the expenses of his journey. His christian friends at Shonenthal made him a present of a handsome suit of new clothes, and offered him further assistance.— Stilling had not yet made any choice of the university, where he should finish his studies. He expected to receive some direction from his heavenly Father for that purpose. After a stay of three weeks at Rasenhime, he took a walk to Shonenthal, to visit once more his friends at that place. A certain lady of the aforementioned city asked him, what university he purposed to attend? His answer was, he had not made up his mind on that subject. "O," said she, "our neighbor Mr. Troost is going to Strasburg, with the intention of attending the winter-lectures, you better go with him."

Stilling believed, that this was the direction, for which he had waited, and while he was yet in conversation on the subject, Mr. Troost entered, and the lady immediately spoke to him about it. Mr. Troost was glad at the prospect of his company, for he had already a slight acquaintance with Stilling. He was a gentleman of about forty years of age and unmarried; he had followed the profession of a surgeon at Shonenthal for better than twenty years; but being no longer satisfied with the knowledge of his profession he had hitherto attained, was resolved to study Anatomy once more at the celebrated university of Strasburg, and likewise to attend other lectures pertaining to the art he practiced: and thus to prepare himself with new strength and ability for serving the public in his calling. In his youth he had spent several years at that university, and laid the foundation of his knowledge in surgery. He was indeed the very man for Stilling; for he had the best heart in the world, formed, as it were, for friendship, bore a most excellent character, and was a friend to virtue and religion. He was acquainted with the world and with Strasburg, and Stilling had to acknowledge it

as a peculiar favor of divine Providence, to become acquainted
with him, at this period. They resolved to go to Frankfort in
company of some merchants, who purposed attending the fair;
and to take a return coach from Frankfort to Strasburg. They
fixed the day of their departure a week from the day of their
meeting in Shonenthal. Stilling's situation was in every respect
highly unpromising. He was engaged to a delicate and pious
girl, whom he tenderly loved, but who had been declared consumptive by all the physicians, who had been consulted, so that
there was abundant cause to fear for her life; he felt with
and for her when he reflected on the load of sufferings,
which her tender feeling heart would have to bear during his
long absence. His own hopes of happiness rested on his becoming a skilful physician; and one thousand rix-dollars
were absolutely necessary, to carry him through his studies, of
which he could not muster one hundred; his prospect in regard to money was therefore very gloomy, for if he failed in
this respect he failed in every other. Though Stilling was not
insensible to these difficulties, his confidence in God's providence
remained unshaken and he drew this conclusion: God begins no-
ting, but what he executes for his glory; he himself has brought
me into my present situation; by his providence alone he has directed me to the study of medicine, and therefore he will likewise execute his plan with me for his glory. This inference inspired him with so much courage, that he frequently observed to his
friends at Rasenhime: "I am anxious to know, how my heavenly Father will procure the means for the prosecution of my studies." But to his other friends he did not disclose his circumstances, particularly not to Mr. Troost; for this tender feeling
friend would have seen a thousand insurmountable obstacles,
had he been acquainted with Stilling's real situation.

At length the day appointed for his departure, approached.
Christina's eyes were constantly swimming in tears, she fainted
several times, and the whole family were deeply affected. The
last evening was spent by Mr. Fredenberg and Stilling in confidential conversation. The former could not refrain from shedding tears when he said to Stilling:

"My dear Son, my heart bleeds for you, and gladly would I provide you with money, were it in my power; I commenced business with little or nothing, and though I have been successful thus far, should I give you the money necessary for the prosecution of your studies, I would severely suffer in my own affair. Besides I have ten children, what I do for one, I owe to all the rest."

"My dear father," answered Stilling with a serene countenance, "I do not ask a penny of you, for I know, *he* still lives, who fed so many thousands in the wilderness, to his providential care I commit all my wants. He will find ways and means. Do not be anxious on my account.—The Lord will provide!"

He had sent his baggage to Frankfort; on the morning of his departure he went after breakfast into Christina's apartment and found her bathed in tears. He embraced her and said: "Farewell, my dear, may the Lord strengthen and preserve you in good health till we shall see each other again!" And thus he left her. Having taken leave of all the rest, he started for Shonenthal, accompanied by the eldest brother of his bride. Here this faithful friend left him likewise. The journey to Frankfort shall not detain the reader, suffice it to say, he and his travelling companion arrived in that city without any accident.

<hr />

CHAPTER IX.

Forty rix-dollars was the amount of Stilling's riches,, when he started from Rasenhime. On his arrival in Frankfort he found it necessary to tarry eleven days for an opportunity of continuing his journey to Strasburg, and during that time his money melted down to one single rix-dollar. He waited however with confidence for the help of his heavenly Father, without disclosing his situation to any of his friends; and the uneasiness, which would nevertheless some times steal over his mind, he suppressed by prayers to God.—One day as he was walking through the streets and had reached the Roemersberg, he met a merchant.

from Shonenthal, by the name of Leebman, with whom he was well acquainted; who inquired very affectionately how he was, and invited him to take supper with him that evening. Stilling accepted the invitation, and went at the appointed time. After supper Mr. Leebman asked him, whence he obtained money for the prosecution of his studies?

Stilling answered with a smile: "I have a rich father in heaven, who will provide for me."

Mr. Leebman looked at him and asked: "how much have you now?"

"One rix-dollar," was Stilling's reply.

"Well, I am one of your father's stewards, and shall open my purse this time." With these words he drew his purse, and gave him thirty-three rix-dollars, as the sum which he could at present conveniently spare, adding: "You will find every where assistance. Should you at any time hereafter be able to return me the money, you may do so, if not, I shall never ask for it." Stilling expressed his thanks to him, while tears of gratitude towards God flowed down his cheeks. This example of the evident interference of God in his behalf, encouraged him so much, that he firmly believed, God would help him through every other difficulty. Before he left Frankfort, he received letters from his friends at Rasenhime, particularly from Christina, who informed him she had taken courage, and was resolved to submit with patience to the will of God. He answered all these letters, but said nothing of the first probation of his faith, and merely told his friends, that he was well provided.

Two days afterwards Mr. Troost hired a return-coach to take them as far as Manhime. On this journey a Swiss-merchant from Luzerne was their traveling companion. In order to pass the time on the road, they conversed on various subjects. The Swiss-merchant was very open hearted towards his traveling companions, which likewise opened Stilling's heart, so that he gave him the history of his life, the recital of which drew tears from the eyes of the noble hearted Swiss. At Manhime they hired another return-coach to Strasburg. On the road between Speyer and Lauterburg Stilling and his friend from Luzerne stepped out of the coach, because its motion in the sandy roads did not agree with them, and walked for a considerable distance together. The Swiss-merchant desired him, when they were alone, to sell him a copy of Molitor's manuscript for five Louisd'ors, and Stilling promised it to him. When they had again entered the coach, Mr. Troost observed in reference to this manuscript, that he would place no value on all these patent medicines, after he should have passed through his studies. Our Swiss friend hearing this, repented of his bargain. Had Mr. Troost known what agreement they had made, he would doubtless have remained silent.

Our travelers arrived safely at Strasburg, and took temporary lodgings at the house of alderman Blesig at the sign of the axe; whence they wrote to their respective friends, informing them of their safe arrival. The next day they were matriculated and Mr. Troost, who was well acquainted in the city, hired lodgings for them both at the house of a rich merchant by the name of R——, whose brother lived at Shonenthal, and who on this account was the more willing. to rent them a well furnished apartment in the lower story of his house for a very moderate sum. A good boarding house was likewise in the neighborhood, where they engaged board by the month. Stilling made the necessary inquiries concerning the lectures, and engaged as many as he could conveniently attend ; physiology, anatomy and chemistry however formed the prominent branches of his studies for the present. The next day they went for the first time to dinner at their boarding-house. They were the first in the dining room, and had the advantage of seeing the other boarders arrive, one after the other. The company consisted of about twenty persons, among whom one gentleman particularly attracted their attention. He was well made, with blue eyes. and an elevated forehead. This must be a fine man, whispered Troost to Stilling. who concurred in his opinion, though he was somewhat afraid he would prove troublesome, on account of his free manners; in that respect however he was mistaken.—His name was Gœthe.—

Two students of medicine, Waldberg and Melzer, the one

from Vienna, the other from Alsace likewise attracted their notice. The first mentioned was a man of superior intellectual faculties, but opposed to religion, and of loose morals. The other was a fine little man, possessed of a noble heart, but somewhat irritative and suspicious. He took his place near Stilling at the table, and they soon became acquainted. A student of Theology by the name of Leose likewise entered the room, a favorite of Goethe, which he richly deserved to be, for he was not only a man of great learning and an excellent Theologian, but he possessed likewise that rare gift, to pronounce in a dry tone the most cutting satire against vice.

Another person took his seat near Goethe, of whom I shall only observe, that he was a raven adorned with peacock-feathers. Another gentleman, but of an excellent character, a native of Strasburg took also a seat at the table, his modesty doth not permit me to praise him, he was the well known Mr. Salzman. If my readers imagine to themselves the most profound philosopher and the real christian united, they will have a picture of Salzman. Mr. Troost whispered to Stilling : "here we ought to be silent hearers for a fortnight." Stilling acknowledged this to be a good piece of advice, and both were therefore for some time silent observers, and no one of the company seemed to take much notice of them, except that Goethe now and then shot a look at them : he seemed to have the government at the table, without seeking it. Mr. Troost was a very useful friend to Stilling, he was acquainted with the world, and therefore an excellent guide through its intricacies. Without him, Stilling would have committed a thousand blunders. So bountiful had his heavenly Father been towards him, that he provided him even with a tutor, who not only assisted him as a friend in the common concerns of life, but who also pointed out to him a suitable plan and method for his studies.

In a short time Stilling felt himself very comfortable at Strasburg, running his race successfully. Messrs. Speelman and Lobstine, two of the professors, whose lectures he particularly attended, soon took notice of him, because he was a diligent student, and sedate and dignified in his deportment. But his thirty-three rix-dollars were now again reduced to a single one, which induced him to offer up fervent prayers for assistance to his heavenly Father, who soon heard him. For in this time of distress Mr. Troost addressed him one morning in the following manner: "I believe, you have brought no money with you, I will lend you six Carolins, till you receive your bills of exchange. Though he had no expectation either of receiving bills of exchange, or money in any other way, he still accepted his friend's offer, who immediately paid him that sum."

Reader! who excited the heart of this friend at the very moment, when Stilling was in the greatest need!!

CHAPTER X.

Mr. Troost was dressed fashionably, and so was Stilling; but the latter had a round whig in his ward-robe, which for economy's sake he one day wore at the dinner-table. No one took any offense at it, but Waldberg. He looked at him, and having learnt before, that Stilling was a friend to religion, asked him: "Did Adam in Paradise wear a round whig?" All the guests laughed, except Salzman, Goethe and Troost. Stilling replied with a look of anger: "Are you not ashamed of this scoffing language? such low and coarse wit is not worth laughing at!" But Goethe took the word, and observed: "Try a man first, whether he deserves derision." It is abominably wicked, it is devilish, to mock an honest, good man, who has given no cause of offense! From that time Goethe took particular notice of Stilling, visited him, and endeavored on all occasions to give him proofs of his good will and friendship.

About the middle of November proposals were issued for a lecture on midwifery, and the students of medicine were invited to subscribe. This lecture was of great importance for him, he therefore went on the appointed day to the Professor to enter his name, under the impression, that this lecture, as well as all others, was to be paid for, at the close of the course. But how great was his astonishment, when the Doctor requested the students, to pay next Thursday evening six Louisd'ors in advance for the lecture. In case he could not have paid this sum at the above mentioned time, his name would have been struck off from the list, which would have lessened his credit materially; and besides would have been extremely humiliating for him; what therefore to do under these circumstances, he knew not. Mr. Troost had already lent him six Carolins, and there existed at present no prospect of repaying that gentleman. As soon as he came into his room, and found himself alone, he locked the door, threw himself into a corner, and prayed earnestly to God for assistance, but no help appeared. The clock struck five, and in one hour's time he must have the money. He almost lost his faith, the anguish of his soul pressed drops of sweat from his forehead, and his face was bathed in tears. While he was walking the floor in utter despair, a knock was heard at the door. At his call "come in," the landlord entered, and after the usual compliments said:

"I come to see, how you like the apartment, you have rented of me?" Mr. Troost was again absent, and totally ignorant of his present critical situation.—Stilling answered:

"I am very much obliged to you, Sir, for the honor you do me, in making the inquiry; and I have the pleasure to inform you, that we are extremely well suited with our lodgings." Mr. R—— replied, he was glad to hear it, but should take the liberty of troubling him with one more question:

"Have you brought money with you, or do you expect bills of exchange?" Stilling felt as doubtless Habakkuk did, when the angel carried him by the hair of his head to Babylon. He answered:

"I have brought no money with me." Mr. R—— looked with astonishment at him and replied:

"How for heaven's sake do you live then?"

"His reply was: Mr. Troost has lent me some money."

"I will tell you, Sir," continued Mr. R—— "Troost wants his money himself. I will lend you as much as you need for the present, and if you receive a draught, give it to me, you shall have no trouble with the sale of it. Do you want money immediately?" Stilling could hardly refrain from betraying his feelings by a sudden exclamation, but suppressing his emotion as much as possible briefly answered: "Mr. R——, I acknowledge, I ought to pay six Louisd'ors this evening if I had them." Mr. R—— observed with some astonishment : "I see, God has sent me to your assistance." With these words he left him, and his feelings may very properly be compared to those of Daniel in the lion's-den, when Habakkuk brought him food. Lost in these sensations, he scarcely perceived Mr. R——'s return, who brought him eight Louisd'ors with these words : "Here is the money you wanted and a little more, when it is gone, you must ask for more." Stilling dared not fully express his gratitude to this gentleman, from fear of exposing himself too much.

In the circle, in which he moved, he was frequently tempted to become a sceptic on the subject of religion ; he heard daily new proofs against the Bible, against christianity, and the very principles of the religion of the Redeemer. All those proofs in favor of religion, which he had hitherto collected, were no longer sufficient to satisfy his reason, the probations of faith alone, of which he had experienced so many in the course of his life, made him invincible. He reasoned thus : "That being, who evidently hears the prayers of the children of men, and who governs their destinies in a preceptible and wonderful manner, must be the true God, and his doctrine the word of God. But I have always revered and adored Jesus Christ as my God and Savior, he has heard me in my afflictions and difficulties and assisted me in a most wonderful manner. Therefore Jesus Christ is undeniably the true God, his doctrine the word of God, and his religion, as he has taught it, is the true religion."

This mode of reasoning, founded on his own experience, could from its nature be no proof to any other man, though it was perfectly satisfactory to himself, and strong enough, to arm him against every attack.

As soon as Mr. R—— was gone, he fell on his face, worshiping God, and thanking him for his gracious interposition, and recommending himself for the future to his preserving grace;

this duty being performed, he went into the lecture hall, and paid his subscription.

While this happened at Strasburg, Mr. Leebman was paying a visit to Mr. Fredenberg; for they were intimate friends; Leebman however knew nothing of Stilling's connection with Fredenberg's family, though he was not ignorant of the friendship which subsisted between them. As they were sitting and talking together, the conversation turned upon their mutual friend at Strasburg. Leebman mentioned, that Mr. Troost could not find words sufficient in his letters to praise Stilling's application, natural talent and progress in his studies. Fredenberg and his family, and especially Christina were rejoiced at these news. Leebman further said, that he could not comprehend whence he obtained the money for the prosecution of his studies. Fredenberg observed, that he neither knew any thing about it. Well, continued Leebman, I wish, some friend would assist me in sending him a handsome bill of exchange. Mr. Fredenberg perceived, that this was a providential hint, he could hardly refrain from bursting into tears; but poor Christina ran into her chamber to pour out her heart in praise to God. Fredenberg replied:

"I will assist you."

"Leebman said:" If you will pay one hundred and fifty rix-dollars, I will give as much, and we will send the draft. Fredenberg agreed to this proposition, and a fortnight after the above mentioned severe probation of Stilling's faith he unexpectedly received a letter from Mr. Leebman, inclosing a draft for three hundred dollars. He laughed, went to the window, looking with heartfelt gratitude to heaven and said: "This is thy work alone, O my Almighty Father!"

My life I dedicate to thee,
My walk shall praise thy name forever.

He then paid Mr. Troost, Mr. R—— and all his other small debts in Strasburg, and had yet money enough left, for his expenses during the winter.

His mode of living at Strasburg was so singular, that the whole university talked of it. Philosophy was the science for which be had always felt great partiality. As a means of self improvement he gave every evening from five to six o'clock a public lecture on philosophy. As he took no pay for these lectures, the faculty made no objection. His auditory was numerous, he obtained by this means many friends, and greatly enlarged the circle of his acquaintances. Neither did he neglect his own studies. He made frequent praeparata on the anatomical theatre, and professor Lobstine, who lectured on that branch with great success, shewed him much friendship and spared no pains to make him master of that part of medical science. During the winter he visited the sick in the hospital, in company of Dr. Ehrman. Here he observed the different diseases, and on the anatomical theatre he learnt their causes. In short he used every exertion in his power, to make himself completely master of the medical art. In belles letters Gœthe opened a new field for him. He made him acquainted with Ossian's, Shakespear's, Fielding's and Sterne's works, and thus Stilling came from nature without a circuitous route back to nature again. There was likewise an association of young men at Strasburg, who stiled themselves "the society of belles letters," of which he became a member. In this society he became acquainted with the best books, and the present state of literature in the world. Mr. Troost introduced him also to Herder, who spent that winter at Strasburg. Stilling admired him more than any other he had seen hitherto, and frequently used to say : "Herder has but one idea, and that idea is the world." He was the better pleased with this introduction because he harmonized more with him than with Gœthe.

Spring was now approaching, and Mr. Troost was preparing for his return. Stilling felt the pang of separation from so dear and valuable a friend, but his present loss had been made up by the many new acquaintances he had formed at Strasburg; he also hoped, in a year's time to see him again at Shonenthal. Before Troost left Strasburg, he was informed of Stilling's connection with the Fredenberg family and received letters for them from Stilling, who desired him to visit his friends as soon as convenient, and to give them a faithful account of all his circumstances.

CHAPTER XI.

Ten days before Whitsun-tide Stilling went to the theatre, to see the performance of Romeo and Juliet according to Mr. Wiss's translation for the German theatre. While there, a great uneasiness of mind seized him, without knowing whence it proceeded. He had received the most encouraging letters both from his relatives in the principality of Salen and from his friends at Rasenhime. He left the theatre to reflect on the cause of this singular state of mind, but could discover none. It however gradually subsided, and he thought no more of it.

On Tuesday before Whitsun-tide the son of one of the professors of the university was to be married, and of course there were no lectures given that day. Stilling resolved to improve this leisure-time for private studies. At nine o'clock in the morning a sudden horror fell upon him, his heart palpitated, and he could find no relief. He rose from his chair, walked the floor for some time, and felt a strong desire to undertake a journey to Rasenhime. He was frightened at the idea, when he reflected on the injury, which such a journey would occasion to his studies, as well as to his purse. At last he persuaded himself that all proceeded from a touch of the Hypochondria; and he therefore endeavored to drive it from his mind by engaging in his private studies, but he strove in vain, his uneasiness increased every minute, so that he could not study in the least. He represented to himself, what people would think of him, should he undertake this journey of more than two hundred miles, and perhaps find all things in the usual order at home. However, as he could not shake off this singular sensation, he prayed to God, that he might give him some sure token, if the journey were necessary, from which he might learn why it was so? While he was thus praying, one of Mr. R——'s clerks brought him the following letter from Rasenhime:

My dear Son!

You will doubtless have received the letters from Mrs. Fredenberg, from my son and from Mr. Troost; the news will therefore not come unexpected, that Christina is very ill. Her former

A a

indisposition has attacked her again, and she is now very weak—very weak indeed. Her sickness has so affected my mind, that I cannot refrain from tears while writing. I do not wish to say much on this subject, from fear, of overdoing the matter; I pray earnestly for the poor child as well as for myself, that we may resign ourselves with filial confidence to God's holy will. May the merciful Redeemer look down with pity upon us all! Your Christina wishes, that I shall tell you, she is so weak, that she can hardly speak!—I have to lay down my pen for a while, may Almighty God enable me to write, what I ought.—In his name I again take my pen in hand to tell you, that according to human appearances—be strong, my dearest son,—I say according to human appearances Christina, won't live to see many more days in this world. O my dearest son! I feel, as if my heart would break, I can't write much more. Your bride wishes to see you once more, but what shall I say, or what advice shall I give you? God! thou knowest my heart, thou knowest, that I would be willing, to defray the expenses of your journey. but dare not advise you, to undertake it. Inquire of the best of counsellors, to whom I commend you in fervent prayer. I, your mother, bride and all the children desire to be affectionately remembered to you.—Your affectionate father—Peter Fredenberg.

Stilling did not know what he should do; he ran like a madman up and down the room; he neither wept nor sighed, but looked like a person in despair. At length he collected his thoughts so far, that he dressed himself, and ran with the letter to Gœthe. As he entered the room he exclaimed: "I am undone, read this letter." Gœthe read, rose hastily, sighed and said with tears in his eyes: "Poor Stilling!" He immediately returned with him to his lodgings. On their way thither, they met another friend to whom he communicated his misfortune, who also accompanied them. Both these friends put the necessary clothes and linnen in his valise, while another one looked out for a conveyance, which was readily obtained, as a boat was going down the Rhine as far as Mainz, and was to start at noon. In the mean time he wrote a few lines to his father-in-law, announcing his intention of visiting him. Gœthe procured the necessary provisions, carried them to the boat, and returned to take Stilling on board. As soon as he was under way, his mind became easy, and he hoped to find Christina alive, and even that she would recover. It happened to be the most convenient time for him to travel, for most of the lectures had been closed for the season. During his journey to Mainz nothing of importance occurred, he arrived there on Friday evening about six o'clock, and on inquiring for a conveyance to Cologne learnt, that a covered boat had set sail a few hours before for that place and that the intention of the captain was, to stay at Bingen all night. Stilling accepted the offer of a boatman to take him to Bingen for four guilders. While the men were getting ready, a lad about fifteen years of age came to Stilling and asked, if he would permit him to go in his company as far as Cologne. Having received a favorable answer, and the men the promise of two additional guilders, our travelers stepped into a small open boat. Stilling apprehensive of danger, expressed his fears to the men, but they only laughed at him. On starting it was perceptible, that the water reached within a few inches to the level of the boat, and whenever Stilling stirred in the least, the water rushed in. All these circumstances made him feel very insecure, he frequently wished himself on the shore : however, to pass the time away, he entered into conversation with his little traveling companion. With astonishment he learnt of him, that he was the son of a rich widow-lady at H——, and that he intended to go quite alone to the Cape of Good Hope, to visit his brother. Stilling asked him, whether his mother had given her consent to this voyage? upon which the lad told him, that she had not at first; but that he had left her house secretly, and that she had pursued and stopt him at Mainz ; yet in consequence of his earnest entreaties she had granted him permission, and had given him a bill of exchange to the amount of eleven hundred guilders. "I have an uncle at Rotterdam," said he, "who is to see me on board a vessel." This declaration quieted Stilling's apprehension in regard to him, supposing his uncle would have orders to detain him. While they were conversing, Stilling felt his feet getting very cold, and on examination found, that the water was penetrating the boat, and that the skipper who sat behind him, was baling with all his might. This increased his uneasiness so much, that he demanded to be landed on the left bank of the river, but though he promised them the full prize agreed upon, they would not consent, but rowed on a head. Stilling and the lad therefore assisted in baling, and it was as much as they could do, to keep the boat free of water. In the mean time it became dark, they drew near the mountains, the wind rose high, and a heavy shower was approaching. The lad was shaking with fear; and Stilling became very melancholy, and the circumstance that the boat-men began to converse with each other by signs, was not calculated to lull his apprehensions, as it indicated, that they had some evil design in view. Night had now set in, the shower was close upon them, it thundered, lightened and the rain descended in torrents, the wind was very high, the skiff was tossed up and down by the waves and nothing but a watery grave seemed to await them. Stilling turned in silent prayer to God, that he might preserve him, especially if Christina should live longer in this world. Engaged in these meditations, he raised his eyes, and beheld the mast of a Yacht—he called for help, and immediately a sailor came on deck, with a lantern and a long hook. The skippers endeavored to avoid the Yacht as much as possible, but wind and water drove them in spite of their exertions towards it, and before they were aware of it, the sailors had fastened the hook to the boat and were drawing it close to the vessel. The captain of the yacht having by the light of the lantern discovered the countenances of the boat-men, said: "Ah, Ah! are you the fellows, who drowned the two travelers a few weeks ago? Wait, you shall have your pay, as soon as I return to Mainz!" Stilling threw them the promised six guilders into the boat, thankful for having escaped so imminent a danger. In the morning at day light they were opposite Bingen; having given the sailors some drinking money, he and his little companion left the Yacht, and soon found the boat fastened to a post, in which they intended to go to Cologne.

There was a tavern not far from the shore, whither Stilling and the lad went. The floor in the bar-room was covered with straw; in one corner lay a man of a very noble appearance. At a little distance farther was a soldier stretched out at full length; a step farther lay a young fellow, who resembled a good for nothing student as much as one egg doth another. In a separate corner in the back part of the room something was lying, which when it began to stir and look up from a multitude of bolsters and pillows he discovered to be some sort of a woman. Having viewed this singular group with much satisfaction he addressed himself to the company in these words:

"Gentlemen, I wish you all a good morning and a successful journey." All three arose from their couches; yawning and clearing their throats they looked about and saw a smiling man standing before them. Having made their compliments to the stranger, one of them asked him whence he came so early? Stilling informed him in a few words, of his last adventure. "You are no merchant, I suppose," replied the stranger, "at least you have not the appearance of one." Stilling answered with a smile: "You seem to understand the science of physiognomy, I am indeed no merchant, I am studying medicine." The stranger gave him a penetrating look and said:

"You study at a time, when others are already settled, you have either been under the necessity of surmounting vast difficulties, or you have made a late choice." He replied:

"Both these things are true. I am a son of Providence, without God's particular interference I would be either a tailor or a collier." He pronounced these words with great emphasis, as he usually doth, when he speaks on this subject. The stranger continued: "I hope, you will give us your history!"

"Yes," answered Stilling, "I will do it with great pleasure." The stranger tapped him on the shoulder and said: "Whosoever you are, you are the man I like." Stilling then inquired, whether the gentlemen wished to take breakfast here? And when all had agreed to have a dish of coffee, he went out to bespeak it. On his return he asked the company, if they would permit him and the lad to join them as far as Cologne? All answered in the affirmative, adding, that it gave them particular pleasure, to receive him as a traveling companion. Meanwhile they went dressing, and the woman in her corner was likewise adjusting her dress very bashfully. He learnt, that she was house-keeper to a Roman catholic clergyman at Cologne, and was of course very reserved in the company of strangers, although she might have saved herself the trouble, being beyond all description ugly. The coffee was now served, and all took their breakfast at one table, excepting the house-keeper, who enjoyed her dish in scrupulous retirement at her own table. After breakfast they all went to the boat, and Stilling observed, that the gentleman, who had pressed him to relate the history of his life, was a stranger to all. Having passed the dangerous place called the Bingerloch, Stilling gave the promised narrative, relating every circumstance, his engagement and the cause of his present journey not excepted. The stranger frequently shed tears during the narration, and so did the soldier, and both wished to learn, how he would find his bride.

The soldier in his turn gave them a brief narative of his life as follows:

"I was born in the Dutchy of Zweybruk, and though my parents were poor, they nevertheless sent me to a good school, that a liberal education might be a substitute for a fortune. After I left school, a certain gentleman under government employed me as clerk. With him I spent several years, became acquainted with his daughter, a mutual attachment was formed, and we promised each other, to marry no other. My patron dismissed me, when he discovered his daughter's attachment. I went to Holland, and enlisted as a soldier. I wrote many letters to my bride, but received no answers, as mine were intercepted. This drove me to such despair, that I often sought for death, though I abhorred suicide. Our regiment was soon sent to South America, where the Indians were at war with the Hollanders. On our arrival in Suriname the company to which I belonged, was stationed at a fort a considerable distance from the capital. I was still wishing for death, and hoped, that in one or the other engagement a ball would finish my life, but I shuddered when I reflected on the possibility, of being taken pri-

soner by the Indians. But being determined not to suffer myself
to be taken alive, I frequently requested the captain, to send me
out on reconoitring parties against the Indians, and being generally succesful in these excursions, I was appointed Sergeant.
At one time I commanded fifty men, we came into a forest at a
considerable distance from the fort; we marched on, carrying our
muskets cocked in our arms. All at once a ball whistled past
my head, and immediately afterwards another. We halted; and
in looking about, discovered an Indian in the act of reloading.
Our guns were in a moment levelled at him, and we called to
him to surrender. Seeing no possibility of escape, he did as we
had demanded. Luckily he understood some Dutch; we compelled him to guide us to their camp, which was not far distant.
We surrounded it, as they were sleeping in perfect security, and
took their chief prisoner. This put an end to the war. I received a commission as Lieutenant, and after some time returned
with the regiment to Holland. I immediately took furlough to
go home, and found that my bride had remained faithful to her
promise. Being in possession of some wealth, and enjoying an
honorable title in society, my application was no longer rejected,
we were married and I am now the father of five children."

The company were pleased with the story; and both the
Lieutenant and Stilling would have been glad to learn now some-
thing of the stranger; but he smiled and said: Excuse me,
Gentlemen, I dare not.

Thus the day passed away in pleasant conversation.
Towards night a storm arose, which compelled them to land at
Leitersdorf below Neuwied, and to stay all night.

The fellow, whom Stilling had taken for a student, was
from Strasburg, and had run away from his parents. While
we others were engaged in conversation, he made himself acquainted with the lad, who had come in Stilling's company.
All warnings to be on his guard, and especially also that of
keeping his bill of exchange out of sight, were of no avail.
Stilling afterwards learnt, that the boy had lost all his money,
and that the student had absconded.

At bed-time it was found, that there were but three beds

for five travelers. It was agreed to cast lots, who should sleep together, and it happened, that the two lads came together, the Lieutenant got a bed to himself, and Stilling and the stranger received the third. At undressing Stilling perceived, that his bed-companion was well provided with jewelry, and concluded, he must be a man of rank. But it appeared to him, that his mode of traveling was incompatible with this idea, he therefore began to suspect him; however observing him to be a praying man, he was ashamed of his suspicions. The next evening they arrived at Cologne. In that place the stranger seemed to have much business; he likewise changed his style of living, hired servants &c. Stilling lodged at the same Hotel. On the morrow Stilling hastened away. The stranger took an affectionate leave of him and said: "Your company, Sir, has given me much satisfaction, continue to pursue your course, I shall not forget you." Stilling once more expressed a desire to know, with whom he had had the pleasure of traveling. The stranger smiled and said: "When you come to Rasenhime and read the papers, and find the name ——, think of me. On his way the name of the stranger occurred again to his mind, it appeared to him familiar, and yet he did not know, what to make of it. In the afternoon he arrived at Rasenhime. In the course of a week he took up a Lippstadt newspaper, in which he found the following article: Cologne May the 24th: Mr.—— Ambassedor of —— at the Hague has passed this day through our city on his way to Holland.

He found Christina in a paroxysm of delirium, she did not recognize him, but pushed him away. He retired for some time to another room, until she had recovered her senses, her friends gave her then to understand, that Stilling had come. Words are insufficient to describe the meeting between the two lovers, but alas! it was too much for poor Christina! Her exertions threw her into fits, and Stilling expected every moment during the first three days and nights nothing else but her departure. She recovered however, notwithstanding the fears of all her friends, and within a fortnight she had recruited her strength so far, as to be able to sit up at least during part of the day. Stilling's engagement with Christina became now generally known. Fredenberg's best friends advised him, to have them immediately married, which was done with the usual formalities by the bed-side of Christina; June 17th in the year 1771.

❧

CHATER XII.

Mr. Dinkler, an excellent physician, a man of great erudition and of an extensive practice, lived at that time in Shonenthal. He was an intimate friend of Mr. Troost's, and had learnt part of Stilling's history from that kind hearted man, and Stilling had likewise found an opportunity, of becoming acquainted with him. This Dr. Dinkler and Mr. Troost were guests at his wedding, and both proposed to him to settle at Shonenthal, particularly, as one of the physicians of that place had lately died. But he could not give a decisive answer to this proposition, because he looked to Providence for guidance and direction in this affair, as well as in all others. But these two friends would not allow any hesitation on his part, and engaged a suitable house for him, previous to his return to Strasburg. Dr. Dinkler likewise promised him, to attend Christina as medical friend during his absence. Mr. Fredenberg also found means to supply him with the necessary sum of money for the prosecution of his studies; and when all things were properly regulated, he prepared for his return to Strasburg. The evening before his departure he entered his wife's chamber, and found her in a kneeling posture with folded hands. He approached her, and perceived that she was as stiff as a corpse, though her pulse was regular. He lifted her up, spoke to her, and thus brought her to her senses again. The whole night she spent in lamentations attended by spasmodic affections. In the morning she had remained in bed, and when her husband came to take leave of her, she threw her arms round his neck, wept and sobbed incessantly. At last he tore himself from her by force. His two brothers-in-law accompanied him as far as Cologne. On the

B b

next day, just as he was stepping into the mail coach, an express arrived from Rasenhime, informing him, that Christina was in a measure resigned. This gave him great encouragement and he began to hope, that on his return he would find her completely recovered. He commended her and himself into the hands of his Almighty Father, and having taken leave of his brothers, continued his journey. In seven days he arrived safe in Strasburg, and went immediately to Gœthe. The noble man hastily rose from his seat, when he saw him, embraced him and said: "Are you here again, good Stilling? How is your bride?" He answered: "She is no longer my bride, but my wife." "That's well done," replied the other, "you are a capital fellow!" The remainder of that day was spent in pleasant conversations.

Mr. Lentz, a man well known in his country by his literary productions, had arrived in Strasburg during his absence. Gœthe, Lentz and Leose formed a circle, in which Stilling found great satisfaction. His religious enthusiasm did not prevent him from preserving a friendly intercourse with men, who entertained freer sentiments on the subject of religion than himself, provided, they were no mockers of religion.

Stilling continued his medical studies with all diligence, omitting nothing, which he judged essential in that science. In the autumn Gœthe returned home. He and Stilling vowed each other an uninterrupted friendship at parting, Leose left the place likewise, but Lentz remained. During the winter he gave a course of lectures on chemistry, made some more præparata for the Anatomical theatre, reviewed several of the lectures, which he had attended, and wrote his inaugural dissertation in Latin, without any assistance. He dedicated it by special permission to his Serene Highness the Elector of the Palatinate, his sovereign, was examined, and was making preparations for his departure.

But here money was again required; he therefore wrote home for some assistance. Mr. Fredenberg was startled. During dinner he put his children to the trial, whether they were willing once more to assist their brother-in-law. All were seated round the table, when the father said: "Children, your brother-in-law stands yet in need of a large sum of money, would you be willing to send him some, if you had any ?" Their unanimous reply was : "Yes, should we even have to sell our own clothes." The parents were moved to tears at this declaration of their children, and when Stilling heard it, he vowed them perpetual love and brotherly affection. In short, a draft was sent to Strasburg, sufficient for the present purpose.

Stilling's inaugural disputation brought him much honor and applause. When Dr. Speelman, president of the Medical faculty gave him his license, he publicly declared, that he had seldom granted license to any one with greater satisfaction to himself, than to the present candidate, who had advanced farther in a very short time, than many others do in five or six years.

March the 24th 1772 Stilling having taken leave of his Strasburg friends, started for home. At Manhime he had the honor of delivering his inaugural dissertation to the Elector of the Palatinate. On that occasion he was elected Secretary of the Manhime philosophical society. At Cologne he found Mr. Fredenberg waiting for him, and half way between that city and their town he met his brothers-in-law who had come out on horseback, and on the fifth of April he arrived in company of these friends at Rasenhime. He found Christina in her room, with her face leaning on the table sobbing aloud. He pressed her to his bosom and asked her why she shed tears at the present joyous moment? "O," said she, "I weep, because I cannot thank God sufficiently for all his goodness." "You are right, my dear," replied Stilling, "but our whole life in time and eternity shall be a tribute of gratitude to him. Rejoice now, that the Lord has helped us thus far !"

At the next faculty day at Strasburg, Stilling was created Doctor of Medicine and received his Diploma from the hands of a notary, and thus his Academical course was finished. His relatives in the principality of Salen heard all this with joyous rapture, William Stilling wrote to him in his first letter to Shonenthal these words : "It is enough. Joseph my son is yet alive, I will go and see him before I die."

Thee I approach—appproach that being,
The Being full of Majesty !
And in the dust before thee bowing,
I offer up my thanks to thee.

Though dust—I join angelic choirs,
In hymns of gratitude and praise,
To Seraph's state my soul aspires,
When Christ from death my dust shall raise.

Yet words are weak—O may life's actions,
Conformed to Christ's example here,
The cross and tears, be satisfactions,
Accepted by my Savior there.

LIFE

OF

HENRY STILLING.

FOURTH BOOK.

𝕳𝖊𝖓𝖗𝖞 𝕾𝖙𝖎𝖑𝖑𝖎𝖓𝖌 𝖆𝖘 𝕱𝖆𝖙𝖍𝖊𝖗 𝖔𝖋 𝖆 𝕱𝖆𝖒𝖎𝖑𝖞.

—◦◉◦—

CHAPTER I.

' May the 1st 1772 Stilling and his wife Christina walked accompanied by Mr. Fredenberg from Rasenhime to Shonenthal, and took possession of their house. I have spoken already of the picturesque situation of that city in the valley of the Wupper, extending from East to West ; during the summer-season the valley is covered in its whole length of about six miles up to the boundaries of the county of Mark, with linnen yarn, undergoing the process of bleeching, and the busy hum of an active and happy people continually strikes the ear. Stilling entered the throng and bustle of the city in the midst of illusive and imaginary hopes of happiness. Soon they entered the house, which Dr. Dinckler and Troost had rented for them. It was built in a recess from the principal street on the banks of the Wupper, the house-lot extended along the shore of the river ; the garden was small but neat, and afforded a charming prospect towards the mountains in the South. Their hired maid had gone thither a few days previous to their arrival, in order to clean the house, and to arrange the small stock of furniture. After every thing had been viewed and criticised, Mr. Fredenberg took an affectionate leave of them and returned to Rasenhime. The young couple were now alone, viewing each other, while tears started into their eyes.—The furniture in the house was very scant ; six wooden chairs, one table, a bed for themselves and one for the hired girl, and a couple of large dishes, six earthen plates, a few silver spoons, a couple of earthen pots and some other cooking utensils, some linnen and the most necessary articles of clothing formed the whole stock of furniture, which could be found in this large house. They divided these articles among the different apartments, but after all, it looked miserably empty ; the third story was left without any furniture and remained in that state during their stay in that house.

And now as to the cash—it amounted to five rix-dollars—and that was all.—

An unbounded confidence in God's gracious providence was indeed necessary, to enable the young couple to sleep in peace during the first night of their abode in Shonenthal ; but I can assure the reader, they rested well and slept soundly, without doubting for one moment, that God would provide for them. The next day he called upon his neighbors, with the view, to form acquaintances, but Christina stayed at home, determined, to live as retired as decency would permit. He found a great difference in the conduct of his fellow citizens and neighbors from that, which he had formerly experienced ; his former religious friends, who used to receive him as an angel of God, and who had always encouraged him and expressed their best wishes for his welfare, received him with coolness, or complimented him with a civil bow. Some attempted to converse with him on religious subjects, but he declared in a friendly but peremptory manner, that he had been talking long enough of duties, it was high time to practice them. Finding that he attended none of their meetings, they considered him at once as a reprobate, and took every opportunity to calumniate him, though in a commiserating tone. In short he was entirely forsaken by his old friends, neither did they employ him as physician in their families. The multitude of rich merchants received him with more civility, as a man, possessed of no wealth, whom they wished to impress with this idea at his first appearance among them, never to look for assistance from them ; that they were willing to pay him for his professional calls, but he must expect nothing else from them. In the midst of these discouragements, he still found persons possessed of noble sentiments, real friends of men, whose very countenance bore the stamp of benevolence.

All these circumstances taken together filled his heart with melancholy forebodings; hitherto he had either found his table spread, or had been able to pay for his meals, and the world, which surrounded him, had scarcely attracted his notice; but now he found himself transferred into a large town, among a population of rich and avaricious merchants, into a world, in which few could harmonize with him, and where learning and sciences were esteemed only as the handmaids of wealth. Stilling therefore found himself overwhelmed with gnawing cares.

Thus two and even three days passed away, without receiving a single professional call; and his five rix-dollars were almost gone, when on the morning of the fourth day a woman from Dornfeld came, and addressed him with tears in her eyes as follows: "Doctor! we have heard of you as being a very skilful physician, we have a great misfortune in our house; we have applied to all the Physicians far and near, but none can help my child, I now come to you, Doctor! O do help my child!"

Good Heavens! thought Stilling within himself; my first patient has been in the hands of all the experienced physicians, what shall I do, who have no experience at all! However he asked her: "What is the matter with your child?" upon which the woman told the story of her child's illness, and Dr. Stilling promised to come and see it. He walked the floor with great uneasiness, assured that every possible remedy had been made use of, the family being rich: what could he therefore do! Troubled in his mind at these thoughts, he took his hat and cane and started for Dornfeld. He found the child, as the mother had described it; the eyes were closed, its respiration was easy, but the left arm was continually swinging backwards and forwards, from the breast towards the right side. Having viewed the little sufferer, he ordered the woman to come to Shonenthal, after the lapse of an hour; he would in the mean time reflect on the case and write a prescription for the child. On his way home, he considered, what he should do with some probability of success? At length it occurred to him, that Dr. Speelman in Strasburg had frequently mentioned Dippel's animal-oil as an excellent remedy against convulsive fits, and he preferred this medicine to any other, because he supposed, that none of the other physicians had thought of it, as it was out of fashion. As soon as he came home, he wrote a recipe, of which Dippel's oil formed the basis, the woman soon came and fetched it away. Two hours afterwards an express came from Dornfeld, calling the Doctor to his patient. On his arrival he found the child well and hearty, sitting up in the bed, and they told him, that it had scarcely taken one tea-spoonful of his medicine, when it opened its eyes, asked for something to eat, and the arm became as straight and quiet as the other. Stilling's sensations on that occasion are indescribable. The house was filled with people, wishing to see the miraculous cure, all viewed him as an angel sent from heaven, and the parents did not know how to express their joy and gratitude to Dr. Stilling, who thanked God in his heart, but blushed at the praise he received, and of which he knew himself undeserving: for the cure was merely accidental or rather providential. Whenever he thought of this cure and heard people praise his skill, he could scarcely refrain from laughing, conscious of having done very little himself; but prudence bade him be silent. He now ordered a gentle cathartic, which completed the cure. His success in this case made a great noise, the blind, the lame, cripples of all descriptions and persons afflicted with all kinds of chronic disorders made application to him, but Dippel's oil did not help all; he had not discovered a specific for every disease; the extraordinay run of business therefore gradually subsided, though the share of practice he retained, was sufficient to procure him at least the necessaries of life. His colleagues however began now to decry him as a quack. A rumor of this nature reached likewise the medical committee at Russelstine, consequently he was summoned to appear before said committee for examination, through which he passed, notwithstanding every chicanery with so much honor, that he received the Diploma of a licensed physician at Shonenthal.

In the commencement of the summer Stilling had issued proposals for a course of lectures on physiology for young surgeons

—Messrs Dinkler and Troost likewise attended them, and from that time to the present Stilling has lectured with very few interruptions ; for when he speaks in public, he feels himself in his element. While he is speaking, his ideas develope themselves so rapidly, that he is frequently at a loss to express them, his whole existence is exhilarated, and all is life and clearness.

When Stilling had spent several weeks in this occupation, the hand of the Almighty fell suddenly and most heavily upon him. Christina relapsed into her former indisposition, spasmodic affections of unintermitted duration for several hours drew her weak body so together, that the very sight excited pity, her fits were sometimes so severe as to throw her out of bed, and her shrieks alarmed the neighborhood : in this situation she continued for several weeks, and the symptoms became daily more alarming, indicating a settled consumption. Stilling trembled. but took his refuge in God. though his strength failed him, and the fear of losing a wife whom he tenderly loved, became almost insupportable, when added to the gnawing cares proceeding from a want of support. He had no credit, all the necessaries of life were very high in this commercial city ; when he awoke in the morning, the question fell heavy upon his heart, how shall your wants be supplied this day ? for there was seldom money in the house sufficient for the support of his family for two successive days : and though his former experience, and the frequent probations of his faith were not forgotten, yet, when he observed, that many persons more pious than himself were suffering and struggling with poverty, hardly able to appease the cravings of hunger, his heart failed him. Nothing else could comfort him nnder these circumstances, but an unconditional surrender of himself into the hands of his heavenly Father, who would not suffer him to be tempted above measure.

Another circumstance augmented his difficulties. It was a principle with him, that every christian, especially a physician, ought to be benevolent, without inquiry into his ability, relying wholly in faith on the assistance of God. Actuated by this principle, he frequently paid the Apothecary-bills of the poor out of his own pocket, and thus incurred debts, which afterwards caused him a great deal of trouble and uneasiness. I dare not say, that the desire of being benevolent alone directed his actions in such cases; I am rather of opinion, that to a certain extent careless-ness and a disregard of money was intermingled with it, a weak side of Stilling's character, with which he was not yet acquaint-ed, but which many severe sufferings sufficiently brought to light. It is not to be wondered at, that he obtained in this manner a great number of patients, though his income remained insufficient. Christina likewise was deeply affected by this circumstance, for she was of a saving disposition, and could not comprehend, how it was possible that so extensive a practice should yield so tri-fling an income; for Stilling never informed her of his generosi-ty to the poor, because he feared her reproaches, and believed, that God would bless him for his acts of benevolence in some other way. In consequence of these anxious cares, Christina became worse every day; and Stilling scarcely entertained a glimpse of hope for her recovery. One forenoon as he was sit-ting by her bedside, the pulse suddenly intermitted, she stretch-ed her arms towards him, exclaiming: "Farewell—my dear —O Lord! have mercy upon me—I am dying." The agonies of death appeared to have settled in her face, her breath was gone and Stilling stood like a criminal before the executioner. After he had regained his presence of mind, he bowed down and kiss-ed her, and spoke a few words of comfort to her; but she gave no signs of life; he was on the point of calling the neigh-bors in, when she suddenly recovered, and felt easier than she had previous to the last paroxysm. He had not yet sufficient practical experience in this kind of diseases, otherwise he might have saved himself many a bitter hour of anguish and terror. Christina did not die, but remained dangerously ill, and the frightful paroxysms returned from time to time, which embit-tered his life, and daily became the source of new tortures to him and his beloved wife. During this time of trial an express arrived from a place fifteen miles distant from Shonenthal, calling him to a person of distinction, who had been attack-ed by a severe illness. Difficult as it was, to leave his own wife in imminent danger, yet the duties of his office call-

ed him away, and he therefore sent word, that he would
come the next day. In the evening Christina had another severe paroxysm, she lost all recollection for some time, and the
cramp drew her quite together. The cup of misery was now apparently full, he ran to the next neighbors for help : men and
women came to assist the poor sufferer, who gradually became
somewhat easier, but continued to lie in a kind of stupor without recollection for some time. The next morning he was obliged to leave her in this situation, and hasten to his patient, the
reader may imagine, with what heart-rending feelings he performed this act of duty. On his return in the evening he
found her still in the situation, in which he had left her in the morning.; and she did not recover her recollection till the next day.
After some time she was restored to her usual health, and he
found, that all these paroxysms had occurred in consequence of
her pregnancy. In the autumn she suffered again much with an
ulcerated breast ; with this single exception, she was uncommonly well and hearty during her pregnancy.

CHAPTER II.

The commencement of Stilling's domestic life was in every
respect thorny and troublesome. There was nothing agreeable
in his situation, except that his wife loved him tenderly, which
circumstance lessened his grief, and often lightened his burden.
But this very love of his wife caused him some times bitter hours;
because it now and then degenerated into jealousy, though after
the first years of their marriage she learnt to suppress this
weakness.

His situation was not unlike that of a pilgrim. traveling by
night through a forest filled with robbers and beasts of prey;
whose noise and howlings he hears with terror on every side.
He was tortured by never ceasing cares for his subsistence,
met with indifferent success in his professional calling ; was un-
popular with the public among whom he lived ; and no one encouraged him ; and those who knew him and his situation, either.

despised him, or were indifferent towards him. When he came to Rasenhime, he durst not say a word about his troubles, because Mr. Fredenberg had become responsible for the debts he had contracted during his studies, and he did not wish to create uneasy feelings in his father-in-law, neither durst he complain to Christina, whose weakly frame of body would not have been able to bear it ; he was therefore under the necessity of encouraging her, and of representing their situation as favorable as possible. In regard to his professional business he found himself in a very critical situation: as long as he practiced among the lower classes, his success was surprising, but whenever he was called to patients in the higher walks of life, whose cases, if successful would have attracted the notice of the world, he had no success : therefore the circle of his practice was generally limited to the poorer classes of society. This apparently singular circumstance admits of a very easy explanation. Stilling's mind was all system, and every thing must be done according to rule and order, his conscience would not permit him the use of that kind of charlatanry, which a practical physician must use, if he wishes to be successful, and to make money in the world. Therefore, whenever he was called to a patient, he examined his circumstances, made his plan accordingly and followed it perseveringly. If his plan failed, he was defeated, without being able to rally again. His method was most successful with robust constitutions, but when high life, weak nerves, a disordered sensibility and imagination opposed him, he found himself not at home.

All these circumstances taken together, produced a strong dislike in his mind towards his profession, and nothing but the idea of being destined to this calling, and that God would still make him happy in its pursuit kept his hopes alive for renewed exertions of activity. Filled with this idea, he formed the gigantic resolution during the first summer of his professional practice, to study until he should have brought the medical system to a Mathematical certainty. While he was laboring to reach this acme of his wishes, he made many valuable discoveries, but the farther he proceeded, the more he found, that his profession was not calculated to render him happy, for he became convinced, that a physician can at most do little in reality : this lessened his hopes, and darkened his future prospects : he felt like a pilgrim overtaken by an impenetrable mist in unknown and dangerous roads, unable to see his path a few steps before him. He therefore cast himself without reserve into the paternal arms of God, hoping, where there was no hope, and continued his way oppressed by many heavy burdens.

Towards the autumn of 1772 the Messrs. Volkraft, two brothers, men of excellent character came from Russelstine to Shonenthal. The elder of them was counsellor of the exchequer, and had some court business to transact at Shonenthal, which detained him several weeks ; his brother, a well known poet and likewise a man of an excellent heart, accompanied him to a place in which he had no acquaintance, except Dr. Dinkler, who gave the two Volkrafts so advantageous a description of Stilling, that they wished an introduction to him. Having become acquainted with their wishes, he went one evening to their lodgings; the counsellor entered into an interesting conversation with him, and was so much pleased, that he embraced and assured him of his friendship ; his brother did the same, both understood him, and their hearts became united from that time. Though he did not discover his alarming situation to them, still his grief found some alleviation in conversation with men of such noble characters, who understood him, and were communicative. The reader may perhaps wonder, why he did not improve this opportunity to open his heart to these friends in regard to his distressed situation ; however if he reflects, that Stilling had been accustomed from his youth to look upon officers of government as beings of a higher order, his reluctance will not appear so strange, though persons of the common cast will unhesitatingly ascribe this reluctance to ignorance and the humiliating circumstances of his low birth.

Frederick Volkraft, the privy counsellor, asked him at the first visit, if he had published any thing? Upon his affirmation and on showing them the manuscript of his own life, they desired him to read it. Both, the style and the declamation, pleased them so much, that they applauded him repeatedly and encouraged

him to continue his publications, and expressed a particular desire, that he should contribute something to the Mercury, a Periodical, which had been commenced a year or two before this time.
He assented to their proposition, and immediately wrote *Asa
Nettha*, an oriental tale, which was published in the first number
of the third and finished in the first number of the fourth volume
of the Mercury, and was generally well received.

Volkraft's acquaintance was of great advantage to him—in
him he had a friend at Russelstine, with whom he frequently
exchanged letters, and when he came to that place, he always
found a welcome reception at his house. No material change
took place in Stilling's situation during the year 1772, and when
at its close he drew the balance of his accounts, found, that
this year had added two hundred rix-dollars to his debts.

January the 5th, 1773, Christina was safely delivered of a
daughter, and though every thing went better, than they had
expected, still her weakly constitution threw her again into convulsive fits, in which she suffered exceedingly.

One Saturday, in the succeeding spring, after he had been
all day riding about, visiting his patients, and was mounting his
horse before the tavern-door of a village, a young, well-look-
ing, but blind and poor woman, was led across the street, inquiring after the doctor.

"What do you want, good woman?" said Stilling.

"O doctor, please look at my eyes, I have been blind for
several years. I have two children, whom I have never seen;
my husband earns his living as a day-laborer; formerly I assisted him in making our livelihood by spinning, but now I can do
it no longer; my poor husband is indeed very steady at his
work, but he alone cannot support us, and therefore we are very,
very poor— please to look, whether you can help me!"

Stilling looked at her eyes, and found she had a cataract.
He told her so, and likewise gave it as his opinion, that she might
be cured, if a skilful physician should undertake the operation.

"Do you perform no operations on the eye, doctor?"

"I have learnt it," said Stilling, "but have never made the
attempt in any living person."

"O then I beseech you, try it on me !"

"No, good woman, I cannot do it—I am too much afraid of being unsuccessful, and in that case, you would have to remain irremediably blind all the days of your life ; no doctor could help you afterwards."

"But if I will venture it?—I am blind now, and cannot get worse—may be, God will accompany your operation with a blessing : O do perform it, doctor !"

At these words a tremor ran through his very bones ; he thought he could not undertake such operations ; he therefore mounted his horse and said : "Good woman, leave me in peace ; I cannot—I cannot do it."

"Doctor, you must—it is your duty—God has called you, to give assistance to the distressed and afflicted, whenever you have an opportunity ; you have said yourself, that you have learnt to perform such operations ; I'll be the first—I'll venture it—and I shall be your accuser on the day of judgment, unless you make the attempt."

These words of the woman entered like so many darts into the heart of Stilling ; he felt, she had reasoned correctly, but at the same time his fear of being unsuccessful, and his antipathy against such operations were almost unconquerable. He therefore made no reply, but rode away in silence. On his way home, he reflected, what he ought to do in the present case, but the result of all his deliberations with himself was, not to operate.

The poor woman went in the mean time to her minister—and why should I not name that noble man—this chosen one among thousands—the pious Theodore Miller ?—He was the father and counsellor of all the members of his congregation ; a prudent, tender-hearted and active servant of Christ ; in short, he was a disciple of Jesus in the fullest sense of the word. His master called him early from his work, no doubt, in order, to set him over many things. Lavater sung his death—the poor wept at his grave, and the rich mourned after him. Sacred be to me thy memory—thy body rests a seed sown for the day of resurection !

The poor blind woman informed this noble man of her distressed situation, and at the same time became the accuser of Doctor Stilling. Miller wrote him a very pressing letter on this subject, in which he represented to him all the blessed consequences of this operation on the one hand, in case of success; and on the other, how inconsiderable the injury would be to him, in case of a failure. With this letter Stilling ran in his distress to Dr. Dinkler and Troost, who advised him, by all means to perform the operation, and Dinkler promised to assist him, which encouraged him in so far, that he resolved to undertake it.

He wrote in consequence to Mr. Miller, that he would operate the woman on a certain day, assisted by Dr. Dinkler. At the appointed time, the two Doctors came to Mr. Miller's house; the woman was called, and a surgeon appointed to hold her head.

After the necessary preparations had been made, and the woman was seated, Stilling took a seat in front of her, seized the instrument, and pressed it at the proper place into the eye. But when the woman, as was naturally to be expected, gave a sudden start, Stilling being frightened, likewise drew the instrument back with his hand, hence the aqueous humor escaping through the wound, flowed down her cheeks, and the front part of the eye shrunk together. He then took the crooked scissors, introduced one leg into the wound, and cut the half-circle as usual, but on examination found, that he had also cut the Iris. He was frightened; but what was to be done? he gave a heavy sigh, and was silent. In that moment, the crystaline lens fell through the wound down her cheeks, and the woman exclaimed in the highest ecstacy of joy: "O Doctor, I see your face, I see the black in your eye!"

All who were present, rejoiced in triumph. In short, he effected the cure; she saw very well with that eye, and a few weeks afterwards, he likewise operated the other with the left hand, and, because his first success had given him courage, every thing was done in proper order, and the woman regained her sight in both eyes.

The fame of this sucsessful operation procured him

a great number of similar patients, with most of whom he was successful. Yet, singular as it may appear, still it is a fact, that notwithstanding the number of these operations, his circumstances were not much benefited by them, for the greater part of his patients were poor, whom he therefore served gratis—only a few were able to pay him. Some of his enemies took even an occasion from these operations, to vilify him, and to rank him with mountebanks and quacks. — "Wait only," they said, "we shall soon see him travel from city to city, and from fair to fair!"

In the month of September, the wife of one of the most wealthy merchants in Shonenthal, was brought to bed for the first time. The case was a very difficult one; two days and two nights had passed on, without the least hope. Dr. Dinkler, the family-physician, proposed Stilling for his assistant, and was accepted. He arrived about six o'clock in the evening. Having made the necessary inquiries, he found, that there was no other way, but to open the fontanel of the cranium of the child. Desirous however of convincing himself of the fact, that the child was dead, he waited till nine o'clock, when he performed the necessary operation. The woman was soon delivered, and in a short time restored to her former health. I cannot describe, what anguish and pity he always felt on such occasions, and how many tears he shed; but he knew it was his duty to go when called; he therefore always trembled, whenever any person knocked at his door during the night; and this dread has been so deeply impressed on his nervous system, that to this day he starts up with fear, whenever a knock is heard at his door during the night, though he is convinced, that he will not be called for any such purpose.

The above mentioned cure made a strong and favorable impression on the public—he met every where smiling faces and a friendly reception, and his practice increased. But his joy was not of long duration—for about three weeks after the cure, he received a summons from the medical committee at Russelstine, ordering him to abstain for the present from acting as a accoucheur, and to appear on a certain day before the committee for examination.

D d

This was quite unexpected, and even incomprehensible to him, until he learnt, that a certain person had sent an unfavorable account of the cure to the above mentioned committee. At the appointed time, he went to Russelstine, and lodged with his friend Volkraft. From him, his noble-minded lady and his brothers and sisters, he received many proofs of a disinterested friendship. But he needed such comfort in his distressed circumstances. He soon called on one of the members of the committee, who said in a sarcastic tone to him: "I learn, you can likewise deprive people of their sight, sir?"

"No sir," replied Stilling, "but I have performed some operations with considerable success."

"That is not so," resumed the counsellor, "you do not speak the truth."

"I do speak the truth," answered Stilling, "I can prove it by uncontrovertible testimony. But I am aware of the regard, which I owe you as one of my superiors, or else I should answer you in the same style, in which you ask me. A graduated person, who endeavors to do his duty in every respect, is deserving of some regard even from his superiors."

"Do you call it doing your duty," said the other with a loud laugh, "when you kill children?"

Stilling was nigh fainting, he turned pale, approached the counsellor with boldness, and said: "Sir—do not say this a second time!"—But in that moment he was so overcome by the knowledge of his dependence on this man, that he sunk back on a chair and sobbed aloud, which however exposed him only to fresh insults; he therefore arose and went away.

During the examination, the most intricate and ensnaring questions were put to him, yet he was able to answer them all; but in the practical part, he was ordered, to draw a puppet from an artificial machine, which he could not effect, because it was held fast on the other side of the curtain. He mentioned the circumstance, but was laughed at. It was therefore decreed, that he had pasesd tolerably well through the theoretical part of the examination, but had completely failed in the practical; he should therefore abstain from the practice of accoucheur, except in cases of extreme necessity.

Notwithstanding the unpleasant feelings, which so unjust a decree excited, he could not avoid laughing aloud, that as an unskilful man, he was forbidden to practice except in cases of *extreme* necessity. With respect to the case in question, the judgment of the court was, that he was guilty of the death of the child, but that the punishment for the crime should be remitted.—Great favor, indeed, for the poor Doctor, to be permitted to murder with impunity!—Not being satisfied with the judgment of the committee, he went the same afternoon to Duisburg, in order to lay his case before the medical faculty of that university, over which the venerable Dr. Lidefrost presided. This faculty pronounced him not guilty, and reversed the decree of the court in such terms, which completely restored his injured honor.

The husband of the lady, whom he had delivered, published the response of the medical faculty at the town-house of Shonenthal. Notwithstanding all this, the real value of the cure lost much in the eye of the public, and it afforded his enemies a pretense for evil speaking.

The fame of his successful operations on the eyes spread in the mean time far and wide; a certain friend inserted an advertisement respecting them in the Frankfort Gazette. This advertisement came to the ears of Dr. Sorber, an eminent lawyer and professor of law at the university of Marburg, who was blind, and in consequence resolved, to undertake the journey from Marburg to Shonenthal, and subject himself to an operation. He arrived at the latter place in the month of April, 1774, accompanied by his lady and two daughters. Stilling was successful, both in the operation and the cure; the patient recovered his sight, and was enabled again to perform the duties of his office as professor at law. During this time, Christina was a second time delivered, and Stilling became the father of a son.

For some time he had entertained an ardent desire of seeing his father again, a satisfaction, he had not enjoyed for several years; for he had not conversed with him since he had graduated, and Christina had never yet seen him. Frequent invitations had been sent to the good man, who had as frequently promised to come; but circumstances had hitherto prevented him from fulfilling it. At length Stilling proposed, to meet his father on a certain day half way at Meinerzhagen, and to take him thence to Shonenthal. This offer was accepted. Father Stilling and his son met according to appointment at a tavern in the village of Meinerzhagen. It would be a vain attempt, to describe their feelings, when they embraced each other. Father Stilling gave vent in broken accents to his joy, that his and Dorothy's son had arrived at the goal of his destination; he wept and laughed alternately, and Henry carefully avoided to make his father acquainted with his trials and sufferings, his narrow circumstances, and all the other difficulties, with which he had to struggle, a discovery of which, he was well aware, would have completely marred the paternal joy.

The exertion he used in suppressing his grief before his father, created a reaction in his mind; his sorrows almost overwhelmed him; he not only knew himself far less happy, than his father supposed him to be, but despaired of ever becoming so. For he still thought himself destined by Providence, to be a physician, and that he therefore ought to abide in that calling, notwithstanding he began to dislike it, because he found on the one hand, that the profession stood on a slender foundation as a science, and on the other, that it did not maintain him and his family—much less would enable him, to make any provision for his children.

The next morning he gave the horse to his father, while he accompanied him on foot, passing the time away in pleasant and soul-reviving conversation. They reached Rasenhime that day, and William Stilling was introduced to Christina's relatives, and kindly received by them. He shook each one by the hand, and his honest characteristic face excited universal respect.—

The next morning the father left Fredenberg's family on foot, in company of one of Christina's brothers, while the Doctor remained, to give free vent to his feelings in the bosom of Mr. Fredenberg's family, which being done, he hastened on horseback after his father. He had never before made the short distance between Rasenhime and Shonenthal with equal satisfaction, and father Stilling likewise rejoiced in his God. When he entered the house, Christina hastened down stairs, to meet and embrace the honest man—tears were shed on all sides ; but such scenes must be witnessed by an eye gifted with the proper organs of sensation, in order fully to relish them. William returned, after having spent a week with his children, and his son saw him safe as far as Meinerzhagen.

A few weeks afterwards the Doctor was early one morning called to a public house, where, he was told, a stranger wished to see and consult him. He dressed in haste, and went to the place assigned. Being introduced into the bed-room of the stranger, he found the patient's head and neck carefully wrapt up. On his approach the stranger held out his hand and said with a weak and hollow voice : "O Doctor, feel my pulse, I am very much reduced and a very sick man." He felt his pulse and found it beating as regular and sound as that of a healthy man. He mentioned this, and immediately Gœthe rushed out of the bed and embraced him. Stilling was rejoiced to see his Strasburg friend, and invited him immediately to his house. While Christina was preparing for dinner, he took his friend to a hill before the city, that he might thence enjoy the beautiful prospect over the city and valley. At that time the two Volkrafts were again at Shonenthal ; in their company was a celebrated author, with whom Stilling however could not harmonize on account of his anti-religious principles, and therefore he had visited his two friends less frequently, than he otherwise would have done. We shall call this gentleman Juvenal. While Stilling was taking his walk with Gœthe, one of the Volkrafts came on horseback to Stilling's door, and ordered the maid to tell the Doctor, that he was on the point of starting for Russelstine, having heard, that Gœthe had arrived there. At their return from the walk the maid told her story, and both were sorry, that this error had been committed, however it was too late to recall Mr. Volkraft.

Gœthe and Lavater were then on a journey to the baths of Ems and to Muhlhime on the Rhine, at which latter place Gœthe had left Lavater, in order to pay a visit to his friend Stilling, promising to return to Muhlhime on a certain day. But during his absence, Lavater resolves, to go likewise to Shonenthal, without informing Gœthe of his intention, who had started immediately after dinner on horseback in the company of Juvenal to Russelstine, to see Volkraft.

Hardly were they gone, when Lavater,accompanied by Volkraft, Hasencamp and Dr. Collenbush came down the street in a close carriage. Stilling no sooner heard it, than he mounted his horse in pursuit of Gœthe and Juvenal with a view to bring them back. Lavater and his companion had meanwhile taken lodgings at the house of a well-known merchant, a sincere lover of the religion of Jesus. Stilling, Gœthe and Juvenal hastened thither likewise, and hardly ever had a company more diversified in sentiment been seated round one hospitable board, loaded according to Shonenthal fashion with all kinds of viands and delicacies. Having spent about an hour in this agreeable company, Lavater, Hasencamp, Collenbush, Stilling and a young merchant went together up the valley, to pay Theodore Miller an evening visit. This walk will always be held in sacred remembrance by Stilling, as it procured him a more intimate acquaintance with Lavater. During their absence Gœthe and Juvenal had gone to Russelstine. Lavater came next morning accompanied by his painter, to take Stilling's likeness for his physiognomy, and then he likewise departed. Though this remarkable visit produced no immediate alteration in his circumstances,it undeniably laid the foundation for several important changes in his life. Before his departure Gœthe obtained from Stilling the manuscript of the first book of his life, with a view, to read it at his leisure, wo shall see in the sequel how Providence turned this apparently insignificant circumstance in his favor.

CHATER III.

In the autumn of 1774 a Shonenthal merchant introduced an acquaintance of his, a Mr. Bouck from Sonneburg in Saxony, who had unfortunately become blind, to Stilling with the hope, that he would be able to restore his sight. The Doctor examined his eyes, and found, that the pupils were dilated, but still somewhat moveable, the commencement of a cataract was perceptible, but the patient was too blind, for the cataract alone to have caused it, and the Doctor therefore concluded, that an amaurosis was coming on and was the principal cause of his complaint, and he expressed this opinion to the patient and his own friends ; but as all of them, notwithstanding, advised him to un-undertake the operation, and said, it was his duty to perform it, so that no means might be omitted, and if the patient, as he thought, was incurable, he would lose nothing, provided the operation should prove unsuccessful. Thus he was prevailed upon, to make the attempt, especially, because the patient was anxious to have it performed. This was however an inconsiderate step, and he found reason enough to repent it. He failed completely in the cure, and the patient's eyes became uncommonly disfigured by soreness and inflammation. Besides this, Mr. Bouck heard, that Stilling was poor, and therefore supposed, he had undertaken the operation merely with the hope of a large fee. The merchant who had introduced him to the Doctor, his landlord and particular friend, attempted to remove these prejudices from the mind of Mr. Bouck ; but other persons less favorably disposed towards the Doctor, visited the patient likewise, and augmented his suspicions, so that he left Shonenthal with much ill will towards him and doubts of his ability, and returned to Frankfort, to consult the most eminent physicians of that city.

About this time a Patrician of Frankfort, von Leesner, a man of an excellent character, who had been blind for some years, heard how successful Stilling had been in the case of professor Sorber ; he therefore wrote to the latter for further information, which being obtained in a very satisfactory manner, he consulted the most celebrated physicians of the city about his case, and as all agreed in the opinion, that the cause of his blindness was a curable cataract, he commissioned his family-physician, Dr. Hoffman, to write to Stilling on the subject, and endeavor to prevail with him, to come to Frankfort, because Mr. Leesner, as an aged and infirm man, could not venture to undertake the journey, promising, to pay him one thousand guilders, whether a cure was effected or not.

This offer was tempting. Christina, Fredenberg's family, and all his other friends, advised him, not to suffer this opportunity of changing his circumstances for the better, to pass away unimproved. Theodore Miller alone did not like it; he observed: "My friend, you will repent of it, and you will pay dear for these one thousand guilders; do not go, Mr. Leesner has time and money enough; *he will* come, when he sees, you won't."

But this advice was disregarded. Stilling's old fault, to play the truant in the school of Providence, prevailed here likewise, and he promised Leesner to come. He believed, that the end of his sufferings was approaching; the sum of one thousand guilders would enable him, to pay his most urging debts, and he hoped, that a successful cure of Mr. Leesner would doubtless procure him a rich and extensive practice. Mr. Bouck, who was still at Frankfort, endeavored meanwhile, to dissuade Mr. Leesner from employing Stilling, whom he described as a needy and unskilful adventurer. Leesner however remained firm, and resolved to attempt the cure.

Goethe, who was then in Frankfort on a visit to his parents, was greatly rejoiced at the prospect of seeing his friend Stilling there; he invited him to make his parent's table his own during his stay, hired a room for him near by, and published the expected arrival of Dr. Stilling in the newspapers, in order to give an opportunity for other sufferers, to make application for operations. And thus the business was resolved upon and regulated.

In the first week of January 1775 Stilling started for Frankfort on horseback, accompanied by a guide. It was a stormy afternoon, he came as far as Waldstadt, where he stayed all night. The next day it seemed as if a deluge was pouring down upon the earth, and every brook and river was prodigiously swelled. Stilling was more than once in the most iminent danger of losing his life, yet he continued his journey as far as Meinerzhagen, where he spent the night. The next morning the sky was tolerably clear, large clouds were flying over his head, and only now and then the sun shot an enlivening ray into his face. All nature was hushed in silence, trees and shrubs were leafless, the fields and meadows were clad in the sombre dress of winter, the brooks were rushing down in torrents, a strong westwind was blowing and not a single bird enlivened the scene. Towards noon he arrived at a tavern, situated in a beautiful and extensive valley. Riding down the hill, he perceived with alarm, that the brook had overflowed almost the whole valley; had it not been for the tops of bushes here and there visible above the surface of the water, he would have imagined himself on the banks of the Rhine. His uneasiness and anxiety increased, when he reflected, that he had promised to write to Christina from Linedorf, and he feared dangerous consequences, should she not receive the promised letter. In this dilemma he observed, that the fence along the road to the bridge reached about one foot above the surface of the water, he therefore resolved, to take the guide behind him on his horse, and endeavor in this way to gain the bridge. At the tavern he found many carters, waiting for the fall of the water, all of whom advised him not to venture across, but he was determined to proceed : he took the guide on the horse, started in and reached the other side without any accident. A few hours afterterwards he arrived on an elevated spot, whence he could overlook the mountains and fields of his native country. Yonder he saw the Kindelsberg before him and at its foot the smoke was rising from the chimneys of Lichthausen ; he soon discovered amongst them his uncle John's house, an indescribable feeling took possession of his heart, while the scenes of his youth were passing through his mind, that time appeared to have been his golden era.

He made his first stop at the house of a son-in-law of John Stilling and was received by his cousin and her husband with the warmest friendship ; thence he went with trembling joy and a throbbing heart to his uncle. The news of his arrival had meanwhile spread through the village ; the windows were filled with people, and as he entered his uncle's house, father William and his uncle met him, whom he embraced with tears, the two aged men likewise wept for joy. "Blessings from the father of mercies upon you, my dear nephew," was the address of the noble hearted John Stilling, "our satisfaction is exceedingly great, to see you at the goal of all your wishes, with honor to yourself you have attained your glory, you have excelled us all, you are the pride of our family." Stilling merely replied: "It is altogether God's work, he alone has effected it :" and gladly would he have added : I am not happy, I am on the brink of ruin, but he kept his sorrows in his own breast and entered the room. Here he found all the chairs and benches filled with inhabitants from the village, who had been acquainted with him when a boy. On his entering all uncovered their heads, a perfect silence reigned throughout, and the eyes of all were respectfully directed towards him. He looked about, and addressed them in broken accents : "Welcome, welcome, dear friends and neighbors, may God bless each one of you.—Cover your heads, or else I must leave the house immediately ; that I am, what I am is the work of God, to him be given all glory !" At these words a joyful murmuring was heard throughout the house : father, uncle and the Doctor took their seats among the people, whose eyes were fixed upon his actions, and whose ears upon his words. It would be impossible to describe the sensation of joy which on this occasion filled the hearts of the two sons of Eberhard Stilling. The next morning he started with his father and uncle for Linedorf. John had loaned his brother his own saddle-horse, while he walked by his side; before the village they met several groups of young men from Linedorf; as his former friends and scholars thy had come out three miles to meet him, they surrounded his horse, and conducted him into the village, whose inhabitants had left their houses, and were awaiting his arrival in the meadow near the brook. Their loud acclamations of welcome reached Stilling's ears, when yet at a considerable distance; deeply affected with these tokens of good will he entered the village on horseback by the side of his father, at whose house he was received by his step-mother and sisters : the latter embraced him with tears of joy. A great body of people came in the house, his aunts from Tiefenbach with their children likewise made their appearance, all was noise and bustle, and no sleep came into his eyes during the first night of his stay under the parental roof. Having sufficiently gratified the curiosity of his former friends and neighbors he hastened away under the repeated farewell exclamations of more than one hundred persons, but had scarcely reached the open fields, when his guide informed him, that his father was coming ; he therefore returned, the old gentleman took his son's hand in both his and said : "I have not yet taken leave of you, my son! may the Almighty Father bless you !" When he was again left to himself,—for his guide had taken a cross-path—he gave vent to his sensations in a flood of tears. The expressions of kindness and good will, which he had received from his friends, relatives and countrymen had indeed been pleasing to him, but it was painful to his feelings, to know, that all this wonder and applause had nothing but a false appearance for its foundation. I am not happy, I am not the man, they take me to be, I am no great physician, I am seldom successful in the cure of my patients, and whenever I am, it occurs by mere accident! I am one of the most unskilled in my profession! and what am I then ?—A physician, regularly graduated at the university.—Well! that is not much ! I am no great light, which shines far and wide, I do not deserve to meet with such a reception as I have!—Such and the like were his meditations till he came in sight to the town of Salen.

Here he merely stopt to dine, and continued his journey as far as Dillenburg, where he arrived late in the evening and lodged with his cousin the second son of John Stilling, the overseer of the mines in that neighborhood. He and his cousin were of the same age, and had always been bosom-friends, the reader may therefore justly conclude, that his reception was kind and affectionate. After one day of rest he continued his journey by way of Herborn, Wezlar, Buzbach and Friedberg to Frankfort ; where he arrived in the evening, and was received with friendship and hospitality in the parental house of his friend Goethe. The next morning he visited Mr. Leesner. He found in him an aged man of a highly respectable character, of pleasing manners, and of enlightened religious views : the state of his eyes was suitable for an operation, so that he as physician believed himself justifiable, in encouraging his patient with the hope of a successful cure. The day was appointed for the operation, and in the interval he had the satisfaction of making the acquaintance of several eminent men. On the day appointed he performed the operation in the presence of several physicians and surgeons, as witnesses, in case of necessity. Every thing promised well, the patient saw and recognized all present after the operation. This news soon spread through the city, friends mentioned it in letters to their correspondents at a distance, and Stilling received letters of congratulation from Shonenthal, before he could receive answers to his own. The Prince of Lowenstine Werthime, the Dutchess of Curland with all the nobility and people of rank in the city made daily inquiries respecting the success of the operation. He had never been better satisfied than at that time; he plainly saw, what a favorable impression this cure if successful would make upon the public, and how much honor and applause and what extensive practice it would procure him. The Senate of Frankfort already deliberated on a decree, granting Dr. Stilling the right of citizenship, with the view of inducing him to settle in that place. The good Doctor was rejoiced at all these auspicious prospects.

During his stay at Frankfort he performed operations on several other persons, among whom was Dr. Hut from Wisbaden, who had become blind in consequence of a cold, which he had caught at night. Stilling was successful; the Doctor was restored to perfect health, and he gained in him a valuable friend. Another patient was a Jewish Rabbi, who had been blind in both eyes for many years; he was sixty-eight years of age; his snow-white beard hung down to his girdle. He was likewise successful in this case, as well as in that of a poor Jewess in the Jews-hospital.

One day, being at Mr. Leesner's, he was called to the door, where a poor, old, blind Jew was waiting for him, led by his son, an interesting youth of about sixteen years of age. The old man addressed him in the following manner: "O dear Doctor, I am an old man, I have a wife and ten children; I have always been an industrious man, and honestly maintained my family; but now I am blind—I and my family have to beg, and you know the situation of us Jews."

Stilling was greatly affected; he gave the Jew his hand and observed: "With the assistance of God you shall have your sight restored."

Both, the old man and his son, sobbed aloud when they heard this, and were on the point of falling on their knees, to express their gratitude, which however the Doctor prevented; he inquired of them. where they intended to take lodgings; that for himself he would ask nothing for the operation, but it would be necessary for them to stay a fortnight in the city.

"O good God," replied the old man, "a lodging will be difficult to be obtained, for though there are many rich Jews here, they nevertheless take little notice of strangers."

"Come to morrow morning at nine o'clock into the Jews-hospital, I will speak to the Directors," said Stilling, and left them.

The next day, as he was in the hospital, dressing the eyes of his patient, the room being filled with Jews, the old man came in, led by his son, and represented his distressed situation to all who were present, but found no mercy; for this hardened people have no feeling for the miseries of a suffering brother. Stilling was for some time silent, until he perceived, that the entreaties of the poor old man were unawailing; he then reprimanded them for their unmerciful disposition, and declared in the most serious terms, taking the living God to witness, that he would not touch either the Rabbi, or this female patient, unless the poor man was provided with suitable lodgings and board for a fortnight. This menace proved effectual, for in less than two hours, the poor Jew obtained all that was necessary.

The next morning he performed the operation in the presence of a surgeon and a few friends. The Jew regained his sight, and when he left the city, ran with outstretched arms, through the streets, incessantly exclaiming: "O ye people, thank God with me! I was blind, but now I see; may God grant long life to the Doctor, that he may be able to cure many blind persons!" Thus Stilling performed eye-operations on seven different people, besides Mr. Leesner; none of whom was able to pay him, except Dr. Hut, who rewarded him liberally.

But now commenced the most unfortunate period in his life. Mr. Leesner did not recover his sight, notwithstanding all the care, which had been taken. An inflammation ensued, and the eyes began to suppurate; and though he had the assistance of several eminent physicians, still their united efforts proved unavailing. Pain, and the fear of an incurable blindness, annihilated all his hopes. Stilling considered himself now a ruined man; he prayed unceasingly to God for help—all the friendly faces, whom he had hitherto met in the streets, disappeared—friend Gœthe and his parents endeavored to comfort him, but in vain. He saw his best hopes disappointed, contempt and misery were staring him in the face; he began to doubt, if God had destined him for his present calling; he feared, he had again followed his own inclination, when he studied medicine, and that he therefore would have to continue in an occupation all his life, to which he now felt an utter aversion.

As he was one day at Mr. Leesner's, lamenting, that the cure had proved unsuccessful, the good old man said: "Do not make yourself uneasy, my dear Doctor, it was God's will, and therefore good for me, that I should remain blind; but I was to be an instrument in his hand, that others might be cured; I shall pay you with pleasure the promised money." Soon after he received it, but with a heavy heart, and after a stay of eight weeks in Frankfort, returned to Shonenthal. His friends there pitied him indeed, but said as little as possible on the subject. Theodore Miller, who had given him the advice not to go, had in the mean time, to his inexpressible grief, departed this life. The generality of his fellow citizens continually slandered him, without regard to his feelings: "Did I not say it," was their language, "the fellow knows nothing, yet he pretends to be a cure-all, it was right good for that mountebank, to have for once been detected."

If his mind had even been strong enough, to make light of such calumny, yet he could not have prevented its consequences. His practice became more and more reduced; those families, whom he had attended as physician before his journey to Frankfort, had in the mean time applied to others, and few showed an inclination of employing him again. In one word, he was almost forgotten ; his debts increased ; for the one thousand guilders were not sufficient, to pay the most urgent debts, and of course his misery was unbounded. He endeavored to bear it alone as much as possible ; but the burden became the more intolerable! Even the family of his father-in-law began to grow cool towards him ; for Mr. Fredenberg seemed to consider him a bad economist, and gave him frequent and severe lectures on that subject; telling him at the same time, that the principal of fifteen hundred 'rix-dollars, which had been expended in the prosecution of his studies, and for the most necessary articles of instruments and furniture, for which Mr. Fredenberg had become security, was soon payable. He did not know, where he could obtain one single penny for the discharge of this debt ; it grieved him to his heart, that the friend, who had given him his daughter, and who had in former times blindly trusted in Providence, was now wavering in faith. Christina highly resented this change in the conduct of her father's family, and resolved to bear up under all difficulties with fortitude and without complaining.

Notwithstanding this great distress, there was never any want of the necessaries of life in the family, and though he seldom had any thing before-hand, still, when it became absolutely necessary, it was not wanting, which circumstance strengthened his and Christina's faith so much, that they were enabled to bear these sufferings with fortitude.

In the spring of 1775, Christina was again delivered of a son, but the child died, when it was but a few weeks old. During her confinement she suffered exceedingly ; and after that time she bore no more children.

In the course of the summer, he received a letter from his friend Dr. Hoffman at Frankfort, in which he gave him the confidential information, that Mr. Leesner was inconsolable on account of his incurable blindness, and was blaming Stilling in some measure ; he therefore advised him as a friend, to visit Mr. Leesner at his own expense once more, since he had so liberally remunerated him for his trouble—and to see, if something effectual could be done for him—that he, Mr. Hoffman, would advertise his intended journey in the public papers, and he entertained no doubt, that it would prove advantageous to him. Stilling felt that he was under great obligations to Mr. Leesner—Christina advised him likewise to go, but all his other friends were opposed to the measure. He followed however in this case his own feelings of right and equity, and started in the mail-coach for Frankfort. A friend lent him one hundred rix-dollars for the journey.

Mr. Leesner was gratified with this unexpected visit, and it removed every prejudice against the Doctor from his mind.— Stilling performed operations on the eyes of a number of persons, some with success, others remained blind; but none was able to pay the heavy expenses of his journey; and consequently he was unable to repay the loan, which he had contracted.

CHAPTER IV.

In the spring of 1776, Stilling found himself under the necessity of moving out of the house, which he had hitherto occupied, because his landlord wished to move into it himself. Mr. Troost assisted him in looking out for another, which he found in the lower part of the town, on the road towards Russelstine, near a number of gardens, very conveniently situated, and commanding a delightful prospect over the surrounding country.— But before he could remove, a severe trial awaited him.

According to the laws of that country, he was not permitted to leave his old habitation, until he had paid his full rent. Hitherto he had always been able to pay punctually the seventy rix-dollars of rent, but in the present case he had not a groat in his pocket; his poverty and want of credit, made him afraid to apply to his landlord for further indulgence in making the payment, and for his permit to remove, but there was no other way; oppressed with sorrow, he represented to him his inability of making present payment. The merchant, a very honest but punctual man in money matters, gave him the desired permit after some moments of reflection, on the condition of paying the rent in a fortnight from that day. In reliance on the assistance of God, Stilling gave his word of honor for the payment, and moved into his new habitation. The serenity of the house, the open view into the country, the convenient situation, in short, every circumstance combined, to alleviate his cares in some measure, though the cause was not removed, and the gnawing worm was still in his heart. The end of the fortnight was approaching, but not the least vestige of help appeared. His distress could not become greater; he frequently ran to his chamber, fervently praying to God for assistance, and whenever business called him away, Christina took his place; but there was no help.

The unwelcome Friday came; he and his wife continued in prayer the whole morning, and the anguish of their hearts forced deep sighs from their tortured bosoms. At ten o'clock the post-boy entered, holding in one hand the receipt-book, and in the other an apparently heavy letter. Stilling looked at the direction; it was Gœthe's hand-writing, and below these words: "Within one hundred and fifteen rix-dollars."

Not knowing, how assistance could come from that quarter, he opened the letter with peculiar feelings, and read, that friend Gœthe had without his knowledge published the first part of his life, under the title: "*Henry Stilling as a Child*," and the one hundred and fifteen rix-dollars the bookseller had paid for the copy-right. He hastened to give the necessary receipt, in order to get clear of the post-boy; after he was gone, Christina embraced her husband, and they praised God with tears of gratitude.

Indelible is the impression, which this interposition of Divine Providence made upon him and Christina; they resolved anew, never to waver in the faith, but with fortitude and resignation to bear all their sufferings; for they saw in the light of divine truth, that the all-gracious Father of men was leading them by the hand; that their walk and conversation were therefore acceptable in his sight, and that he was preparing them for higher purposes by these severe trials.

How trifling and how detestable are all the sophistries of

the philosophers of this world, when the christian has made an experience of this kind? What do I care, though they say ten thousand times : "God's providence extends not to individuals—he has unalterably established the plan of the world—no changes can be effected by prayers!" Jesus Christ is the governor of the universe ; Stilling has called upon him a hundred times, and has received help. Of what use are the cobwebs of the clearest logical conclusion, when one experience follows after the other, and puts them down? In the sequel of this history, the reader will meet with still more surprising proofs of a divine interposition, than those already mentioned.

His friendship with Gœthe, and the visit of the latter to Shonenthal, had been vehemently cried down by those, who styled themselves the Elect of God—they looked upon Gœthe as a free-thinker, and found fault with Stilling, that he continued on intimate terms with him ; and yet all this was the plan of everlasting love, that he might be tried and convinced of God's faithfulness, and might be prepared for his other gracious purposes. I have said and written it a hundred times, and cannot repeat it too often : whosoever desires, to become a faithful servant of God. should not separate himself from men, but from sin ; he ought not to connect himself with any society, whose avowed purpose is to serve God better than others do, for a cloak of this kind generally covers a proud spirit, creates hypocrisy, and becomes an abomination to the pure and holy God. I have been acquainted with a number of such societies, all of whom ended in disgrace, and became a reproach to true religion. Young men and young women! will you walk the true path of life, distinguish yourselves by a holy life, and by actions in accordance with the precepts of the gospel, confess Jesus Christ by faithfully following his example, and profess him wherever it is profitable and necessary ; but then be not afraid of acknowledging, whose disciple you are. Confide in him in every situation of your life ; pray to him in full confidence, and he will guide you to your high calling and destination.

About this time, counsellor Eisenbart at Manhime, a very active and influential man, had established a statistical and agricultural society in the ancient town of Rittersburg, in the Palatinate. Many learned and estimable men were among its members ; the object of the society was the encouragement of agriculture, manufactories and commerce. The Elector of the Palatinate had taken this institution under his own protection and patronage, and had endowed it with suitable revenues. Among other projects, the society had planned and commenced a manufactory of Siamois, a kind of goods, fabricated in perfection at Shonenthal. Counsellor Eisenhart, desirous of receiving every possible information on that subject, and having some acquaintance with Stilling, wrote to request him to make the necessary inquiries concerning the best mode of manufacturing this kind of goods, and to give him the desired information. Though Stilling was pleased with the institution, and was desirous of promoting its benevolent designs, yet it appeared to him an undertaking fraught with danger to himself, should he act as a spy in this affair. For he could expect nothing else, but that his situation would become very unpleasant, and in a pecuniary view, more unpromising, should the people of Shonenthal discover, that he had meddled in the business. However, in order to give a satisfactory proof to Mr. Eisenhart of his being a well-wisher to the society, he represented in his answer on the one hand the danger, to which he would expose himself, should he comply with his request, but on the other asked him, if he could serve the society by ocasionally writing a treatise on subjects of their deliberations ? being under the impression, he had collected in the course of his life many practical observations on agriculture and manufactories.

He soon received an answer, that such treatises would prove very acceptable ; he therefore wrote several, and sent them to counsellor Eisenhart, who read them in the meetings of the society at Rittersburg. These labors received an unexpected applause, and he was elected an honorary member of this society, a circumstance, which gave him great pleasure ; for although this connection did not increase his income, still he was pleased to be engaged in labors, which had a tendency to promote the happiness of mankind.

CHAPTER V.

Stilling had acquired some celebrity from the publication of his life, as well as from his treatises; the community began to look upon him as worthy of a share of the public favor, which encouraged him to continue the history of his life to his settlement at Shonenthal, the publications of which considerably increased his income, without however enabling him to pay off his debts. They were still increasing, though in a less proportion than formerly. But who would have imagined, that many inhabitants of Shonenthal supposed from the publication of his life, that he was a free-thinker! And yet this was actually the case; they charged him with making himself the hero of a novel, and the principles expressed in the history of his life, they considered as totally averse to the system of the reformed church, and hesitated not to denounce him as a man without religion. In order to do away these prejudices and suspicions, he wrote "the history of Morgenthau;" but without the desired effect; he still remained an object of reproach and defamation, which rose in the autumn of 1777 to the highest pitch of malice.

He perceived about this time, that the people were staring at him, whenever he passed through the streets; wherever he showed himself, he observed them running to the windows, and frequently heard them whisper: "Look, there he goes!" He could not assign any reason for such strange conduct towards him, but he noticed, that whenever he spoke with any person, he was strictly watched; others turned their eyes with pity from him, in short, he appeared to himself like a spectre, of which people were afraid. This new species of suffering was so insupportable, that an extraordinary strength of mind was requisite to bear it. In addition to this he perceived, that scarcely any patients made application to him, and that apparently he would shortly be deprived of all means of support.

One afternoon his landlord entered, and having viewed the Doctor for some time with a compassionate look, addressed him as follows:

"My dear Doctor, I hope you will not take it ill, if I tell

you, that a general rumor has spread through town, that you
have become insane last Saturday a fortnight ago; that this derangement is imperceptible in your outward behavior, but that
you had nevertheless completely lost your senses; all patients
have of course been warned from making application to you under these circumstances. I beseech you, tell me how are you! I
have closely watched you all this time, but I cannot perceive the
least vestige of derangement."

Christina covered her face with her apron, sobbed aloud,
and ran out of the room. Stilling stood aghast; sadness, anger
and innumerable other sensations were furiously rushing from
the heart to the head, a derangement might actually have taken
place, if his constitution and organisation had not been extraordi-
narily strong and regular. At length tears gave vent to the
sensations of the heart, and he burst out in these words: "No
Adramelech could ever have invented such malice—devilish—
such Satan like cunning was necessary to deprive me of my living!
But God my avenger and provider lives, he will not leave me always in this hell! he will save and protect me! I need not give
an account to any living person of the state of my mind. you may
observe me and my actions, they must speak for themselves.
This whole thing is so extraordinary, so inhumanly malicious,
that I cannot speak a word more about it."

"I beg you, dear Doctor," continued his landlord, "do not
think ill of me for making the inquiry, I did it from regard and
love towards you."

"No," replied Stilling. "I am obliged to you for it."

From this time the rumor of his insanity gradually subsided;
but like a stinking monster, its odor remained; Stilling and Christina were compelled to breathe in its pestiferous air; his practice decreased, and with it the hope of making a living for himself and family, but he could never learn, whence the rumor
had originated. If the reader wishes to have a correct view of
his situation at this time, let him represent to himself a pilgrim
traveling on a lonely and narrow foot-path; to his right a fa-
thomless abyss, and to his left a steep mountain, towering towards the clouds, whose declivities are covered with loose rocks,

suspended over his head, and threatening momentarily to crush the weary wanderer; before him the path narrowing with every step, and at last entirely ceasing,—every where an unmeasurable precipice.—Had he been a follower of the fashionable religion, he would have left wife and children, and would have gone into the wide world; but not even a temptation of this kind entered his mind, on the contrary he was resolved to look with increasing confidence to Providence, believing, that God could readily point out a way, where human wisdom could discover none; and thus he proceeded on, groping his way along the narrow path step by step in utter darkness.

In the beginning of the year 1778 he again struck the balance of his accounts, and found to his grief and astonishment, that during the past year he had fallen still deeper into debt: his creditors began now to threaten him with executions, and it seemed, as if it were impossible, to obtain relief. In addition to all these troubles, his mental agony was increased by this circumstance, that as agent of the statistical and agricultural society he had received subscription money for the publications of said society to the amount of twenty-eight guilders, which he was unable to pay, and for which he had to account to Mr. Eisenhart. In this distress and anguish of his soul, he ran to his chamber, praying to God for relief; afterwards he wrote a letter to Mr. Eisenhart, in which he disclosed his situation, and his present inability of paying the subscription money. Mr. Eisenhart soon informed him, that he should say no more about the twenty-eight guilders, that he had hitherto imagined him perfectly satisfied with his present calling, but now learning the contrary, he proposed to him the acceptance of a professorship of Agriculture, Technology, Commerce and the Veterinary art, at the new Academy at Rittersburg. The salary would be six hundred guilders a year, the fees for lectures would probably amount to two or three hundred guilders more; that living was cheap at Rittersburg; he expected to obtain the Elector's consent to his call without any difficulty.

Reader! represent to thyself Stilling's sensations at the perusal of this letter. He sat down in a deep reverie, Christina be-

ing frightened, looked over his shoulders and read; she clasped
her hands, sunk down upon a chair, wept aloud and gave praise
to God. Having recovered somewhat from the first shock, he
beheld through the door, which Providence had opened, splendid
hopes for the future; he supposed he now saw his true and real
destination. As a criminal, having escaped condemnation, by receiving full pardon from the judge, which again excites in his bosom the hope of life, sinks on his knees, stammering forth his
thanks, thus Stilling sunk down before God, uttering inexpressible words. Christina's courage likewise revived, she longed to
escape from her present situation, into a country, in which she
was a stranger. As soon as the tumult in his heart had in some
measure subsided, his debts again rushed to his recollection—
scarcely was he able to look through this confusion. How do
you suppose it possible to leave this place, thought he to himself,
without paying your debts. This was a gordian-knot, which
must be cut in some way or other. He encouraged himself however by the resolution to trust with implicit confidence in God,
being convinced that he was preparing this way for his escape
from danger. He therefore wrote to Eisenhart, that a call as
professor at Rittersburg would be very acceptable, and that he
thought he could fill that station with honor, but feared, that his
creditors would not permit him to move, and inquired, if it were
not possible to obtain a loan for the payment of his debts in Shonenthal; promising to mortgage his salary for its repayment.
But Mr. Eisenhart informed him that he could give him no such
hopes, that his creditors would be willing to wait, as soon as there
should be a prospect on his part to pay them. Stilling however
knew, that his credit was so completely sunk, that eight hundred
guilders at least must be paid, before his creditors would permit
him to remove, still he took courage, and hoped, where there
was no hope.

He freely mentioned to his friends what had occurred, and
they related it again to others. Thus it soon became a towns-talk,
that Doctor Stilling would receive an appointment to a professorship, and nothing appeared to the Shonenthalers more ridiculous.—How doth he come to this?—He knows nothing.—This is

a story of his own invention to appear big.—But notwithstanding this talk, all things proceeded in the usual order: the Academical Senate at Rittersburg chose him to fill the chair as professor of Agriculture, Technology, Commerce and the Veterinary art; they proposed him in that capacity to the Elector of the Palatinate, who acceded to the wishes of the Academical Senate and nothing was now, wanting but the formal call, and it was to be expected, that this would occasion some delay. Stilling withdrew himself gradually from all professional business, by receiving no new patients, excepting such as were afflicted with the cataract, and devoted himself wholly to his future agreeable destination. The knowledge which he possessed of the branches he was to teach was to be brought into a systematical order, which he effected without much difficulty. The summer was spent in this delightful occupation, and autumn came on, when he expected to receive the call. In the first week of September a letter arrived from Mr. Eisenhart, in which he was informed, that as the Elector had moved his court to Munich in Bavaria, he had given orders for a translocation of the Academy from Rittersburg to Manhime, where there were persons sufficient, who could honorably fill the professorship designed for him, and that therefore he ought to lay aside all prospects of a call for the present. This was a severe damper for poor Stilling, he and Christina sat together weeping in the chamber, every thing appeared to be lost, but he humbled himself under the all-powerful hand of God, and surrendered himself, his wife and two children to the paternal direction of his kind providence, resolving without murmuring to recommence the practice of physic, and to bear with resignation whatever Providence might send. He went again amongst his friends and acquaintances, relating to them the misfortune, which had befallen him, accepted patients again, and it seemed, as if every thing were going on better than before.

Those who are acquainted with the ways of Providence from self experience, know that this is exactly the method, God pursues with his children. Stilling had passionately desired this change. not from the purest motives ; had he received the office when he expected it, he would have come to Rittersburg with an overbearing spirit, and could not have been happy. It is a maxim of eternal love, to render its pupils pliable and obedient to the divine will, when this is effected, God delivers them from their troubles.

In the mean time the people of Shonenthal blew again the alarm, for they believed now, they had sufficient reason to consider the business of this call as a matter of his own invention, proceeding from his love of vanity; but he cared little about it, the frequent occurrence of similar trials had rendered him callous; he was resigned to the will of God, visited his patients from morning till late in the evening, while Christina' prepared for the winter, by purchasing and housing the necessary vegetables, by whitewashing the house, and such like things. In the latter part of September however, the call unexpectedly arrived. He received it with a calm mind, but with heart-felt satisfaction ; he and his good wife praised God, and began to make preparations for the journey. The Academy remained at Rittersburg, because insurmountable difficulties had presented themselves in its translocation to Manhime. He now made a full stop to his medical practice, excepting the operations on the eye, which he however resolved in future to perform gratuitously.

At lengt the moment of his removal from Shonenthal arrived, it was late in October, the days were short, the weather stormy and the roads very bad. With the beginning of November he had engaged to commence his lectures at Rittersburg. But one severe trial awaited him yet; eight hundred guilders were to be paid, before he could move. Several of his friends advised him, to assign his goods to his creditors, but this step he would not take. His answer was :

"Each of my creditors shall be paid to the last farthing, this I promise in the name of God, he has led me thus far, and he will surely not put me to shame." When they replied, this is all very well, but what will you do, should you be arrested ?

"I leave it to God," was his answer, "it is his business." He packed up all the goods he intended to take with him, and sent them on to Frankfort, and appointed a day for the sale of the rest by auction. Every thing went on without any hindrance, he received and paid out monies without interruption, and even engaged the post-coach as far as Russelstine, for himself and family for the next Sunday. A friend of his informed him in the mean time, that some of his creditors had agreed to arrest him before his departure, supposing, that if they should stop him from removing, some one or other would come forward and pay his debts for him. Stilling inwardly trembled, yet he trusted in God for deliverance.

On the last Thursday before his intended departure Mr. Troost entered with a cheerful countenance.

"Friend," said he, " matters go on again in Stilling's fashion," with these words he drew from his pocket a linnen bag, pouring its contents on the table.

"How is this ?" inquired Stilling.

"I went to a certain merchant," replied Troost, "knowing, that you owe him sixty crowns, and asked him to forgive you that debt. He answered with a smile : I will not only do this, but I'll make him a present of sixty crowns besides, for I know, he is in great distress. He then paid me the money and here it is. Now you have already the eighth part of what you" want, my advice to you is, that you take leave to morrow of all your acquaintances in town, then you have Saturday to yourself to prepare for your journey. Be of good cheer, and with patience and resignation see what God will do." He followed his advice. The first to whom he came was a rich merchant, who met him at the door and addressed him in the following words : "My dear Doctor, I know you come to take leave, I have always considered you as a man of rectitude and of a good character ; I could not employ you as a physician, for I had reason to be satisfied with the one we had, previously to your arrival ; God has lifted me likewise from the dust, and made me, what I am, I am sensible of the obligations. I owe to him. please to receive this trifle from me in his name, do not commit a sin by refusing its acceptance through false pride. With these words he embraced him, and put a roll of twenty Ducats into his hands. Stilling did not know, what he should say, but his benefactor left him abruptly.—But why should I detain the reader by giving details !—Presents were forced upon him with the greatest delicacy from all sides, and when he came home in the evening and counted—he had exactly eight hundred guilders, neither more nor less!

Such scenes lose by the most splendid descriptions—I am silent and adore—God knows you, my kind benefactors at Shonenthal! On the day of retribution I shall declare : Lord! these were the persons, who saved me from my troubles, reward them exceedingly according to thy promise, and he will do it. But not a word to thee, friend Troost, chosen among thousands, not a word to thee—When once we shall walk together through the fields of heaven, the occurrences of that time shall form a theme for our conversation.

Mr. Fredenberg was not only indifferent to the call of his son-in-law to Rittersburg, but even averse to it; looking upon him as a bad economist, he believed, that a fixed salary would avail him as little, as the earnings of his profession at Shonenthal ; and in as much as he had become responsible for his debts, he was afraid, he would have to bear the burden alone, and perhaps finally be compelled to pay the whole. Stilling's heart suffered exceedingly at the reproaches of his father-in-law, the more so, as he was unable, to remove his suspicions : sighs and prayers to his heavenly Father for help were rising continually from his heart but his confidence did not waver, he firmly believed, that God would finally deliver him from his troubles, according to his faith. He however promised Mr. Fredenberg, to pay yearly two hundred guilders, which would gradually lighten the burden ; this promise satisfied him in some measure. On Saturday he went with his family to Rasenhime, in order to take leave of his wife's relatives. He was fearful of a heart-rending scene, which would prove injurious to Christina's weak constitution, but he was mistaken, she felt more deeply than he did himself, how unjustly she and her husband had been treated by the family. She knew, she had been as saving as possible, that she had been moderate in her expenses for dress, and that their furniture and mode of living had always been within proper bounds : this consciousness filled her heart with courage and peace. Towards evening when the whole family were assembled and lamenting the departure of their brother and sister, Christina, after having sent both her children out of the room, arose from her seat and addressed her relatives in the following words : "We are about to go into a strange country, we leave parents, brothers, sisters and other relatives behind us, and we leave them willingly. God has sent us many sufferings and crosses, but none of our relations have assisted or comforted us ; the grace of God alone has made strangers instrumental in delivering us from utter ruin. I depart hence with pleasure. Father, mother, brothers and sisters ! farewell ! and live so in this world that I may meet you again before the throne of God !" Having said this, she kissed them all, without shedding a tear, and left them. Stilling also took leave of his friends, and hastened after her. The next morning he started with his family for Rittersburg.

CHAPTER VI.

The farther he removed from the theatre of his trials and sufferings, the more he felt his heart enlarged; his very soul was filled with gratitude and ecstatic joy. The experience we draw from past sufferings is the source of heartfelt satisfaction ; we come from every new trial more refined and more enlightened, and the religion of Jesus has this inestimable merit, that it teaches us to know sin and to shun it.

If we add to this general experience, his pleasing prospects, which promised him not only subsistence, but gave him likewise reasonable hopes for the gradual extinction of his debts, and brought him before a new public, which could not be prejudiced against him ; the reader will not find his satisfaction extravagant or unnatural.

A number of his friends from Shonenthal surprised him at noon in a tavern, where they had ordered a farewell-dinner to be prepared. Having spent a few hours in the company of these excellent men, he took his leave of them, and reached Russelstine that same day. Here he hired a hackney-coach as far as Co-

logne, and thence another one to Frankfort. At Coblenz he paid
a visit to the well known Madame Sophia de la Roche, who already knew him through the publication of the first part of his
life. At Frankfort he spent a pleasant day in the conversation
of his old friends, and after a day of rest, continued his journey
by way of Mainz to Manhime, where he was received with the
greatest cordiality by Mr. Eisenhart. In the latter city he found
many friends and patrons, all deeply interested in his behalf on
account of the publication of his life.

These pleasant occurrences were like precious drops of dew
on the hearts of Stilling and Christina, which had been parched
for so long a time by the drought of continued disregard and contempt. Mr. Eisenhart however gave him some very useful hints.
The publication of his life, notwithstanding the interest,
which it excited, had given rise to a suspicion in the minds of
many, that he was an enthusiast and a dangerous man. His
friend therefore advised him, not to *talk* much of religion, but to
let his light shine by rectitude of conduct and by noble actions;
for, added he, in a country, where the Roman Catholic religion
is predominant, it is necessary to be extremely cautious. Stilling
was conscious of the truth of these remarks, and promised to neglect none of his admonitions. But he could scarcely forbear
smiling, when he reflected, that the same book, which had drawn
upon him the suspicion of libertinism at Shonenthal, drew upon
him that of enthusiasm at Manhime. So little truth do the judgments of men contain.

From Manhime the road passed through the mountainous
Austrasia. Notwithstanding the unfriendly season of the year,
and though nature wore her most gloomy aspect, he admired the
steep mountains and rocks to his right and left, and the ruins
of knightly castles on the tops of them; every thing reminded him
of his native country, and he felt very comfortable. Soon the
ancient turrets of Rittersburg presented themselves to his view
above the tops of the forest. His heart beat in stronger pulses,
the nearer he approached the place of his future destination. It
was twilight, when he entered through the gate of the town. As
the coach was driving through the narrow street, on turning a

corner, he heard a male voice exclaim: "Halt! Is professor Stilling in that coach?" A redoubled *yes* was the answer. "Well then, step out, my dear friend and colleague, you are before your future residence."

This mild and affectionate address affected Stilling and Christina greatly; they alighted, and embraced professor Siegfried and his lady. Soon afterwards his other colleague, professor Stillenfeld, made his appearance, who attracted Stilling's attention particularly by his urbanity and placid manners. Stillenfeld was not married, but Siegfried had a child; they were beloved for their amiable disposition and excellent character; they were friends of religion, and almost enthusiasts in their desire to promote the welfare of their fellow men. The professor was a learned, deep-thinking man, who had studied theology, but was now engaged in lecturing on the laws of nations, on finances and political economy. Stillenfeld was a man of a refined and noble character; all was system, order and mathematical accuracy with him; few surpassed him in mathematical knowledge, in physiology, natural history and chemistry. Stilling was delighted with these men, and his wife found a friend in the companion of professor Siegfried, with whom she soon became intimate, and from whom she profited much in matters relating to economy.

Stilling wrote as soon as possible to his father-in-law at Rasenhime, as well as to his father at Linedorf, and to his uncle at Lichthausen; giving them a full account of his situation, not forgetting to mention the agreeable prospects, which brightened his horizon for the future. John and William Stilling were highly gratified to hear of the new honors, which their Henry had attained, and asked one another with astonishment: "What will yet become of him?" Mr. Fredenberg, on the other hand, was not so overjoyed; his answer was filled with paternal advice and exhortation, to manage matters well; he appeared to have no sense of the honor, conferred on his son and daughter in their new station; for rank and honor were but little regarded by him.

As the completion of the system of political economy, which

he had formed, was an object near his heart, he was engaged during the first winter of his residence at Rittersburg, to form a compend of it, and to lecture on the manuscript copy. This work was published at Manhime in the spring, and notwithstanding its faults and imperfections, was well received by the public; he therefore believed himself at length to be in the calling, for which Providence had designed him; he felt himself at home in his business, and could do with pleasure, what his duty required. He was happy in his connections, for the circle, in which he moved, loved, honored and esteemed him and Christina. Slander and revilings had ceased; and he would have been completely happy, had it not been for the tempest, which threatened him from Shonenthal in consequence of his debts. During the summer-session he lectured on the forest-laws, on husbandry and technology, for he was desirous of giving to his system of political economy the widest possible extension, and as the compends in use did not suit his plan, he resolved to compose new ones on all these sciences.

God had hitherto prepared him by many severe trials to become a useful instrument in his hand, but His providence saw yet many imperfections in him, which opposed the accomplishment of his gracious plan with him. The rough material was there—filing and polishing was still necessary, and he neglected not to finish his education by these means.

The society of political economy, of which he had now become a regular and active member, continued its operations and labors with evident success and blessing to their country, and the Palatinate on the Rhine will always remain indebted to this society for various improvements, introduced by the society into that country. A school was established by them, in which all the sciences connected with financial operations were taught; a manufactory was established, which is still in a flourishing condition, and gives bread to several hundred persons. Of all these improvements, counsellor Eisenhart was the prime mover. The society possessed likewise an estate in the village of Siegelbach, about five miles distant from Rittersburg, which was intended for experiments in agriculture, with a view to set a good example to the farmers in the neighborhood. This estate had hitherto been in the hands of a steward, who by mismanagement had ruined it.

When Stilling came to Rittersburg, the administration of this estate was given into his hands as professor of agriculture; and believing himself qualified to undertake the management of it, willingly accepted the trust. This took place immediately after his arrival at Rittersburg.

When he came for the first time to Siegelbach, with a view thoroughly to examine it, he found handsome stables built, according to the latest improvements in agriculture, and paved with hewn stones; twenty skeletons of Swiss cows, a true and faithful picture of Pharao's seven lean kine, collectively giving daily about three quarts of milk; besides there were two working-horses and two colts, and in separate sties a considerable number of hogs; and though it was but the beginning of November, there was not a mouthful of hay for all these creatures to be found, and straw for litter was entirely out of the question.— It was difficult to ascertain, what ought to be done in such a state of affairs; immediate application to the society for relief, appeared to him the shortest and only effectual remedy. But here he found deaf ears; all were tired of the continued claims upon their purses, and they advised him, to manage as well as he could. Stilling ought immediately to have given up the management of the farm, but he was wanting in the necessary prudence; he was deeply interested for the institution, and believed his own honor to be connected with that of the society, and that he must therefore go through with the business; a resolution, which prepared new misfortunes for him.

The first thing he undertook was the sale of half the stock, hoping, that with the money arising from it, he would be able to purchase the necessary fodder for the remainder. For this purpose he made a vendue, and was pleased to see so many bidders, who raised the price of the cattle not a little; he therefore entertained good hopes, of being able to overcome all difficulties. But great was his disappointment, when he perceived, that most of the buyers were creditors to the estate! The rest were for the

most part poor people, who could not make immediate payment,
so that he received very little cash, and if he wished to keep up
the establishment, he was under the necessity of drawing upon
his own purse, and wherever that was wanting, upon his private
credit. In the mean time he kept his hopes alive with the prospect of a plenteous harvest the next summer, and that the revenues from the artificial clover-meadows, and of other grass,
would rid him of this burden ; and thus far he was excusable,
but that he continued to have any thing to do with the management of the estate, after he had become acquainted with its true
situation, indicated after all an extreme carelessness and neglect
of his own interest in the circumstances, in which he was placed.
But it is easy in taking a retrospective view to hit upon the very
thing we ought to have avoided, in order to save ourselves a
world of trouble.

The performance of his official duties in the Academy was
nevertheless agreeable to him, and accompanied by the divine
blessing. But in the administration of the estate at Siegelbach,
none of his expectations were realized ; every where he found
a curse instead of a blessing ; he had to contend with unfaithful servants, with thievish neighbors, with debts and want of
support from the society, so that he saw himself at length compelled from motives of self-preservation, to throw up the administration, and render his accounts to the society. Thus he was
honorably liberated from that burden, yet not without an increase of his personal debts ; for he had spent a great deal of
money, which he neither could nor would bring into account, to
avoid suspicion of self-interest.

Misfortune after misfortune seemed now again to fall upon
his head. He had contracted new debts at Rittersburg, and was
scarcely able to pay the interest of his old at Shonenthal, much
less any part of the principal. Many false and unfavorable rumors, concerning his mode of living, were propagated at Shonenthal; for instance. it was said, that he was keeping a carriage
and servants, lived very extravagantly, without troubling himself about his debts. With almost every mail he received importuning letters, either from his father-in-law, or from some
other one of his creditors at Shonenthal.

Mr. Fredenberg was indeed in a very unpleasant and critical situation. Having become security for him, he was threatened with arrest by a man, who had in former times rendered assistance to his son-in-law from the purest and most humane motives. Stilling expected therefore nothing less, than to see his father-in-law and benefactor involved in a bankruptcy on his account.

Dreadfully alarming was this situation—and to whom could he complain but to his heavenly Father!—This he did incessantly; he endeavored to overcome his unbelief and want of confidence, by recalling to his mind the many wonderful proofs in his own life, that God is a prayer-hearing and prayer-answering Father, and this effected so much, that he did not utterly fall into despair. All letters to his father-in-law breathed devotion and resignation in the ways of Providence, but without producing the desired effect. Counsellor Eisenhart, who became in some measure acquainted with his situation, made several attempts, and proposed various plans, to effect a change for the better. Stilling wrote novels: "Florentin of Fahlendorn" and "Theodore von der Linden," and endeavored to stem the current with the amount he received for the copy-rights, but all this was no more than a drop of water in a bucket. He addressed himself to several wealthy friends, but some could not help him, others were even offended at his presumption, others again exhorted him to patience, and a few assisted him with some drops of dew upon his parched tongue. Every attempt proved fruitless, while the severest threatenings from Shonenthal continued to arrive. During this time of extreme distress, the Almighty prepared himself to hold judgment over Stilling, and to decide his fate.

August 17th, 1781, on a very warm and sultry day, while Christina was assisting the maid in raising a heavy basket on her head, she felt something burst in her breast; an acute pain, accompanied with alternate paroxysms of chills and flashing heat, soon followed. When Stilling returned from his lecture-room, and entered her chamber, she met him, a death-like paleness had spread over her face, and she addressed him in the following words:

"My dear husband, I have attempted to lift a heavy basket, I have thereby injured my breast; may God have mercy on you and me! I shall not be able to overcome it."

At these words Stilling lost his presence of mind; he stood in utter astonishment, and being worn out with grief, supposed, that death was about to hurl his last and sharpest dart at him.— His head fell upon his shoulder; both his hands were folded over his breast; he stood, the picture of despair, yet without being able to weep, or utter a single word—for he too was of opinion, that the last hour of his dear Christina was approaching. After some time, however, he recovered in some measure; endeavored to comfort her, and brought her to bed. Towards evening the malady attacked her most violently. Christina, patient as a lamb under the hand of the shearer, exclaimed:

"Lord, do with me, what is pleasing in thy sight! I am thy child—if it is thy will, that I shall no more see my parents, brothers and sisters in this world, I commend them to thee—lead and direct them in such a manner, that I may see them again before thy throne."

Christina's principal disease for the present was an inflammation of the breast, accompanied with hysterical paroxysms, the symptoms of which manifested themselves in a very severe cough; several physicians were called, and all the means applied, which possibly might save her. After a fortnight it seemed, as if hopes might be entertained of her recovery, and as if immediate danger were past. Stilling mentioned these joyful news to all his friends; he sung hymns of praise; but alas! he had deceived himself; her malady assumed the character of a settled consumption. His distress had now reached its acme; the idea of losing the dear partner of his joys and sorrows, was altogether insupportable; for she was a most excellent companion, agreeable and pleasing; her conduct, yea, the very tone of her voice, was prepossessing; her cleanliness extreme; in her plain dress, order and neatness were conspicuous, and every thing she undertook, was done without parade and with great ease. Among her intimate friends she was jocose and witty, and yet withal very pious—free from all hypocrisy. Stilling knew her worth, and therefore dreaded her loss the more.

Sometimes she expressed a hope of recovery, but soon the most dreadful paroxysms returned; she coughed with such violence, that small pieces of the lungs were expectorated with severe and painful struggles. Under all these sufferings, she never manifested the least impatience, but merely exclaimed in the agony of her distress: "Lord! spare me, according to thine infinite mercy!"

When her husband and the nurse were on the point of giving out, being overcome with pity and watchings, she would sometimes look at them with the most expressive countenance, saying: "O my dearest husband! my dear Mrs. N.....! I pray you both, have yet a little patience with me, I know, I cause you a world of trouble!"

Stilling was wrestling day and night with God; one of the corners of his study had become smooth with kneeling; but heaven appeared as if shut to his entreaties, and as if his sighs and fervent prayers remained unheard. As Christina could not bear the least noise, he continually walked about on his stocking-feet, and in the anguish of his heart ran from one corner of the room to another, till at length the soles were completely torn to pieces. In the midst of these troubles the most threatening, insulting and humiliating letters incessantly arrived from Shonenthal. Mr. Fredenberg's heart was almost broken in consequence of the expected death of his daughter, but still his reproaches were unceasing. He was prepossessed with the idea, that Stilling was the cause of his own misfortunes, and apologies were of no avail. His situation at that time beggared all description, yet, the greater the anguish of his heart was, with the greater fervency he did cleave to the all-merciful love of God. After the lapse of several weeks he stood one evening—it was the beginning of October—at the window of his entry, in the act of prayer, when he suddenly felt comfort in his mind, and resignation to the will of God; he was still sensible of all his sufferings, but at the same time had strength to bear them; he went into the sick-room, but Christina gave him to understand, that she wished to be left alone for the present; after some time she called him in, desired him to sit down by her bed-side, and with some difficulty turned her face towards him. She viewed him with an indescribable look, and said: "I shall depart, my dearest and best Henry, and I depart resigned; our married life has been one continued chain of sufferings, it doth not please God, that I should see you delivered from your troubles, but he will deliver you, be of good courage, and submit with resignation to his will. God will not forsake you!—I do not commend my two children to you, you are their father, and God will provide for them."

Having said this, she made yet some arrangements in regard to family affairs, then turned towards the wall, and was very quiet. From that time he frequently spoke with her of her departure, and her expectations after death. Now and then her paroxysms returned, and in such moments she wished for an easy death, and that it might happen in the day time, for she was afraid of the night. Mr. Siegfried visited her frequently, his lady would gladly have done the same, but indisposition and family circumstances prevented her. At length the moment of her dissolution approached; on the evening of the 17th of October he observed in her countenance the traits ot death; towards eleven o'clock, being overcome with fatigue he retired to another room to take some rest, at five o'clock in the morning he returned to Christina, and found her very composed and resigned. "I have overcome!" exclaimed she, "I behold the joys of another world before me, I am free from every thing which this world contains." Stilling sat down by her bedside watching the last moments of his bosom-friend and companion: frequently she pressed his hands, uttering merely these words: "My dear husband! my all in this world!—She did not wish to see her children, she only commended them to the protection of God. More than once she repeated these words: "Jesus! thou canst lead me gently through the gates of death." Towards ten o'clock she said: "My dear husband! I feel very sleepy, and at the same time very happy, should I perhaps awake no more, I bid you farewell!" Once more she looked at him with her large black eyes, and with smiling lips pressed his hand and soon fell asleep. About an honr afterwards she gave one groan and quivered. In that moment her respiration ceased, the traits of death were fixed in her face,—once more

she smiled—Christina was no more.—A tender-hearted husband
alone can feel, what Stilling felt on this occasion! In that very
moment professor Siegfried entered the room, looked at the bed,
embraced his friend and both shed tears in silent mourning.

"Loving angel!" exclaimed Siegfried after a while, looking
at the corpse, "thou hast then triumphed over all thy sufferings!"
But Stilling kissed once more her pale lips with these words:
"Dear sufferer, thank to thee for all thy faithfulness, enter thou
into the joy of thy Lord!" When Siegfried was gone, Stilling
led his two children to the corpse of their departed mother. As
soon as they beheld it, they sobbed aloud. Stilling took one upon
each knee, pressed his children to his heart, and all three shed
many tears. At length he regained strength and courage, he
arose, in order to make such preparations as the circumstances
required. October the 21st, early at dawn of day his friends at
Rittersburg, accompanied Christina's corpse to the grave. The
two Protestant ministers of the town faithfully assisted him in
overcoming this last separation, by entertaining him with comforting views of eternity.

CHAPTER VII.

An important period of Stilling's life had closed with the
death of Christina and another one as momentous as the former
still farther discovered the views of Providence with him.

After the death of his beloved wife he endeavored to make
arrangements, as suitable to his present solitary situation as circumstances would admit. In the first place he went to Zweybruken, the residence of several of his most intimate friends, to
hold a consultation with them, in regard to a convenient place
for the education of his children. Such a place offered in
that town, he therefore made the necessary arrangements and
brought his children thither. His daughter Hanna was in her
ninth and his son Jacob in his eighth year. On his return to his
solitary dwelling he felt his loss with redoubled weight, and some

time elapsed before he became fully resigned. He had relinquished the thought of housekeeping for the present, had
discharged the maid, and was boarding with his landlord. He
now almost repented of having taken this step, but his circumstances absolutely required it, he knew his children ought to receive their education, which he could not give them himself, on
account of his professional calling, which left him no time to
engage in the education of his own children.

His father William Stilling sometimes endeavored to give
him comfort, by reminding him of what he had suffered at the
death of his beloved Dorothy, and that time had gradually healed
this wound; he therefore hoped, it would produce a similar effect on him. But this also was of little avail; he remained greatly
afflicted, without any prospect of a speedy deliverance. One Saturday afternoon, in the middle of November, his distress had reached
its highest point, prayers to his heavenly Father were his accustomed and only resource. In the evening at six o'clock, having
finished his last lecture for that day, the hired girl in the house
informed him, that a young gentleman had inquired for him and
had just left the house. Not long afterwards the young man returned; he appeared to be of a friendly and prepossessing mien,
and addressed himself to Stilling in the following manner: "Professor Stilling, I come from R—— and have the expectation of
a place in the department of the finances of the Electoral service,
but agreeable to the Elector's orders, have to qualify myself for
it, by studying here in Rittersburg at the least for half a year:
though this falls heavy upon me,—being a married man, though
without children—it is a source of consolation to me, that these
circumstances give me an opportunity of making the acquaintance of Professor Stilling. I have heard, that Mrs. Stilling has
departed this life, and that you are deeply afflicted on that account; if you would permit myself and wife to live with you, it
might prove a means of removing your despondency at least in
some measure; we shall in that case have the advantage of your
conversation, and you will feel less solitary. I venture to flatter
myself with the hope, that my wife will be deserving of your
friendship, for she is good hearted and noble minded." At these

words Stilling's soul revived; it appeared to him, as if some one had taken the oppressive load of grief from his shoulders, scarcely was he able to conceal the ecstacy of his joy. He immediately went with Mr. Kuhlenbach—the name of the above mentioned gentleman—to the public house, to wait upon his lady, and to announce to her his readiness to receive them. The next day they moved into his house. Every thing now took again its ordinary course without interruption, and he felt himself comfortably situated. He published during this winter all his compends, which enabled him to think of a gradual discharge of his debts. his yearly income amounting to the sum of fifteen hundred guilders: he likewise sold all the furniture he could spare, and with the money arising from the sale he paid the most urgent debts. This mode of living continued till the spring of 1782, when Mr Kuhlenbach began to talk of removing from Rittersburg, which created a fear in Stilling's mind, that after his departure he would relapse into his former melancholy. Mr. Eisenhart thought he ought to marry again, and Stilling himself believed that this would be the most advisable step he could take. His fiirst intention was, to make proposals of marriage to a certain widow of an excellent character, who had one child and some property, and whose family was unexceptionable; she was acquainted with him, and had already given him sufficient proofs of her ability of managing the affairs of a family. He therefore addressed himself to her by letter, but in her answer she gave him such important reasons for the determination she had taken, never to marry again, that he relinquished all hopes of succeeding in his addresses.

About this time he began to entertain doubts whether his first marriage had been really and purely the work of Divine Providence, or whether human weakness and even impurity of sentiment had not a considerable share in that engagement? A conviction, that neither his father-in-law nor his departed Christina nor himself had followed either the precepts of religion or of reason, was the result of this deliberation. For the first duty of the christian ought to be, to examine every step he takes in life in conformity to the rules of sound sense and propriety, under the direction of Divine Providence and prayerfully, and more particularly the important one of marriage ; and then confidently hope for the blessing of God. This however had been neglected : Christina was an innocent and inexperienced girl, she loved Stilling almost without knowing it, and when she became aware of it, prayed to God for the accomplishment of her wishes ; and thus religion and love were interwoven with her hysterical paroxysms. This circumstance was unknown to Stilling and her parents, both parties looked upon this marriage as a work of Divine Providence. The imprudence and impropriety of this step became apparent too late in its disastrous consequences. Christina was without property and so was Stilling. He was necessitated to study with borrowed money, was afterwards not skilled enough in economy, to manage business to advantage, and of course was unable to maintain himself and family, and possessed still less ability to pay his debts. Christina on the other hand, being educated as a merchant's daughter, expected from her husband, that he would manage the general concerns of the family, and that her business only was, to keep house with what came into her hands ; she would therefore have made any merchant happy, but not a person in Stilling's situation. But notwithstanding all this, he had to acknowledge, that these ten years of difficulties and probation had been highly beneficial to him. God had made use of his own faults as a means of purification, his dear Christina had passed through the same fiery ordeal, and had passed it with honor. He therefore found abundant reason to be thankful to God, who had overruled evil for good.

Mrs. Sophia de la Roche, her husband and their still unmarried children lived at this time in the town of S——. Stilling had called on her when business had brought him the last time to the place of her residence, but not being on terms of intimacy in that family, he had made no mention of his intention of marrying again. Soon after his return he received very unexpectedly a letter from the above mentioned lady. in which she expresses herself concerning his intended marriage as follows :

"Your friends in this place have not observed the same caution, which you did, when at my house, for it is generally reported, that Stilling has made proposals to several young ladies without success. I do not like this at all. Must you then absolutely have a rich wife? or would one of my female friends suit you? She is a very virtuous and handsome girl, of an ancient, noble family, in which there have been many individuals distinguished for their learning, her own parents were persons of excellent character; the father is dead, her mother is still alive, though in a very delicate state of health: she herself is about twenty-three years of age, and in this short period of life has passed through many trials and sufferings; she is well educated, well skilled in all female work, a saving housekeeper, pious, and will make an excellent mother for your children, she is not rich, but will receive a handsome outfit. . . .

If all these qualifications, the correctness of which I attest with my word of honor compensate you for the lack of a few thousand guilders, you will please to inform me of your approbation in your answer, I shall then name her, and tell you, what you ought to do. . . . .

Stilling forthwith communicated the contents of this letter to his friends, professor Siegfried and the Lutheran minister at Rittersburg. They were both agreed in considering this proposition as a providential hint, and encouraged him to follow its direction. He therefore expressed his thanks to Mrs. de la Roche, for the interest she had taken in his affairs, and begged her, to name the amiable lady, whose character she had so charmingly described, because he was resolved to follow her suggestion and salutary counsel. A week afterwards Mrs. de la Roche informed him, that her friend's name was Selma de St. Florentin, that her brother was Attorney to the city authorities; she once more confirmed all she had said of her in her first communication and told him, she had shewn her his last letter, and that she had given her to understand, she had no objection to a visit from Stilling.—She therefore advised him, to come to S——, as soon as his circumstances would admit, and that she would take it upon herself to introduce them to each other.

Stilling had always manifested a certain rashness in all his undertakings, in this spirit he likewise acted on this occasion;

the very next day after the receipt of Mrs. de la Roche's last communication, he started for S——, and arrived June 25th 1782 at her house, where he was received with much cordiality and friendship. She forthwith made the necessary preparations for an interview between Selma and Stilling; wrote a billet to the colleague of Selma's brother and his lady, a Mr. and Mrs. P—— her own intimate friends as well as of Selma, informing them of Stilling's arrival, and requesting them to come next morning about ten o'clock with Selma and her brother into Mrs. de la Roche's garden, and that Mr. P—— should accompany Stilling from his lodgings to the same place.

All this was done according to request, Mrs. P—— called for Selma and Mr. de Florentin and Mr. P—— for Stilling. The latter conducted him through the gate of the town along the wall into a beautiful garden. On entering he saw Selma dressed in an orange coloured silk-gown and a black straw hat walking in apparent uneasiness among the fruit-trees, wringing her hands in extreme agitation. In another place Mrs. P—— and Selma's brother were walking arm in arm. As Stilling approached them, they all stood still, that Mr. P—— might have an opportunity of introducing him. After the usual compliments were passed, Mr. and Mrs. P—— and Selma's brother hastened into the garden-house, leaving Stilling and Selma to themselves. He approached her, offered her his arm, walking slowly forward. After a short pause he addressed her rather abruptly in the following manner: "Miss de St. Florentin, you are in some measure acquainted with me from the published history of my life, you likewise know the object of my coming hither; I am poor, but have a sufficient income for a comfortable living; my departed wife has left me two children, and my character is exactly as I have described it in the publication of my life. If you can make up your mind to become my wife, I would ask it as a favor of you not to detain me a long while in doubt and uncertainty, being wont to take always the shortest possible course for the attainment of my wishes. I hope you will not find any cause for repenting of your choice, I am endeavoring to walk in the fear of God, and shall do all in my power to make you happy."

Selma, after having recovered from her surprise, raised her expressive eyes full of sweetness upwards, covered her face with her fan and replied: "The will of Providence is also my will."— During this conversation they had reached the garden-house, where Stilling was examined from all sides. Selma alone kept her eyes fixed on the ground, without speaking one word. Some time being spent in mutual discourse, the company separated after agreeing, that Selma and her brother should come that afternoon to Mrs. de la Roche, in order to have further conversation on the subject which Stilling had proposed to her that morning.

As soon as Mrs. de la Roche and Stilling were alone, she asked him: "how were you pleased with Selma?"

"She exceeds by far my most sanguine expectations," was Stilling's reply.

"I am glad to hear it," said Mrs. de la Roche, "and I hope, Providence has destined her for you."

After dinner Selma did not arrive as it had been expected, which created much uneasiness both to Stilling and Mrs. de la Roche; but just as he began to give way to the most gloomy despondency, Mr. de St. Florentin entered with Selma his sister. Mrs. de la Roche took Mr. de St. Florentin by the arm and led him into an adjoining parlor, while Stilling conducted Selma to the sofa.

"What has prevented Miss de St. Florentin from giving us the pleasure of her company somewhat earlier? I really began to fear, you would deprive us altogether of this satisfaction;" was Stilling's address.

"I had promised to call on an acquaintance, and therefore could not be here before this time. But my sensations on the present occasion are indescribable!"

"Have you come to a determination in regard to the subject I introduced to your consideration this morning? and may I hope for a favorable conclusion?"

"If my mother makes no objection, I shall accede to your wishes."

"But your mother?"

"I do not expect she will make any objections."

This declaration of Selma created the more lively joy in Stilling, the greater his fear had been of a different solution of the drama. He arose, kissed her, and in that moment Mrs. de la Roche and Mr. de St. Florentin entered the room.

"Are you so far already?" asked she, with a countenance beaming with joy.

"Yes!—yes!" and with these words he led her to Mrs. de la Roche, who took both by the hand and said with eyes lifted up to heaven:

"May God bless you, my children!" "If angels in heaven regard the things of this sublunary world, I have no doubt, your departed Christina views the present scene with heavenly rapture."

This scene was indeed deeply affecting. Selma's brother now joined the group, his and Stilling's heart united forever in the tender bonds of brotherly love. Mrs. de la Roche seated herself on the sofa, took Selma on her lap, who hid her face in her friend's bosom, bedewing it with tears. This silent but affecting scene having continued for some time, they entered into conversation, and Stilling's heart was drawn towards Selma with an almost irresistible force, though his acquaintance with her was short and he knew as yet little of the interesting incidents of her life. She on her part declared, that she entertained the highest regard and esteem for him, and added with dignity: "I am resolved, so to supply the place of your departed Christina in regard to her children, that on the great day of accounts I may meet her with them in the consciousness of having done my duty. After they had separated, Selma went to Reichenberg, whence she intended to go to her aunt at Kreuznach, to spend her bridal days in that place. When he had returned to Rittersburg, and maturely reflected on the occurrences of the last few days, his mind was greatly agitated, because he had not mentioned a word of his debts; he acknowledged it was an almost unpardonable fault, if you please to give that name to an omission of duty, which it was morally impossible to fulfill. Selma knew Stilling merely as an author and from general report, she had seen him on the day of their engagement, for the first time; what is generally called love among young people, was here out of question, he therefore was aware, that Selma would never have consented to marry him, should he have disclosed the state of his finances at that time; but he also felt, how fatal to their future happiness the discovery of his debts would prove, if made at a time, when it would be no longer in her power to retract, and yet he had not resolution enough to make the disclosure.

While he was troubled in his mind on account of these things, he received a letter from her, and was astonished at the spirit which it breathed, the free flow of sentiment it contained, and at the correctness and order of style, which were imprinted on every line.

Soon after, the consent of Selma's mother arrived, and was communicated to him. He accordingly went to Kreuznach, with the intention of spending a few days with his bride, and of becoming better acquainted with her. This visit proved a new source of satisfaction to him in observing, how richly the paternal love of God had rewarded him for all his severe and long sufferings. Still he could not prevail with himself, to disclose his debts, he therefore supplicated God in frequent prayers, to direct matters in such a way as to take a favorable turn.

Two days previous to his departure from Kreuznach, as he was sitting with Selma and her aunt in the hall in the morning, the letter-carrier entered, and handed Selma a letter, which she immediately opened; after she had read part of it, he observed, that paleness was spreading over her countenance, she arose and called her aunt into the adjoining room, but soon returned, and walked up to her own chamber. After a while her aunt likewise came back into the hall, and informed him, that a friend of Selma's had mentioned to her, that he was deeply involved in debt, that Selma had expressed some surprise at it; it was therefore highly necessary he should give her a suitable explanation of the subject; she also added: many men of excellent character have the same misfortune, this circumstance ought not to create any unpleasant feelings much less a separation—and so forth.—Stilling therefore went up stairs to her, but with a sensation not unlike that of a criminal, who is brought before his judge, to hear his sentence pronounced. When he entered the room, he found her seated behind a small table, her head resting on her hand.

"Pardon me, my dearest Selma," he began, "that I have said nothing of my debts, I have wished to unburden myself but have not been able to muster sufficient courage, for if I had, I am sure, you would never have consented to become mine. Yet in my distress, I have this great consolation, that they have not arisen from prodigality and extravagance; in my present situation I am able to make considerable money, and I am unremitting in my labors; if we are economical, we have a prospect of paying the debts, and should I die before they are paid, you know, that no one can make a lawful demand on you in regard to them.--You will therefore lose nothing, except that you will have some hundred guilders less income per year, which must go towards the payment of the debts, the remaining thousand guilders will be amply sufficient for our subsistence. However, dearest Selma, I do not hesitate to declare you free from your engagement to me, I give up every claim—whatever may be the consequence to myself—in case, you repent of your promise."

Selma arose from her seat in great emotion, and with an affectionate look replied: "You need be under no apprehension that I shall retract my promise, God, as I believe, has destined me, to bear the burden with you—only have courage, with his gracious assistance, we shall overcome this difficulty."

The reader may probably represent to himself Stilling's sensations at this address, tears rushed into his eyes, and overcome by his feelings, he embraced her with these words: "You are indeed an angel of God!" They then went down stairs together; her aunt was delighted with the fortunate turn this very disagreeable and dangerous affair had taken, and comforted both from the treasury of her own experience.

How wisely did Divine Providence again direct Stilling's affairs, on this critical occasion!—Will any one say, that God is not a prayer hearing and prayer answering God?—An earlier discovery would probably have deprived him of Selma, and a later one would doubtless have created much uneasiness and vexation.

CHAPTER VIII.

Stilling returned perfectly satisfied and happy to Rittersburg, where he made the necessary preparations for the wedding, which was to take place at the house of Selma's aunt at Kreuznach.

All things being in readiness, he went to Kreuznach August the 14th 1782. On his arrival he was received in the most affectionate manner by Selma, who now not only esteemed but also loved him. The marriage-ceremony was performed August 16th by Inspector W——— a friend of Stilling, in the presence of a few mutual acquaintances. The next day a jaunt of pleasure into the Rhinegow was proposed and accepted by the wedding guests. It was a truly delightful excursion, every where objects met the eyes, calculated to give the highest gratification and entertainment to minds possessed of sensibility. In the evening on their return, one part of the company among whom was Selma, were in imminent danger of losing their lives from the carelessness of the boatmen who were intoxicated, and therefore most shamefully neglected their duty. But the eye of Providence watched over his wife and her companions, so that they finally landed without receiving any injury.

A few days afterwards he returned to Rittersburg, accompanied by Selma and her aunt; when they had reached half way, they were met by the students, who manifested their participation in his joy by the delivery of a well written poem. Thus commenced a new period in his domestic life, Selma immediately sent for his two children from Zweybruken, and undertook their education with the faithfulness of a mother. At the same time she represented to him the necessity of taking upon herself the superintendence of the household expenses, which he willingly gave into her hands. The beneficial consequences of this arrangement soon became visible, his children were well clothed, and every thing was conducted with the greatest order and economy. Every friend was welcome at his table, his house became the asylum of a number of young men, many of whom were there preserved from danger, while others were called back to the path of virtue, and snatched from impending ruin.

Notwithstanding all this, his purse was never empty, and Selma now laid a plan for the liquidation of his debts; the interest of the whole was regularly paid, and a part of the principal of that contracted at Rittersburg. The whole of the latter was discharged in less than three years, after which money was sent to Shonenthal, which silenced his creditors in that city in some measure; in short, his long and severe sufferings in consequence of his debts at length terminated. And though importuning letters still arrived from time to time, Selma answered them in a manner, which could not fail to satisfy every reasonable creditor.

While these things were going on, many circumstances occurred, which greatly circumscribed his sphere of action: his activity and the number of his publications, which had been well received by the public, produced much envy: many attempted to place him in an unfavorable light as much as possible, and though he was very active in promoting the best interests of the institution and the welfare of the community, among which he lived, either no notice was taken of it, or his most salutary measures were decryed; and whenever the court or any other bodies politic were willing to acknowledge his merits, persons were always found ready to prevent it. To this ought to be added, that he was very desirous of executing and teaching his system of political economy without the interference of others, which in his present situation was impossible. Besides his income was too small, to enable him to make provision for his family, which became a favorite project with him, now that his debts were no longer oppressive to him. These circumstances combined excited a wish in his mind, that a more advantageous situation might offer; though he was satisfied and pleased with his present calling, as long as it should please Providence to continue him there, for his difficulties could not be called sufferings, as they only limited him in his activity.

In the year 1784 the Elector resolved, to unite the Acade-

K k

my at Rittersburg with the ancient university at Hidleberg, which had always been the universal wish of its teachers. This translocation actually took place in the autumn of the same year. Stilling's situation was thereby in some measure improved, his sphere of action was enlarged, and his income somewhat increased ; but not so as to enable him to make provision for his family ; and envy, the baneful effects of which he had experienced in some measure at Rittersburg, fell with redoubled weight upon him at Hidleberg ; though he also found many and important friends in the latter city, and enjoyed the good will of the public, chiefly on account of his success as oculist, performing all operations gratuitously. To this ought to be added the esteem which he enjoyed from all the members of the university, and that at length his unremitting zeal and faithfulness reached the ears of the Elector, who assured him of his protection and favor by sending him the diploma of privy counsellor without his previous knowledge, and without the payment of any fees.

About this time Mr. Fredenberg departed this life. The immediate cause of his death was dropsy in the chest. Selma had succeeded previous to his decease in convincing him of Stilling's honorable intentions, and of the prospect he had of paying his debts; he therefore died perfectly satisfied and with the resignation of a christian, which he was in the full sense of the word. Peace be with his ashes !—

The German society at Manhime elected Stilling as a sitting member, a circumstance which obliged him to go every fortnight with his friend the church counsellor Mieg to Manhime to attend the sessions of the society, which journies afforded him an agreeable relaxation from his studies and an opportunity of still enlarging his acquaintance with gentlemen of learning and respectability.

In the autumn of 1786 the university of Hidleberg celebrated her fourth centennial Jubilee with great splendor, on which occasion a vast multitude from all parts of Germany assembled. Stilling was chosen orator of the day by the statistical-economical Academy, and having prepared himself carefully for the occasion, he delivered his oration with uncommon applause. Having left the rostrum his Excellency the minister de Oberndorf, the representative of his Electoral Highness expressed his thanks to him for the oration in the most obliging terms, and the first men of the Palatinate who were assembled on this occasion embraced him, whose example was followed by the deputies of the imperial free cities and of the universities.

Stilling was much gratified at these marks of attention and respect ; he perceived that God was with him and permitted him to enjoy a portion of honor, after many bitter cups of trials and sufferings. At the same time he was fully sensible, that to God alone was due all praise for this enjoyment : since his talents were his gift, and he likewise had enabled him to cultivate them. Henceforth he enjoyed the esteem and regard of all influential men in the Palatinate, and this moment appeared likewise to have been fixed upon by Divine Providence to place him in that situation for which he had been preparing these last fourteen years.

The Landgrave of Hessecassel had resolved, to place the university of Marburg on a respectable footing, and for that purpose had called a number of learned men, to fill professor's chairs at this seat of the Muses: and desirous of having also the Statistic-economical department filled with a teacher, had invited several gentlemen, to accept this professorship, but various circumstances had prevented them from acceding to his wishes.

In the autumn of 1786 Mr. Leske of Leipzig accepted the call, but on his journey to Marburg was seriously injured by a fall, the consequences of which occasioned his death one week after his arrival in that city. Stilling had been frequently talked of, as a man, capable of filling the chair, but several persons of influence had been opposed to him on the ground, that a novel-writer would not be a suitable man to fill so important a station. But in vain are the attempts of men, to resist the plans of Divine Providence. In the month of February 1787 he received the call from the Landgrave, notwithstanding all opposition, with a salary of twelve hundred rix-dollars or two thousand one hundred and sixty imperial guilders, and the promise of an ample provision for his widow in case of his death.

He accepted this call with gratitude towards his heavenly guide, father and protector; all his wishes were realized, he could now complete his system and teach it without any interruption, and hoped, that his salary would afford him means of making suitable provision for his family. His children were three in number: the son and daughter of the first marriage were nearly grown up. He permitted his daughter to stay a year among the relatives of her departed mother, but placed his son in a private Academy under the care of a respectable clergyman in the neighborhood of Heilbron. Selma had brought him three children, of whom however one son and a daughter had died at Hidleberg, his youngest child, a girl of about one year old, he took with him to Marburg.

He started for the place of his destination about Easter 1787; in Frankfort he stopt with his tried and faithful friend Kraft, who rejoiced at the pleasing termination of his severe trials: at Marburg he met with a most affectionate reception from all the members of the university: it appeared to him, as if he were returning to his own acquaintances and country. Even those, who had been opposed to his call, became his warm friends, as soon as they knew him, for their opposition to him had originated in the purest motives.

Having entered upon the duties of his new office in reliance on the divine assistance and all matters in his household being properly arranged, his heart urged him, to send for his father, whose place of residence was only a few leagues distant from Marburg; he therefore invited him by letter to spend some time with him, as his own engagements prevented him from visiting his father. The good old man having assured his son, that he would be pleased to come, he made the necessary preparations through his cousin, the son of John Stilling, who was overseer of the mines at Dillenburg.

Great would have been his joy if his uncle John could have been of the party, but God had called him a year previous from his labors into his rest, and had assigned him another sphere of activity in a better world.

On a fine summer day's afternoon, 1787, as he was engaged in lecturing on Technology, several young gentlemen, students of the University, entered his lecture-room, announcing the arrival of his father. He forthwith closed the lecture, and sensations of various kinds rushed through his mind, while he walked down stairs in deep silence, accompanied by all the students. Selma had meanwhile received her father-in-law most affectionately at the door of the house, and conducted him and his companion the overseer of the mines into a parlor, and was gone for her child to present it to its grandfather, when Stilling entered with his retinue. Opposite the door stood his cousin, and a little to his left William Stilling, bent down with age, his hat in his hands, and his venerable face, marked deeply by care and various troubles with furrows and wrinkles. Cautious, and with that bashfulness peculiar to himself, he looked at his approaching son, who drew nigh his father with ardent affection, while the crowd of students had arranged themselves behind him, smiling with participating joy. Having for some moments viewed each other, they met in a silent and affectionate embrace. Being somewhat composed, Henry began :

"Father ! you look a vast deal older than when I saw you thirteen years ago !"

"Very true, my son."

"Honored father, I hope you will address me in your accustomed language, I am your son, and I am proud of it.— Your prayers and your education have made me what I am, without your help I would be nothing."

"Well, well ! let this be so.—God has done all ! To him be all the praise !"

"It appears to me, as if I stood before my grand-father, you resemble him indeed very much."

"I resemble him in appearance, as well as in mind,—I enjoy that inward peace, which he enjoyed, and in my actions I endeavor to take him for my example."

"How rough and stiff are your hands—my dear father! have you to work so hard for your subsistence?"

He smiled in father Stilling's fashion and replied : "I am a farmer, and accustomed to work, it is my calling, be not uneasy about it, my Son !" I have, t'is true, to labor hard for my subsistence, however I am not in want.——

Stilling then shook hands with his cousin, and while in the act of conversation with him, Selma entered with her little daughter in her arms. The aged father took hold of her hand, and said with great emotion : "May the Almighty bless thee, my child."—Selma sat down, cast a scrutinizing look over the whole circle, and shed silent tears.

Gradually the crowd dispersed, the young gentlemen left the house, and Stilling's friends at Marburg commenced calling on his father, who was treated by them with great politeness and respect. God will reward them for this kindness, so worthy their benevolent hearts.

William spent several days with his son, and repeatedly declared : that this short season appeared to him like an antepast of heaven! Content and happy he returned home accompanied by his nephew.

Stilling's abode at Marburg was perfectly happy, and his professional labors were crowned with success. His married life was a continued source of the most refined enjoyment, which can be found on earth ; for Selma loved him with her whole soul : and as his long continued sufferings had excited his nervous sensibility to such a degree, that he was always dreading some terrible evil, her constant endeavor was to exhilarate him and to wipe away his tears. Unconscious and without affectation, she is the life of every company ; and a faithful mother to his children of the first marriage.—Though she is opposed to my saying any thing publicly in her favor, yet I own it to myself and to my readers, that I should say something more of the excellency of her character to the praise of God ; I have therefore, unknown to her, drawn the following picture of her person and character, which I herewith present to the reader. She is rather short in stature, of a pleasing and animated countenance, and her sweet blue eyes beam with beneficent tenderness towards every noble heart. She possesses an excellent judgment in all things, so that her husband frequently asks her advice when he fears, that his precipitate disposition will lead him to rash and inconsiderate actions, and he has never found cause to regret it. She is an enlightened christian, enthusiastic in love to God and the Redeemer; and charitable towards mankind, and her economical disposition doth not prevent her from performing those acts of beneficence and liberality, which the religion of Christ inculcates. She is of a modest and retiring disposition, and always desires to appear dependent on her husband, even when he follows her advice; she never attempts to shine, but still she pleases wherever she makes her appearance, and possesses the happy art of making every one feel at ease in her company. But I must refrain my pen: "May God give such a wife to all, whom he loves!" said Gœtz of Berlichingen of his Maria, and so says Stilling of his Selma.

Besides this domestic blessing, Stilling has also a considerable income, so that all gnawing cares for his subsistence are banished from his dwelling. God's blessing accompanies his professional calling—but little ought to be spoken on this subject, the honorable man and the christian is attentive to his calling, and leaves the event to God.

He continues at Marburg the operations of the eye, and more than one hundred persons afflicted with the cataract — for the most part from the poor and laboring classes—have, with the assistance of God, received their sight, and with it, the ability of making a living for themselves and families. The assurance, of having been the instrument in the hand of God of restoring comfort to so many families is to him a source of never failing satisfaction. His heart beats with rapture, when the poor man, who has for a long time been deprived of his sight, with grateful feelings squeezes his hand and directs him for his reward to the rich inheritance of the spiritual world. Blessed be the remembrance of that woman, who compelled him to perform the first of these beneficent operations. Without her he would not have become so useful an instrument in the hand of the father of the poor and the blind! Blessed be the memory of the worthy Molitor! May his spirit in the fields of light in the paradise of God enjoy the blissful sensation of the friend of man!

Young man, whosoever thou art, that readest this, carefully watch over and cherish every germ of virtue in thy soul! nurse it with the greatest care, that it may grow into a tree of life bearing twelve kinds of fruits: if Providence assigns thee a useful calling, pursue it with diligence; but if a desire arises in thy heart to sow the seeds of happiness for thy fellow-creatures, in a manner unconnected with thy profession, or if Providence opens a door to thee for that purpose, do not neglect the heavenly call, though it should be connected with much labor and trouble to thyself, for nothing brings us nearer to God than beneficence.

But beware of *false* though *fashionable* activity. The slave of sensuality covers his uncleanness with the white-wash of humanity; he professes to do good every where, without in reality knowing what is good; he raises the unworthy to office, by which he doth infinite mischief to the community. In a similar manner acts the proud priest of his own reason, which though in itself frail, weak, and often erring, he elevates above every thing else; he would be an Autocrat in the moral creation, and builds up his system with unhewn stones and untempered mortar.

Young man! open thy heart, and suffer thy understanding to be enlightened by the divine light of truth! Be pure in heart, and thou shalt see God! and when thou beholdest this fountain of light, thou wilt also see the straight and narrow path, which leadeth to life; pray every morning to God, that he may give thee an opportunity of doing good, and if thou findest one, embrace it with all thy heart, and rest assured, that God will assist thee; and if thou hast succeeded, return thanks unto him in thy closet for it.

Before I close I feel I ought to say a word to my reader. It is a difficult task, to write the biography of one still living; every man has his foibles, faults and follies, and even sins accompany him through life, which are frequently of such a nature, that they cannot well be laid before the public; therefore the man, whose life is described, appears in a more favorable light than he ought : on the other hand it is likewise impossible to say all the good he does or has done, lest he should appear ostentatious. However I do not mean to write Henry Stilling's whole life and actions, but rather how Providence has led him through the difficulties and dangers of life. The great Judge will on the day of account lay his many faults on the golden scales of the sanctuary, his little good in the other, and thy eternal love, O merciful Saviour ! will accept him through the atonement which thou hast made on the tree of the cross.

L l

LIFE

OF

HENRY STILLING.

FIFTH BOOK.

Henry Stilling's apprentice years.

CHAPTER I.

Dear Reader and friend of Stilling ! You may take the title, "Henry Stilling's apprentice years" in what sense you please. He has hitherto been a teacher himself and has served in that capacity from the ranks upwards; he commenced as village schoolmaster at Zellberg, and ended as Professor at Marburg. But he has been at the same time a scholar and an apprentice in the work-shop of the best and greatest of masters, time will soon show, whether he may become a journeyman—to rise higher, would be impossible, in as much as we all have but one master and can have no more.

Stilling was at that time firmly persuaded that the professorship of Political Economy was the calling for which Providence had prepared him from his youth, and that Marburg was the place where he was to labor, until the Lord should see fit to call him from the field of action. This conviction was very satisfactory, and stimulated him to exertions in faithfully discharging the duties of his calling: he wrote his large work on State polity, his compend on the Science of Finances, his Compendium Camerale Practicum, his Fundamental Doctrine of State Economy; Henry Stilling's domestic life ; besides many other small treatises and pamphlets on various subjects ; he likewise relieved many, who where afflicted with deceases of the eye and the cataract. He lectured daily four and even five hours, and his correspondence increased from year to year, so that he was obliged to labor hard, that no part of his duties might be neglected; but in the multiplicity of his engagements he found great relief in the friendly and neighborly disposition of the inhabitants of Marburg. This ancient city is situated on the declivity of a mountain, the brow of which is adorned by an ancient castle. Its narrow streets & indifferent buildings leave an unpleasant impression on the mind of the passing stranger, but whoever has an opportunity of becoming acquainted with the pleasant state of society in that city, will acknowledge, that similar cordiality and disinterested friendship are seldom to be met with in any other place. The beauties of nature, which surround the town likewise contribute their share in making an abode at Marburg pleasant and agreeable. The first family, which opened the arms of friendship to Stilling and Selma was that of Professor Coing. Dr. Coing was professor of theology, and a real christian, a man of a friendly, mild, pleasing and benevolent disposition; his lady was likewise an eminently pious woman, and resembled her husband very much in disposition and character; her family name was Duising. They were both descendants of French refugees. They had four children, one son and three daughters, all of whom had reached the years of maturity; the names of the daughters were; Elisa, Maria and Amelia, the son was called Justus, he was a student of divinity: They all resembled their parents in character, were examples of christian and domestic virtue; and the whole family led a very retired life.

Many were the causes which cemented the bond of friendship between the families; Coing and Stilling were countrymen, relatives on both sides had intermarried; Parson Kraft at Frankfort, Stilling's old and faithful friend was a brother-in-law of Mr. Coing; and what is more than all, the families on both sides were christians; for where the spirit of christianity reigns, hearts become united by this bond of perfection in a manner, which far exceeds every bond of consanguinity: and happy is he, who has made this blessed experience. Selma became particularly attached to Elisa Coing: equality of age, and probably other causes depending on the character of these two ladies, laid the foundation of the closest friendship and intimacy. Stilling's mind was much affected during the first winter of his stay at Marburg by his overwhelming business and by the cramp in the stomach, so that he lost his cheerfulness and became extremely melancholy. Selma therefore persuaded him to undertake a journey during the Easter-vacation to her relations in Franconia and Suabia. In the spring of 1788 he sat out on this journey accompanied by a student from Anspach. In this city he visited the lyric poet Uz. He entered the house with some reserve; the poet, a man of small stature and somewhat corpulent met him with distant politeness and naturally waited for the stranger to introduce himself. No sooner was this over, when the worthy, aged man embraced him with these words : "You are then Henry Stilling ; I am glad to see the man, whom Providence so wonderfully directs, and who with so much frankness professes the religion of Christ and so courageously defends its principles." They then conversed about poets and poetry; on taking leave Uz embraced him again with these words : "May God bless, strengthen and preserve you! Cease not to defend the cause of religion and to follow our head and redeemer in bearing his cross! Our present time requires such men, and the rising generation will need them still more! In a better life, we shall meet each other again with joy!" Stilling returned to his lodgings deeply affected and strengthened by this visit.

Uz, Cramer and Klopstock will probably be the Asaphs, Hemans and Jedithuns in the temple of the New Jerusalem.

The next morning Stilling rode fifteen miles further to Kemathen a village not far from Dunkelsbuhl. Having arrived at the parsonage, he knocked at the gate, which was opened by the parson, a handsome man of a dark complexion, who was exceedingly surprised at seeing his brother Stilling, having no intimation of his visit. His wife meanwhile was engaged in domestic occupations, and was not much pleased to be interrupted by a visitor, she however received the stranger with her usual politeness; but when he called her sister and saluted her in the name of Selma she sunk in his embrace. Stilling spent several happy days with brother Hobach and sister Sophia, who accompanied her brother-in-law to Wallerstine, the residence of her own brother; at Oettingen they passed the church-yard, where Selma's and Sophia's father sleeps, and at Baldingen they visited the grave of their mother and in both places paid the tribute of grateful remembrance to the memory of these dear relatives. When prince Ernst of Wallerstine had heard of his arrival, he invited him to the princely table during his stay; which invitation Stilling accepted in regard to dinners only, but reserved his evening hours for the circle of his friends. After an agreeable stay of ten days at Wallerstine he sat out on his journey for home. At Frankfort he found his daughter Hannah at the house of his friend Kraft. She had been for some time with her relatives in the country of the lower Rhine, both were rejoiced to meet again after so long a separation. From Frankfort they traveled together to Giessen, whither Selma, Mr. Coing and Elisa, had come to meet them, in whose company they returned to Marburg. About this time the tutor of two young counts arrived at Marburg where his pupils were to study under his direction and superintendence. I shall call him Rashman. He was a candidate of Theology, a man of extraordinary talents, of a penetrating judgment, highly polished manners, and of great mental powers. He was likewise a severe critic of all men with whom he came in contact; to study a man's character was his favorite occupation; in every company he watched the words and actions of all persons present with an eagle's eye, and then gave a decided opinion of their character; exercise in this art had enabled him to judge with much precision, though his judgments were not always guided by charity. He had however given the young counts a most excellent education, and they now rank among the best characters of the age. Mr. Rashman had been in close connection with a certain secret society, and had there chiefly obtained his knowledge of human nature. He was fond of parade and of a good table, and always drank the best wines. In his intercourse with others he was very exact, difficult to please, choleric, and a hard master to servants. This singular man sought Stilling's friendship, he and the two young counts attended his lectures, and paid weekly several visits at his house. Stilling was frequently invited to dine with them, and found much pleasure in his conversation, though their religious sentiments were not in harmony. In the course of the summer of 1788 Mr. Mieg, church counsellor at Hidleberg and his lady paid a visit to Stilling and Selma. The honesty, the unceasing activity in doing good and the affectionately beneficent heart of counsellor Mieg, had made a favorable imprression upon the mind of Stilling, and a similar disposition had led Mrs. Mieg and Selma into the bonds of the most intimate friendship. This visit not only united the two families still more closely, but had likewise an important influence upon Stilling's philosophical System and whole manner of thinking. In consequence of having adopted the system of Wolf's and Leibnitz's Philosophy, he could not rid himself of the doctrine of fatalism: for twenty years he had been contending with this giant by prayer and supplication to the Lord, without being able to slay him. The freedom of the will and of human actions he had always asserted in his writings and believed against all the objections of his own reason, and continued to pray, though fatalism whispered into his ear, thy prayers are of no avail, for what God has decreed, must come to pass whether thou prayest or not. And though he had experienced various proofs of answers to his prayers, fatalism would reply: "These are mere accidental incidents." What a temptation ! All the delights of religion, its promises for the present and the future world, our only comfort in life, in sufferings and in death, become a deluding image of the imagination, as soon as we listen to the insinuations of fatalism. Mieg effected Stilling's enlargement from the horrors of this prison, by accidentally mentioning a certain treatise on Kant's Philosophy, which had pleased him much, and by adducing one of the postulates of Kant's ethical system: that we should always act in such a manner, that the maxim of our conduct may be universally right and applicable.

This excited Stilling's attention, the novelty of the sentiment made a deep impression on his mind, and he resolved, to read Kant's works, which he had hitherto refrained from doing, because the study of a new system of philosophy and especially that of Kant, had appeared to him incompatible with his duties.

He naturally commenced with Kant's Critique of pure reason, he readily comprehended its meaning, which at once ended his conflict with fatalism. Kant proves in that work, that human reason knows nothing beyond the boundaries of that world to which our senses reach; that this reason always contradicts itself in attempting to judge of supernatural things according to principles applicable only to sensible objects, in short, this book is a complete commentary on the words of the Apostle: "the natural man i. e. the unconverted man, receives not the things of the Spirit of God, for they are foolishness unto him." To describe the satisfaction which Stilling experienced in consequence of this discovery would be in vain; hitherto it had been grievous to him to think, that human reason, this inestimable gift, which distinguishes us from the brute creation, should be opposed to religion, which was dearer to him than life; but now he found every thing as it ought to be; he discovered the fountain of every spiritual truth, in the revelation of God to man, i. e. in the Bible, and the fountain of all those truths, which belong to and are necessary for this natural life, in nature and in reason. In a letter which Stilling wrote to Kant, he expressed his approbation of this principle: and in Kant's answer he found the following important expression: "You do well to seek peace and rest of mind solely in the gospel, for it is a never failing fountain of all those truths, which, when reason has exhausted all her resources, are no where to be found, but in that blessed volume." Afterward Stilling read Kant's Critique of practical Reason and then his Religion within the bounds of Reason. At first he thought he had found probability in both these works; but after a closer examination he observed, that Kant did not seek the fountain of supernatural truths in the gospel, but in the moral structure of our nature. But how is it possible, that this moral sense which bids the Mexican to bring human sacrifices to the Gods; which urges the Iroquois or Delawar Indian to scalp and murder innocent women and children, could be considered as the fountain of truths which lie beyond the sphere of our senses? But if it be objected, not the corrupt but the pure moral sense is this fountain, I answer: The pure moral principle is a mere imaginary, theoretical capacity to discern good from evil; but where is the man, who is in possession of this pure capacity ? for all are by nature depraved and oft times led astray by many errors, so that they mistake evil for good, and good for evil. But before our moral sense can be regarded as an infallible guide in human actions, our moral nature itself must be corrected, which can be done only through the influence of revealed truth. It is undeniable, that every postulate of morality is an immediate revelation from God ; and what the wisest of pagans knew on this subject, they derived indirectly from the light of revelation. Stilling however was thankful for the knowledge which he had gained from the reading of Kant's critique of pure reason, and it is his sincere opinion, that this book is and remains the only possible philosophy, this word being taken in its usual acceptation.

Though Stilling was perfectly satisfied on that head, a still greater danger threatened him : his connection with Rashman familiarized him with ideas, which singly considered, did not appear dangerous, but which, when taken as a whole and in their consequences were calculated to lead him first to Socinianism, then to Deism, thence to Naturalism, and finally to Atheism. His heavenly guide however did not suffer him to fall so low, but it was bad enough, that he began to consider the atonement of Christ as an oriental figure of the moral merits of the Messiah.

Rashman represented these ideas with so much warmth and reverence toward the Redeemer, and with so much apparent love to him, that Stilling began to be convinced of their truth. But his religious ideas and experience were so deeply rooted in his whole existence, that his defection could not well proceed any farther.

This situation lasted almost a year, and a certain lady of great piety will still recollect of having received about that time a letter from him, in consequence of which she withdrew her friendship and esteem, until he again adopted more scriptural sentiments on this subject. When he began to come to himself, he observed with astonishment, how far his heart had removed from the simplicity of the gospel ; that sinful and

M m

sensual inclinations again were rising in his mind, and that
the peace of God, which passeth all understanding, was becoming daily more faint in his soul. The faithful Shepherd however led him again into the right path, and the sequel of his history will show, what means were employed to effect this purpose.

CHAPTER II.

In the winter of 1788 the countess of Stolberg-Wernigerode
invited Stilling, to pay her a visit during the next Easter-vacation. He replied, that if there were any blind in that neighborhood afflicted with the cataract he would come, but on no other
condition. This caused the count of Wernigerode to publish in
his territories, that all persons afflicted with this disease should
assemble the week before Easter at his castle, as he expected a
visit from an eminent oculist from Marburg.

When Stilling received the assurance that such patients
might be expected, he undertook the journey on horseback and arrived on Good Friday evening at the castle
of Wernigerode, where he was received with uncommon
condescension and friendship by the whole family. Eleven persons afflicted with the cataract were quartered in the
castle, on whom he performed the operation on Easter-morning.
Among them was a woman, twenty-eight years of age, who in
going from Andreasberg to Ilsenburg had stuck fast in a snow
drift as she passed the Brocken. The snow had fallen so deep
that it finally reached over her head, and she could proceed no
farther. She had remained for twenty-four hours in the snow
in a kind of lethargy, and the only injurious consequence of this
accident had been that a cataract was formed over her eye, from
which she was relieved by the operation. There was likewise
an aged man and his sister among the blind at the castle of Wernigerode, who had not seen each other for twenty years. When
both were cured and met for the first time, they stared at each
other for several minutes in utter amazement, because they
looked so old.

The time which Stilling spent at Wernigerode in the circle of this excellent and pious family will never be forgotten by him. A week after Easter he returned to Marburg. A few weeks afterwards the count of Wernigerode with his family passed through Marburg on his journey to Switzerland; they visited Stilling and Selma and the count promised to be back by the 12th of September, to assist in celebrating Stilling's birth-day; and he kept his word. Selma received the news of their coming a few days previous, and had a dinner prepared, to which likewise Rashman and the young counts his pupils together with many other Marburg friends were invited. His birth-day had never before been celebrated with so much splendor, his lecturing desk was handsomely decorated, and Mr. Rashman pronounced an oration in honor of the day. It was somewhat singular, that his Jubilee was so formally celebrated, without any particular reference to it; every thing happened as it were by chance: he thought afterwards of it, and it soon appeared, that this celebration was his initiation to a new period of his life.

Soon after in the autumn of 1789 the vacation commenced, during which Stilling made a journey into the Dutchy of Darmstadt, and thence to Newwied, to perform operations on persons suffering with the cataract. Rashman, the young counts and Selma accompanied him as far as Frankfort, whence he went to Russelhime on the Mayn, where Mrs. Sartorius the lady of the minister of that place, was cured of the cataract. He spent nine days in the happy circle of this christian family, and here he discovered for the first time his imminent danger of apostatizing from religion, which he however providentially escaped. Parson Sartorius was a man of the old Halle or Franke's school, and spoke with him on religious subjects in that style, especially of the atonement and the imputed righteousness. Without intending it, he was involved in a dispute with him on these subjects, and here commenced his return to the truth. At Darmstadt Stilling performed operations on a number of persons; one man however would not consent to the operation, but preferred, as he said, to remain blind to the glory of God; for when he was informed of Stilling's arrival, and that with God's blessing his sight might be restored, he answered very calmly : "The Lord has given me this cross to bear and to his glory I will bear it !"— What a mistaken notion ! From Darmstadt he went to Mainz, and thence in a covered boat down the Rhine to Newwied, where he arrived about four o'clock in the afternoon, and was surprised to find that Mr. Rashman, the two young counts and Professor Erxleben from Marburg had arrived there before him. Stilling's journey to Newwied is remarkable in the history of his life, because he saw there one of the settlements of the Moravian brethren for the first time. On Sunday he was present at their religious exercises. Mr. Duvernoy preached an excellent sermon. Every thing he saw and heard made a deep impression on his mind, to which Rashman greatly contributed: though widely differing from this society in religious sentiments he spoke with much esteem and enthusiam of the brethren. His Highness Prince John Fredrick Alexander of Newwied, celebrated for his wisdom and maxims of general toleration, was then with his lady at his country-seat Monrepos, about nine miles from the city, situated at the upper end of the valley on the side of a mountain, from which there is one of the finest prospects in the world. He invited Professor Erxleben and Stilling to dine at his country-seat and sent his equipage for them. A christian friendship commenced between the aged princess and Stilling, which was kept up by a frequent correspondence, until this pious and noble minded lady exchanged this world for a better ; and Stilling anticipates with joy her welcome in the happy fields of everlasting bliss. Having performed several operations at Newwied he returned in company of his friend and colleague Erxleben to Marburg. At Wetzlar he expected to find a letter from Selma, but was disappointed. Entering the parsonage-house of friend Makenhower he perceived a certain uneasiness in his and his wife's countenance and of course immediately inquired whether any letter from Selma had arrived ? They answered him : Selma is not very well, though not dangerously ill ; this we are commissioned by her to tell you. He hired immediately a post-chaise and arrived in the afternoon at Marburg. He met Hannah unexpectedly in the hall, who had been sick for some months at Selma's sister in Suabia and had returned during his absence. From her he learnt, that Selma was not dangerously ill. Going up stairs he saw her standing at the head of the stairs, pale and weak ; but smiling through her tears, she observed with a tender look : "My dear, be not uneasy, nothing particular is the matter with me."

This assurance composed his mind in some measure and he entered the room with Selma. She had been the last spring unfortunate in child-bed. A very handsome boy was still-born. An alarm of fire in our neighborhood had probably been the cause of this misfortune and its consequences. She was now again expecting to be confined, and Stilling thought her present indisposition was owing to that cause, in which opinion he was confirmed, as she soon became better. One day, soon after his return from Newwied he was sitting with Selma on the sofa, when to his great surprise she addressed him in the following manner : "My dear husband ! I beg you to listen tranquilly to what I have to say ; I am sure, that I shall die during my next confinement. If you wish me to spend the remaining part of my time with any kind of comfort, or if you wish me to die in peace, you must promise me to marry my friend Eliza Coing, she will suit you better than I do, and I know, that she will make a good mother for my children and an excellent wife for you. Lay every thing aside which custom and the laws of society require, and give me your promise ! My dear Henry, you won't refuse me !"

The reader may judge of his feelings at that moment and may readily think, that he did not give her the desired promise. When he had recovered in some measure from his great surprise, he gave her the following answer : "My dear child ! you know yourself, that whenever you have been in circumstances like the present, you have been sure of your death, and you still live ; I hope, and trust to Providence, that you will get through this time also, and even should this not be the case, do you not see, that it would be against all the rules of common decency for me to give you such a promise?" Selma appeared to be greatly distressed at this declaration and replied : "It is a pity, that you cannot lay all these things aside to satisfy me ! I am sure, I

shall die, every thing is very different from what it used to be."
During the whole winter Selma prepared herself for her death
as for a long journey, and endeavored with great serenity of
mind to arrange every thing in proper order. At the same time
she continued importuning him to give her the promise she so much
desired, and even went to extremes in order to accomplish her
object. One evening for instance it happened that Eliza was
at supper at their house, and none of the children were
present ; towards the end of supper Selma looked with
much tenderness at her and said : "Will you my dear Eliza, marry my husband when I am gone?" The situation of Stilling and Eliza at that moment was indescribable. She blushed
deeply and said: Selma, "I beg you don't talk so !" and Stilling
lectured her severely on account of this unbecoming behavior.
When she saw, that she could not prevail with her husband, she
made application to such of his friends as she knew had the greatest influence with him, and continued to intreat them to see, that
her wishes might be accomplished after her death.

In the spring of 1790 the important moment of Selma's delivery was approaching, Stilling began to pray earnestly for her
life, but she remained undisturbed and unmoved. May the 11th she
was delivered of a son; she was as well and better than she
had been in similar circumstances. He rejoiced thanking his
God, and began to tell Selma how vain and idle had been
all her forebodings, but she looked at him very seriously and said : "My dear husband, we are not over all difficulties yet." For five days she was quite smart, and gave suck
to the child, but on the sixth day an eruption broke out on her
skin, she became very sick, and Stilling's soul was overwhelmed
with grief. Friend Eliza came to nurse her, Hannah helped
all she could, and Mrs. Coing came daily to relieve her daughter.
Stilling however still entertained hopes of Selma's recovery, but
one afternoon as he was sitting alone by her bed-side. he observed, that she became flighty and began to pick the bed-clothes.
He immediately left the house and town, and ran to a solitary
place on the castle hill. and prayed fervently, not for Selma's life,
for he demanded no miracle, but for strength for his weary soul,

to enable him to bear this severe dispensation of Divine Providence. His prayer was heard, he returned to his house resigned to the will of the Lord. From this time he saw Selma only twice for a few moments, for his constitution suffered too much, and his friends therefore insisted on his keeping from the sick chamber. The next day in the afternoon he went to her bedside; she was then afflicted with the lockjaw and Eliza sat nodding on the sofa, to take a little rest; Selma raised her half broken eyes, looked tenderly at her husband, and pointed with her finger to Eliza.—Stilling cast his eyes to the ground, and left the room. The next morning he went again to her bed-side—that moment Stilling never can forget. She seemed like a being, which belongs to another world. When he asked her, how she was, she audibly breathed through her teeth : very well ! He could not long bear this scene, his frame was too weak, and his heart too much affected, he left the room and saw Selma no more. Eliza could neither bear to witness the last struggles of her friend, but Mrs. Coing assisted her in her last moments. She departed the next night May the 23d at one o'clock in the morning ; the friends came weeping to Stilling's bed-side to bring him the melancholy news—his answer was: "Lord ! thy will be done !"

CHAPTER III.

Selma —— dead ! the wife which was Stilling's joy and pride —— dead ! God however had given him more than resignation, heavenly peace pervaded his heart, though his constitution was suffering. The continual attacks of the cramp in the stomach had shattered his nervous system, and this severe stroke might have done great injury, if God's paternal goodness had not peculiarly supported him. All was now dead and silent about him. For Christina's departure he had been prepared by long and tedious sufferings, but now matters were very different. Selma had indeed frequently declared that she henceforth would not be a suitable companion for him in his walk through life, and the sequel proved that she had spoken the truth, but her departure was heart-rending and almost insupportable! She had been a valuable treasure! A noble instrument in the hand of her heavenly father to him! and now she was no more! She had been an angel to him in his economical affairs. She was an excellent house-keeper; notwithstanding a moderate income at Lautern and at Hidleberg she had paid better than two thousand guilders of his debts, and the remaining creditors became willing to wait, when they saw a prospect of receiving their money. But what was more to him than all this, she had taken every care upon herself so that from the time he married her he was like a ship-wrecked mariner, who had been in imminent danger of drowning, whom a benevolent hand has assisted in drawing to the shore. *"Mind your business,* she used to say, *and nothing else, the cares I'll take on my shoulders."* And she faithfully kept her word, during the nine years, she was his wife. I have to beg the reader, not to take Selma's words, that henceforth she was no longer a suitable companion for Stilling, in a way that they were not intended to be taken. The plan according to which God led Stilling, was so plainly visible, that every person attentive to the ways of Providence could observe it. Even Rashman saw it, and frequently said: "Providence must have something particular in view with you; every thing, which happens to you, seems to have a bearing to one great end, which is yet hidden in the dark recesses of the future. Stilling was convinced of this, and it bowed him down in the dust, but it gave him likewise courage to fight the heavenly fight, and to increase in faith and love towards the redeemer of the world.

Selma was a corpse—Hannah, a girl between sixteen and seventeen years of age, undertook with courage the helm of affairs, and a faithful good servant, whom Selma had hired at Lautern, assisted Hannah in all things. Of six children which Selma had born, three were living viz: Lisette, Caroline and the little orphan. Lisette was better than four, Caroline two and a half years old. Selma was not yet full thirty years old when she died. In her bridal days she had told him: "You will not have me long, for I have forebodings that I shall not reach my thirtieth year."

Though Hannah was a good girl, and did all she could to aid in the education of her younger brothers and sisters, still her task was too great; Providence however provided a place for Lisette with friend Mieg in Hidleberg, and for Caroline with a female friend not far from Marburg.

Counsellor Ries of Marburg an intimate friend and colleague of Stilling, invited him after Selma's death to his house, and undertook the management of the funeral. His Lady procured a good nurse for Selma's infant, so that Stilling was free from all cares of that description. The child was baptized in Mr. Ries' house and Mr. Ries, Coing, Rashman and the two young counts stood god-fathers.

As soon as Stilling had removed again to his own house, he sent for his aged father William Stilling, whose resignation under sufferings, likewise imparted comfort to his son. Father William stayed about a fortnight in Marburg. During this time Stilling recovered his strength, to which Selma's last will greatly contributed. It was a matter of course that he should marry again, for the education of his small children, and the superintendence of his domestic affairs required it; for it could not be expected, that Hannah should refuse a suitable offer of marriage, because her father wished to retain her as housekeeper. How satisfactory was it therefore, that the legitimate possessor of his heart had appointed her successor in such a manner, that Stilling himself would not have made another choice.

Whoever has not had the experience, can scarcely believe it, how consoling it is for a widower to know, that his departed wife approves of his choice! And in his case it was more than mere approbation.—

After the expiration of the time, which decorum and the laws prescribe, he solicited the hand of Eliza, and both she and her parents gladdened his heart by their consent: the assurance of the approbation of God, of the accomplishment of Selma's last wish, and the knowledge that this marriage was approved by all good men, imparted an indescribable tranquility to his mind.

N n

Henceforth Eliza took the education of Caroline upon herself; she also visited Hannah from time to time, assisting her by counsel and advice, and Stilling himself had found again a friend, to whom he could communicate every secret of his heart.

The 12th day of September was now approaching, which as the anniversary of his birth-day had been so splendidly celebrated the last year, which had been a time of sufferings and affliction to him. The hereditary Prince of Hessencassel was at that time studying at the university of Marburg, to whom Stilling gave weekly four lectures. On his birth-day he and Mr. Coing received an invitation to dine with the Prince, the evening was spent in Coing's family.

The 19th day of November was fixed for their marriage. He first gave his usual four lectures, attended to the lessons of the Prince of Hesse, and afterwards went to Coing's house, where the wedding was to take place. A number of friends were invited to the wedding dinner, and the reformed minister Starbaum performed the marriage-ceremony.

Calm and joyful was this evening —— with it commenced a new period of life, which greatly distinguished itself from all the preceding, and which brought Stilling nearer his final destination. Eliza likewise entered cheerfully and in reliance on God's gracious assistance on her new sphere of action, and she soon experienced, what a certain friend had told her before her marriage, "that it was difficult, to travel the same road with Stilling."——But she has hitherto faithfully and firmly performed her pilgrimage, and has always evinced by her actions, that she knows her duty and how to perform it.

A few weeks before his wedding Rashman and the young counts had left Marburg. He was a comet, which had accompanied the planet Stilling for some time in its orbit, and whose atmosphere had exercised a detrimental influence upon the latter. But in the new family circle in which he was moving every injurious consequence soon disappeared, and by means of some other co-operative causes he became more firmly established in the doctrine of Christ's atonement than he had ever been before, and the sequel proved, that Rashman in a remarkable manner became one of the instruments in the hand of God for the completion of Stilling's education: through Rashman he learnt many great secrets and made important discoveries;—what Barruel and the triumph of Philosophy desire to relate, and in substance correctly relate, though they err in minor circumstances, became thus known to him.

The reader however ought not to suppose, that Rashman designedly instructed him in all these things: he was very talkative, and whenever any of his friends dined with him, some fragment or other would make its appearance, and Stilling, who was gifted with an excellent memory, perfectly retained, what he had heard, and thus he learnt during the three years of Rashman's stay at Marburg the whole connection of all that. which since has produced those great and terrible phenomena both in church and state; and uniting his own experience, and what he had read on this subject, with the fragments he learnt from Rashman, he obtained a correct view of the whole. How useful and necessary this knowledge was, is, and in future will be to him, *he* only can judge, who has a clear view of the designs of Providence with Stilling.

———◆———

CHAPTER IV.

The first few weeks after Eliza's marriage were days of happiness, her way was strewed with flowers. Stilling likewise enjoyed a reprieve from his sufferings, but a fortnight before Christmas trials of various kinds were visiting him again.

Hannah had from her childhood severely suffered from a tetter on her left cheek, Selma had employed every possible means to relieve her, and Eliza was faithfully treading in her footsteps. About the above mentioned time a celebrated physician came to Marburg, who was consulted on the occasion, and ordered the use of sublimate as an exterior application. It is difficult to say, whether this application, or a predisposition inherited from her mother, or both together produced the terrible consequences—certain it is, that Hannah was afflicted about this time with severe paroxysms of the cramp. These fits, deeply afflictive to every spectator were so in a peculiar manner to Eliza: nevertheless she gathered sufficient courage faithfully to nurse poor Hannah, and God preserved her from all injury.

This was the first act of the tragedy, the second, which followed, was a severe trial for Stilling, Eliza and Hannah. I will relate it as a warning example to young people of both sexes, yet in such a manner, that the feelings of a worthy family may not be wounded by the recital.

Hannah being one day in company had been particularly requested to play and sing—what could be more harmless than this —and yet it became the sole cause of painful sufferings to the family, which continued for more than six months. A young man, who was studying Theology, whose will had never been broken, whom Hannah had never seen before, happened to be in the company, and became so enraptured with her music, that from this time he employed every means, the most desperate not excepted, in order to obtain her. In the first place he made application to her parents, and receiving in answer, that there would be no objections on their part, after he should have a suitable situation, and should have obtained Hannah's consent, he was still dissatisfied, and insisted on it, that the parents should give him a positive promise. Hannah on her part declared, that she could never love and would never marry him, and that she had never given him the least encouragement. But all this was of no avail, he again applied to her parents, endeavoring to prove, that it was their duty, to compel their daughter to marry him. Not being able to effect any thing in this way, he attempted force, came one day quite unexpectedly into Stilling's house, at a time, when he was engaged in lecturing, and rushed into Hannah's room; luckily a female friend was with her, their screams were heard by the father, he and brother Coing hastened to Hannah's relief and both severely reprimanded the foolish fellow. He then took lodgings in a tavern opposite her parent's house, that he might repeat the tragedy whenever he pleased; but Hannah was taken to a place of safety at a distance, and the fellow quitted his lodgings. At another time he came again unexpectedly to the house; Hannah happened to be absent; he behaved so savage and unmannerly, that Stilling thrust him out of the house; he forthwith ran to Mr. Coing's, where Mrs. Coing was lying very sick in bed; Eliza pushed him out of the house, which brought to him such despair, that he rushed to the river Lahn to drown himself, he was however brought back, and threw himself on the ground before Stilling's house; with great trouble he was induced to return to his parents, who lived several miles from Marburg; afterwards he wandered about in the country, overwhelming Stilling with threatening letters, so that the latter was finally compelled to seek aid from the police. The poor fellow then traveled from home, and died in the flower of his age.

This severe and fiery trial was made up to Hannah by a blessing. A young minister by the name of Schwartz, having charge of the congregation at Derbach, a village about fifteen miles distant from Marburg, had for some time lived on a familiar footing with Stilling. Being yet unmarried, his mother and sister Caroline kept house for him. Caroline was an intimate friend of Hannah, and was on a visit to her, when the above mentioned candidate of Theology suddenly entered her room, and she had taken Hannah to her mother as to a safe asylum. While there, Schwartz and Hannah became attached to each other, the parents gave their consent, and the goodness of God crowned this union with his favor.

CHAPTER V.

The struggle with the candidate had taken place in the early part of 1791; and this portion of that year became further distinguished by two death's in Stilling's family. In the month of February little Francis, Selma's last child died with the dropsy in the head. Mrs. Coing was likewise gradually approaching her dissolution. She had been for some time very weakly and asthmatic. By works of love and watchings at sick-beds she had probably caught a severe cold, which brought on a consumption. Stilling visited her frequently, she was always resigned and happy, and whenever she thought with some anxiety of her children, he gave her the assurance, that he would consider them as his own, if the parents should die before him.

All these mournful occurrences, exercised a detrimental influence upon Eliza's health, she likewise became sick, though not dangerously, yet so, that she was confined to her bed, which troubled her the more, because it disabled her from seeing her mother. But they both sent daily messages to each other with the comforting assurance, that neither was dangerously ill.

One morning early towards the latter part of March the message arrived, that Mrs. Coing had fallen asleep in the Lord, and it became Stilling's duty, to break these mournful tidings to Eliza—a difficult task,—he performed it however, and then hastened into the paternal house. As he entered the room, the corpse immediately met his eyes—she had been a handsome woman, and her continued walk in the precepts of the christian religion, had enobled as it were, all the traits of her countenance; the lineaments of her face expressed—not the hope, but the enjoyment of everlasting life.—Her bereaved husband stood before the corpse, looked at Stilling with a smile, and said: "God be praised, she is with her Savior"—he mourned, but as a christian mourns.

To know that our dear departed friends have gone to a place of happiness fills the soul with comfort and joy.—Mr. Coing, who had celebrated his birth-day about this time, had prayed to God to grant him the life of the partner of his griefs and joys as a birth-day present, but he did not obtain his wishes; Stilling had prayed during half a year for the life of Selma and was not heard.—But christian readers! Let not such examples deter you from offering up your prayers and supplications to God—our heavenly Father wills, that we his children shall ask him for every thing,—because such prayer preserves our attachment to him and the sense of our dependence on him: if he sees not fit to give us what we ask, we may rest assured, he will give us something better for it. The Lord answers every prayer which is offered up in faith, we always receive some good

by means of it, which we otherwise would not have obtained, and
we receive that which is best for us.

If the christian is so far advanced, that he continues to walk
always as in the presence of God, and has sacrificed his own will
without reserve to the good will of God, he will then be praying
without ceasing, and the Spirit of the Lord will make intercession
for us with groanings which cannot be uttered; for the holy
Spirit knows what is the will of God; if *he* therefore excites
the heart to pray for something, he also gives us faith and assurance of being heard; the christian prays then and is heard.

Stilling and Eliza had resolved immediately after their
marriage to take Jacob his eldest son home again; he was now
seventeen years of age; of course old enough to enter the university; he had hitherto received the private instructions of the worthy and learned pastor Grimm near Heilbron. As Stilling could
undertake no journeys except in vacations, he desired Jacob, to
come on a certain day during the Easter-vacation to friend
Mieg at Hidleberg where his parents would meet him and take
him home. They also resolved to bring Lisette back at the
same time, for Eliza was desirous of having all the four children together, in order to be enabled to perform her maternal
duties with regard to them in the manner she desired. Wishing
also to give the elder Mr. Coing and his children some diversion,
they agreed to take them all as far as Frankfort to friend Kraft's.
This plan was in all its parts executed during the Easter-vacation of 1791. Soon after their arrival in Hidleberg Jacob made his
appearance: he had become a good young man, in whom his parents
could rejoice, and he was glad on his part at having the prospect of
living once more in the bosom of the family. Difficulties however
arose in regard to the plan of taking Lisette home, Mrs. Mieg,
who had no children, was desirous of keeping her, and she likewise declared, that her mother's life would be endangered, if
the little girl should be taken away, in consequence of her attachment to her. Both Stilling and Eliza were very sorry that
they were obliged to leave their little daughter at Hidleberg, for
Eliza believed it to be *her* duty to educate the children of her departed friend, and that they would be demanded from her hand

alone; however at length both parents consented to leave the dear little girl in the care of friend Mieg, and the sequel will show, that she was well taken care of. They then returned with their son to Frankfort, and after a short stay in that city, the whole company returned to Marburg.

In the autumn of 1791 Eliza was delivered of a daughter, who received the name of Lubecka. On Newyears-day of 1791 Stilling was chosen Provost by the university; this office is at Marburg held in high estimation, but at the same time connected with greater difficulties than in any other university: he entered upon it in reliance on the divine assistance, and truly! he needed it during the year more than ever. About Easter Hannah's marriage approached; uncle Kraft with his wife and children, and father William Stilling were invited to the wedding. All came, and Stilling reckons these days among the happiest of his life: to his poor suffering father, this time was—as he expressed himself—a foretaste of heaven. Schwartz and Hannah were united in the bond of marriage in the house of their parents, with the blessing of all their relatives; their married state is happy, and they are doing well.

A young nobleman, the Prussian counsellor Vinke had for some time pursued his studies at Marburg, he lodged and boarded in Stilling's house, and was one of the best young men, that ever came to that university. In the spring of this year his father the Dean Von Vinke at Minden wrote, that in the course of the summer he intended to pay Stilling a visit with his wife and children. This visit took place according to promise, at the time, when the German Princes were making the campaign in Champagne, and when the Duke of Weimar came to Marburg with his regiment. Stilling made on that occasion the acquaintance of the Prince, he and the Dean spent an afternoon in his agreeable company. After the visiters had departed, the fatigue which Eliza had undergone, brought on a miscarriage; on the ninth day however, as the weather was very fine, she was again able to leave the room, a promenade in the garden was resolved upon, and Schwartz and Hannah who were on a visit to their mother, and old Mr. Coing participated likewise in this party.

The latter was uncommonly cheerful; but being afraid of the evening air, which was also injurious to Eliza, he went home with her at an early hour; and as he passed below along the garden-wall, the young people strewed flowers upon him from above.

The next morning at five o'clock Stilling's maid came into his bed-room to call him out; when he opened the door he saw Schwartz and Hannah standing in the open door of the opposite chamber, both very pale and with downcast eyes. "Dear father," said Schwartz, "what you have supposed, has taken place, father Coing has departed." These tidings were a severe affliction to Stilling,—how should he make them known to Eliza, who was still very weak, and loved her father tenderly!—but he endeavored to muster all his courage, went to her bed-side and said : "Eliza! one of our dear relatives has departed"—she immediately replied : "Good God! is it Hannah?"— "No" was his answer, "it is father Coing." — Eliza mourned, yet as a christian she soon recollected herself. — But this shock laid the foundation of a severe affliction, which she has still to bear. He then hastened to his dear brothers and sisters. All three stood in the room close together like a clover leaf, giving vent to their tears. He embraced them and said: "You are now all three my children ; as soon as possible, you shall remove into my house." This took place as soon as the funeral was over. The sequel will show, that this circumstance of having his wife's brother and sisters living with him became a source of great comfort to him. Mr. Coing had been suddenly attacked by an apoplectic fit ; a physician had been immediately called, and all possible means had been employed to save him, but in vain. He calmly assured his children, that he was willing to depart. He had been a man of an excellent character, and his blessing rests upon his children.

Here commences the most important period of Stilling's life, changes took place in and about him, which gave it a very remarkable direction, and which prepared him for his true and real destination.

O o

CHAPTER VI.

Soon after Mr. Coing's death it became necessary for Stilling as Provost of the Marburg university to attend the princely commissary in a journey to Lower Hessia, to inspect the bailiwicks, and to sell the tithes belonging to the university, to the highest bidder. The two friends Ries and Stilling therefore went together and the latter took Eliza along for the recovery of her health and spirits, which her last illness and the sudden death of her father had greatly impaired. After the business had been transacted, he returned by way of Cassel to Marburg. At Cassel Eliza began to observe a disagreeable sensation in the muscles of her neck, and on the right side of it an involuntary motion of the head towards the right shoulder became observable.

When the autumnal vacation approached, uncle Kraft informed him, that a rich blind Jewess in Frankfort was desirous to have an operation performed by Stilling, and offered to pay his traveling expenses if he would undertake the cure. He expressed his readiness to come, but because the Provost of the university is not permitted to stay a night out of town without special permission, he was under the necessity of applying to Cassel for leave of absence, which he soon received. His predecessor in office promised to do the official business for him until his return, and Eliza went with him. Having arrived towards evening at Vilbel a handsome village on the river Nidda about six miles from Frankfort, and stopt before a tavern, to bait the horses, the land-lady came in haste to the coach and exclaimed with great anxiety of mind : "Do you know, that the French have entered Germany, and have already taken the town of Speyer?" This news was like an electric shock to Stilling, but still he hoped it was a mere empty rumor, or that it was at least greatly exaggerated ; he therefore continued his journey to Frankfort, and arrived at Mr. Kraft's. Here he learnt, that the news were but too true, and the whole city was in fear and terror. It is here absolutely necessary, that I should make some observations on the singular impression which this news made upon him.

Lewis XIV king of France, after him the Regent, Duke of Orleans, and finally Lewis XV had in the space of a century led the French nation into an unexampled luxury; a nation sunk deep into voluptuousness will readily receive the witticisms of a Voltaire for Philosophy and the sophistic dreams of a Rousseau for religion: hence a national character will arise which is highly pleasing and enticing to the unconverted man, and as this character at the same time has an external polish and appears systematic, it likewise becomes interesting to the thinker, and thus obtains the approbation of every civilized nation. Hence it came, that the German nobility and literati considered France as the High School of fashion, politeness and morality. The vigorous and powerful German language was despised, every body spoke French; — French adventurers, even barbers, no matter who, provided he was a Frenchman — became the educators of our Princes, and French milliners the governesses in the first families of our country. The German character and with it religion, were thrown among the rubbish.

Some of the literati, especially the Theologians—seeing the danger—wished to extricate us from our troubles; and to do this effectually, chose the way of accomodation. They proposed peace between Christ and Belial, each one was to yield a little. Christ was to give up the doctrines of faith, Belial was to prohibit the grossest vices, and both should henceforth acknowledge nothing as the fundamental law of religion, but morality; for in that one article all were agreed, that morality must be believed and taught, but in regard to its practice it was left to the liberty of each individual, how much or little of it was necessary; for this liberty must by no means be infringed. This system of union was to be called—for honor's sake—the christian religion, in order not to give too great an offense to Christ and his true worshipers. Thus arose our famous system of enlightened religion, and the neology of the present day. But here I must intreat the reader not to misunderstand me! None of these men purposely intended to make peace between Christ and Belial; in as much as the very existence of the latter was no longer believed: but the spirit of the times had from our youth imperceptibly exercised an influence over our mode of perceiving, thinking and judging, whereby the moral sense of the nation was changed, so that many portions and narratives of the Bible were considered as superstitious, ridiculous and absurd, and that under the influence of such adulterated principles and organs of examination a revision of the Bible was undertaken. This was the commencement of the great apostacy, which Christ and his Apostles have so clearly foretold, and concerning which they have observed, that soon afterwards the man of sin, the incarnate Satan would make his appearance and would be cast into the abyss at the sudden arrival of our Lord.

Stilling had formed this view of the state of religion and of the kingdom of God, during a long series of years, partly by a careful study of history, partly by an attentive observation of the signs of the times, partly also by a diligent reading and reflection on the Biblical prophecies, and partly by communications, which he received from great and learned men: and its importance filled his soul; to all this ought to be added another observation, not less important, in complete harmony with all what has now been mentioned.

He had noticed the origin of a confederacy of men of all ranks, he had watched its growth and progress as well as its principles, and had found that its aim was no less, than an exchange of the christian for natural religion and by a singular direction of Divide Providence he had learnt through Rashman how far this confederacy had already succeeded, and all this took place at the very time, when the French revolution was commencing. He knew that the German members of this league were intimately connected with the French Jacobins, and was therefore sufficiently at home in the History of the times and in their relation to the Biblical prophecies.

The result which this knowledge produced in Stilling's mind was as follows: that Germany would be severely chastised by France, for having adopted the impious principles of this nation, he foresaw the great contest, by means of which this chastisement was to be given; for wherein a man sins,thereby he is also punished, and in as much as the apostacy in Germany continually increased he thought he could observe the gradual preparations for the establishment of the kingdom of the man of sin. That all these ideas really existed in his mind, before any one thought of the French revolution and its consequences, several passages in his writings testify and especially the oration, which he pronounced in the year 1786 before the German Society atManhime, which however has never been published for reasons, which may readily be deciphered. But notwithstanding all these convictions, he had no idea, that the storm would break loose so soon and so suddenly over Germany; he indeed suspected, that the French revolution would lay the foundation for the last great contest between light and darkness, but he did not suppose that this conflict was so near at hand; for he entertained no doubt, that the united powers of Germany would prove victorious in France—but events turned out very differently—Stilling's feelings on the occasion were therefore indescribable; to have on the one hand the accomplishment of the highest expectations of the christian approximating, on the other the prospect of unheard of afflictions and persecution, which would be the unavoidable consequences of the approaching conflict. Truly! a state of mind, which might easily have crushed a man, who during his life had labored so much, and was still laboring, unless Providence had preserved him for important purposes.

We might suppose, that these trials were severe enough, but during this time of anguish and high excitement, God laid another affliction upon him, for reasons which are only known to him: it has been already observed, that terror had brought upon Eliza an involuntary motion of the head towards the right side of her body, at a time when her constitution had been impaired by a severe illness; hitherto this evil had not manifested itself in its full malignity, but during the stay at Frankfort, it took an alarming turn. A rumor was spread during the second day of their visit in this city, that the French army was approaching; the city council assembled at the Rœmer, hogsheads filled with water were ordered to be kept ready in each house, so as to enable the inhabitants to extinguish the fires in case of a bombardment; in short, the general terror was indescribably great; but in regard to Eliza a peculiar circumstance greatly increased it. The university of Marburg, of which Stilling was Provost, was one of the States of Hessia, and the Landgrave was at war with France. Nothing was therefore more probable, than that the French would send Stilling as a hostage to France, should they enter Frankfort; this was too much for Eliza, who affectionately loved her husband, her head was in continued motion and drawn towards her right shoulder, the whole upper part of her body was thereby distorted; Eliza suffered a great deal and Stilling knew not how to bear these complicated afflictions: Eliza was naturally well shaped, and to see her now so disfigured,— it was almost more than could be endured; at the same time it was utterly impossible to leave the city, they had to stay there yet two full days, until it became apparent, that the French were endeavoring to take Mainz before they would advance any further; he then found an opportunity of departing, and as the Jewess was incurably blind, he immediately returned with Eliza to Marburg. Every possible means were here tried, to deliver the poor sufferer from her misery, but alas! all applications have hitherto proved ineffectual, she has borne this affliction now better than eleven years—she has indeed recovered in some measure, her illness is however still a severe cross for herself as well as for her husband.

He continued active in his office as Provost as well as in his professorship, and Eliza bore her misery with the resignation of a christian. to this trouble must be added the continued fear of an irruption from the French; the Elector returned indeed in the month of October, but his troops arrived very slowly on account of the bad roads and weather. Hessia remained unprotected; the French General Custine might therefore have fearlessly advanced if his courage and sense had equaled his whiskers and his mustachios, the greater part of Germany would have lost its political existence, for the general sentiment was favorable to a revolution and friendly diposed towards France.

But at that time the plan of Custine was still unknown, and the worst was to be expected, his troops were laying waste the

Weteraw, and from time to time the thunder of cannons was heard, every one prepared himself for flight, except the heads of departments, who could not leave their post; of course Stilling was likewise compelled to remain were he was.

One Sunday morning towards the end of October the rumor was spread through the city, that the French were approaching and were coming down the Lahn-mountain—Stilling took his refuge in prayer, asking comfort and strength from the Lord, who heard his petition; his fear of the French vanished, none came, and soon the Prussians and Hessians approached, Frankfort was retaken, and the siege of Mainz commenced.

During the next Easter-vacation Stilling received an invitation from the worthy family of Vinke to pay them a visit at Minden, which invitation was accepted, his friend, the son of Mr. Vinke and some acquaintances from Cassel accompanied him. He performed this journey on horseback and suffered much during this time from the cramp in the stomach. While on this journey he increased the circle of his acquaintance considerably, and with many of them he entered into an intimate friendship. Arriving at his door on his return, Eliza came out to meet him. But alas! what a spectacle!—She was drawn almost double, the involuntary motion in her neck had communicated itself to the upper part of the body — all the means, that could be thought of, were employed for her recovery, but with little effect.

In the spring of 1793 young Coing entered upon the ministerial office, having received a call as minister of the Reformed congregation of Gemund a town in Upper-hessia about twenty-five miles distant from Marburg. He had lived for more than six months in Stilling's house—Coing would have been his brother, had no bond of relation-ship existed. The most remarkable occurrence in Stilling's history during this and the succeeding year was the publication of two works, which have become the instruments in the hands of Providence of leading him to his proper calling; these works were : "Scenes from the spiritual world" in two volumes, and "Longing for heaven" in four volumes besides a key.

The "Scenes from the spiritual world" had an astonishing effect, for they made him known to the whole religious public that could read the German language; and being thus prepared, the next work entitled "Heimweh" — in English "longing for home," was received with eagerness and completely decided his fate as the sequel of his life will show.

The origin of both these works is very remarkable and proves incontestibly that he was absolutely passive in the hands of his heavenly Father. The origin of the "Scenes from the spiritual world" was as follows: when Rashman was at Marburg, the conversation turned one evening upon Wieland's translation of Lucian ; Rashman read several passages of the work, which were very comical, the whole company burst into a roar of laughter, and all agreed in admiring the translation as an inimitable master-piece. Some time afterwards this work was again brought to Stilling's recollection, and he resolved to purchase it. After a while his conscience smote him for having taken this hasty step. "What"— was the language of this reproving voice — "thou purchasest so dear a work of seven volumes!— and for what purpose— merely for thy own amusement — and yet thou art still deeply involved in debt— and a large family to provide for — and supposing, all this were not in the way, the money for which thou hast bought this work, might have materially benefitted some poor person ! —thou purchasest a book, which is of no use, much less necessary to thy calling." He stood before his judge like a poor sinner, who surrenders himself at discretion. It was a severe conflict, a hard wrestling for mercy—at length he obtained what he sought, and from that moment endeavored on his part to atone as far as possible for the fault he had committed. "If Lucian and Wieland"—such were his thoughts — "have written Scenes from the realms of imaginary Deities, partly with a view to point out the folly of heathen mythology, and partly for the diversion of the reader, I will write "Scenes from the true, christian spiritual world" for serious reflection, for the conversion and edification of the reader, and will apply the money arising from the sale of the copy-right to the benefit of poor blind persons; this idea he immediately adopted and this was the origin of a work, which had the above mentioned effect.

The work entitled Heimweh——English : Longing after Heaven—was likewise produced as it were by chance. Stilling had read Stern's "Tristram Shandy." This work is written in a sententious, humorous style, and in reading it, he had not the most distant idea of what Providence designed. He had also been in the habit of daily translating a verse from the Hebrew as also one from the Greek Scriptures with the intention of forming both into a brief sentence in the lapidary style. He had collected a considerable number of such sentences, with no other view but the study of the scriptures. Who could therefore suppose, these insignificant things should lay the foundation for the development of his destination ?—*He* certainly entertained no such idea.

Soon after the reading of the above mentioned work—it happened towards the end of July 1793—the bookseller Krieger at Marburg came one forenoon to him, and requested him to write a novel, wishing to purchase the copy right, being desirous of receiving something from his pen,which would sell better than those dry compends, which he had published. Stilling approved of this proposition and promised him some work of this kind which he would forthwith begin.

Meditating on what he should do, the thought occurred to him, that he had from his youth nourished the idea of describing the way of repentance, conversion and sanctification of a christian, under the figure of a journey, after Bunyan's example, he therefore resolved now to execute this idea, and to imitate in this work the style he had admired in Tristram Shandy, and to incorporate into the book whenever suitable his collection of scripture sentences. A sentiment, he had written a short time before in a friend's Album : "Blessed are they who *long after heaven*, for they shall reach their home." gave him the idea of a suitable title to a book which was intended to describe the wearisome journey of a christian towards his eternal home.

Thus prepared, he commenced writing; but fearful he should

P p

not succeed in the style and method he had proposed to himself, he read the first six sheets before two of his most intimate friends in Marburg, Michaelis and Starbaum, who were delighted with the beginning and encouraged him to continue the work. However to be quite sure on this subject, he selected seven from the number of his friends, who met every fortnight at his house, to whom he read what he had written during the interval, and subjected it to their judgment and criticism.

His state of mind, while he was engaged in this work was peculiar indeed; his spirit seemed to be elevated into ethereal regions, and an indescribable sensation of a happy tranquility pervaded his soul. When he sat down to the work the ideas rushed so rapidly into his mind, that he was scarcely able to write fast enough, hence the work received a very different form and tendency from that at first contemplated. And this state of the author's mind lasted exactly as long as he was engaged in the work, viz: from August 1793 until December 1794.

This work was uncommonly well received, many copies were sent to America, where it is frequently read. It became known in Asia, wherever there were Germans, friends to the christian religion. The author received testimonials of approbation from Denmark, Sweden and Russia as far as Astracan. A large number of commendatory letters from persons of every rank in the different provinces of Germany poured in upon him; many learned sceptics were thereby gained over to the christian cause; in short, there are few books, which have excited so general an interest.

It is a remarkable circumstance, that in this very period of time three distinct and unconnected voices plainly declared. that the professorship in the university was not his proper calling. The first was a conviction of his own mind for which he could assigns no particular reason. That impulse, which he had felt from his youth, of becoming an active instrument in the hand of the Lord, for the propagation of religion and which always had been the efficient cause of all his religious labors, stood at that time more clearly before him than ever, and excited an ardent desire, to rid himself of every earthly care so that he might devote himself with all his powers to the service of the Lord and his kingdom. The second voice spoke the same language from all the letters, which he received about this time. In all of them he was called upon, to devote himself exclusively to the service of the Lord and of religion, and that he ought by no means cease laboring for the good cause. The third voice finally was, that about the same time secret societies and a revolutionary spirit among the students at Marburg became general, by which means they were filled with sentiments and principles in direct opposition to those doctrines, which Stilling inculcated; hence the number of his hearers continually decreased, and the spirit of the times, left him not the least hope of being useful in future by teaching the principles of Political Economy, which he professed.

I now intreat the reader, calmly to reflect what must have been the feelings of a conscientious man in such a situation! But clear as all this was, still the way to reach the goal was involved in mist and obscurity. For in the first place his family was numerous, his son was pursuing his studies, the war and other circumstances had raised the price of every article, the number of indigent persons, who were looking to him and others for assistance, was continually increasing, his high salary was scarcely sufficient to maintain his family, many debts were still to be paid, though Eliza, treading faithfully in Selma's footsteps, had paid within the last few years several hundred guilders in despite of sickness, heavy expenses and Hannah's outset: the interests were likewise regularly paid, but under present circumstances it was impossible to think of any considerable diminution of debts, he was therefore under the necessity of remaining in his office for the sake of the salary. His situation was of course by no means enviable. Insurmountable obstacles prevented him from entering upon that career, in which he might have been cheerfully active, and for which he had felt a strong bias from his youth; on the other hand the calling in which he had to labor without hope and without a blessing was indispensably necessary for his subsistence. To all this ough to be added the sad reflection he frequently made, what his sovereign would say, should he learn, how little Stilling was doing or rather could do for the large salary he received?—

The year 1794 strewed again many thorns over Stilling's course of life; in the month of February Eliza's eldest daughter Lubecka died, and during the summer other trials awaited him, which shall be related in the sequel.

In the month of July he received a letter from Lavater, informing him, that on his return from Copenhagen, he would pass through Marburg to pay him a visit. This was a cause of great joy to him, he had hitherto had but one personal interview with this beloved friend and this had taken place twenty years before at Elberfeld, though they had kept up a constant correspondence. He was glad of another opportunity of conversing with this witness of the truth on various subjects, which could not well be treated of in a correspondence. Lavater arrived on Sunday afternoon at Marburg in company of his pious and amiable daughter, who afterwards married parson Gesner at Zurich. He stayed only till the next morning, when he continued his journey.

History scarcely presents another example of a learned man, who has equally excited the attention of the world without entertaining the least wish of so doing. On the evening, as he was at supper in Stilling's family, the place before the house was thronged with people, and the windows were crowded with spectators. But he was in more than one respect a remarkable man, a dear witness of the truth, as it is in Jesus Christ. The bond of friendship, which had hitherto subsisted between him and Stilling, was on that occasion more closely knit together, and they resolved that neither ignominy nor shame nor death itself should ever alienate their hearts from Christ, hated and despised as he might be by the world.

Soon after this the severe trials and sufferings came on, of which I have spoken above. It was his custom during the vacation of Whit-suntide to make a journey with his students to Cassel to show them at Wilhelmshohe the different kinds of foreign forest trees. This year to his great satisfaction, the Elector granted him the accomplishment of a wish, he had long entertained, of establishing a school for young foresters. On his return, he dropt the following expression before the students: "I have at length obtained, what I desired," without further mentioning the object of his wishes. There was a private teacher at Marburg, much beloved by the students, a great friend of Kant's philosophy, which at that time was the fashion of the day. The Elector, who was no friend of this philosophy, transferred the young man from Marburg to Hanau as professor of Philosophy with a salary of one hundred dollars. This order displeased the students at Marburg, and their suspicion rested on Stilling of having been the means of his removal, for they supposed, that the expression which he had dropt on the journey from Cassel, of having obtained what he desired, had reference to this circumstance. The fermentation rose at length to the highest pitch, and they resolved to serenade the above mentioned teacher, but to attack Stilling's house and break the windows. Jacob, who was a student of law and never entered into such combinations, learnt with terror what was going on. He knew, that his mother Eliza expected soon to be confined and that his aunt, Amalia Coing, Eliza's youngest sister was very sick with the dissentery. Fearing for the lives of his parents and his aunt,—for the spirit of the times, being in harmony with the terrorism reigning in France, breathed nothing but death and murder, and the students were filled with revolutionary sentiments,—he informed his parents of the danger which threatened them, and besought them to take measures, which might prevent so great a misfortune. He then went round among the students and begged them to give up their plans, but at first without success. At length it was promised him on condition, that he would join their secret society. For two hours the poor fellow was hesitating between two evils, at last he concluded, that his becoming a member of the society was the less of the two, he therefore consented to join it, the attack was averted, and they took no other revenge of Stilling, except that they spat in the street as they passed his house in procession—— this was harmless, for the street was wide enough for it.

Stilling was wholly unacquainted with the circumstance, that his son had joined one of the secret societies of the students, he was informed of it a year afterwards, but in such a manner, that it occasioned him neither grief nor uneasiness. Jacob strongly solicited his parents, to permit him to study for half a year at Gœttingen, declaring that this step would be very advantageous to him. His parents gave their consent with some reluctance. Jacob's secret intention in going to Gœttingen was formally to renounce all connection with the society and to inform the Provost of it, which he could not do at Marburg, unless he wished to rouse again the ire of the students. About this time all Academical secret societies were prohibited by the diet at Ratisbon, and inquiries concerning them were instituted at all the universities; fortunately Jacob had already renounced all connection with the order, and obtained a testimonial for that purpose, and thus he escaped censure. The next summer, after his return to Marburg the judicial inquiries into the nature of these secret institutions commenced there, and to the astonishment of all, Jacob's name was likewise found on the list. He then came forward and produced his testimonials; the business was referred for a final decision to the Elector, whom Stilling informed of the true cause of his son's having entered the society; the Elector was perfectly satisfied and cleared him from every responsibility on this account.

A new connection was formed in the course of this year in Stilling's family. Stilling had always considered the two sisters of Eliza, Maria and Amalia, two amiable young ladies as a valuable gift of God, he as well as all his friends, who were admitted into the family-circle, were charmed with their society. Amalia had made a deep impresssion upon Jacob by her excellent character and beauty. At first he had been of opinion, that it was wrong to marry the sister of his step-mother, and thinking himself not able to conquer this attachment, he was on the point of leaving the paternal house. He however entrusted the secret of his heart to his brother-in-law, who advised him, to make his wishes known to his parents. Stilling and Eliza had no objections, but gave their consent to the marriage, provided Jacob obtained a situation, which would enable him to maintain a family. However seven years elapsed before it actually took place. In order to prevent slanderous reports, he left the paternal house and engaged to direct a young gentleman in his studies of the law at the university.

In the autumn of this year the Elector gave to young Mr. Coing a call as chaplain to his embassy at Ratisbon, which office he filled with honor and applause for several years.

CHAPTER VII.

Thus situated Stilling entered into the year 1795; on the 4th of January Eliza was safely delivered of a son, whoreceived the name of Frederick, and is still alive. A fortnight afterwards he received one Sunday afternoon the sad intelligence, that his intimate friend and uncle Kraft had suddenly departed this life. The manner in which this real christian and celebrated preacher died, was very remarkable. He was seated at the supper table, with his wife, one daughter and a few friends, all, who were present, had enjoyed themselves in his agreeable company, for he was that evening uncommonly cheerful. After supper he arose from his chair, raised his eyes to heaven, commenced a prayer, and in that moment his spirit departed, he dropt down and was instantaneously dead.

Kraft had been a learned Theologian and though his oratorial powers had not been of the first order he was nevertheless a celebrated and an interesting speaker; he kept the attention of his auditory always fixed and irresistibly affected the heart. I was once in church at Frankfort, a Prussian officer took his seat by my side; the indifference, depicted on his countenance plainly indicated, that he was merely there. in order to be able to say he had been to church. The Sexton laid a hymnbook before each of us; the officer barely looked once into it; of me he took no notice at all; at length Kraft entered the pulpit—the officer looked up with indifference—Kraft commenced his prayer, the officer became more attentive.—The minister began to preach, and very soon his eyes were steadfastly fixed upon him, his mouth was wide open as if ready to devour every word Kraft was uttering; at the word *Amen*, he turned to me and said : "I have never before heard such a sermon."

Kraft was a man endowed with wisdom, and consistent in all his actions, he was a zealous christian, both theoretically and practically. He was uncommonly charitable, and his pious wife was a faithful helpmate in the exercise of that virtue; whenever it was necessary, and he knew, that the gift would be well applied, he gladly spent a hundred guilders in one charitable act, and that in such a manner, as if the receiver were doing him a favor in accepting the present. When he was yet a student, one day a poor man asked an alms of him ; having no money in his pocket, he took his silver buckles out of his shoes, and gave them to the beggar. Though he was very orthodox, he was one of the most tolerant men in existence.

Blessed art thou, dear man of God ! The assurance of meeting thee again in the kingdom of heaven is a cordial to thy friend, in his painful pilgrimage through this vale of tears.

Mr. Passavant from Detmold was appointed to take charge of Kraft's congregation. Three daughters besides his widow, survived him; the two eldest were married to two worthy clergymen, the youngest married a young lawyer after the death of both her parents. Kraft's widow moved with the remaining part of her family into her native city Marburg, where they live in Stilling's house in christian love and friendship.

He hired this summer a country house at Ochershousen about one mile from town, for the benefit of his and Eliza's health, where they spent the greater part of the summer season. But his lectures he continued to give in his house in the city.

In the spring of 1796 a young man came one morning to Stilling at Ochershousen. He addressed him politely, and when he inquired for his name, learnt, that he was the remarkable N——. In expectation, what this singular man might have to say, he invited him to take a seat. The stranger at first consulted him concerning a friend, who was afflicted with weak eyes, but the real cause of his visit being uppermost in his mind, he soon took hold of Stilling's hand, kissed it and said :

"Mr. Stilling! are you not the author of the work entitled: "Longing for Heaven ?"

"Yes, Sir, I am."

"Then you are one of my unknown superiors !" (Saying so, he again kissed his hand.)

"No my dear Sir, I am neither *your* unknown superior, nor that of any *other* man. I am engaged in no secret Society !"

The stranger looked in deep emotion at him, and said : "Dearest Mr. Stilling ! do not conceal yourself from me, I have been tried long and severely enough ; as you well know."

"My dear Sir! I declare to you before God, that I am not engaged in any secret society, and that I comprehend nothing of all you mean or expect to learn from me."

This declaration was too strong and too serious, for a doubt to remain on the stranger's mind, it was now *his* turn to be astonished, and he continued: "How does it happen, that you are so well acquainted with the society, which exists in the East, and describe it so accurately in your work, and point out so minutely their places of meeting in Egypt, on mount Sinai in the monastery of Canobin, and under the temple of Jerusalem ?

"I know nothing about it ; these ideas presented themselves very lively to my imagination; It is mere fiction."

Pardon me, you have related nothing but the truth.—It is incomprehensible to me, how you could so exactly hit it !

He then gave a circumstantial account of this society in the East, which astonished Stilling beyond measure: for he learnt some remarkable and extraordinary circumstances, which however are not suitable for publication, I only assure the reader upon my word of honor, that, what he learnt from the stranger, has not the most distant relation to politics.

About the same time a certain Sovereign asked Stilling in a letter, whence he had obtained his information concerning the society in the East? for what he had written in his late work concerning it, was correct. His written answer was of course in substance the same, which he had given to the above mentioned stranger.

The disclosure of the Oriental secret Stilling continues to look upon as a circumstance of the greatest importance, because it has a reference to the kingdom of God. But many things in regard to it are still in the dark, for he obtained afterwards from a respectable source some hints concerning another Oriental society, established upon different principles, likewise unconnected with politics. It is still uncertain whether these two societies are in any connection with each other.

CHAPTER VIII.

The year 1796 was for a great part of Germany a year of terror and misery, the crossing of a French army over the Rhine, their march into Franconia, and afterwards their retreat, filled the whole country with indescribable misery, and as Hessia was at peace with France, all fled into the neighborhood of Marburg. A census being taken of the fugitives, who had fled to that town and its vicinity the number was found to amount to forty-five thousand persons. It was a pitiful sight, to behold all the roads lined with waggons, coaches and carts carrying baggage; men, women and children on horseback and on foot, blessing the prince, who had made peace. All these occurrences greatly affected the mind of Stilling, but in particular the spirit of the day, which insults and tramples upon every thing, which is sacred; and his anxious desire, to be actively engaged in the cause of religion, increased daily. This ardent wish had induced him in the year 1795 to commence the publication of a periodical entitled "The Grey Man," which met with a reception from the public beyond his most sanguine expectations wherefore it is still continued. It is not only read in all Germany, but in every part of the world. I myself have seen German American papers, in which parts of "The Grey Man" were inserted with the promise of a continuation.

I must recall William Stilling again to the recollection of the reader, by giving a short relation of the remainder of his life. His second marriage had not been blessed; in despite of hard labor and economy, he had every year become more reduced in his circumstances, had involved himself in debt, and the four children, which he had with his second wife, three daughters and one son, all very honest and well-meaning, were unfortunate and poor in the world. The old patriarch saw them all in their misery about him, without being able to assist them. Stilling meanwhile was living at a distance, and knew but little, how matters stood in his father's family, and could not even suspect the wretchedness of his situation. His father however had several reasons for wishing that the true state of his situation might be kept from his son. In the first place he had frequently declared, that he would rather put up with the meanest fare than receive assistance from any of his children. In the second place, the reader will remember that Stilling had received many bitter reproaches from his father in the days of his calamity. His father could not have forgotten all this and it was natural therefore he should feel some reluctance in accepting his support from this child.

After he was settled at Marburg he was opportunities of receiving more correct information concerning his father's troubles, and though a heavy debt was still to be paid, he resolved, after mature reflection and consultation with Eliza, to contribute weekly one Dollar towards the support of his father, and to send him from time to time as much sugar and coffee, as the two old people would need. Eliza likewise sent as opportunities occured a bottle of good wine to Linedorf, to invigorate the good old man.

After the death of his wife, William Stilling gave the management of the house into the hands of his youngest daughter, who had married a carter, and he boarded with her. But this poor woman, whose husband was always on the road with his waggon and horses, was too poor to hire help in the house, to nurse her old father, and she herself had to labor hard in field and garden from morning till late in the evening, and thus little care was taken of William. The other children were likewise unable to do any thing, for they could not help themselves, much less assist others; in short the misery was great indeed.

William Stilling was then in his eightieth year, and in all respects perfectly healthy, excepting his legs and feet, which were full of running sores. The strength of his mind was likewise nearly gone, as well as his memory.

In the month of August 1796 Stilling received a letter from one of his relatives, who had visited the good old man, and had seen the misery in which he lived. The description of the sufferings of his father contained in the letter, induced Stilling, immediately to send a waggon to bring him to Marburg. Learning at Ockershousen the news of the arrival of his father in town, he forthwith hastened thither, to welcome him. But alas! in what a wretched situation did he find him! When he entered the room, where he was, such a pestilential odor struck upon his olfactory nerves, as he had never experienced in any anatomical theatre. Scarcely could he approach to embrace him. It was really a blessing for the good old father, that the strength of his mind had so far decreased, that he was not very sensible of his sufferings. A few years before, this great misery would have appeared to him an intolerable burden with his nice sense of decency and love of cleanliness. Stilling's heart was bleeding at this spectacle, but Eliza, who had frequently expressed the wish, that she might be so fortunate, as to have an opportunity of nursing her parents in their old age, commenced the necessary and burdensome labors with courage and resolution. — Dear and noble wife — thou forbiddest me, to say a word in thy praise — well! I shall be silent! But father William who was here in a great measure insensible of thy filial love and services, and could not impart his blessing to thee, will hereafter meet thee, faithful bearer of thy cross! in the fields of bliss, and richly return thee the thanks, he was unable to express on earth! Dorothy too will approach with him, to welcome her daughter Eliza. Father Eberhard will smile peace to thee, and Selma will embrace her friend with these words: *"Blessed art thou, who hast so completely fulfilled my expectations!"* All these glorified saints will lead thee to the throne of thy merciful Saviour, who will incline the sceptre of the universe towards thee and say: *"What thou hast done to this my servant, thou hast done unto me, enter thou, citizen of the new Jerusalem, and enjoy the consummation of bliss."*

Eliza continued to perform her works of love until October, when she was delivered of a daughter who is still alive, and was called Amalia. Amalia Coing who was the engaged bride of William Stilling's grand-son, undertook to nurse him during Eliza's confinement; she also will reap in eternity her reward for her faithfulness.

The close of 1796 brought mourning into Stilling's family; in autumn two brothers of Mr. Coing — both unmarried — departed this life. Mrs. Kraft likewise left us on Christmas-day, to join her brothers and husband in a better world. Her daughter married the next summer, and the remaining three persons of the Kraft family still lived together at Marburg.

This year had also been a year of suffering to Schwartz and Hannah; he had left his place at Derbach, and accepted a call as minister at Eckzell in the Wetterow, where he was exposed to all the horrors of the war. Hannah was *one* of the forty-five thousand fugitives of whom I have spoken before. In her parent's house she was delivered of her third child, and then returned again to her post.

The year 1797 was not remarkable in Stilling's life, every thing went on as usual, except that a deep gloom overhung his spirits, which deprived him of every enjoyment. His pleasant family circle alone, in which every one, who moved in it, was comfortable, kept his mind from totally sinking. Eliza and her two sisters were the instruments, which the Lord employed to aid him in bearing his cross, though Eliza herself was almost sinking under her burden.

Their Father was insensible to all this, he was a child, and became more imbecile every day; in order that every attention might be paid him, Stilling sent for Mary the daughter of his eldest sister, who faithfully performed her duty towards her grand-father, until his circumstances required another nurse, which was found in an old widow, who attended him by night and day. Mary's character developed itself greatly to her advantage, she enjoys the regard and love of all the good, and

Stilling and Eliza love and treat her as one of their own children. William Stilling gradually lost all recollection so much, as even not to recognize his own son, he remembered hardly any thing of his second marriage and children, but of his marriage with Dorothy and the years of his youth he sometimes spoke in unconnected sentences. But if any one turned the subject to religion, his mind seemed to revive, he then spoke connectedly and rationally, and when this also ceased, his imagination was still attached to some Bible passages treating of the forgiveness of sin through the sufferings and death of Christ, which he repeated again and again, with many tears and wringing of hands, and with which he comforted himself in his sufferings. From this example we may learn, how important it is, to fill the memory of children early with edifying passages from the Bible and with hymns ; for the first impressions upon the memory of a child are indelible. During the years of their youth, these sentences and verses are perhaps of little practical use, but when in old age their pilgrimage leads them through William's desert, where they are devoid of all enjoyment of social life, and almost of the consciousness of their own existence, have scarcely a glimmer of reason for their guide, and have forgotten almost their course of life, such scripture sentences and verses become spiritual food, which strengthens them for their passage through the awful gulph of death.

During the Whit-suntide-vacation of 1797 Stilling and Eliza again experienced a remarkable proof of the care of Divine Providence. He enjoyed indeed a handsome salary, but his family expenses were also very great ; for every article was at that time exorbitantly high at Marburg, and every father of a family will recollect periods in the time of his housekeeping, when various circumstances combine, which when united, occasion a press for money while his situation is such, that he neither can nor dare make debts. Such was at this time the situation of Stilling or rather of Eliza, who had taken upon herself the family cares and the administration of the income. A worthy lady in Switzerland had some time previous to this consulted him in a letter concerning the blindness of her husband. But at the time when he was in these straightened circumstances and on his yearly journey with the students at Cassel, he received a letter from this lady inclosing a bill of exchange for three hundred guilders, requesting him not to suppose that she expected a recompense or any services for this trifle; the cause of her sending it was merely, that she felt it her duty to do so, and begged him to say not a word about it. Thus he was at once relieved from his embarrassments, and Eliza's faith was greatly strengthened.

The year 1798 is in Stilling's history remarkable, as he wrote during that period his "History of the triumph of the christian religion," in an explanation of the Apocalypse ; and also by a journey to Bremen with Eliza.

The origin of "the triumph of the christian religion" was as follows : the important consequences of the French revolution, and the great events, which were taking place in the world about this time, made every where a deep impression on those true worshipers of the Lord, who were attentive to the signs of the times. Several of them undertook to apply certain parts of the Apocalypse to these events, without reference to the whole connection of this prophecy and its spirit contained in the Bible. Some very sensible men supposed the French cockade to be the sign of the beast and therefore believed, that this beast had already arisen from the abyss and that the man of sin had actually made his appearance. This opinion being very generally received among the true christians of this time appeared dangerous to Stilling, and he intended to warn them against it in one of the numbers of "The Grey Man." He considered it however an extremely important circumstance, that the learned Dr. Bengel in his explanation of the Apocalypse, written more than fifty years before, had difinitely declared that the great conflict would commence in the last decennium of the eighteenth century, and that the Pope of Rome would then lose his power. An anonymous writer at Carlsruhe had gone a step farther and in a more definite explanation of Bengel's Apocalyptical system of calculation had fixed upon the years of the last decennium, when Rome should fall, and this he did eighteen years before it actually took place. These circumstances attracted Stilling's attention to Bengel's works and particularly to that of the above mentioned anonymous writer at Carls-ruhe. To these occurrences which made a deep impression up-on his mind the following circumstances must be added, which prepared him for so important a work ; "the Heimweh" had made a deep and salutary impresson upon numbers belonging to the Moravian church, Stilling became better known in that socie-ty, his life and his other works were read more generally, es-pecially "The Grey Man." Brethren, passing through Marburg, visited him, he likewise read many works, which had been pub-lished by them ; in short he esteemed and respected this society the more highly, the better he became acquainted with it and its publications, especially with their congregational and missonary accounts, which were sent him ; and he believed, that all their establishments and their activity in the spread of the gospel had been peculiarly directed and were accompanied by the blessing of Divine Providence, but what united him more than any thing else to this society was an intimate correspondence between him and Brother Erxleben, who was stationed first in Bremen, then at Norden in Eastfriesland and lastly at Herrnhut. This corespon-dence still continues, and will probably not cease until one of them is called to join the church triumphant above. Stilling be-lieved he had discovered in this society an important preparatory step for laying the foundation of the kingdom of God, it appear-ed to him to be the Seminary of this kingdom, and this idea gave him an important view in regard to one of the principal figures in the Apocalypse.

The second circumstance, which prepared him for this work, was the extensive and unexpected awakening, which had taken place in England, in consequence of which the great Mis-sionary Society had been established. The occurrence was so striking and the period of its origin so remarkable, that no true christian could remain indifferent. This awakening likewise strengthened the idea in his mind, that the kingdom of God would speedily be revealed, and the true christian from every quarter looked after the golden hand of the clock on the pinnacle of the temple, and he, who was rather dim-sighted asked his sharper-sighted brother : "What o'clock is it?" But notwithstanding all these reflections in Stilling's mind, he did not entertain the most distant idea of venturing to write an explanation of the sacred prophecy of the Apocalypse, but rather to warn his fellow christians in "The Grey Man" against so daring an attempt, because many had missed the point. However as in the leadings of Providence throughout Stilling's life, that which is most unexpected appears always to be the theme and maxim of his heavenly Father, so it was likewise in the present case.

One Sunday morning in March 1798 Stilling had resolved not to go to church, but to write for "The Grey Man" and especially to impart to the christian reader something useful about the Revelation of St. John. With this view he took up the above mentioned anonymous explanation of this last book in the New Testament, and began to read. Suddenly he felt an impulse to translate the Apocalypse from the Greek, to explain it verse by verse, and to retain Bengel's system of calculation, because it had hitherto been applicable, and had been remarkably fulfilled in our times. He therefore commenced the labor immediately, hoping, that the spirit of the Lord would enlighten him in all difficulties, and would lead him into all the truth. His "History of the triumph of the christian religion" is therefore no previously meditated work, but was written in leisure-hours, with prayer and supplication for light and grace, and forthwith sent to Nurnberg to friend Rowe for publication. As soon as he shall find leisure, he will in a few supplements to the work rectify, explain and more clearly define several things which may need elucidation.

Whoever is not inclined to a malicious interpretation of every thing, but is willing to judge honestly and equitably, will not accuse Stilling of wishing to excite the idea that he was writing by divine inspiration, my only aim is to convince the reader, that his works—more or less defective—were published under a peculiar direction of Divine Providence; the course in which God led him throughout his whole life, and the uncommon and unexpected blessing, which accompanied his practical works answer sufficiently for the truth of this assertion. This was

R r

likewise the case with "the history of the triumph of the christian religion," for scarcely had one year elapsed after the first edition had been published, when a second was demanded.

Stilling's melancholy had reached its acme during the summer of this year, he sometimes endeavored to investigate its cause by means of his medical knowledge, but all attempts were fruitless. It was not melancholy in the usual acceptation of the word, but what I would call a complete void of enjoyment, a state of mind which even the purest earthly pleasure could not affect, he was a stranger in the world, every thing which gives satisfaction to other good men was totally indifferent to him—Nothing—Nothing but this one great object, to become useful in extending the Redeemer's kingdom—which however appeared to him partly dark and partly unattainable — filled his soul: towards it his view was directed and to nothing else. His soul, heart and understanding were attached to Christ with fulness of love, but accompanied by a sensation of sadness. What increased the evil was, that he durst not disclose his grievous situation to any one, because no one understood him—in a few instances he discovered himself to some friends in the Netherlands, but they took umbrage at it, because they fancied he believed himself in an exalted mystical state, since he had called the situation of his mind: "the state of mystical truth." Good God! it is difficult to travel the path of the holy cross—but afterwards it brings inexpressible blessings!

The true cause why his heavenly guide permitted him to fall into this sad state of mind, was doubtless in the first place, to preserve him against religious pride and vanity, which kills every sense of religion, into which he would have fallen without this thorn in the flesh, as he received from every quarter assurances of approbation; in the state in which he was, these things gave him pleasure for a moment, like a warm ray of the sun on a cold December-day, but immediately afterwards all was again as before, and he felt, as if it were nothing to him. In the second place, the heavenly smelter probably brought him into this oven of purification, in order radically to burn out certain remains of corruption.

Though Eliza herself had a heavy cross to bear, still she was the only one among all his friends, to whom he could discover himself and impart his feelings without reserve; which indeed increased her own sufferings, without her being able to extricate him out of his, but her faithful care and participation in his trials were inestimable blessings to Stilling, and her animating conversation made his burden lighter.

CHAPTER IX.

His operations of the cataract and cures of diseases of the eye were peculiarly blessed; he had continued them without interruption though he did not meddle with medical practice in any other way; but a twofold inconvenience attended them. The maxim which he had adopted, and from which he cannot depart, to demand no pay for any operation and cure of the eye, but to serve all without remuneration, unless a patient makes him a present of his own accord, and can do it without injuring himself, brought him a great number of applicants, he was every moment exposed to interruption, and his patience was frequently tried to the utmost. The second still greater inconvenience was this, that poor, blind persons with testimonials of their poverty were sent to him from all quarters, without having sufficient money for their maintenance during the cure—what was to be done in such cases ?—— he could not send these objects of pity away for the sake of a few guilders. The Directors of the two Protestant orphan-houses at Marburg had agreed, to receive patients of this description during the cure for a very moderate compensation, but even this moderate compensation had to come out of Stilling's pocket; and besides in consequence of this benevolent arrangement citizens and foreigners sent their needy patients the more frequently without money; of course many a trial of faith took place, but the Lord most gloriously legitimated them all, as the sequel will show.

About the middle of the summer of 1798 Dr. Wienholt in Bremen invited Stilling to come to that city, since a number of persons, afflicted with the cataract wished to be operated by him. Stilling replied, that he would come during the autumnal vacation. This was done accordingly, and Eliza resolved to accompany him, notwithstanding her indisposition, for she did not like to leave her husband for so long a time alone, who greatly stood in need of her care and support: besides this, she was desirous of seeing the city from which her ancestors on the maternal side had descended, for one of them Duising came from Brabant and had settled at Bremen during the religious persecution of the Duke of Alba. Two cousins, by the name of Meyer both Doctors of Law were still residing at Bremen; the elder was one of the four ruling Burgomasters of the city, and the younger Secretary in one of the Departments of government. These relatives were likewise very anxious to see their Marburg friends.

On the 22d day of September 1798 Stilling and Eliza commenced their journey to Bremen. In consequence of Eliza's illness, they were compelled to travel very slow, because she could not bear the jolting of the carriage. On the 28th late in the evening they arrived at Bremen, and were hospitably received by Secretary Meyer; he and his excellent wife were in perfect mental harmony with Stilling and Eliza, and the latter soon felt at home and comfortable in this family. His brother, the Burgomaster likewise omitted nothing, which he supposed would be agreeable to his Marburg friends.

Stilling performed twenty-two operations of the cataract in Bremen, and besides gave to many afflicted with weak eyes, his advice as oculist. Among the patients, on which he performed these operations, was an aged man, a citizen of Bremen, who had been blind for many years, and in consequence of this affliction had been reduced in his circumstances. Several ladies requested Stilling to permit them to be present at the operation, wishing to be witnesses of the satisfaction, which a man must feel, at the recovery of his sight who has been blind for years. The operation was successful, and Stilling permitted him to look about—the patient looked round clasping his hands exclaiming: "Ah!

yonder are ladies, and every thing is in great disorder in the room!" The good ladies did not know, what they should say or think, and hastily left the place.

Stilling made many highly interesting acquaintances in Bremen, and also renewed several old friendships; among others with Doctor and Professor Meister, with whom he had become acquainted at Elberfeld, and with Ewald, who was minister of a congregation in Bremen. The celebrated Dr. Olbers became his friend and at his house he also made the acquaintance of the great Astronomer Schroeder.

Bremen is blessed with many pious inhabitants, and the character of the people is more refined and more moral, than in other commercial cities. This is in particular to be ascribed to the excellent preacher's, with whom this city has always been blessed and whose pious services it still enjoys.

After a very pleasant stay of three weeks and some days he and Eliza left Bremen on the 21st of October. The Lord had blessed his hand, and the rich patients had presented him with sums which not only covered the expensive journey but left something in his hands, which was a great help in his numerous family. Their relatives at Bremen accompanied them as far as the Asseler Damm. The road to Hoya was in a dreadful condition, however they arrived without any accident though late in the evening in that city; at Hanover they stopped again a short time at Mr. Falk's, where they met with a brotherly reception; they then continued their journey, and arrived at Marburg and found all their friends there in the enjoyment of health.

CHAPTER X.

This journey to Bremen enlarged the number of Stilling's friends and acquaintances but it also increased his correspondence. Consultations concerning diseases of the eye and letters on religious subjects arrived daily, so that he was scarcely able to answer them, In addition to this labor ought to be reckon-

ed the throng of patients either afflicted with the cataract, or
wishing to consult him about some defect in their sight, so that
it appeared next to impossible, to fulfil all his duties, yet God
aided him, that he neglected no part of his calling.

Under these circumstances he commenced the year 1799.
On the 22d day of Feb. Eliza was safely delivered of her youngest child which was a girl; the countess of Waldeck had expressed a desire to become its god-mother, which offer was of
course thankfully accepted; and she gave her the name Christine; it still lives a blessing to its parents.

Stilling had become more intimate with Lavater since his
visit to Marburg. They differed in opinion on certain subjects,
which gave rise to a lively and spirited correspondence; which
however did not in the least lessen the brotherly love subsisting
between them. Both lived and labored for the Lord and his
kingdom, and this great aim was likewise the bond of their mutual love. At that time the celebrated physician, Doctor Hotze
was in Frankfort with his excellent son-in-law Doctor de Neuf-
ville. Stilling had made Hotze's acquaintance several years previous; the reader will also remember, that Passavant was stationed in Frankfort, both were friends of Lavater and Stilling,
and united by the same bond among each other. Lavater was
in the habit of sending all his letters to Stilling open to these two
friends in Frankfort, and the latter sent his answers likewise
unsealed to them, whence a very agreeable and innstructive controversy arose. The subjects treated of in these letters were
the most important articles of faith; for instance, the doctrine of
atonement; the answering of prayers &c. In the year 1799 this
interchange of letters had ceased, for Lavater had been arrested
and exiled to Basle, and Hotze had removed from Frankfort.
All this I mention for the sake of a singular phenomenon, which
occurred to Stilling on the 13th of July. Before his journey
to Bremen a friend had given him the confidential information,
that a certain celebrated and worthy man was struggling with
want and poverty; Stilling mentioned this circumstance to several friends in Bremen; Doctor Wienhold undertook to make a
collection for him, and in the course of the succeeding winter

sent him about three hundred and fifty guilders; Stilling by making inquiry, how this money could be safely transmitted, learnt that his wants had in a measure been relieved, and that this kind of assistance would wound his feelings. This induced Stilling to retain the money, and to make inquiry at Bremen, whether it should be given to the English missionary society or whether it should be employed to assist the unfortunate inhabitants in the canton of Underwalden in Switzerland?—the contributors approved of the latter application, and Stilling entered into correspondence on this subject with the worthy and pious Antistes Hess atZurich, because he had been particularly interested in those unfortunate people. This letter as already mentioned was written the 13th of July; while in the act of writing, and meditating on the situation, in which Switzerland then was, he received a strong impression on his mind, that Lavater would die a violent death, that he would die a martyr. This last word was properly speaking the one which made the strongest impression on his mind. It was very natural, that he should be much surprised at this unaccountable feeling and that in consequence he should mention it in his letter to Hess, desiring him at the same time to tell it to Lavater, as soon as an opportunity might offer. Hess very soon returned an answer, expressing his own astonishment at what Stilling had mentioned, and promised to inform Lavater at a suitable time of it, which I think he did. My friend Hess will recollect this circumstance very well. Stilling had this impression — as has been observed — on the 13th day of July; and ten weeks and a few days afterwards, viz: on the 26th of September, Lavater received the deadly wound, the consequence of which was a protracted suffering of fifteen months, when death released him from his earthly troubles.

In the autumnal-vacation Stilling took his wife and children to the village of Munster near Buzbach in the Wetterow, whither Schwartz had moved from Eckzell; afterwards he made a journey to Frankfort and Hanau, where patients awaited his arrival; but Eliza remained at Munster. From Hanau he went to Budingen. Having there spent three very pleasant days, he traveled in company of a certain Mr. Grafenmeyer, who was on a journey to Gœttingen as far as Buzbach. The road led them through a swampy country, which at that time was said to be infested by robbers, many stories were told of a certain pewterer or coppersmith as captain of the band; and these tales gave the coach-man and servant on the box rich materials for conversation. Burglaries, robberies and stories of murders and executions, were their continued theme, until they came to the forest of Florstedt.—Here all at once the coach-man gave the servant a knowing look, and said: "Sure enough, there he is!" Stilling looked out of the coach, and observed a tall, strong, thickset man, dressed in a blue coat with metal buttons, a cocked hat fixed on one side of his head, and a heavy cane in his hand walking towards the woods; the coach-man turned round and whispered significantly and with evident marks of fear into the coach : "Yonder he goes !',

"Who goes yonder ?"

"Who else but the pewterer."

"Ah ! is that the pewterer?"

This was certainly rather alarming, but Stilling who was no coward got out of the coach on account of the bad road, before they reached the forest, and walked on before; for he was more afraid of bad roads than of all the pewterers or coppersmiths in the world. The forest appeared to be full of people, who were cutting wood, but no robber was to be seen.

In Buzbach he met his son-in-law Schwartz, both stayed that night with Mr Beck the forester, whose father-in-law submitted the next morning to an operation, afterwards they went together to Munster where they found Eliza and all their other friends in tolerable health.

After a pleasant visit of six days at Munster he started with his family for home, Schwartz accompanied them on their return as far as Buzbach, this happened on the 16th day of October. Here they made a short stop, and took breakfast with the forester; just before starting Schwartz was gone out for something, but soon returned in great haste and said : "Dear Father, Lavater has been severely wounded by a gunshot." This piece of news created a very strong sensation in Stilling's mind; yet notwithstanding his grief and pity he was calmly resigned to the will of God; and the remarkable circumstance that his presentiment had been fulfilled, gave him a strong assurance, that the Lord had salutary designs in view, the journey was continued, and in the evening of that day they arrived safe at Marburg.

CHAPTER XI.

Though the year 1800, the last in the eighteenth century was fraught with the same mental agonies for Stilling as some of the preceding ones had been, nothing of great importance occurred, which could interest the general reader. During the Easter-vacation he was again obliged as an oculist to make a journey to Frankfort, Offenbach and Hanau. Eliza did not accompany him this time. At Hanau he spent four pleasant days at the house of Mr. Ries a brother of Mr. Ries at Marburg, who together with his lady are among his most intimate friends. With the celebrated merchant Wirshing from Nurnberg he formed a highly interesting acquaintance; this worthy old gentleman had come once more with his children to the Frankfort fair, and it was a particular source of satisfaction to him to meet Stilling, whose life and other works he had read with approbation and practical benefit. Wirshing had been a poor orphan-boy left destitute by his parents: by industry, filial piety, confidence in God, by a complete knowledge of his business and extensive travels he had gathered a large estate; he showed his friend Stilling with praise and gratitude towards God his two large ware-houses, filled with Nurnberg toys. Wirshing's character made a deep impression upon Stilling, he particularly admired his humility, modesty and practical knowledge of religion.

Lavater's wound was not instantly mortal, though it proved so in the end. Pity for his misfortune induced his friends to unite in their respective places of abode to offer up their suppli-

tcations to the throne of grace in his behalf, which also had a
en dency, to knit the bond of friendship more closely between
each other. In Stilling's letters to Passavant, to Achelis the Reformed minister at Gœttingen, and to a female friend, Lavater
formed the principal subject. His works had been particularly
blessed to the edification and building up in the faith of this pious lady; this had induced her, to enter into a correspondence
with him, but having her reasons for preserving an incognito, she
never told him who she was; he therefore corresponded for a
long time with a certain Julia in the North of Germany, without even suspecting her real name. He sent her several tokens
of rememberance according to his fashion, but they as well as
his letters passed through the hands of Passavant in Frankfort,
who alone knew her. During Lavater's illness Stilling heard
for the first time of her, and desired his friend Passavant, to
tell him, who she was? After some time he received the following sketch of her life. She is the daughter of Burgomaster
Eike at Minden in Hanover, she had been married to the well
known Theologian Richerz, who had formerly been the University preacher at Gœttingen, and afterwards Superintendent
at Giffhorn in the Electorate of Hanover; he had distinguished
himself by several theological works, and died with the consumption after a lingering illness. Julia had always been weakly and subject to frequent indisposition, and suffered still more
from being obliged to nurse her husband; during his long sickness she would have sunk under her many and severe trials,
if her resignation and piety had not been her support. She
never had any children; after she had become a widow she removed to her native city Minden; her own father was then very
old and stood in need of his daughter's fostering care, she therefore considered it her duty to nurse and attend him.

From this time Stilling corresponded frequently with Julia,
and the subjects of their letters were the sufferings of Lavater,
and likewise the one thing needful, which ought to be every
christian's chief concern.

Were I permitted, to say all the Lord does for his people—

Yes — the unbeliever too — would be astonished — and yet not believe.

Lavater continued on the sickbed his correspondence with Stilling. The subjects on which they communicated their thoughts to each other were the most important doctrines of the christian religion, yet did they not handle them as matter of controversy, but as brethren in perfect harmony, the last letter he received was written a fortnight before his death : this great man departed this life on the second day of January 1801, as a witness of the truth in Jesus Christ. A short time afterwards Stilling composed the well known poem, entitled: "Lavater's transfiguration." Several reviewers denied, that Lavater had been a martyr of the truth, as Stilling called him, and others contended, that the wound he had received was not the cause of his death, however nothing is more clear than this.

Lavater's sanctified heart forgave his murderer without hesitation, he used to say, that he would search heaven and hell, until he could find him, in order to thank him for the wound, which had been an excellent school for him: he likewise most earnestly desired, that his friends would make no further inquiry about the unfortunate man, but would leave him to divine mercy; his relatives consider this request of their departed friend as binding; but still I hope, I may be permitted to say a few words, as a proof of my assertion, that he was a martyr.

The soldier, who gave Lavater the deadly wound, was a Swiss from the French part of the Canton of Bern; he and a fellow soldier were making a great noise before a house adjoining that of Lavater ; he heard that they demanded something to drink, he therefore took a bottle of wine and some bread, and went out to take it to them ; the grenadier, who afterwards shot him, was particularly friendly, and called him *kind hearted*, (Bruderherz) for he spoke the German language as well as the French, which was his mother tongue. Lavater then returned into his own house. Meanwhile the soldier spoke with some citizens of Zurich, and soon after Lavater came out again, to ask the apparently well disposed soldier for protection against an unruly companion of his; the fellow then acted very different from what he had done before, used threatening language, levelled his gun and shot him.

I now ask upon what principle this sudden and terrible change in the mind of the wretched young man can be explained unless upon the following. The soldier was a well informed man, acquainted with Lavater's works,—for every Swiss read them—at the same time he was in favor of the revolution, as the greater part of the inhabitants of the Pays de Vaud were, of course he was opposed to Lavater in every respect, especially in regard to religion and politics, for his letters to Mr. Reubel and the French Directory had been published not long before. When Lavater brought him bread and wine, the soldier did not know him, but after he had returned into his house he learnt from the bystanders, that the charitable person had been no other than Lavater; upon this information he became enraged, and being heated by wine, shot him, when he unfortunately came to him a second time. Believing this to the he fact, I contend, that Lavater died as a martyr for the truth; for he was wounded on account of his religious and political sentiments.

CHAPTER XII.

The death of Lavater was in a measure the signal for the great and wonderful development of Stilling's fate, which hitherto had been hid by the impenetrable veil of futurity. I find it necessary, to give the reader a full view of Stilling's situation at this time, so that he may be able to judge for himself, whether it was possible for him to continue longer in the station he then occupied as professor of Political Economy at Marburg. His household consisted of the following fourteen persons:

1. His father, whose state of health and weakness were such, that a girl like Mary was no longer able to attend him, and it became therefore necessary to hire

  2. an old widow, to take care of him. Occasionally he was

also visited by Mary's mother, but as she had to manage her own family, the burden chiefly rested on this widow.

3. and 4. Stilling and Eliza. 5. Mary Coing. 6 Amalia Coing, betrothed to Jacob. These two sisters faithfully assisted Eliza in the management of all family concerns. Mr. Coing's children had surrendered their property to their brother-in-law, and were therefore boarding and lodging with him.

7. Jacob. Though he had succeeded in obtaining the office of government-attorney in Marburg, yet it was not sufficient to maintain him, he therefore had his board still in the paternal house.

8—11. Caroline, Frederick, Amalia and Christine. Caroline was to be sent to a good school to receive instruction in all things necessary for a well educated young lady.

12. Mary Stilling's half-sister's daughter. 13. An elderly widow by the name of Bapp. Her husband had died when she was young. She had for some time maintained herself and her three children by her labor, when Eliza engaged her as maid; the child-like simplicity of her character, her unshaken faithfulness, her pure morals, and true piety had made her a valuable acquisition in Stilling's family, where there was always enough to do. 14. A maid to do the ordinary housework in the family. His household consisted thus of fourteen persons, and every reader who is somewhat acquainted with the expensive mode of housekeeping in a city, where every article must be bought for ready money, will comprehend that it was impossible to pay any debts, especially if he takes into consideration Stilling's principle in regard to poor patients; though the interests were regularly paid, and no new debts contracted.

In addition to the difficulties of paying the expenses of so large a family, the reader ought to recollect the throng of business which pressed upon him from all sides. For in the firt place there were daily applications, both written and personal of patients, suffering with diseases of the eye, sufficient to occupy the attention of any one man, which however added little or nothing to his income, unless during journeys, which he seldom made, and only when called. In the second place a very extensive religious correspondence, must be attended to the importance and benefit of which he alone is able to judge, who has seen the letters : then the demands from every quarter to write religious works, and to be solely active for the Lord and his kingdom ; an occupation in which he delighted and to which he believed himself called ; but which was very expensive, without adding any thing to his income : how could he therefore follow this inclination without injuring the interests of his numerous family, unless he received a salary for these labors, sufficient to enable him besides the maintenance of his household to pay a debt amounting to more than sixteen hundred guilders ? In the third place his office as public instructor became more and more unfruitful and his auditory continued to decrease for reasons, which have already been noticed : neither his lively manner of delivery, nor his perspicuity and flowing style were of any avail,—in short, the study of the sciences of finance was out of fashion in Marburg, and yet was Stilling for the sake of his family compelled to accept a salary without ability to perform equivalent services. To all this ought yet to be added the following stern demand of conscience; that he ought as a moral man, and still more as a christian, to resign his office and salary, as soon as he found himself unable conscientiously to discharge its duties, even though no blame attached to himself. This demand of conscience, which no sophistry could eradicate from his heart, created a great deal of uneasiness in his mind, without his being able to submit to its dictates. I ask every reasonable reader, how it was possible to find the way out of this labyrinth? In the present state of his family he needed the full sum of two thousand guilders, without thinking of the payment of his debts. This sum he either must receive from the Elector of Hessia, and at the same time resign his office, or he must receive a call as oculist and author of religious works from some other quarter with a similar salary. Whoever is but superficially acquainted with the state of Hessia, will know, that the first proposition contained a moral impossibility; and to entertain any hope of the execution of the second plan would have been altogether fruitless ; and even supposing, that such a plan had been feasible, it would have been impossible for Stilling to leave Marburg, because his father's situation was such, that he could not be removed; and neither he nor Eliza could entertain for a moment the idea of leaving him in the hands of strangers. Jacob likewise was as yet in no way able to maintain himself, to leave him at Marburg and assist him from a distance would have been connected with insurmountable difficulties, and to take his bride Amalia away, would have been a severe stroke to him; in short, in whatever view the case might be considered there appeared no possibility of a removal from Marburg. In this unpleasant situation, being overwhelmed by a multiplicity of duties and a host of cares, he was besides afflicted with his constitutional melancholy, so that he needed all his religious experience to support him under this oppressive burden.

The work entitled: "Longing for Heaven" and the "Triumph of the christian religion" had procured him many friends and correspondents from every province of Germany, but particularly from Wurtemberg and Switzerland. At St. Gallen, Schafhousen, Winterthur, Zurich, Bern and Basle, and here and there scattered throughout the country were many friends of Stilling and readers of his works; a particular bond of friendship had connected the family of Mr. Kirchhofer at Schafhousen with Stilling's family, since young Kirchhofer had studied Theology at Marburg, during which time he boarded in the professor's family. By this means he had made the acquaintance of Kirchhofer's four pious and well informed sisters, who kept up a very extensive correspondence with many true worshipers of the Lord in Switzerland, whereby Stilling's acquaintance and correspondence were likewise in a most interesting manner enlarged. All these circumstances together prepared his way for a journey into Switzerland, which through the guidance of Providence proved to be more important and interesting to him than any other he had hitherto undertaken.

During the month of March 1801 he received very unexpectedly a letter from parson Sulzer at Winterthur, requesting, he would come that spring to him, to perform an operation on a highly respectable lady who was afflicted with the cataract; and was very anxious to receive her sight through his instrumentality, she offered to pay all his travelling expenses and loss of time. This offer was very pleasing to Stilling, but still he thought that in undertaking so expensive a journey too much caution could not be used, he therefore answered, that he would like to come, but not being able to travel alone, Eliza must accompany him, and as the regular stage was going night and day, he would be under the necessity of taking an extra-conveyance on account of their delicate state of health, which would considerably increase the expenses of the journey. Sulzer briefly replied: he should come, every expense would be paid.

Having obtained leave of absence from the Elector, he and Eliza made every necessary preparation for this interesting tour; the children were sent to different friends, where they could stay until their parents return; Mary and the other members of the household were to nurse her grand-father and take care of the house.

They started from home March the 27th; at Buzbach they paid a flying visit to their children Schwartz, and arrived in the evening at Frankfort at the house of pastor Hausknecht, who received them with hospitality. In Frankfort they purchased several articles, which they deemed necessary and started March the 29th for Hidleberg. During the first day of their journey he had several severe attacks from the cramp in the stomach, though he had been free from it for some time before; and this evil followed him until his return home. Though sickness thus deprived him of every pleasure during the journey, yet he afterwards discovered, that Providence had sent it in kindness, because without it he would have been too much exalted by the friendship with which he was received, and the honors which were shown him.

Both he and Eliza were very anxious to get to Hidleberg, partly on account of their friends, Mr. and Mrs. Mieg and partly for the sake of Lisette, who was now fifteen years old, and whom they had not seen in ten years. By her amiable disposition, she had gained the hearts of all, who knew her; and the Marburg friends who had seen her at Mr. Mieg's house in lidleberg could not speak enough in praise of her on their returnt retiring from the noise of the world, she only lived in spiritual things.

She had looked for the arrival of her parents with so much anxiety, that it was found necessary in the evening, when it was delayed beyond the expected time to administer a composing draught to quiet her nerves. Monday was spent in the bosom of this pleasant family; on Tuesday they went as far as Heilbron, and arrived on Wednesday about noon at Ludwigsburg; here they found several friends from Stuttgard, who had come to meet them; it was a particular gratification to Stilling, to find among them his old friend Israel Hartman, teacher at the orphanhouse, of whom Lavater used to say, if Christ were now on earth, he would choose him for an Apostle. The whole company dined in the orphan-house, happy in each other's society; after dinner the journey was continued as far as Stuttgart. Stilling here again formed many acquaintances with pious and learned Wurtembergers, among these were Storr, Rieger, Moser, Dann and many others. On Thursday in the afternoon he went as far as Tubingen, on Good-Friday to Tuttlingen, and on Saturday before Easter to Schafhousen, where he was joyfully received by Mr. Kirchhofer's family.

On the road from Tuttlingen to Schafhousen is a spot of ground from which you enjoy a prospect, which is highly interesting to a German, who has never before been in Switzerland. Having arrived on a hight of ground after leaving Tuttlingen the most sublime scenery presents itself to the wondering eye. On your left about three miles distant in a straight line and in a South Easterly direction you behold the ruins of the fortress of Hohen-Twiel situated on a high rock; on your right in a South Westerly direction and at the same distance, you see the lofty ruins of the fortress of Hohenstaufen. Between these two points on the right from Hohen Twiel you behold the lake of Constance, glittering like melted silver for about nine miles towards your right; on the South-side of the lake you overlook the charming country of Thurgow, and beyond it the Alps of the Grissons; further to the right appears the canton of Appenzell with its

T t

snow clad mountains; further on the canton of Glarus and its gigantic mountains, among which you notice particularly the sevenpronged Kuhfirsten, the Sentis and the Glarnitch towering above all the rest; next to these a long row of snowy mountains stretching into the canton of Bern; thus your eye overlooks a large portion of Switzerland.—If one views the whole chain of the Alps, as it lies along the distant horizon it appears to the eye like a monstrous saw made to saw planets asunder.

Stilling remained at Schafhousen until the 7th of April, he performed several successful operations, among which one excited a particular interest. A youth, fifteen years old, the son of pious parents, being born blind, submitted to an operation on Monday after Easter in the presence of several persons; when the first ray of light darted into his eye, he exclaimed in an ecstacy of joy : "I behold the Majesty of God."— This exclamation made a deep impression on all present; but a slight inflamation prevented his receiving the full benefit of a cure though his sight was in some measure restored, and Stilling hopes with the blessing of God to be more successful in a second operation. I ought yet to notice one pretty idea of this young man. His parents had purchased a golden ring, in which was set a full sheaf of hair, to which each member of the family had contributed, heavy with golden fruit; Eliza received this ring as a present after the operation, and the young man desired to have the following devise engraven on it : "written in faith, delivered in sight." but unfortunately the ring was not large enough for this appropriate motto.

While at Schafhousen Stilling and Eliza accompanied by Mr. Kirchhofer's family visited the celebrated falls of the Rhine, but the cramp in the stomach caused him frequently to lag behind the company, and prevented him from enjoying this splendid scene of nature, as he otherwise would have done. They went on the balcony so near the falls that they might have washed themselves in it. It would be a fruitless attempt to give a description of this sublime scenery of nature, one must see and hear, in order to obtain a correct idea of it: the incessant roar, the trembling of the ground on which you stand, and the im-

mense mass of water, which rolls with irresistible force in milk
white foam at least eighty feet down the rocks and throws itself
rearing and bellowing into the extensive and boiling caldron,
presents an idea to the mind of proud man, which humbles him
to the dust.— The next day in the afternoon our travelers started for Winterthur; at Andolfingen, a village romantically situated on the banks of the Thur, they met their friend parson
Sulzer and several persons from the family of the lady who had
sent for him, who received him with open arms, and in this company he and Eliza continued the journey to Winterthur, where
they arrived in the evening. It was a Mrs. Frey who had desired
Stilling to come into Switzerland, she and her two sons kept a
large hotel in the town aud were besides engaged in extensive
mercantile business. Here Stilling and Eliza were received
—if I dare say so—like angels from heaven. The next morning he performed the operation successfully on Mrs. Frey but an
inflammation unfortunately destroyed the sight of her right eye,
the other was perfectly restored.

During his stay at Winterthur he was uncommonly thronged with business. Hundreds afflicted with diseases of the eye
called to consult him, besides the operations he performed every
day for the cataract. He was at times very ill with the cramp
in the stomach, which embittered his every enjoyment. On the
10th of April however, he received a visit, which for a short
time caused him to forget cramp and pain of all kinds. The pious brother of Lavater, Alderman Diethelm Lavater, Gesner,
Lavaters son-in-law, Louise his wife, the indefatigable nurse of
her father, and a Mrs. Fuessli from Zurich, a pious suffering
saint, now uniting her Hallelujah with the songs of those, who
clothed in white robes and palms in their hands triumphantly
rejoice before the throne of God and the Lamb, crowded together into Stilling's room. Similar to his feelings on this occasion will be *our* sensation, when we shall have overcome, and
arrived in the fields of light in the kingdom of God; the blessed saints of former times, all those eminent christians, whom
we here have longed to know, will then hasten to our embrace

—and then—to behold the Lord himself—with the glorious signs
of the son of man! — my pen drops from my hand.—

On the 13th of April Stilling went in company with Sulzer,
young Kirchhofer and Mrs. Fuessly to Zurich, to visit his
friends there, and also to see the well known manufacturer and
merchant Mr. Esslinger, who was afflicted with the cataract.
He expressed his resolution to submit to an operation in the following words: "I was resigned to my fate, expecting help only from the Lord; he now sends it to my own house, I will therefore accept it with gratitude."

At Zurich Stilling also saw the widow of his departed friend
and brother Lavater— a woman, worthy of such a husband—a
stricking image of the most exalted christian virtue.—In the
evening he returned accompanied by Sulzer to Winterthur. Here
he received a letter of thanks from the authorities of the city of
Schafhousen, for the successful operations of the cataract on several citizens of that place. On the day of his second departure
for Zurich he was particularly honored by the magistrates of
the city of Winterthur. While he was seated at table in Mrs.
Frey's house, Dr. Steiner a member of the city authorities delivered to Stilling in the name of the city of Winterthur an address accompanied by a very beautiful silver medal in a neat case,
the latter fabricated by a lady of that town. On the cover of
the case the following words were written :

To dry the tear in the eye of the blind,

To gladden his heart with the cheerful ray of light,

And to cause him to behold—instead of dread darkness

The lovely image of the king of day;

Is a talent, noble Stilling, intrusted to thee by the Lord,

For which the pious christian with heartfelt gratitude

Thanks his God.

On the one side of the medal were engraven the following words:

To

the christian friend of man,

HENRY STILLING

Court-Counselor and Professor at Marburg,

This medal is presented

by the Wardens of the congregation of Winterthur

as a trifling memorial of his visit so richly crowned with blessings,

which he made in the month of April 1801 ;

And as a mark of the respect and grateful love

of its citizens.

On the other side :

Indefatigably active
In the cause of suffering humanity
He is sowing a glorious seed
For the great day of remuneration.

The reader will easily imagine, with what deep emotion and humble gratitude towards God he received this honorable testimony of regard, and in what manner he replied to the affectionate address of Dr. Steiner.

On this day, the 16th of April, ever sacred to Stilling, he and Eliza left Winterthur for Zurich, after having bid an affectionate farewell to all the dear friends in the former city. In Zurich they were received with open arms by Mr. Gessner and his excellent wife the daughter of Lavater.

The first operation he performed in this city, was on Mr. Esslinger; it succeeded and he regained his sight, but not long afterwards he was afflicted with amaurosis, which caused an incurable blindness.

To this famil'ys kindness and friendship among many others Stilling feels himself deeply indebted, may they receive their reward in eternity.

Gladly would I mention all the christian friends, with whom he became acquainted in Switzerland and particularly in the city of Zurich, and all who honored him with their intimacy, but this would be impossible. Hess, the two Dr. Hirzel, father and son; professor Meyer, and the celebrated engraver and designer Lips, who also drew and engraved Stilling's likeness, vied with Lavater's family and relatives in acts of friendship towards him.

On the 21st of April Stilling and Eliza left Zurich after having taken an affectionate leave of their friends; Dr. Steiner and parson Kirchhofer accompanied them.

They traveled from Zurich by way of Baden and Lenzburg to Zofingen in the canton of Bern, where he was to perform an operation on judge Senn. He was a venerable pious man, modesty and every other christian virtue formed the principal traits in his character as well as that of his family. The operation succeeded, as also that performed on a poor servant maid, They then traveled through the beautiful valley of the Aar, by way of Aarburg and Olten, and thence over the Hawerstine; a mountain which would pass in Germany for one of the highest, but in comparison with the Alps of Switzerland scarcely deserves that name. The road on its summit is cut through the solid rock, and after you have passed the highest elevation, you enjoy an extensive prospect into Germany. Towards the Northwest you have a glimpse of the Vogesian mountains, towards the North you see part of the Black Forest, and turning to the South the whole chain of the Alps presents itself on the south-eastern horizon. At Laufelfingen they took lodgings at the public house of Mr. Fluhebacher. With Mrs. Fluhebacher Stilling has kept up an edifying correspondence from this time. In the evening about six o'clock they arrived in the city of Basle, where they met with a cordial and hospitable reception from Alderman Shorndorf; and spent several happy days in the midst of this christian family.

Here again Stilling found much for him to do, he also made many important acquaintances, especially with the members of the German society for the advancement of true happiness, and with several pious ministers of the gospel. After a stay of four days he and Eliza left Basle on the 27th of April.

And now dear reader, who among you has ears to hear let him hear! and who has a heart to feel, let him feel!—

Stilling owed a debt of one thousand six hundred and fifty guilders,—among the seventy-two patients, on whom he had performed operations, was one, who knew nothing of his debts, at least. who had no means of ascertaining, to what sum they amounted, and who nevertheless paid Stilling for the operation and cure the exact sum of one thousand six hundred and fifty guilders. When Stilling and Eliza in the evening came into their bed-room, they found the money partly in cash, partly in bills of exchange lying on their bed. Both sunk down upon their knees in humble gratitude to God, to offer up the sacrifice of praise to him, who had given them this proof of his particular care and providence. Eliza said : "We may well say here, to his friends he gives it while they sleep ;" and she declared that in future she would never distrust him.

But I have still more to say—The kind hearted Lady, who a few years before had sent him the sum of three hundred guilders, in a time of great pressure, was visited by him, in order to thank her for her kindness; he now removed the cataract from her husband's eye and when he protested against receiving any pay, the patient said: "that is my look out:" and sent him the sum of six hundred guilders, which paid the expenses of the journey.

One remarkable circumstance more—Stilling's heavenly guide knew that in a few years he would be in want of a considerable sum of money, but he himself was totally ignorant of it. This sum several wealthy patients paid him. Besides this money he received a great number of presents and testimonials of love and friendship in jewelry, so that he and Eliza returned from Switzerland like two bees, retur ning from a rich bed of flowers.

The omniscient God knows, that all this is pure unadulterated truth. But if this is so, what consequences ought we draw? At the close of this book we will push the inquiry farther.—

Our travelers took their way through the Breisgau to Carlsruhe. On this route, or rather until they arrived at Rastadt, Stilling was troubled by an uneasiness of mind, which at length arose to agony, he felt as though he were exposing himself to certain death. The cause of this anxiety was the following :

when at Basle he received some hints that he would subject himself
to danger should he travel by way of Strasburg; and this warning came from the latter city, in a letter from a certain friend.
Another circumstance deserves likewise notice as co-operating
in producing this melancholy feeling. A dangerous man had
thrown out severe threatenings against Stilling, while at Basle;
the cause of all this is to be sought for in the works, he had published, which contain a great deal, which must appear highly
exceptionable to a freethinker. I know there are some, who
abhor the very name of Stilling.—Strange—Stilling feels no enmity much less abhorrence against any one! — Friends! on
which side lies the truth? Surely not on that where there is
enmity!

Stilling's sufferings were indescribable especially at Freyburg
in the Breisgow, at Offenburg, and at Appenweyer; for he thought
if he should be attacked it would probably be at one of these places, when however he found himself safe at Rastadt he became
more composed, though he suffered severely from the cramp in the
stomach. On the 29th of April they traveled to Carlsruhe; on
this part of their journey his bodily pains became excru-
ciating. He wished for rest and on his arrival in the city he
did not intend to go to the Elector; but afterwards reflected, as
that pious prince had read his works and especially "Longing for
Heaven," and highly approved of it, and had written him several
letters on this subject, it was his duty to call on him though he
knew not if he would be received. He therefore went to the
palace, was announced, and immediately admitted, and had
to promise to return in the evening at five o'clock, to spend some
time in religious conversation. I shall say no more of this visit,
but that it paved the way for such a call as he had long wished
to receive, by means of which he was at liberty to devote himself
without reserve to religion and the extension of the Redeemer's
kingdom.

On the 30th of April they went to Bidleberg; Lisette had
during the absence of her parents offered daily prayers to God
to grant them a prosperous journey. On the next morning, the
1st of May they continued their journey; Mr. Mieg and Lisette

accompanied them as far as Heppenheim, and here they saw, Lisette for the last time in this life. Mr. Mieg returned with her, to Hidleberg, and Stilling and Eliza continued their course to Frankfort where they arrived May the 2d. From Frankfort they went to the Schlangenbad. In this pleasant solitude they had leisure sufficient to recapitulate their long journey, and having recovered from their fatigue, returned to Marburg, where they arrived on the 15th of May, and found their family in the enjoyment of health and comfort.

CHAPTER XIII.

The payment of his debts was the first object of Stilling's care after his return from this journey. The greater part of the principal which had been loaned him at Shonenthal immediately after his return from Strasburg, and for which his father-in-law had become security, was still unpaid; this debt was now cancelled. Stilling had left Hidleberg and moved to Marburg, in hopes of paying his debts by means of the large salary which he was to receive at the latter place; such at least was his and Selma's plan, but it was not the plan of his heavenly guide, for the largest debt he had contracted, was not paid by means of his salary, but from the treasury of Providence. The views of the Lord in bringing him to Marburg were to offer him an asylum from the horrors of war, and then to crown his unshaken confidence in such a wonderful manner, that all must confess: "The Lord has done it." Should any of my readers find fault with the above observation, that it had been the Lord's plan to offer him an asylum from the horrors of war, while so many thousands perhaps much better christians than he was, had been for years exposed to this evil, I answer, that a good shepherd preserves the weakest of his flock more carefully than any of the others from the injury of storm and rain.

Providence always executes her plans fully and not by halfs like short-sighted mortals, thus it was in the case of Stilling. A friend in Strasburg had loaned him while he was studying, a

U u

sum amounting to about forty-five guilders, and had never pressed him for the payment. His other creditors being less generous, he was gratified by this man's forbearance; thus the debt remained unpaid, until the French revolution and the war came on. The communication between France and Germany being thereby interrupted, he had almost forgotten it. But his heavenly guide whose attribute is justice did not forget it; for soon after Stilling's journey to Switzerland a friend paid the brother of the Strasburg creditor, he having long since departed this life, not only the principal but also the interests for thirty years, which raised the sum to near one hundred guilders. Stilling received from an unknown hand the receipt for the payment of this debt, but never learned, who had performed this act of friendship for him. "But he will find thee, nobleminded man! in these regions, where every thing shall be made known, and then only he will be able to express his gratitude to thee."—

A few weeks after his return from Switzerland, he was one forenoon engaged at his desk, when a knock was heard at the door, and at the word "walk in," a young man between twenty-seven and thirty years of age entered. He had a wild and agitated appearance, looked with shyness about the room and frequently cast an uneasy glance at Lavater's likeness. "You have been at Zurich" he commenced, "I have been there too, I must get away."—He walked about the room with a restless step, and again looked at Lavater's picture. All at once he said: "I cannot stay in Germany, I am not safe here, they might arrest me.— O, Mr. Stilling, will you not aid me in getting off?"—Stilling was somewhat embarrassed at the strange conduct of the man, and asked him, if he were a Swiss?—"O yes," he replied, "I am a Swiss!—but I have no rest, I want to go to America, can't you give me your advice, how I may get there?"—He said much more, while he hurried up and down the room, and occasionally cast glances at Lavater's portrait. All this excited the suspicion of Stilling, that he was the murderer of Lavater. He therefore advised him to go to Hamburg, where he would find opportunities enough to get to America, and that he should set off as soon as possible, lest he should fall into the hands of the police. Suddenly the poor fellow rushed out of the door and hastened away.

On his journey from Switzerland, he and Eliza spent one night with their children Schwartz at Munster. After they had told them, how the Lord had blessed them, Schwartz and Hannah proposed, that their parents should now consent to Jacob's and Amalia's marriage. They were quite willing it should take place, and to surprise the two lovers the more and to increase their joy, they resolved, to keep all the preparations for the wedding as secret as possible, to invite friend Slarbaum and his family to tea, who should then unexpectedly arise and offer to perform the marriage ceremony. This plan could however be executed only in part; the secret some how or other transpired; they were married July the 12th 1801. Jacob moved back to his parents, and he and his wife lived with them upon the same footing as before.

During this summer Stilling wrote the second volume of "the Scenes from the spiritual world." On that occasion a very remarkable circumstance took place, which I think will interest the reader. I have mentioned before, that he had written a poem entitled "Lavater's transfiguration," soon after Lavater's death; in this poem, two of his friends, who had departed before him, Felix Hess and Pfenninger, are represented as receiving the soul of the weary combatant in the form of angelic beings after his death and accompanying it to the New Jerusalem. About six months after the publication of that poem the reformed minister Breidenstein at Marburg came to see him; they conversed on various subjects, and among others on this poem. "One could almost say," observed Breidenstein, "you had redeemed the promise, which Felix Hess gave to Lavater before his death." "What promise do you refer to?" said Stilling. "Lavater," replied Breidenstein, "was standing, some twenty odd years since at the death-bed of Felix Hess, and said with many tears, I can no longer hope that you will close my eyes when I depart!"— Hess replied: "I shall then fetch you away!"—Stilling said: "I have never, never heard this before—it is singular indeed—where is it mentioned? I must read it myself!"—"So you shall," replied Breidenstein, "this is a very strange circumstance!"

The next day he sent him Lavater's miscellaneous works, which contain among other things a brief description of the life of Felix Hess, the conversation between Lavater and Hess is also mentioned, exactly as Breidenstein had related it. I can assure the reader, that Stilling had never before seen or heard any thing of this occurrence, or if he had read it once, which however I doubt, he had not thought of it for many years. If this took place accidentally it is certainly one of the most singular accidents which ever has occurred. For in the first place Hess says about thirty years before to Lavater, a short time before his death, "I shall fetch you when you die:" Lavater dies so many years afterwards,—Stilling resolves to write a poem on his death—resolves, to form the design of the poem so, that two of his friends come to fetch his soul when liberated from the tenement of clay, and he choses for that purpose the very man, who had promised to do it almost thirty years before.—One circumstance more. During Stilling's stay at Zurich he was asked, since Lavater had stood on a more intimate footing with another friend than with Felix Hess, why he had not used the name in the poem for calling Lavater away? Upon Stilling's inquiry who that friend had been? he was told it was Henry Hess. This information induced him to introduce him in the second volume of the "Scenes" in the following manner: "Henry Hess is represented as an angelic being in heaven, commissioned to bring Lavater to the mother of Jesus, because she wished to know him, who on earth had been such a faithful disciple of her son;" Lavater asks her in this interview concerning the character of the Lord during his life here on earth &c. Long afterwards, when the work was published, Stilling happened to read by chance the twenty-sixth chapter of the first volume of Lavater's work, entitled: "JESUS THE MESSIAH" which treats of the privacy of the life of Jesus until his thirtieth year; and here he found to his astonishment, that Lavater, on account of our present want of means for obtaining information concerning this portion of the life of Jesus, consoles himself with the idea, that in the happy abodes of the blessed Mary would give him the desired information on this subject as well as on every other particular of his life and charac-

341

ter, during his earthly pilgrimage. I solemnly assure the reader,
Stilling had not read this before he wrote the Scenes.

In the autumn of 1801 he and Eliza undertook another
journey. A pious person in the North of Germany was afflicted with the cataract, she was to poor to come to Marburg, or
to send for Stilling. After some consultation with Eliza it was
resolved—because God had so richly blessed their journey to
Switzerland,—to make this tour at their own expense. They
therefore made preparations for it, and Stilling wrote to the patient that he would come. At the receipt of this letter she made
his expected arrival known in her neighborhood. As their way
led through Brunswick, they received a friendly invitation, to
lodge during their stay in that city at the house of Mr. Stobwasser, who does an extensive business in japaned ware, and is
a member of the Moravian church. Stilling thankfully accepted the offer; and on their way thither they intended to stop at
the town of Munden to pay Julia a visit, and make her personal
acquaintance; she invited them to lodge at her house, which
invitation they accepted with pleasure.

Stilling and Eliza commenced their journey, Ssptember the
18th; and took Caroline with them as far as Cassel, where she
was to stay, until the return of her parents. At Cassel they
lodged with counsellor Kunkel, whose lady is a near relation of
Eliza.

The next day they went as far as Munden where they spent
the Lord's day. Julia received them in the fulness of christian
affection ; and the reformed minister Klugkist and his excellent lady likewise manifested towards our travelers great kindness and civility. Julia and Eliza covenanted together, to continue in the path, which our adorable redeemer has pointed out
and on which he himself has preceded us, as the captain of our
salvation. Julia has two sisters, ladies of excellent character, who by their presence increased the friendly circle. At
Gœttingen they found their friend Achelis on the point of moving into the neighborhood of Bremen, whither he had received
a call, he however accompanied them as far as Nordhime. In
this town the deepest gloom fell upon Stilling, it commenced

when he bid Achelis farewell, but I do not know, whether his friend observed it. This distressing state of mind originated in a fear of the bad roads, and of being upset in the carriage —but it was almost insupportable and lasted during the whole journey, though not always with an equal degree of violence. On the 22d day of September they arrived at Stobwasser's in Brunswick, and though he and his lady were gone to Berlin, the two travelers were kindly and hospitably received by that part of the family, which they found at home. From Brunswick Stilling went to the lady, for whose sake the journey had been undertaken. The operation was successful, and her sight was restored. In the city itself he performed operations on twelve persons, and at Ampleben a village about twelve miles distant from Brunswick on a Mrs. Bode, who with her husband belongs to the followers of Jesus. After a stay of four days with Mrs. Bode, who was restored to her sight, Stilling and Eliza returned to Brunswick,

The Duke who sent twice for Stilling, conversed with him on various subjects, among others on religion, concerning which he expressed himself in a very edifying and satisfactory manner. He also told him: "All, you have done here to my people, I consider, as having been done to my own person"—and the next day he sent him the sum of sixty Louisdors, (about two hundred and fifty dollars,) to his lodging, which more than paid the expenses of the journey. During his stay at Brunswick he was informed that the young count and countess of Wernigerode wished Stilling to stand god-father at the baptism of a daughter; he therefore resolved to take that route in his way homeward, and arrived in the evening of the ninth of October at the castle. The succeeding three days they spent in the pleasant circle of this noble family. A gentleman from Saxony, who was there on business and sat at table by the side of Stilling observed: "One ought to come from time to time to this place, for the sake of receiving new strength and vigor for the prosecution of our journey through this vale of tears."—And he was right—for religion, good manners, elegance, cheerfulness, a pleasing address free from all affectation are the characteristics of every

member of this family. On the thirteenth of October, after
having taken an affectionate leave of the count and his family,
our travelers left Wernigerode.   Count Stolberg sent them in
his coach as far as Seesen, whence they took an extra-conveyance as far as Gandershime, where the countess Fredericke of
Ortenburg was canoness, who had been for many years a friend of
Stilling and who had informed him that a number of patients
were waiting for his arrival.   The countess was rejoiced at his
visit and here also he received many proofs of kindness. He was
consulted by many afflicted with various diseases of the eye, and
cured a poor old woman of the cataract.   In the evening before
his departure his melancholy rose to an alarming degree, but towards midnight he turned himself in earnest prayer to God,
slept quietly till morning and continued his homeward journey
with Eliza; late in the evening they arrived at Munden were
Julia, Klugkist and other friends emulated each other in acts of
friendship towards them.   As it was thought Julia's aged father
could not live much longer, Stilling and Eliza invited her to pay
them a visit at Marburg, after the old gentleman's death, which
she promised to do. In Cassel much bussiness waited for him,
from morning till night he had to write recipes and give his
advice to patients, he likewise performed a number of operations.

The reader will recollect, that Mr. Coing Eliza's brother
had received a call as minister to Braach near Rothenburg on
the river Fulda and that his sister Mary and the two children
Frederick and Amalia were there at that time.   It was Stilling's
intention, to bring these two children home again as well as
his sister Maria, if she desired it, and to pay a visit to his
brother-in-law ; they therefore left Cassel on the twenty- second
of October. As they were passing through the Leipzig gate he
said to Eliza : "I would give a great deal, my dear, if we were
on our journey to Marburg."   Eliza replied : "Well let us go
there"—but Stilling would not consent, as he thought if any misfortune awaited him it might overtake him in one place as well
as an other, so they continued their route. Mr. Coing met them
on horseback and in the evening they arrived safe at Braach.
They stayed a full week in this pleasant place; during all which

time Stilling felt like a poor malefactor, who expects his execution in a few days. Maria who was not very well consented to return to Marburg with them and the children; the twenty-ninth of October was fixed upon for their departure, for this purpose horses were ordered at the post-office in Morschen. On Wednesday evening, the day before their departure, his melancholy rose so high, that he said to Eliza: "If the torment of the damned in hell is even not greater than mine at present, it is horrible indeed."

The next morning the postillion came at the appointed time with four very lively horses. He drove with the empty carriage through the river Fulda; Stilling, Eliza, Mary, the children and Mr. Coing were ferried over in a boat, meanwhile the postillion drove up the meadow on the other side of the river and waited for them on the shore. They all got into the carriage; Stilling took his seat behind on the right side, Eliza sat by him with Amalia on her lap; when Coing had taken leave, the driver cracked his whip, the horses gave a sudden start, the carriage turned short, the forewheels caught and threw the barouche with such force on the ground, that the body broke in two pieces. Eliza, Maria and the two children were thrown out in the meadow, but Stilling being seated on the side on which the barouche fell, remained in it, and was badly bruised and wounded. Happily the bolt flew out, so that the hind part of the carriage was not dragged along by the horses, though he was so squeezed in, that he could not stir. But it was remarkable, that notwithstanding the severe pain he felt over his whole body his melancholy had entirely left him, peace and serenity filled his mind, and though he did not know what the consequences of the accident might be, he was fully resigned to the divine will, there was no trace of any fear of death. Much as the driver deserved a severe scolding, yet Stilling only said mildly: "Friend, you have turned too short." The rest of the party escaped uninjured.

Mr. Coing came back, when he observed the accident; the coach was raised up, and Stilling, wounded and bruised as he was, limped back to Branch leaning on Eliza's arm. The driver likewise returned to the village with his horses and broken carriage, and the farmers were near giving him a severe drubbing. They were all eager to lend their assistance, one of them rode full speed to Rothenburg for the Doctors, while others offered refreshments to Stilling and his family. The right side of his breast was very much swollen, one rib was broken, he felt a severe pain under the right shoulder-blade, a wound on the temple of the right side of his head was bleeding freely only one eighth part of an inch from the great artery, and his right side and hip were extremely painful when he moved his leg.

Several physicians soon arrived, whose united care restored him in a few days so far, that he could return to Marburg. On the second of November they left Braach a second time, Stilling rode on horseback, because he distrusted the coach as the roads were very bad ; this precaution proved fortunate, for his family was upset again though without receiving any injury. It was a long time before he recovered fully from this accident. It affected his head and brought on a vertigo. Mr. Coing accompanied them as far as Mabern where Caroline waited for her parents. The next day they returned to Marburg.

CHAPTER XIV.

The commencement of the year 1802 brought sadness and mourning into Stilling's family. On the third of January he received a letter from Mr. Mieg at Hidleberg, informing him, that Lisette was sick, but he did not think, that any serious consequences need be apprehended, because the physicians entertained good hopes of her recovery. At the reading of this letter, Stilling received an impression, that she was dead. He always has an agreeable sensation, when he learns, that a child or a pious person has departed this life, because he knows, that a soul has again reached the desired haven. This sensation is likewise an unspeakable comfort to him, when one of his family or children dies; yet being endowed with a very feeling heart, his physical nature has on such occasions to undergo a severe conflict;

this was the case now, he greatly suffered for several hours, but then he gave up his Lisette to the Lord, who had entrusted her to him, and on the sixth of January, when the news of her death arrived, he was so strong that he could comfort her deeply affected foster-parents; but Eliza suffered much on this occasion.

Mr. Mieg gave Lisette a very honorable burial, and published a little book containing her course of life, character, death, funeral and several pamphlets and poems, which had been written on the occasion. Mr. and Mrs. Mieg had given her a most excellent education. and God will reward them for the many pious instructions they have given her. It is remarkable that the aged mother Wilhelmi followed her favorite a few weeks after.

About the same time the Burgomaster Eike, Julia's father died also. Stilling and Eliza repeated the invitation, which they had given her to visit them, after the death of her father. She came about the middle of January, and was so much pleased, that she resolved to spend her life in their family. Matters were all arranged, Julia paid for her board and lodging, and employed herself in leisure-hours with the education of Amalia and Christine: Eliza protested at first against receiving pay for her board, but Julia persisted in it, declaring, that she would not come on any other condition, and therefore Eliza was obliged to submit. In the month of March Julia made a journey to Erfurt to pay a visit to a friend, and returned in August. Since this time she has been a member of Stilling's family, to which she proves a real blessing from God, by her piety, serenity of mind, experience in afflictions, and especially by the unremitting care she takes in the bringing up and education of the two youngest girls.

This spring Stilling received letters, desiring him to come to Fulda ; he complied with the request, and Eliza accompanied him. On their return, they traveled by way of Hanau and Frankfort and paid a visit to prince Frederick of Anhalt and the countess Louise, who had left Marburg last autumn and had removed to Homburg on the Height. After an absence of four weeks, they arrived again at Marburg.

The important period of Caroline's confirmation was approaching. She was now in her fifteenth year and very large for her age. Her father's worthy friends, the reformed ministers Slarbaum and Breidenstein had given her religious instruction for the last two years, which had made a deep impression on her mind, which was imbued with the most pious, christian sentiments; and it was highly satisfactory for her father to know, that not only Caroline but his three eldest children were in the way of becoming true christians. Julia wrote a letter to Caroline from Erfurt, which she inclosed in one directed to Mrs. Duising, desiring her to deliver the inclosure to Caroline on the day of her confirmation, and it is well worth inserting.

My dear and beloved Caroline!

On this most solemn day of thy life, on which all thy friends press thee to their bosom with renewed marks of love and attachment, my prayers also shall unite with those of thy parents and relatives, perhaps in the very hour, in which thou by the most solemn vows shalt promise eternal faithfulness and love to him, who has first loved thee. I shall also pray for thee, that he may grant thee faith and perseverance in this love.

O my dearest, best Caroline! I beseech thee most ardently, carefully to consider and to keep, what thou promisest on this day so important to thee for time and eternity! Love the Lord, as thou lovest no other being!—Thou canst do nothing greater, nothing better, nothing more important.—Suffer neither pleasure nor pain, neither flattery nor the derisions of the world, to deprive thee of that crown of glory, which thy faith beholds to day as reserved in the hand of the Lord for thee, and remain faithful unto him even unto death.—

The confirmation took place on the day of Pentecost, amidst the prayers of all her relatives and the congregation.

The unpleasantness of Stilling's situation increased daily; on the one hand his religious sphere of activity enlarged, and became more important and beneficial; and the Director of the Tract-society in London wrote him an affectionate letter, encouraging him to establish a similar society in Germany; and at the same time his religious correspondence and practice in diseases of the eye increased from day to day; on the other hand his professional calling became daily more unproductive; the change of territories, which at that time had taken place in Germany, brought those provinces, from which most of the students were expected, under the government of princes, who had universities in their own dominions; thus their number decreased at Marburg, and those who still attended, directed their attention to mere professional studies among which cameralistics had no place. In short, his auditory became so small, that he frequently had not more than two or three hearers—this was deeply afflicting,—his conscience smote him, for accepting so large a salary, while he was doing so little for it, and yet necessity compelled him to receive it. At the same time, that great principle, which he had kept in view from his youth—to labor and to live alone for the Lord and religion filled his soul, he daily heard and saw, how extensively beneficial his religious sphere of activity was and yet was constrained to neglect it, in order to labor in a calling, by which he gained his living, but which was wholly unproductive in itself. Another circumstance made his situation still more unpleasant. The Elector of Hesse was inclined to support religion, but he held this opinion, which abstractedly considered, is very correct: that every servant of the State ought to devote his whole time to that branch in which he is engaged, and was not pleased if an officer endeavored to serve two masters. But such was Stilling's situation, that he was compelled to act against this principle, which produced many sad reflections in his mind—his conflict was severe—but a kind Providence was now paving the way for the execution of its plan.

About the middle of summer he received a letter from parson Konig at Burgdorf in the canton of Bern, desiring he would come and perform an operation on him and promising to pay the expenses of the journey. He and Eliza began therefore to make preparations for their second tour into Switzerland.

During these occurrences William Stilling's state of health unexpectedly changed. His mind and judgment had entirely left him, while his bodily constitution had still appeared healthy, but suddenly the members of his body refused to perform their offices; having lain so long in bed, his whole body was sore, a surgeon attended him daily to dress his sores, which was such a painful operation, that the poor man screamed and lamented so loud, that the whole neighborhood was deeply affected. Stilling could not bear this scene, he generally left the house as the time approached for dressing the sores. But towards the close of his life his sufferings appeared to be without intermission and his groans almost incessant. At length the day of his redemption drew nigh; in the evening of the sixth of September he departed to the blessed habitations of his forefathers. His quiet unobtrusive piety—though unobserved by the world—was seen and marked by his heavenly Father. Not the man, who is celebrated far and wide,—not he who does much, is always a great man, but he is truly great, who sows here and reaps a thousand fold above. William Stilling sojourned here sowing in tears, now *he* will reap in everlasting joy. His children, Henry and Eliza think with rapture of his welcome in the fields of bliss and when they reflect, that they were unremitting in their endeavors to smooth his bed of suffering, they are comforted.

A week after their father's departure from this world, Stilling and Eliza commenced their second journey into Switzerland. In Frankfort he found patients, who detained him several days. On the sixteenth they reached Hidleberg early in the afternoon. The welcome of their friend Mieg and his family was deeply affecting. Mieg happened to be absent on business in the country when they arrived, and returned only towards evening. He said he had dined that day with a gentleman of high standing in society, and the conversation turning upon Stilling, his friend observed that some prince ought to pay him a salary, that he might pursue his beneficial calling as oculist, without involving himself in difficulties. This expression, though insignificant in itself, made, when taken in connection with other circumstances, for instance, the death of his father and a second journey into Switzerland, a deep impression on his mind, and produced high expectations.

The next day our travelers continued their journey as far

as Carlsruhe. In this place I find it necessary to go a step back in my narrative, to bring every thing under the proper point of view.

Jacob's marriage had been blest with a child during the last spring—but notwithstanding his skill and integrity and the best testimonials from the officers of government at Marburg, he could obtain no office sufficient to maintain his family; and with his mode of thinking in regard to law it was impossible, that the practice of this profession could procure him a living; his father had therefore to assist him considerably: these things greatly troubled him, he therefore requested his father, to recommend him to the Elector of Baden on his passage through Carlsruhe, supposing as he was born in his dominions, he had some claim to a settlement in them. To ask such a favor of a prince favorably disposed towards him was a difficult task, though the settlement of his son was very desirable.

Stilling and Eliza arrived, as has been said late on Friday evening the eighteenth of September at Carlsruhe. It is his custom to carry the *Daily Word* of the Brethren's church with him during his journeys for his instruction and edification. This little book contains two passages of the Bible for every day in the year with an appropriate verse from the hymnbook attached to each, in general expressive of this application of the Bible passage either to any individual or to the church at large. The first part of these texts is properly styled the *Daily Word*, the other is called the Doctrinal Text for the day. When on the following day he opened the book, he found the Daily Word to be 2 Sam. 7. v. 25. &c. "And now, O Lord God, the word, that thou hast spoken concerning thy servant and concerning his house, establish it forever, and do as thou hast said." In the Doctrinal Text were these words: "Be faithful unto death and I will give thee the crown of life." These remarkable passages of scripture strenghtened his hope, that the long desired change in his situation would take place this day. Soon after a message was sent from court, that the Elector wished Stilling to come that morning at nine o'clock, and stay to dinner.

In consequence of this request he went at the appointed hour to the palace, was announced and immediately admitted. After some conversation he felt at liberty to recommend his son. He commenced with observing, that he had always been reluctant to lay requests of this nature before princes, who were kindly disposed toward him, but his situation was of such a nature, that he found himself under the necessity to make an exception to this rule ; he then gave a true representation of the character of his son, and offered to produce the most satisfactory proofs of what he had said, viz : the testimonials he had received from the government officers at Marburg, and finally begged the Elector, to let his son serve from the ranks, and advance him only according to his merits, he would consider it as a great favor, if his salary would barely support him with proper economy, and at last concluded in these words; he hoped, that his Electoral Highness would not ungraciously look upon this first and last recommendation, which should ever come from him. The Elector expressed himself in the kindest terms and said : "He would endeavor to find a place for him in the organisation of the Palatinate, Stilling should in the mean time mention his request to his counselors and ministers, that they might be acquainted with the circumstance, when his son's name should be brought forward, which Stilling promised to do.

This conversation had given him an opportunity to speak of his own situation; and the Elector inspired him with so much confidence, that he gave him a plain statement of it, upon which the good prince observed : "I hope, God will grant me means to assist you in getting out of this unpleasant situation, and to place you so that you may only concern yourself with the publication of religious works, and attend patients afflicted with diseases of the eye ; for you ought to be disengaged from every worldly care. A description of his feelings on this occasion would be impossible! "Are you anxious, that this plan should be put into immediate execution?" continued the Elector. Stilling replied : "By no means, and I intreat your Highness, to wait until Providence opens a door, so that no one may be injured and that I may not interfere with the promotion of any other person." The Prince replied : "Do you think you can wait six months or a year longer?" Stilling answered : "I can wait as long as it pleases God, until your Highness shall have found the way which Providence may point out."

Whoever is acquainted with the Elector of Baden, will know that his Highness conscientiously keeps his pledged word, and in fact doth generally more than he promises. Every christian, feeling heart will therefore be in accordance with Stilling's grateful sensations.—Praised and blessed be the Lord! his ways are holy, blessed is *he*, who surrenders himself without reserve to his guidance and direction! Whoever trusts in him, shall not be put to shame.

CHAPTER XV.

On the nineteenth of September having performed an operation on a poor aged peasant, whom the Elector had expressly sent for, Stilling and Eliza continued their journey towards Switzerland. The nearer they approached, the more terrifying became the rumors of revolutionary movements in that country; this was unpleasant, but they knew, that they had undertaken this journey for benevolent purposes, and therefore placed their confidence in Divine Providence, and this was not in vain.

At Freyburg in the Breisgow they were informed of the calamity, which had befallen the city of Zurich on the eighteenth of September but at the same time learnt, that its inhabitants had experienced the powerful protection of Divine Providence in the midst of danger. On the twenty-fifth of September they arrived at Basle and took up their abode in the hospitable mansion of the Shorndorf family, whence they mentioned their arrival to parson Konig, and that they would tarry there until they received information from him, that they might undertake the journey with safety.

How pleasing would it be were it possible to relate every trait of the mercy and goodness of God, which occurs in the life of man, but as this impossible, because many are not proper to meet the public eye, the christian rejoices, whenever he can mention such an instance to the praise of God. One of this de-tion occurred to Stilling while at Basle. The reader will remember the kindness which he had experienced from Mr. Isaac at Waldstadt, how he clothed him, when he was in the greatest distress and misery. He had indeed paid the expenses which Isaac had incurred, but the thought frequently troubled him, that he had never been able practically to manifest his gratitude to the family of this friend in need. An opportunity now offered, and he resolved not to neglect it.

The eldest son of Mr. Isaac had learnt the tailor's trade with his father, and as a journeyman-tailor had come to Basle, and lived several years in that city; afterwards he had settled at Waldstadt,—Rade-vor-dem-Walde in the Duchy of Berg—his native town, and kept house with his brothers and sisters; but as a sedentary life did not agree with his state of health, he had given up the trade, and commenced storekeeping, and thus made a living for himself and his family. On the twenty-fourth of August a fire broke out in the village, which raged with so much violence, that the whole town in a few hours was reduced to ashes; and poor Isaac's children not only lost their own property, but also the store-goods, part of which had been taken on credit. Mr. Becker—the real family name—did not himself inform Stilling of this misfortune, but another friend reminded him of his obligations to this family. It was an embarrassing case; for whatever even with the greatest exertion he could do for them in his present circumscribed situation would be of little avail to them, nevertheless he made up a small sum and sent it, and as he had previous to his departure from home finished the twelfth number of "The Grey Man," he added at the close a notice of this misfortune, and ventured to implore the aid of christian friends in behalf of the family. While at Basle, he was invited by the members of the German society to address them in one of their meetings, which he did, and at the close of his address, reminded them of their former friend, and related the misfortune which had befallen him; a collection was immediately taken, which amounted to near one hundred guilders. The notice published in the above mentioned periodical produced about one thousand guilders for Mr. Isaac's children and to his native town five hundred; which sums were sent to Stilling for distribution.

In a few days the information was received from Burgdorf, that peace was restored in that neighborhood; Stilling and Eliza therefore left Basle September the twenty-ninth; at Liestal he performed the operation for the cataract on a person, and arrived in the evening at the house of Judge Senn in Zofingen, who had come as far as Aarburg, to meet them. As they were traveling down the valley of the Aar, and the evening sun was spreading its light over the landscape, the rays struck a distant glacier situated in a south-easterly direction, which gave it the appearance of a meteor glittering in the most beautiful purple light. But it would be impossible to give a full description of this splendid spectacle of nature to any person, who has not viewed it himself; you feel as if you had a glimpse of the realms of celestial glory. Judge Senn, who rode before them in his gig, turned round and observed: "What a majestic sight!"—I have seen yonder glacier frequently illuminated by the rays of the sun, and still the spectacle is new to me as often as I view it." The next morning they started for Burgdorf, where they arrived at six o'clock in the evening, and took their lodgings at the parsonage. This town is situated on a hill, which has the form of a saddle; on its western point stand the church and parsonage, on the eastern the castle; between these two points and on the saddle itself is built the town which hangs down the hill similar to a splendid housing. On the northern side a violent and rapid stream called the Emme rushes down the mountain, and from the two points afore mentioned the traveler enjoys a most delightful prospect. Towards the north-west the chain of the Jura here called the Blue Mountain, presents itself to the eye; in the South appears *again* the noble chain of the Alps, from the Mutterhorn and Shreckhorn in the West until far beyond the Jungfrau in the East. Stilling performed in this place several operations besides that on Mr. Konig, one eye of the latter was perfectly cured. I cannot refrain here from relating the circumstances attending the operation performed on one of the patients, because they throw much light on the character of Swiss peasants. Two very

stout, handsome men, dressed after the fashion of the country but
neatly and cleanly, came one day into the parsonage with an old
grey-headed man, and inquired after the strange Doctor. When
Stilling came, one of them said in the Swiss dialect: "We bring
here our father—he is blind—can you help him?"—Stilling replied after viewing his eyes: "With the blessing of God, my
friends, your father shall recover his sight." The two men
were silent, but large drops rolled down their cheeks and be-
spoke the emotion of their hearts; the lips of the old man quivered and a moisture spread over his eyes. During the operation they arranged themselves on each side of their father so as
to see the whole proceeding: when it was over, and their father
had obtained his sight, they did not speak but expressed the sensation of their heart by means of the silent but expressive language of the eyes--after a pause the elder of the sons asked: "Doctor! what do we owe you?" When Stilling answered, that though
he was not in the habit of receiving money for his cures, yet being on a journey, and his expenses great, he would accept a recompense, provided they were able to give it without injuring
themselves, the elder son pathetically replied: "It must be a
large sum indeed which we would not willingly pay when
the health and comfort of our father is in question—" and the
younger added: "our left hand doth not receive back, what
the right has given." Stilling replied with a shake of the hand:
"This was well spoken—you are worthy men, God will bless
you, if you retain such sentiments towards your father!"

Stilling and Eliza again enlarged the circle of their friends
in Burgdorf. Here they likewise became acquainted with the
celebrated Pestaluzzi and his institution. The principal trait of
his character is benevolence towards man in general and towards
children in particular. Properly speaking not his method of education, has given him his great celebrity, but his method of instruction. The progress, which children make according to his
system of instruction in all those branches of learning, which in
their detached or analysed form can be brought under the scrutiny of the eye and mind united, is really astonishing. But
time can only show in how far this system of tuition is appli-

cable to the development of abstract ideas, and of our moral and religious sentiments, and what an influence it will exercise on the practical life of man. Caution is therefore necessary, as experience ought to show us, how far the children taught according to this system will become useful in society, before we place implicit confidence in a new method of instruction. It is rather inconsiderate to favor a general introduction of any new system of education, before we are fully aware of its practical utility.*

October the fourth our travelers went to Bern, and took their lodgings at Mr. Niehans, a pious and faithful friend of God and man. Their stay in this beautiful city, which lasted four days, was thronged with business. On the ninth of October they left Bern. At Hindelbank, a village between that city and Burgdorf, they visited the celebrated monument of Mrs. Langhaus a work of the great Hessian artificer Nahl. At Burgdorf Stilling again performed operations on several patients, and then went by way of Zofingen, to Zurich, Winterthur and St. Gallen. On the twenty-seventh of October they passed through the Romantic Thurgow, along the lake of Constance to Shafhousen, where they again met with much hospitality from the dear family of parson Kirchhofer. On the first of November they left Switzerland ; having received an invitation by express from a merchant at Ebingen, afflicted with the cataract, they were under the necessity of taking a circuitous route by way of Moskirch and the Suabian Alb ; from Ebingen they were sent for

---

*Observation of the translator. The American public ought seriously to reflect on the truths, which Stilling pronounces here in regard to education. The welfare of our children, the continuance of our republican institutions, and the happiness of children's children depend chiefly on the education of the rising generation, and on the manner, in which this is done. And yet there is no country, in which more experiments in methods of teaching are made, or rather, in which parents allow every empiric in the art of instruction, to follow his own inclination without limitation or reserve. There is no system prescribed or adopted either in our country schools or in our Gymnasia or colleges, and though custom has introduced a certain routine in the latter, yet there are not two or three among these high schools of our country in existence, in which the system of instruction is alike, wherever an alteration has been admitted from that course of studies which the pilgrims of the seventeenth century brought with them from England.

to Balingen, thence they went to Stuttgardt, here they took up their abode in Mr. Seckendorf's hospitable mansion, and Stilling found many opportunities of serving suffering humanity.

In this place he made the acquaintance of Mr. Goldman, a member of the Elder's conference of the Moravian brethren, with whom he entered into an intimate friendship. From Stuttgard they took again a circuitous route over the Black Forest to Calw, where Stilling visited the pious Mr. Havlin minister of New Bulack, with whom and whose family consisting of his wife and daughter he was already acquainted by an interesting correspondence. Here likewise a circle of precious souls collected round our travelers, in the house of Mr. Shille. On the ninth of November they left Calw for Carlsruhe. To this latter place he went by the express desire of the Margravine of Baden who had informed him. that a number of patients expected his arrival. The Elector repeated the promise, he had before given him, and on the twelfth of that month they went by way of Manhime to Frankfort. Here and at Vilbel he found three patients, and on the sixteenth they arrived at Marburg.

The fruit of the first journey to Switzerland had been the payment of his debts, that of the second was the solution of the enigma of the views of Providence with Stilling.

CHAPTER XVI.

In the spring of this year Mr. Coing had married an excellent young lady, who was altogether worthy of him. Stilling, Eliza, her sister Maria and Jacob, were at the wedding, which was celebrated at Homberg in Lower Hessia at the house of the bride's mother, Mrs. Wiskeman. Here counsellor Cnyelm a widower, a pious and wealthy man became acquainted with Maria, who was much pleased with him. The necessary rules of caution and decorum being observed, they were married, and Maria,—the noble, mild, affectionate and pious soul—obtained a husband, in every respect suitable for her, with whom she is as happy, as it is possible for mortals to be on this sublinary globe.

At the close of this year his cousin, master of the mines at Dillenburg, John Stilling's second son, paid him a visit. He was always glad to see this friend of his youth, whom honesty and skill in business had made a valuable member of society. On this occasion the bond of friendship was renewed, which had so long subsisted between them.

In the commencement of the next year an occurrence took place, which in a great measure loosened the bonds, which had connected him with Marburg. An order was issued from Cassel, according to which no professor at the university should publish any thing, without previously submitting it to the inspection and censure of the Prorector of the university and the Dean of that faculty to whose province the subject belonged.

This restriction of the liberty of the press, which was confined to Marburg alone, excited much sensation, and no one could imagine the cause of such a proceeding. Stilling therefore immediately applied to Cassel for information, respecting this singular and extraordinary order, and to his astonishment received for answer; the periodical entitled "*The Grey Man*" had been the cause of this restriction of the liberty of the press. This circumstance soon became generally known, which made his stay in Marburg very unpleasant, and created a strong desire in his mind, that the Lord might soon open another door for him. A remonstrance of the university against the said edict was soon sent to the Elector, in which he was petitioned to withdraw this order. Stilling availed himself of this opportunity, to make the proposition of submitting in as far as he was personally concerned to the full severity of the restriction, provided it should fall upon him alone; but the law remained in force.

During the Easter-vacation he and Eliza undertook a journey to Herrnhut in Upper Lusatia. His friend Erxleben had informed him, that many persons in and about Herrnhut, afflicted with the cataract, were desirous of his assistance, and that the expenses of the journey should be paid. They left Marburg on the twenty-fifth of March; at Eisenach, Stilling visited his friend Director Gechhausen, but found him much indisposed. Our travelers made no stay on the road; their way led them through

Gotha, Erfurt, Weimar, Weisenfels, Leipzig and Meissen to Dresden. Here they paid a visit to the venerable minister von Burgsdorf; and were received by him as one christian friend should receive another. On the first of April they entered Lusatia and arrived that afternoon at Klinewelke, a colony of the Moravian brethren, where he found his friend Nitchke, the minister of the place in deep mourning; his wife having been called from time to eternity a fortnight previous to his arrival. Stilling formed here many new and interesting acquaintances, and visited several patients. whom he promised to attend on his return from Herrnhut. On the second of April he and Eliza arrived by way of Bauzen and Lobau at Herrnhut. This place is situated on an elevated piece of ground between two hills called the Hut and the Heinrichsberg; each of these hills is crowned with a pavillion, from which the prospect is uncommonly beautiful, towards the East you have a view of the Silesian Giant-mountains, and to the South the chain of the Bohemian mountains bounds the view towards Bohemia. Kind and affectionate was the reception of Stilling and Eliza in this congregation. I would utterly fail, were I to attempt a description of it; neither could I give the history of their stay at Herrnhut, because it would too much enlarge this volume; and besides he was requested by the members of the Directory not to say or write a great deal in praise of the Brethren's congregations, as they prospered best under oppression, contempt and oblivion.

Erxleben and Goldman were particularly glad to see Stilling and Eliza at Herrnhut, the first was a correspondent, the second a personal acquaintance from Stuttgart. I shall say nothing of the many friends of Stilling in this place, as I find it impossible to mention them individually; and I should be sorry to wound the feelings of any of them.

The celebration of the passion-week is affecting and edifying in all the Brethren's congregations, but particularly so at Herrnhut. Stilling and Eliza attended all the meetings held in that week, with great spiritual benefit to themselves. They also received permission from the directory to participate in the communion on Maundy Thursday. This communion is, what it ought to be;—a solemn union of Christ as head of his church, with all his members among all religious denominations. What a pious heart feels in this sacred hour, cannot be described but must be experienced. Stilling performed many operations in Herrnhut, and gave his advice as oculist to several hundred persons. The throng of patients was exceedingly great. On the 12th of April our travelers left Herrnhut for Klinewelke. Having performed operations on several persons, they arrived on the 13th at Dresden, whence after a stay of three days, they returned by way of Waldhime and Grimma to Leipzig. They had several reasons for taking this circuitous route, the principal was the desire expressed by the Saxon minister von Burgsdorf, a kind father of the poor, that he would pass through Waldhime, which contained the largest poor-house in Saxony, for the purpose of removing the cataract from several blind persons in that place ; another cause for their going this way was a pressing invitation received from Mr. Burgsdorf's children at Coldiz; in this place the last operations were performed during this journey.

April the 21st they left Leipzig, and passed through Weisenfels, Weimar, Erfurt, New Dietendorf and Gotha to Eisenach, where they found their friend Gochhousen recovered from his illness and spent an agreable evening in the company of his family and that of Dr. Muller and arrived on the 26th at Cassel: here they rested for several days. Their brother and sister Coing came also; and in their company time passed pleasantly away. On the second of May Coing and his Julia returned to their station, and Stilling and Eliza to Marburg.

Many solemnities took place on the accession of the Landgrave of Hessencassel to the Electoral dignity. On the 20th of May Stilling received by an express from Cassel an invitation to come without delay to court, that prince Charles the brother of the Elector had unexpectedly arrived from Denemark, and wished to see him. The preparations for the journey were soon made, and on the 21st in the evening he and Eliza were at Cassel. The next two days were chiefly spent in company of prince Charles, subjects important to the welfare of the kingdom of God formed the principal part of their conversation. His Highness is doubtless a true christian, his heart is filled with veneration and love to his Saviour, and his knowledge and experience in religion are of an extraordinary kind. Having on the 23d taken a christian farewell of this enlightened Prince, Stilling and Eliza left Cassel and arrived in the evening again at Marburg.

CHAPTER XVII.

Stilling's lectures were badly attended through the summer-session. During the White-suntide-vacation he visited with Eliza his friends at Wittgenstein; and as Tiefenbach and Florenburg are only fifteen miles from Wittgenstein, they resolved to go to all these places which the days of Stilling's childhood and youth had stamped with the seal of interest to them both. Stilling particularly anticipated great satisfaction in revisiting those places with Eliza, which had been the theatre of his childhood and youth, and which he had not seen for the last thirty-eight years. After a stay of several days with their friends at Wittgenstein, the journey to the hamlet in which Stilling had first seen the light was to be undertaken, and their friends were to accompany them. But as the hour of departure approached, an inexpressible horror seized on his mind, which increased every moment, he felt, as if great dangers awaited him there, God alone knows the cause of this singular phenomenon. His friends respected his feelings, and the journey to Tiefenbach was given up.

While at Wittgenstein, he received a letter from his son Jacob, which informed him, that the Elector of Baden had given him a call as counselor of justice and assessor at the Electoral court of justice at Manhime—a call, which by far exceeded the expectation of all his friends—to the call was added the inquiry, whether Stilling himself would come for a yearly salary of twelve hundred guilders for the present, with a promise of increasing it as soon as practicable.

The joy at Jacob's permanent settlement, and at the near and certain prospect of being extricated from his own critical

Z z

situation filled their hearts with gratitude towards God, and they hastened home, to make the necessary preparations for Jacob's departure, as he had been directed to enter immediately upon the duties of his office. But in Stilling's soul a conflict arose between reason and faith. If he considered his situation merely in an economical point of view, it was at best a hazardous undertaking to exchange a salary of twelve hundred rix-dollars for one of twelve hundred guilders, and the more so, as the expenses of his family left him nothing of his present high salary, and prudence suggested many reasons, for his remaining where he was ; there is no crime,—were her suggestions—in continuing as you have heretofore. — Perform the duties of your office and travel during the vacations, if you have few hearers at your lectures it is not your fault. And in regard to your sincere desire of being active in the cause of religion, you may succeed in the way, in which you have hitherto, and if the effect does not wholly correspond to your wishes, it is reasonable to suppose that God will not require more of you than you are able to perform.

But Stilling's conscience judged very differently. According to the demands of this monitor, he ought to resign his office, and give up his salary into the hands and channel from which he derived it, when he could no longer earn it to the satisfaction of his own conscience, and the approbation of the authority which paid it. This proposition is general, and admits of no limitation, whoever entertains principles differing from these, judges incorrectly. Stilling was now so situated, that he might venture to act according to this principle, a way being open, as soon as he chose to take it; and his experience of the last years had taught him, that the Lord has means enough to assist and to save without recourse to a high salary. Besides it is the first duty of the true christian, if he has a choice of callings, to give the preference to that in which he can be most useful, without regard to a difference in his income. Stilling therefore believed it his duty to accept the call ; for there could be no doubt, but he would be more useful by attending to his profession as oculist and by continuing to publish religious works, than by remaining Professor in a university ; and those branches, by which he could make himself most useful to the community would come within the compass of his calling, if he accepted the vocation of the Elector of Baden.

To all this ought to be added the dealings of Providence in regard to Stilling from his very childhood; for that man must be blind indeed, who could not see, that God in the most systematic manner had paved the way to the door, which the Elector of Baden now opened. Had he entertained a desire of waiting for some other opportunity, with which a higher salary might be connected, it would have been culpable distrust of Providence, after having so repeatedly experienced his goodness. Besides this vocation was so singular, so unique, that it would have been unreasonable to expect ever to receive a similar one, and finally, the enlightened christian will see, that Stilling's guide had no other aim in view than to give him opportunities for excercising his faith. Influenced by these considerations, he accepted the call in the name of God; but in order to do what could be done in his case, he wrote to the Elector of Baden, asking him for an augmentation of salary at least in grain and such like things; in consequence of which letter the call arrived with the promise of an increase of salary, as soon as practicable.

The great question concerning his final establishment was now decided, the enigma of his wonderful leadings was solved—it could now no longer be said, that his faith and confidence in Jesus Christ and his government of the world were but fanaticism and superstition; on the contrary, the Redeemer had gloriously and evidently legitimized both himself and the faith of his servant, and in addition to this gave him at this time the following mark of his gracious approbation. A lady who lived above two hundred miles from Marburg, who knew nothing of Stilling's present situation, and had no other acquaintance with him than through the medium of his writings, felt an inclination, to send him twenty Louisd'ors.

She followed this impulse and wrote him, that he would know what use to make of it. This money with what he had still remaining from his tour to Switzerland was enough to facilitate his removal from Marburg and settle his family comfortably at the place of his future residence.

Gracious God! how kindly leadest thou those who trust in thee! how much might we learn, were we carefully to study the ways of Providence! If but one of all these occurrences had been wanting he could not have accepted the call; if he had only received in Switzerland a sufficiency to pay his debts and the expenses of his journey it would have been a glorious display of the grace of God, but he would have been compelled to stay at Marburg, because the means would have been wanting for his removal and the expenses of a new settlement; for in Marburg he was not able to lay up any part of his salary.

Blessed be the Lord! He is still the God of the Bible! — Yes he has truly said: *"I am who I am, and shall be always the same." "Jesus Christ the same yesterday, to-day and for ever."*

After Jacob and Amalia had removed to Manhime June the 25th, accompanied by the blessing of their parents, Stilling and Eliza commenced preparations also for their departure for Hidleberg, the place, which the Elector had recommended to them as their future residence, where Stilling as witness of the truth was to be actively engaged for the propagation of religion and the extension of the kingdom of Christ, and also to serve his suffering neighbor as an oculist. His next duty was to apply to the Elector of Hessencassel for his dismission, which he soon after received. About the time of his departure Stilling once more expressed his thanks to the Elector for all the favors he had hitherto shown him and recommended himself for the future to his kind remembrance and protection, of which he graciously assured him in his answer.

Stilling's departure excited much regret in all Hessia but especially at Marburg; the citizens in general expressed their sorrow, and his immediate neighbors were bathed in tears on the day of his removal. Stilling's and Eliza's hearts were deeply affected, especially when they passed the church-yard, the resting place of so many of their dearest friends and relatives. Their friend Julia removed with them. The first day they went as far as Munster, where Schwartz and Hannah resided; here they stayed Sunday and Monday, which latter day was Stilling's birth day, and was now celebrated in a very splendid manner. On the thirteenth of September they took leave of their children, and went to Frankfort, where they rested two days; on the sixteenth they went as far as Heppenhime, and on Saturday the seventeenth they entered Hidleberg.

Remarkable was the daily word for that day: Exod. XV. 17. "Thou shalt bring them in and plant them in the mountain of thine inheritance, in the place, O Lord, which thou hast made for thee to dwell in, in the Sanctuary, O Lord, which thy hands have established." The reader must not suppose that Stilling applied these scriptural expressions to the town of Hidleberg, or his own temporal situation; he understood the mountain of Iehovah's inheritance, the place which he had made for himself to dwell in and the Sanctuary, to mean the spiritual Zion, and the Mystic temple of God, in which he was now employed as a servant.

His friend Mieg had provided a very convenient and pleasant dwelling and other friends had supplied other wants. Stilling with his Eliza, Julia, Caroline, the three children, Frederick, Amalia and Christine, the faithful and pious Mary and a hired servant were soon settled in their new habitation, and Stilling waits upon the Lord and submits with cheerfulness to his gracious guidance and directions.

How gladly would I here have expressed my gratitude to a number of dear and intimate friends! But how could I do this without wounding the feelings of some one whom I either inadvertently passed by, or whom to name other circumstances forbid?— All the inhabitants of the friendly Marburg are my friends, and and I am theirs, and in this relation I trust we shall remain until our final consummation.—Dear friends! you all know us, and we know you. The Lord our God knows us all. May he be your great reward! Amen!

RETROSPECTIVE VIEW

STILLING'S LIFE.

In the first place I earnestly intreat all my readers, impartially to peruse the following pages; for they contain the true point of view, from which Stilling's life throughout ought to be seen and judged.

The reading world knows, that I, Doctor Young, the author of this work am Henry Stilling, and that it contains my own life; it is therefore of no use any father to retain a borrowed name. I lay it aside and speak henceforth in my own.

I can answer the first and principal question which ought to arise, viz: whether the history of my life as it is related in the foregoing five books, is really and actually true, most conscientiously in the affirmative, and if this is so, if the history of my life is true in its whole extent, results arise, of which few readers are aware. I consider it therefore a duty incumbent on me, most conscientiously and logically to develope and to represent these results and consequences to the reader; I therefore once more entreat him carefully to peruse and examine my observations on this subject.

The destinies of man from his birth until his death either happen from a blind chance, or agreeably to a wise plan, made by God, in the execution of which men co-operate, either as really free beings, or mechanically, as nature does; yet supposing, they act as free agents. This idea, viz: that men only appear to act freely but are in reality nothing more than machines, contains the substance of that doctrine which is termed Fatalism. It is not here the place to refute this horrible doctrine, but I refer the reader, who is desirous of seeing a refutation of it, to my work entitled "*Longing for Heaven.*"

Here I shall take it for granted, that God governs the world with infinite wisdom, in such a manner, that men cooperate as free agents.

The phrase, "blind chance" in itself sufficiently shows, that this nonentity is incapable of forming any plans for preparing with wisdom the means for their execution, and afterwards of carrying them into effect; wherever therefore,—as for instance in the history of my life—such a plan and execution thereof is evidently visible, it would be nonsense, to think of a blind chance; and whereas in the destinies of every man—consequently in my life also—many other persons cooperate, it is impossible, that all these cooperating beings could act under the direction of a blind chance, I therefore draw the conclusion that nothing does nor can happen by chance.

That man in general may be at least in part master of his destiny and has for the most part to ascribe his happiness or unhappiness to himself, none of my readers will doubt, unless he is a fatalist, but with these I do not here contend: but whether I have cooperated in my destiny, whether I have methodically and consciously contributed any thing to the leadings of Providence, who brought me sted by step to the desired haven, is a question, on which every things depends ; for if I can prove, that this is not the case, consequences of the greatest importance will arise therefrom.

There are men, who feel a natural impulse from their youth which remains with them until the day of their death, and they make use of all their rational powers, and labor diligently, to reach the goal to which that impulse points. For instance, one possesses a strong mechanical bias, he struggles, strives, labors and invents, until he produces some work of art, which fills the mind of the beholder with astonishment. This is the case in every calling, in all arts and sciences you will find such aspiring men ; the world calls them great men, great minds, geniusses &c. Many however do not succeed, notwithstanding all their striving, and notwithstanding the strength and ardor of that impulse ; because their success suits not in the plan of the government of the world—again many succeed, and among them some who do immense evil in the world, and they are successful, because their activity with its consequences may be applied for salutary purposes. It is therefore certain, that such men, have formed and executed the plan of their life at least in a great measure themselves, and the impulse, which they felt, was natural to them. The reader must recollect the lives of many great and celebrated men, which will warrant the truth of my assertions.

But now the principal question is: Am I such a man? do I belong to the class of remarkable men, who in a great measure have formed their own destinies?

Let us strictly and impartially examine and then answer this question. Every thing depends upon this, whether I had such a powerful impulse? I answer, yes, I possessed it and do possess it still.—It is no other than to be extensively engaged in the service of Jesus Christ for the propagation of his religion and the extension of his kingdom.—But let the reader observe, that this was not my natural disposition—for I rather possessed an uncommon levity of mind, and an ardent desire after the most unlimited enjoyment of physical and intellectual pleasures; and I beseech the reader, not to lose sight of this my natural disposition. The religious inclination entered my heart wholly from external causes and in the following manner:

The early death of my mother laid the foundation for it, with it my heavenly guide commenced in the second year of my life; if she had remained alive, my father would have attended to his farming business, I would have been under the necessity of laboring in the field, would have learned to read and write, and no more; my head and heart would have been filled with the every day concerns of life, and God only knows, what would have become of my moral character. But in consequence of my mother's death, the pious disposition of my father was strongly excited, and through his connection with mystics he was induced to withdraw from the world; he therefore confined himself to the tailor's trade, and I received an education, corresponding with my father's principles; no other objects were suffered to enter my senses except such as were of a religious character; he gave me the lives of men and women to read, who had distinguished themselves by their piety and activity in spreading the gospel, in addition to this I repeatedly read the holy Scriptures; in short, I heard and learnt nothing in the house of my father but of the religion of Jesus and of men who had become pious and holy by means of it, who had lived and labored for the Lord and his kingdom, and some of whom had even sacrificed their lives for his sake. It is a well known fact, that the first impressions upon the soul, especially if they are lasting and powerful, are indelible; and this was exactly my case; the desire of being constantly engaged in the extension of the kingdom of God and the spread of the religion of the Savior, was so deeply impressed on my mind, that the afflictions and trials of many years have never been able to weaken it, on the contrary it has continually increased, and though at times saddening prospects removed this principle for a season it soon returned with redoubled force. Let no one suppose that in my childhood I was determined on this course, or that I sought to prepare myself for the future execution of such a plan—and it would be ridiculous to suppose, that my father had it in view—*his* wishes extended no farther, than to make me a good, pious christian and an able schoolmaster, but as this calling in my country does not maintain a family, he wanted me to learn his trade, that I might make an honest living. His view in giving me these books to read, was to procure entertainment for my mind and to induce me to become a pious christian. But that this kind of reading produced the effect already mentioned, was the intention of the great ruler of the world, who designed to employ me in his kingdom.

From what has been said I consider it demonstrated, that God implanted this ardent desire for his service in my mind without my having a natural predisposition for this service, but that it was effected by his wise direction and government.

But the principle which was natural to me, viz: an uncommon levity of disposition, and a desire for the most unlimited enjoyment of physical and intellectual pleasures, was in direct opposition to that which he wished to engraft in my heart; my heavenly guide began therefore early to contend with this dangerous enemy; and the instrument he used for this purpose was again my father, without his having the most distant idea of it; he was wholly unacquainted with my natural disposition, else he would surely have endeavored to avoid many cliffs and rocks in my education on which

I would have suffered an unavoidable shipwreck, if the paternal hand of God had not led me over them in safety. But my father suspected nothing of all this. He caused me almost daily to feel the rod, according to his mystical principle, that it was necessary to crucify the flesh; and I know with certainty, that he sometimes chastised me for no other reason, but to deny and crucify his paternal love to me. Almost with every other child this kind of discipline would have had most pernicious consequences, but with me—the reader may believe me upon my word—it was an absolutely necessary method of education; for my levity and sensuality were unbounded; no one, but God and myself, know, what abominable thoughts, wishes and desires arose in my soul; it seemed, as if a potent inimical power was exciting persons, who had no evil in view, to cast me into the most dreadful temptations and dangers destructive of every moral principle, but all snares were laid in vain—not my religious principles—for a child has no principles—but the severe discipline of my father and God's gracious dealings preserved me from falling into the abyss of destruction. The same natural depravity which was always warring against my religious desires compelled my heavenly guide to exercise me for more than sixty years in the school of adversity, before he could make use of me, and the attentive reader will find in the sequel, that all my afflictions were intended to destroy and root out my levity and sensuality.

Now we will examine, whether I am a great man, have a great mind and am a genius? that is, whether I have obeyed the religious principle which God had planted in my soul by my own strength and my natural disposition? My father wished to educate me for a good schoolmaster and tailor, and he attained his wishes in so far, that I became a schoolmaster and tailor, but the predominant desire of my heart was, to be a minister of the gospel. My religious principle produced this effect. I wished to study Theology, and my father would have liked it to, but as his whole property would not have been sufficient to maintain me two years at a university, I durst not think of the possibility of accomplishing my wishes. There was therefore no choice, I must remain a schoolmaster and tailor; and my natural disposition gave me a strong bias for reading and research in all branches of knowledge. For as my mind had once acquired a taste for abstract ideas and sciences, it continued without intermission in this course, and was always endeavoring to find opportunities for reading and research. I might perhaps ascribe to diligence and activity what I gained in knowledge in the various branches of sciences which I studied, and I must own, that the Lord made use of this progress in learning as preparatory means: but it was unavailing in reaching the goal which my spiritual principle had in view.

I was opposed to the tailor's trade and was also heartily tired of teaching a. b. c. spelling, reading and writing to little boys and girls, and began gradually to consider the occupation of a tailor and schoolmaster as very disagreeable; and from this period my mental sufferings commenced, for I saw no possibility of being any thing but a schoolmaster and tailor. The severe discipline of my father in the mean time had not changed; and though he no more chastised me every day as formerly, yet I was never comfortable in his presence; his unbounding severity excited in me the desire of leaving his house as often as possible; hence I accepted every call with great joy, yet as I did not perform the work of instruction with pleasure, but as a task, and even frequently pursued my own favorite studies at the expense of my duty, I was not a good teacher, neither could I bear during my leisure-hours to work at my trade, and trifled away my small earnings as schoolmaster, so that my father had to find me in clothes and maintain me: he observed with sorrow, that I would never be an acceptable teacher, in consequence of which his heart became more and more alienated from me, and after having married a worldly minded woman, who peremptorily demanded, that her step-son should perform the labors of the field, my troubles reached their acme, for I suffered exceedingly, as I had never been accustomed to such kind of work. My hands were full of blisters from handling the rough tools, and I was so stiff from thrashing and mowing that I could move with difficulty. Days and weeks appeared to me an eternity; my future prospects were as gloomy as the present, I saw no possibility of extricating myself from of my present situation, as I received no new calls to fill the office of schoolmaster; if I therefore wished to leave my father's house I was compelled to seek employment with master-tailors in the country; but then my earnings were so small, that I was unable to procure the necessary clothes to appear with decency in public; I was of course considered a vagabond deserving no confidence. My religious principle however still presented to me the character of a Spener, a Franke and other pious ministers, as the ultimatum of all my wishes, but the reflection, that it was impossible for me in my present situation ever to become a man similar to them, almost sunk me in despair.

The views of Providence, in bringing me into this sad state were twofold: In the first place it was necessary to keep down my corrupt nature, and secondly, to expel me from my native country, because no opportunity existed there of executing those plans which Providence had formed in my behalf; though I was in some measure aware of the first mentioned view, yet of the latter I had not the most remote idea, for I loved the environs of my native village so well that any thing short of absolute necessity could not drive me from them; this necessity however did take place, and I left my country.

Here I would beg the reader to observe, that this first step toward attaining the aim of my religious principle was taken against my will and wishes: I was driven from my country by the power of Providence, as the history of my life plainly shows.

My first intention was, to go to Holland, and look for employment with some merchant. But at Solingen-Schauberg in the dutchy of Berg, I was persuaded to desist from that plan, I stayed, and worked at my trade. This occupation I heartily disliked; for my corrupt nature always demanded amusing changes, my greatest pleasure consisted in reading novels and works of this description; my imagination was always engaged in creating with incredible vivacity the most romantic pictures, and my levity cast off every serious impression. But eternal love took pity on me, and determined me by a singular but powerful and efficacious call, to devote my whole future life to the Lord; still my natural corruption was by no means rooted out, Jesus Christ my

Savior had to combat and conquer this evil through his Spirit, by means of long and severe sufferings and trials; this great object is not yet completed, neither will it be, until my soul shall be delivered from this body of sin and death.

Notwithstanding that my mind had now taken its direction towards the great goal of man's destination, I was still guilty of numerous aberration, and very soon after the powerful call at Schauberg I went sadly astray; my disinclination to the tailor's trade was the cause of my readily accepting the offer of a place as private tutor in the family of a merchant; and I was too thoughtless to reflect on the consequences. My misery became here unbounded, no one who has not himself experienced it, can form an idea of the state of torment and deprivation of every human enjoyment in which I there found myself. Here my corrupt disposition was attacked at the very root, and at length my wretchedness became so great, that I ran away, wandering about in the wilderness until I recollected myself and returned to Rade-vor-dem-Walde (Waldstadt) and John Jacob Becker (Mr. Isaac) received me kindly, gave me work and clothed me. I was now completely cured of my former disgust to the tailor's trade; so that afterwards Mr. Spanier and Mr. Becker could hardly persuade me to accept the situation as private tutor in the family of the former, and even now I am so far from any antipathy to this trade, that—were it necessary—I would cheerfully lay hold again of the needle.

During my abode with Mr. Spanier it seemed, as if Providence had designed me for a merchant; I was daily employed in mercantile business, every thing I undertook appeared to succeed, and though I had no particular inclination to become a merchant, I nevertheless began to think, that it was God's will, which I ought to obey, especially as I was told in confidence, that a rich, handsome and pious daughter of a certain merchant was destined for me, that her father was willing to give her to me, and then to enter into partnership with me. While my mind was filled with these ideas and expectations, I received a strong impression, that I ought to study medicine, a circumstance, which I have noticed in the history of my life. I was pleased with the idea, neither

were those persons, who wished to get the reins of my destiny in
their hands averse to this plan. For it was singular, they observed
—that a wealthy family should give their daughter in marriage to
a fellow, who till lately had been nothing but a journeyman-tailor;
but after I should have been at the university, and received my
Diploma as Doctor of Medicine, the case would be different.
Such was the plan of man, and also that of my heavenly guide:
For soon after I had formed the resolution of studying medicine,
pastor Molitor at Attendorn communicated to me his arcana
concerning the cure of diseases of the eye, and immediately afterwards became sick and died. God knows, that I never in
my whole life thought of becoming an oculist, and that neither
I, nor any of my relatives laid a plan for obtaining these recipes
—and now I beg the reader to consider what a powerful effect
these cures of the eye have exercised upon the development of
my final destiny.—Whoever doth not recognize in these things
the all-governing hand of an omniscient almighty Deity, has
no eyes to see, nor ears to hear.

I commenced practice as an oculist, and by this means became acquainted with the worthy family of my departed father-
in-law Peter Heyders of Ronsdorf in the Dutchy of Berg (Mr.
Friedenberg of Rasenhime) and against all my expectations and
plan engaged myself there to a weakly person, while sickness confined her to her bed. I thought I must obey God, for
I believed it was his will. I bethrothed myself to Christina,
though I knew, her father was not able to assist me in my studies, and that I could then no longer count opon any support
from Mr. Spanier. With forty rix-dollars I had left Rasenhime and with half a french-crown I arrived at Strasburg; but
it is known from the history of my life, how gloriously the Lord
has been my support. And now I ask again: was it my plan to
marry Christina or to study medicine at Strasburg?

On my return I settled as physician and oculist at Elberfeld; (Shonenthal) I expected to have uncommon success in my
practice, for I looked upon myself as peculiarly prepared by the
Lord for this profession; I also hoped to have opportunities of
being active for the Lord in connection with my calling; I be-

lieved, that I would be a very useful instrument in the hand of God in the sick chamber; that I would be serviceable to my patients in regard to their souls as well as bodies: I also intended to write religious works; but none of these expectations were realised; my practice was not only circumscribed but was confined chiefly to the lower classes; only as oculist, I was eminently successful; but even this success I owed not to any skill of mine: I had indeed learned the art at Strasburg, merely because it was a branch of surgery, but I had such a horror of the practice, that I never shall forget my feelings, when the poor woman at Wichlinghausen, pastor Muller, Doctor Dinkler at Elberfeld and friend Troost compelled me to venture on an operation: with a trembling hand I performed it and most miserably—but the woman was perfectly restored to her sight—this gave me more courage; but even now, after I have performed operations on above fifteen hundred patients, I feel my heart palpitating when I am about to perform one.

It is therefore apparent, that I have contributed nothing towards becoming an oculist, and particularly, to my uncommon success. The Lord has done this.

It would be impossible for me to attempt a description of that deep melancholy, which seized upon me, when I plainly saw, that the profession of medicine did not suit me, that the heavy load of my debts was yearly increasing and I not able in any wise to prevent it. This was an efficacious antidote to my natural corruption—and God be praised—it was completely rooted out—I saw no way of escape, I had a wife and children to maintain, my debts were continually increasing, while the proceeds of my profession were daily decreasing—I was not wanting in knowledge and learning, I diligently searched every corner of medical literature, but I found in this fluctuating science nothing but want of science, all was mere probability and conjecture; I was heartily tired of the profession, but how was I to maintain myself and——wherewith was I to pay my debts?—— All I could do, was to surrender myself at discretion into the hands of Providence; this I did with all my heart and forever; this covenant has not been broken, but it became continually stronger, more unlimited and unconditional on every occasion.

I wrote religious books, but without much success. "The eulogy of the shepherd-boy;" "The great Panacea in doubts of religion;" and "The Theodicy of the shepherd's-boy" met with an indifferent reception from the public: but "Stilling as a child," an essay, which I had not intended for publication, but had written merely to read before a society of young men, and which Gœthe published without my knowledge excited an unexpected and incredible sensation, I was strongly urged to publish the continuation of my life, and wrote while yet at Elberfeld "Stilling as a Youth" and his "Peregrinations." I can without hesitation declare, that few books have procured for their authors an equal share of celebrity, and even now, after twenty-eight years have clasped, after so many changes in taste and literature, Stilling remains a popular book; it is read with the same avidity as at the time of its first publication; the Omniscient God knows and in part I also, how blessed its effects in regard to religion have been; for I can produce a multitude of testimonials in confirmation of this truth. The publication of the life of Stilling therefore shewed me for the first time clearly the path my heavenly Father wished me to take.

I now entreat the reader again carefully to observe, that I have formed no plan for that important period of my life which led me towards my final destination, which was: to follow the dictates of my religious diposition, but that the whole was the plan of Providence.

Does any one ask why my heavenly guide did not at that time place me in the situation he intended I should fill, I answer: There were still many things to file and polish away, neither were my principles firmly enough established, I was still in conflict with fatalism, nor had the period of my religious activity yet arrived.—When my troubles had reached their full measure, and there was none on earth to help, I received deliverance in a manner which I could not anticipate. In consequence of a treatise entitled "the most beneficial improvement of the forests in the principality of Nassau Siegen,"—my own native country —which I had written as I thought, merely to gratify a friend, I received a call to the newly established Cameralistic Academy at Kayserslautern—Rittersburg—in the Palatinate, as Professor of Agriculture, Technology, Commerce and the Veterinary Art with a salary of six hundred guilders, and at my departure from Elberfeld my most urgent debts, amounting to eight hundred guilders, were paid in as unexpected a manner as all my debts were discharged several years afterwards in Switzerland.

Every candid reader will acknowledge that neither here had I any premeditated plan, but it was altogether the work of my heavenly guide and director.

It was my belief at that time, that the study of political economy was the calling, for which Providence had designed and prepared me from my youth; for I had enjoyed every opportunity of becoming practically acquainted with it in all its branches; I had studied medicine, because its auxiliaries were indispensably necessary to my present calling. By this view of things my desire of becoming a religious instructor was by no means extinguished, but I hoped to combine it with my vocation; in this conviction I continued for twenty-five years, and faithfully labored to do justice to my profession; of which I can adduce as proofs the number of compends and treatises which I have written on the subjects connected with the sciences I was teaching, and even after I had attained the fiftieth year of my life I thought of no change, until the work entitled "Longing for Heaven" became the means in the hands of Providence of placing me in my proper station.

. The reader has learned from the fifth book of the history of my life, that I did not write it with the view of executing any plan of my own, but that I formed the resolution in consequence of the urgent solicitations of the bookseller to publish some work of taste, and when I commenced, I had no idea of composing such a work as it became under my hands, and as it proved itself afterwards in its effects; — these were wonderful, it operated like electricity in every part of the world—a circumstance which I can prove.—From that time I was called upon from every quarter, to devote my time wholly to the writing of religious works;—"The Grey Man;" "The Scenes from the spiritual world," and "the History of the triumph of the christian Church"

increased these calls from the generous and christian community
which had found edification in these works ;—but how could I
attend to this unanimous call?—a multitude of domestic difficulties prevented me,—my debts were not yet paid—and where
could I find the person, who would pay me a salary expressly
for this purpose ?—The Lord however removed every difficulty
out of my way—he paid my debts most gloriously ; and my religious writings, especially "Longing for Heaven" had brought
the good and pious Elector of Baden to the determination of
placing me in the station for which the Lord had designed me.

Behold ! my dear Reader, in how wonderful a manner the
Lord has at length brought me to the goal of my wishes, the desire of which he had engrafted in me from the first years of my
childhood. My present occupation is therefore ; First : a continuation of my profession as an oculist : for this calling has
been assigned me and has been confirmed by the Providence of
the Lord. Secondly : a continuation of writing religious
works ; and Thirdly : the publication and gratuitous distribution of small religious tracts, through the liberality of pious,chris-
tian friends. Whether the Lord has something yet in view
with me I know not; I am his servant, may he employ me, as
seemeth good in his sight—but without knowing his will I shall
not take a step.

All my readers will now be convinced, that I am no great
man, have no great mind, or genius—for I have contributed nothing systematically towards the attainment of that situation in
which I am now placed, even my natural disposition and character were to be subdued by means of long protracted trials and sufferings. I was passive as the clay in the hands of the potter.
Whoever therefore looks upon me as a man possessing great talents and virtues, or who judges me to be a great saint, de-
ceives himself; he might just as well praise a rough old box as
a master-piece of workmanship, in which a rich man preserves precious treasures for his use and convenience. Whoever will wonder and rejoice over me, let him wonder how Providence has led me through the difficulties of life, let him worship the Father of men and thank him, that he still prepares

his witnesses, and sends his laborers into the vineyard at the eleventh hour.

I now entreat the reader carefully to examine the following proposition :

First : Does not the history of my life irrevocacably prove, that I was not educated and directed by human wisdom and reason but by him, who knows how to direct the heart, the actions and destinies of man, without doing violence to their free will, has he not done all this after a plan, which is visible in my life from the beginning to the end?

Secondly : Does not the same history of my life evidently show, that on my part nothing has been contributed either to the scheme or its execution ? that neither fanaticism nor error had any share in it ? for in whatever point I have been either visionary or in an error, time and circumstances have improved my knowledge.

Thirdly : If then the all-wise, all-merciful and omnipotent ruler of the world has prepared and directed me, without either myself or any other human being having any participation in his plan, is it possible that his work should mis-carry ? would he guide and direct an errorist or a fanatic, as he has guided me, in order to deceive men ? He may perhaps permit a fanatic or an impostor to struggle through difficulties by the powers of his own mind and impose upon the public ; for he suffers free agents to act free as long as it is consistent with his divine counsel, but can any one show me in the history of my life that in any one part of it I have by my own exertions overcome difficulties of this kind, or have endeavored to impose upon the public ?

Fourthly : Does it not follow from all this, that the system of religion, which I teach and which is no other, than that which Christ and his Apostles, and afterwards all orthodox fathers of the church have taught, is correct and has again been confirmed by God's dealings with me ?—It is possible, that I may entertain some private opinions in non-essentials which are still erroneous, but in the essential parts of our religion, I am as certain I am not in an error, as I am sure, that God has conducted me through my whole life, and has prepared me to become a witness of the truth. In the mean time I am conscious before God, that none of my religious ideas have arisen from laborious research or are the result of a deduction drawn from premises—the dictates of my reasoning powers—but all are the result of discoveries of my own mind, which have occurred to me during the reading of difficult passages of the scriptures. And according to my conviction the essential parts of the christian religion depend on the following principles :

First : The sacred writings, as we now possess them, contain from the first chapter of Genesis to the last of Maleachi, and from the first chapter of the gospel of St. Matthew to the last chapter of the Apocalypse the history of the revelations of God to man ; and are therefore the only authentic source of all supernatural truths, which are nesessary for man to know.

Secondly : The first human beings were created by God in a perfect state but they sinned by disobedience to God, in consequence of which they lost that perfection with which the Creator had endowed them. the sensual appetites became more and more preponderating and hence every imagination of the thought of the human heart was only evil continually among their posterity.

Thirdly : Previous to this however, a class of higher spiritual beings had revolted from God, and had become wicked ; the prince of these beings tempted our progenitors to disobedience and rebellion against God ; and these evil spirits may exercise an influence upon the spiritual part of man, when the latter gives them an opportunity for it ; but there are likewise good spirits attending man, and exercising an influence upon him, whenever circumstances require it. Those evil spirits with their prince Satan and all wicked men, I call the kingdom of darkness.

Fourthly : God has from eternity begotten a Being, equal in nature with himself, which stands in regard to him in the same relation in which a son stands towards his father, hence the Bible calls him the Son of God, the Logos, the Word of God : this Son of God took upon himself the government and redemption of the fallen human race ; in the days of the Old Testament he revealed himself under the name of Jehovah, in the New, as true man in Jesus Christ. He is God and man in one person.

Fifthly: This God-man Christ Jesus redeemed the fallen race of Adam by his vicarious atonement,from sin, death and the punishment of sin. This vicarious atonement forms the basis of reconciliation with God, for the forgiveness of sins, and of course for eternal happiness. The moral doctrines of Christ (christian ethics) which are also contained in all their parts in the Old Testament, and have been taught even by pagans are only a criterion by which we may know, whether and how far the vicarious atonement of Christ has been effectual in us. This christian morality is a natural consequence of the work of redemption, without which it is as impossible, that it could be performed in a manner pleasing to God, as it is for a sick man to perform the duties of a man in health.

Sixthly: Jesus Christ arose from the dead, and became thereby the fundamental cause of the resurrection of man, he ascended into heaven, and took upon himself the government of the world. He therefore governs all things, directs all the destinies of men, conducts and finally executes all things which pertain to their salvation. For this purpose he together with all his true worshippers and the holy angels stands as the kingdom of light in opposition to the kingdom of darkness and these wage a continued and an uninterrupted war, until the latter shall be finally subdued, and thus the work of redemption will be finished; then the Son will again deliver the kingdom to the Father, that *he* may be all in all.

Seventhly: God will and must be worshipped in the name that is, in the person of Jesus Christ. God out of Christ is a metaphysical non-entity, which daring reason has abstracted from the idea of a perfect man; and to worship this non-entity which exists merely in the heads of philosophers, is idolatry. Through Christ alone we find the Father of men, in him alone he will and can be worshipped.

Eighthly: The Holy Spirit, the Spirit of the Father and of the Son, is truly one Being with the Father and the Son and of the same divine nature. He proceeds from both as light and warmth proceed from the sun; his influence has been continually exerted since the great day of Pentecost ; every one who truly believes in Christ, accepts his doctrine of salvation, repents sincerely of his sins, and desires earnestly to be liberated from sin, and to become a true child of God, receives the gift of the holy Ghost in proportion to his faith and the sincerity and ardor of his desire after this gift, whereby his moral abilities are gradually strengthened, and his worldly and corrupt desires are in the same proportion subdued.

This is my system of faith, confirmed to me as true by many trials and much experience. It contains in my view the pure, unsophisticated Dogmas of Holy Writ, upon the certainty and truth of which I will live and die.

The new system of enlightened Theology stands in direct opposition to this ancient christian Doctrine of faith and practice. Many ingenuous, candid and truth-loving men, give preference to the enlightened system as it is called, because they are convinced, that this modern system of Theology is more in accordance with human reason, than the old christian system ; they have therefore invented a new Exegesis, a mode of explaining the Bible, which suits their philosophy : however these men either perceive, or do not perceive that the tendency of the new Theology is toward natural religion alone, whose dogmas consist in moral theses and doctrines, which represent the mission of Christ as needless, and the Bible as a useless book. But as neither these sense of right and wrong, nor the beauty of virtue can restore those moral abilities to man, which have been lost by the fall of Adam, immorality continually increases with the reign of this enlightened Theology, depravity grows in accelerated proportion, humanity sinks again into the darkest barbarism, and divine judgments exercise a severe but just vengeance over a people, which despises all the means of its moral improvement.

On the other hand the experience of every century proves in the example of millions of human beings, that the old christian doctrine of faith has formed its votaries into good and holy citizens, husbands, wives, friends and children; the modern system of enlightened Theology may here and there form an honorable man, and produce civic virtues, and such a man may at times perform splendid actions, but to be benevolent in secret at the expense of self-interest and from love to God and man, even towards enemies, is only possible where the Spririt of Jesus Christ reigneth.

Now arises the very important question, whence it happens, that such ingenuous, candid and truth-loving men, notwithstanding all this incontrovertible experience persevere in their system of enlightened Theology as it is called? My answer is, there are two principles or foundations from which every religious proof must necessarily proceed, if these premises are false, every demonstration founded upon them, if otherwise mathematically and logically correct, must be false and incorrect, and this is here exactly the case.

The christian doctrine of faith is founded upon the following principle: God created the progenitors of the human family as free agents with a tendency to a progressive moral improvement; and with it, to a proportionate enjoyment of moral happiness: but they suffered themselves to be tempted by an unknown evil being, whereby they were induced to direct their tendency to a progressive sensual improvement, if I may be permitted the expression, and with it to a proportionate enjoyment of temporal happiness. Sacred writ teaches us this principle, and the experience of six thousand years proves that it is incontrovertibly true. Hence it follows: If man had continued in his original state, obedience to the moral law would have been natural to him; his reason would have instructed him, and his heart would have obeyed this instruction, and natural religion would then have been the only true religion. But in man's present fallen state, in which corruption reigns triumphant and his moral powers are in subjection to the former, it is impossible that the latter should rise superior, of course there is no way of redemption in nature, but the Creator must interfere, if mankind shall be saved.

Whoever builds upon these premises a correct logical system, will find the christian doctrine of salvation very reasonable, and the modern system of enlightened philosophy very unreasonable. The principle of the latter is as follows: All creation is one connected whole, which the Creator has endowed

with mental as well as physical powers, and has given it eternal
and immutable laws, so that no divine interference is any longer necessary, of course all things proceed in creation after certain unchangeable and fixed laws, the aim of which is the general utility of all beings. The human race is a part of the whole,
and the eternal laws of nature act in such a manner upon the
free will of all human beings, that every action receives such a
direction, that he does what these laws require. The science of
moral philosophy teaches these laws according to which the
free will of man is necessarily directed. This is the principle
of Determinism or Fatalism, and you may guard your expressions in what way you choose, it is either open or concealed at
the bottom, and as it were the foundation of all ratiocinations of
neologists.

If we inquire, from what source reason has drawn this system,
we will find that it happened very naturally. Reason endeavors
to convince itself of the existence of a Supreme Being, and also
to investigate his nature and properties : but not being acquainted in the whole visible creation with any other rational being be-
side itself, it separates all bounds, limits, imperfections and infirmities from the human soul, it creates an infinitely rational,
omnipotent, omniscient, all-good and omnipresent human soul,
which it calls God ; and as the work of a human artificer would
be considered imperfect, if he were necessitated to turn
sometimes a little wheel here, and another one there, in short, to
lend a helping hand from time to time to keep the machine in motion, so likewise has the great artificer of the universe formed
a machine, which coming from the hand of a perfect master, must
necessarily be perfect in itself, and therefore needs not the inter-
fering or helping hand of the master.

But is this dreadful principle true ? 'No—Our own sensation of the freedom of our will, and our reason itself must
convince us that it is incorrect. For if it were correct, it
would logically follow, that every human action is the result
of the determination of the Creator. Agreeably to this horrid
principle the God of the new Theology has willed and does will
the most abominable deeds, which men are able to commit, and

C c c

the most dreadful sufferings, with which men afflict men, all the oppressions of widows and orphans, all the abominations of war and tyranny ; for he has formed the machine of nature, so that all these things are the result of necessary consequences.

No one will deny, that reason, when it follows up the results of its own system must recoil at the consequences, which present themselves to view ; of course reason is in contradiction with itself, and wherever this is the case, the empire of reason ceases, it has come to those limits, which it durst not overstep. A more alarming idea cannot occur to the mind than this, that human reason is directed and guided into that channel, especially in our days, in which the most unbounded luxury vies with the most abandoned immorality—and particularly, when this system receives the name of the christian religion—O horrible blasphemy!

My dear frinds! either be christians in the full sense of the word, and agreeably to the true old evangelical system, or be wholly naturalists; mankind will then know, to what class you belong. Think of Laodicea! That course is a trap, which Satan has laid for men.

Dear christian Brethren and Sisters! we will remain faithful to the Father of our Lord Jesus Christ, to our blessed Savior and to his holy Spirit, we will continue to receive the holy scriptures of the Old and New Testament, as the common sense of man interprets and understands them, as the only fountain of faith and spiritual knowledge : that when he comes—and he will come soon,—he may look with favor upon our faithfulness ! Amen.

LIFE

OF

HENRY STILLING.

SIXTH BOOK.

𝕳𝖎𝖘 𝖔𝖑𝖉 𝖆𝖌𝖊 𝖆𝖓𝖉 𝖉𝖊𝖆𝖙𝖍.

—•●•—

CHAPTER I.

I shall soon arrive at the goal of my pilgrimage, being in the commencement of the seventy-seventh year of my life, after a long season of corporeal sufferings from spasmodic affections in the stomach and general debility. I am filled with reverential awe when I review this long series of years, which have passed away like images reflected on the wall from a magic lantern. The present moment of my life appears to my mind like a large but sacred picture, part of which is still covered by a veil, which I shall not lift until my tenement of clay shall rest in the silent grave, and shall there ripen a seed sown for the day of resurrection. Grace, mercy and happiness through the atoning blood of my heavenly guide will then radiate from this picture upon my whole being—Hallelujah!

How different is the scene around me from that which I have described in Henry Stilling's youth. No longer do I sit at the oaken folding table between sun-dials in the small and dark room engaged in making a stomacher for neighbor Jacob's wife, or buttons for the Sunday coat of Shoemaker's Peter. No longer do I see the stately form of Eberhard Stilling moving about dressed in his clean linnen-frock; nor Margaret entering the room in busy haste, to fetch salt for the soup from the flowered box behind the stove. No longer is heard the hum of the spinning wheel of my full and red cheeked aunt, and the voice of her song is long since hushed in the silent grave. Uncle John no more comes, to communicate to us, his astonished hearers, his discoveries in Electricity, Mechanics, Optics and Mathematics, which he has made. No! the scene which now surrounds me is different indeed.

Here I sit in a convenient armchair before my well used desk, on the walls of my room are fixed the pledges of remembrance from my near and distant friends. My Eliza tried by many severe afflictions and sufferings walks through the house with feeble steps, engaged in her domestic avocations, my youngest daughter Christine the only one of my children, who still resides in the paternal mansion assists her mother and frequently rouses me from melancholy by her play and song.

My daughter Hannah lives with her husband Schwartz and ten children at Hidleberg, their oldest daughter is married to Professor Voemel in Slanen, and has presented me with a great grand-son, whose god-father I am ; his eldest son William was Rector at Winehime, and is now the instructor of the only son of our minister of State de Berkhime. The university of Hidleberg has given him the Diploma as Doctor of Philosophy, in consequence of his persevering diligence, his knowledge and his good moral conduct ; he visits me almost daily.

My dear Jacob lives at Rastadt with his wife and six children blessed of the Lord ; who leads him through many difficult paths, but he treads them as becometh the christian, His eldest daughter Augusta lives with me, and attends the Grauenberg institution for the education of young Ladies ; she too assists in cheering my heart in the gloomy days of old age and infirmity. As the worthy foundress of this institution has taken upon herself the education of the two daughters of the Grand Duke and has invited my third daughter Amalia to share in that labor, Caroline has taken upon herself the superintendence of the institution, and both daily visit their parents. My second son Frederick has spent the last six months in my house previous to his entering on the duties of financier and economist in Russia, and during this time has enlivened many a melancholy hour by his guitar and his melodious voice and song. But I must not forget that grand-fathers and grand-mothers generally become talkative when their children and families are the subject; to avoid this common error, I will break off and resume the thread of my history from the close of Stilling's apprentice years.

On my arrival at Hidleberg in September 1803 I learnt, that the Elector was at Manhime, I therefore went thither the next day, to announce my arrival and to recommend myself to his protection. He received me most graciously and observed : "I am glad to learn, that you have arrived in the States of Baden, it has been my sincere desire from my youth to devote all the powers of my mind and body to the service of the religion of Jesus, Christ, but God has called me to the throne, and I must turn my attention to the duties of that office : you are the man, whom God has prepared for usefulness in his kingdom, I therefore absolve you from all other obligations, and desire you in my place to promote the cause of religion by your correspondence and the publication of religious works; for this purpose I place you in this situation and give you the salary connected with it.

This declaration of the Elector gave me a legal right to my present vocation, a written instrument alone was wanting, which however I considered in my case superfluous, as no one had a right to interfere in my calling. Perfectly satisfied I returned to Hidleberg; for the ardent desire, which I had felt from my infancy, was now fully realized. One circumstance still disturbed my peace of mind, though I had the most unshaken confidence in my heavenly guide. On my return to Hidleberg I found every thing far different from what it had been ten or eleven years before ; every article I wanted in the family was as dear, as I had found it at Marburg. Our friends had advised us to sell our furniture, because we would be able to purchase it as cheap and of better quality at Hidleberg; but we found, it was quite different. Our handsome furniture at Marburg was sold for a trifle, and we were obliged to purchase at Hidleberg an inferior kind at a higher price, in short, our moving and settlement cost us near one thousand guilders, which consumed all our savings from the different journeys we had made. At Marburg my income had amounted to two thousand five hundred guilders, this sum had barely sufficed to support us, without enabling me to make any provision for my family; circumstances, which I can neither explain nor mention to the public, greatly increased my expenses. At Hidleberg I was nearly in the same circumstances, and my present salary amounted to hardly half of my former. When I and Eliza made these discoveries towards the end of 1803, dark melancholy seized upon my soul, and I reasoned in the following manner: You have heretofore taken no step of your own accord, to extricate you from a situation, in which Providence had placed you, and thus you always experienced the powerful aid of your heavenly guide. But is this the case now?" Have you contributed nothing to the call, which the Elector has given you? Was your desire to labor and to be active in the cause of the Lord free from impure motives? In the depth of your soul was there not some vanity lurking? Did you not hope, to shine as a great light in the church of God, and to become celebrated in the world by means of your religious publications? And finally, are there any higher duties to be fulfilled than to provide for our families, so that they do not come to want and poverty? How will you be able to answer for rejecting the means which Providence had provided, and throwing yourself into a situation, in which, notwithstanding the best intentions, many things are precarious? —All these questions arose like severe accusers to my soul, and I could not produce one word in my own defence. — I saw no other way, but to undertake an accurate and impartial self-examination that I might learn the real state of both. During this examination I found, as all the children of Adam will find in similar cases, that every thing they undertake, and in whatsoever they co-operate is all contaminated by sin; though in the main points which determined my removal, I was free from reproaches; for reflecting on all the circumstances connected with my situation at Marburg I was led to the conclusion, that my stay in the latter place ought not to have been prolonged, when a prince was willing to engage me, who was desirous of laboring for the Lord and his kingdom, a prince too that knew and loved me, circumstances, which impressed the seal of a divine call to the dictates of reason. As early as the last summer, when the Elector informed me, that he was now enabled to give me a salary of twelve hundred guilders, and that he would endeavor gradually to improve my situation, I frankly told him, that my family could not subsist on so small a salary; but receiving no reply to this my representation, I once more considered every circumstance, and sincerely believed that it was my duty to accept the call, it being in all probability the only one, which I could expect. On examination of the question, whether my desire to be active in the cause of the Lord was free from impurity, or whether the vain thought of becoming a celebrated man was not in a measure stirring up this desire, I found, that our best works will not bear a strict scrutiny when considered in the light of God's word, but I also found, that if vanity should have occasioned this strong bias, I would surely not have selected a calling, which is most exposed to the contempt and contradiction of the great men of our times. Having taken this view of the subject, the question could no longer be, how to make provision for my family, for I was convinced, that I had obeyed the will of my heavenly guide, and therefore was unconcerned in this respect. The sequel of the history of my life will show, how fully the Lord confirmed my confidence.

During the latter part of 1803 I was engaged with the arrangement of my library, though frequently interrupted by the necessity of answering letters and attending to a multitude of patients, who came to consult me. The year 1804 I commenced with writing Henry Stilling's apprentice years, the publication of the fifteenth number of the Grey Man, and several narratives for Ashenberg's pocket-book. It was a season of many trials and sufferings for myself and family; Caroline became dangerously ill and our youngest daughter Christine was afflicted by an ulcer on her left arm, which threatened to affect the bone, and even her life. However Caroline recovered, but Christine, then in her fifth year, showed symptoms of consumption; my stock of money too was nearly exhausted, it was therefore necessary, that assistance should come soon from a higher hand; and this help was not delayed; for towards the end of

March I received a letter from Upper Lusatia inviting me to come and assist a number of persons afflicted with the cataract, promising that the expenses of the journey should be paid: for which purpose I would receive on my way an order for two hundred rix-dollars. With gratitude towards the Lord we began to prepare ourselves for this long journey, for the distance from Hidleberg to Gorliz is not less than four hundred miles. My first duty was to give the Elector notice, who desired me, as I passed through Herrnhut, to apply to the Directory of the Brethren's church in his name to form a Moravian settlement within the States of Baden.

Although we knew that my friend Julia Richerz would take the most tender, motherly care of our two little girls, yet Eliza was very loath to leave poor little Christine for so long a time, however there was no alternative, for I could not travel alone on account of the frequent paroxysm of cramp in my stomach.

On the third of April we commenced our journey; at Hidleberg and down the Bergstrasse the almond and peach-trees were in full bloom, the weather was delightful, all nature appeared to smile and to announce to us a pleasant journey. But we were disappointed; for between Darmstadt and Frankfort we came in sight of the Feldberg wearing still the garb of winter; further on we discovered the mountains of the Wetterow covered with snow; these circumstances alarmed me, for I was not unacquainted with the road to Herrnhut; in the evening we arrived at Frankfort.

The reader of this part of my history can feel no interest in the particulars of my journey; suffice it to say, that it was very troublesome, the cramp in my stomach and danger from the weather and bad roads were the order of the day; now and then we felt the genial influence of spring, though these seasons were short and far between, but they were the more welcome and refreshing. We spent a few days at Cassel, one at Eisenach, and one and a half at Erfurt. On the nineteenth we arrived at Kleinwelke, a congregation of the Moravian brethren near Bauzen in Upper Lusatia. Many operations of the cataract were here performed, and a number of patients consulted me on divers complaints of the eye, whom I served as well as any weakness would permit. The twenty-third we started for Herrnhut, where we lodged in the public house, and were soon visited by several of our friends. I made known the Elector's proposition to the Directory of the Brethren, of forming a settlement of this society in the territories of Baden; but as they intended to establish one in the Black Forest in the Kingdom of Wurtemberg, the wish of the Elector could not be gratified for the two following reasons : first, because the forming of such an establishment is very expensive, and secondly, because the congregation of Konigsfeld is near the Baden lines, and two settlements so near together would be superfluous. It is however singular, that a few years afterwards the colony of Konigsfeld by an exchange of territory came within the States of Baden and that thus the desire of the Elector was finally gratified. We stayed in Herrnhut till the ninth of May; on which day we left the place for Gorlitz, where a number of patients were waiting for me. Gorlitz is a very pleasant and flourishing city, situated in a fruitful plain, watered by the river Neisse. The splendid church of St. Peter and Paul is celebrated far and wide for its large and elegant organ its immense bell and subteranean church; the rising of the sun over the Giant-mountains is a noble sight when viewed from the city. At a small distance toward South-West is the Landscrone, a solitary mountain, which does not appear to be of great height and yet is seen from every rising ground in Lusatia. Gorlitz was to me an interesting place on another account. The celebrated Jacob Bœhm was a citizen of this town. I was delighted to find, that he was still remembered by his townsmen; they are proud, that he was a citizen of their town, though he died near two hundred years ago, and in his life-time was cruelly persecuted by the clergy and particularly by the Pastor Primarius Gregorius Richter. Bœhm teaches nothing in his publications in contradiction to the Augsburg confession, he was a constant attendant on divine service and came frequently to the Lord's table; in his walk and conversation he was blameless; he was a faithful subject; an exemplary father of his family, and a kind neighbor; and yet a proud

D d d

priesthood treated him as an incorrigible heretic. One morning he came to Pastor Richter on some business; as he entered the door, Richter threw his slipper at his head; but Boehm took it quietly up, and carried it to its owner. When he died in 1624, the ministers of the city would not allow him to be buried in the church-yard; the case was brought before the high-consistory at Dresden, which ordered, that the corpse should be buried with all christian honors, and that the clergy should follow it in procession. The church-yard in which Boehm is buried lies on the North-side of the city, his grave is marked by a small square, hewn stone, on which is engraved the year of his birth, his name and the day and year of his death. A private gentleman of Gorlitz told me, that during one of his walks he observed two Englishmen, filling their snuff-boxes with soil from Boehm's grave, which circumstance induced him to put a new stone on it, as the old one was much defaced.

We received many marks of attention and friendship in this pleasant city, and I had many opportunities of serving suffering humanity. After a stay of six days we went to Niesky a considerable settlement of the Brethren, in which place they have established their Theological Seminary. I became here acquainted with many excellent and learned men, and other interesting members of the brethren's congregation. The next day I rode about six miles into the country to perform an operation on a nobleman; on this excursion I saw the highest point of the Giant-mountains, called the Shnakuppe at a distance before me; it appears to me however, that the Blauen at the upper end of the Black Forest is much higher, than either the Broken or the Shnakuppe and yet are the mountains of the Black Forest merely hills in comparison with the Alps of Switzerland. During my stay at Niesky we received an invitation from a neighboring nobleman, to spend a few days with him in order to give me an opportunity of performing an operation on an old, blind woman, belonging to his estate. On the evening of our arrival the lady of the nobleman took my arm, and led me through several hilly orchards to a pleasant cabin at the end of the village; in a dark room on a chair sat an aged woman, who was totally blind.

"Good evening, mother," said the countess, "God sends you a friend, through whose instrumentality you may recover your sight."

The woman hastily rose from the chair, stretched her hands out, endeavoring at the same time to take a few steps forward.—"Where are you, angel of God," she exclaimed.—The countess kissed her and said, sit down, mother, here is some medicine, which you must take to morrow, and the next day I shall come again with this friend, who will open your eyes. After I too had spoken a few words of comfort to the aged peasant, we returned home. On the appointed day in the morning the countess and I went again to her, and I performed the operation.; when it was done I placed her with. her open eyes before the countess. But such moments are indescribable.—It was a feeble representation of that scene, which I shall soon behold in full glory, when I a poor sinner, shall appear before *him*, and shall with open eyes see *him* as he is. With tears of joy the countess embraced the happy woman before we returned home. The cure was eminently successful. In the most delicate manner the countess presented me with the sum of two hundred Dollars, which she had destined for that purpose.—Happy art thou now, my friend, in the mansions of the blessed, after thy pilgrimage through this vale of tears! Enjoy thy rest in the arms of thy Savior, soon we shall meet again!

. . . After a stay of nine days at Niesky, we went to Kleinwelke where I was thronged with business. On the twenty-ninth of May we returned to Herrnhut to attend the minister's-conference for which I had received an. invitation. A description of this singular and useful institution is worth the reader's attention. It was exactly fifty years, since Bishop Reichel had first proposed such a society; this venerable servant of God was still living and able to assist in celebrating the Jubilee of this ministerial conference. On the thirtieth of May about seventy ministers of the two Protestant confessions assembled at Herrnhut from the adjoining provinces. All ministers of the gospel are admitted, and it matters not, whether they are in connection with the Moravian church or not. Candidates of the ministry are likewise

occasionally admitted, but no laymen, without special permission.
At eight o'clock in the morning the meeting is opened with singing and prayer. The conversations do not embrace scientific
subjects, but the official duties of the minister, and the most suitable manner of performing them, the walk and conversation of
ministers and their people, and particularly the manner in which
the pure doctrines of practical christianity may be preserved and
spread. . ....

Letters not only from all the different countries of Europe
but from every quarter of the globe are addressed to this ministerial conference; as it is impossible, to read them all in one day,
the most important are selected and read; observations are
made on their contents, and they are afterwards answered.
The transactions of the day are minuted, and these minutes are communicated to the distant members and friends
of the Brethren's church. The celebration of the Jubilee made
this yearly meeting of the conference peculiarly interesting, the
two Bishops, Reichel and Rissler, were present, who had been actively engaged in the service of the church, before count Zin-
zendorf's decease, and who had been to Asia, Africa and America in the service of the Lord. The former as original founder
of the institution and Pastor Baumeister from Herrnhut opened
the session with some short addresses full of unction. . . . .

The next morning we started for Dresden by way of Klein-
welke, Ponnewitz, Konigsbruk and Hermsdorf. and arrived there
June the fourth.—At Wurtzen, Leipzig, Erfurt and Cassel, I had
to perform many operations for the cataract, and was consulted
by a number of patients, suffering from diseases of the eye. At
Cassel I learnt with joyful astonishment, that the Elector of
Baden had given to my son-in-law Schwartz a Professorship of
Theology at Hidleberg, and that he had accepted the call. Though
I had taken no step to induce the Elector to call Schwartz and
it was my determination never to make use of any influence I
might have with his Highness for the recommendation of any
one and especially of a child or near relation, yet it was very satisfactory to me, and I thanked God with all my heart, that his
kind Providence had led my two eldest children with their families

into my neighborhood, and that they were so well provided for.

At Marburg, where I was obliged to make a stay of several days, Schwartz came to see me; he gave me a particular history of his call, and we conversed long on its importance. On the fourth of July we arrived at Hidleberg in the enjoyment of health, enriched with temporal and spiritual blessings. We likewise found our little Christine completely restored. All these circumstances tuned our hearts to praise our heavenly guide and protector.

During our long and dangerous journey Providence had so graciously protected us, that no misfortune had come nigh us, on the contrary, he had loaded us with loving-kindness and blessings innumerable. With a cheerful heart would I enter into a detailed narrative of these favors, as well as of the edifying conversations with so many dear children of God, but the fear of being misunderstood bids me to be silent, and I shall therefore say no more on the subject but that this journey has been highly profitable to me and Eliza for our advancement in practical piety.

Our stay at Hidleberg did not last long at this time; the Elector sent one day for me to dine with him—which he frequently used to do—and during dinner spoke to me as follows: "Dear friend, I am soon going to Baden for a few weeks, to which place you must accompany me, for I wish to have you in my neighborhood. I replied: "Your Electoral Highness need only speak the word; but in reality I was frightened at this address, for whence should I be able to defray the expenses of my stay for several weeks at such a celebrated bathing place. My last journey had indeed added some hundred guilders to my stock, but these I would want for the coming winter; but I soon recollected myself by calling my old symbolum to mind: "The Lord will provide." After dinner the Elector took me into his cabinet and handed me three hundred guilders with these words: "This is intended for your stay at Baden."

My occupation in the mean time consisted in continuing my correspondence, in writing a number of the "Grey Man" and the "Christian friend of man," besides attending to many operations and consultations of patients.

On the 21st of July I went to Baden in company of our friend Julia, my wife, our little Christine and my niece Mary, who was to wait upon us. The bath proved very salutary to my wife, Julia and Christine. Carolina remained at Hidleberg as housekeeper with Frederick and Amalia. Baden is a very ancient bathing place, celebrated as such even since the days of the Romans; it is situated in a charming valley and is a very pleasant place of abode, it is twenty-one miles distant from Carlsruhe and six from Rastadt; the valley runs in a north-westerly direction, and is watered by the river Ohse, which is important to the inhabitants as a means of transporting their wood to the Rhine. The horizon is bounded by the lofty and pointed mountains of the Black Forest, at the foot of which on both sides of the valley fruitful hills, covered with gardens, vine-yards and fields delight the eye. On the South-side of one of these hills, which lie towards the North, the town of Baden is built, and on the summit of the hill stands the palace, in which the Margraves of Baden resided previous to the founding of the town of Rastadt. Through the wide opening of the valley towards the North-west your view extends over the charming plains of the Grand-dutchy of Baden and the rich country of Alsace; the romantic Vogesian mountains close the horizon in that direction, and the majestic, glittering river Rhine winds through the broad valley, like a silver ribbon thrown over a variegated field of flowers. When in mid-summer the sun sets behind the Vogesian mountains, and illumines with his setting rays the valley of Baden up to the summits of the Black-Forest, a prospect presents itself to the eye which undoubtedly is to be reckoned among the first beauties of nature, but it must be seen, it cannot be described. The air is so pure and balsamic in this charming valley, that many persons come hither merely to breathe the air, without using the baths.

My readers will doubtless believe, that I was not one of those bathing guests, who come hither merely for amusement and to enjoy themselves once a year ; for which there is otherwise every possible opportunity.

I was occupied in the same manner as at home in answering the letters of my friends, writing religious works, and performing operations of the eye, however I did not neglect, to walk as often as the weather would permit into this garden of God, to listen to the voice of eternal love not audible to every ear. Gradually also a circle of friends of religion gathered round us, in which we were at home, and who enjoyed with us the blessings of nature.

In this place I wrote the first pocket-book for the year 1805 ; which contains the portrait of the Elector of Baden, but unfortunately it is not a good likeness. That prince had his abode at his summer palace called the Favorite about six miles from the town of Baden ; where I frequently visited him.

Towards the end of the month of August I was again called upon to undertake a journey. Pastor Faber at Gaisburg in the neighborhood of Stuttgart, who had been afflicted with the cataract wished me to remove it. — —

THUS FAR DR. YUNG HAS WRITTEN HIS OWN LIFE, THE RE-
MAINDER IS SUPPLIED BY HIS GRAND-SON.

The active and useful life of Dr. John Henry Yung, called Stilling, has become generally known by his own description to believers in Jesus as a striking testimony of the paternal Providence of God. He has forbidden us to publish a continuation of it; we shall therefore in these pages confine ourselves to a narrative of the occurrences of the last days of his illness to the moment of his departure.

My venerable grand-father began to feel in the commencement of the year 1816 a considerable decrease of bodily strength and vigor, being then in the seventy-seventh year of his age. His children, grand-children and friends observed with apprehension his gradually increasing debility and far and near many a fervent prayer arose to the throne of God for a longer continuance of his life. God in his mercy heard our prayers and granted us the blessings of his society longer than we had dared to hope. Several excursions which he made to visit his children at Hidleberg, at Baden and Rastadt seemed to invigorate his constitution, so that he was able in the course of that summer to restore sight to seventeen persons who were afflicted with the cataract. But the incessant attacks of cramp in the stomach and pain in his side, which he ascribed, together with a certain organic defect, to a fall from a coach some twenty years since, had reduced him so much, that he was confined to his bed since the beginning of the winter of 1816—1817 ; notwithstanding the recourse to strong and powerful medicines. From this time he was no longer able to continue his correspondence, though the most important letters were still answered through the medium of his children, but when dictation became too burdensome, he was obliged to leave all letters unanswered. However this was not his only cause of grief, he deeply sympathized in the sufferings of his beloved wife, who had been afflicted for many years by a spasmodic affection in her neck, to which now were added a severe pain in her breast and ulcers on her lungs. The venerable couple suffered with pious resignation to the will of Providence, the sight of which, though highly edifying, was frequently heart-rending to their friends and relatives.

Now and then his vital vigor seemed to return ; during such seasons he attempted to continue those labors, which most required his attention. but his hand soon sunk under the infirmities of the body. It was during some of his more cheerful hours, that he commenced writing his Old Age as far as it has been published. His feeble body permitted him to do no more, and he prohibited his friends from giving the continuation. What he has written of his old age, is sufficient for the reader to become acquainted with his external circumstances in the latter days of his life, and at the same time to admire his strength of mind at so advanced a period. What we shall say here of his latter days, is not to be considered so much a continuation of his history, as a testimony for the truth of the christian faith, and at the same time it is intended to fulfil the wishes of his friends, who desired to obtain a knowledge of the last hours of his earthly pilgrimage.

In the commencement of the winter, when he received the last number of his Biblical narratives and his golden Treasure from the press, he observed with visible joy: "Well, I have been enabled to finish my Biblical history." Towards Christmas the weakness of our venerable grand-father and the disease of our grand-mother increased so much, that we could not hope to keep them much longer with us. They endeavored to disencumber themselves from every temporal care, and to prepare for their journey to their eternal home. In the mean time God granted us the enjoyment of their endearing presence a few months longer; for in the beginning of the year 1817 both gained strength, so that they were sometimes able to leave their bed. When our grand-mother affectionately expressed her concern for her husband, he replied: "I am perfectly satisfied with whatever may happen; whether God pleases, that I shall continue in activity or not." This complete resignation to the will of his heavenly Father he manifested to the end. Once in a severe paroxysm of the cramp he exclaimed: "God has led me from my youth by his kind Providence, I will not murmur, but glorify him likewise in my sufferings!"

His mind during his last illness was constantly occupied with subjects relating to the kingdom of God ; these formed his favorite conversations with his wife, children and friends, and for the same reason he read with indescribable satisfaction the work of Kanne: "Lives and reminiscences from the lives of awakened christians" and that of Shubert: "Old and New things from practical Psychology." Once he said in reference to these works: "These men have been chosen by Providence as powerful instruments of much good in the present century." When he had read Blumhardts "Magazine for the latest history of Protestant Missionary and Bible societies ;" and we conversed with him concerning the extension of the kingdom of God in our times, he observed: "I am rejoiced, and it is a source of consolation in my old age to be informed of the spread of religion." He spent the greater portion of his time in reading religious works, and especially in the perusal of the holy scripture, which was the constant companion of his bedside, he also delighted in the singing of hymns. Thus occupied he never felt the misery of languor and ennui. It was seldom his weak-

E e e

ness would permit him to converse with his friends and family, but on such occasions he manifested the same cheerfulness, which had always made his conversation so interesting and agreeable in every circle of social life. At such times he delighted to converse about his youth and frequently with spoke affection of his relatives in the countries of the lower Rhine. He did not like to hear of his recovery. On a young lady observing, that it was reasonable to hope, the milder season of spring would recruit his strength, he said : "Don't say so, for I cannot bear to think that my friends should be disappointed." To the physician he frequently said, "I feel the approach of death." His favorite recreation was singing accompanied by instrumental music; when his children and other young friends sung, tears would steal down his cheeks. As the diseases of the venerable couple required different temperatures, he was removed from the room occupied by his wife, but visited her for some time daily, and was either supported to her bed-side or rolled in an arm-chair; and it was a great satisfaction for the friends to listen to their edifying conversation. As he had always shown by his walk as well as by his numerous publications, notwith-standing the extensive learning, he had acquired, that he was persuaded, the knowledge of Jesus Christ far surpasses all other, so he confirmed this sentiment a short time before his end, when we were speaking of the effect of his publications, by saying: "For our knowledge, our capability of expressing our ideas acceptably to the public, and such like gifts, we are in-debted to Divine Providence ; and there will be no question con-cerning these things before the throne of God. But their ap-plication, and the small portion of humility and faith we possess will be imputed to us for righteousness through the grace of God." We might quote many declarations of his, indicative of his love of activity and of his faith in Jesus Christ, were it not for the fear of becoming too prolix. Besides it is known to all, that our venerable father praised and glorified the Redeemer by his walk and conversation, as well as by his publications, and that he in connection with other worthy men, was chosen a distin-guished instrument of divine grace for the support of religion during times of infidelity and false illumination.

As spring approached the symptoms of dissolution became more and more alarming in regard to both our parents. But they with great self denial, being perfectly resigned to the will of the Lord, strove to hide their sufferings and their increasing weakness from their friends, though it was impossible to mislead us in that respect. Our mother departed in the Lord on the twenty-second of March, in consequence of the breaking of ulcers on her lungs. Two days previous to her death, her venerable husband, well aware as a physician, that her end was approaching. had taken an affectionate leave of her, by reciting some suitable verses, and closed with these words: "May the Lord bless thee, thou suffering angel! May the Lord be with thee!" When he received the intelligence, that she was gone, he folded his hands, and raised his eyes towards heaven with this exclamation: "God be praised she has finished her course!" From this time his thoughts were more and more engaged with things pertaining to the spiritual world, he preferred being alone, well aware, that the departure of his wife was a summons to himself. When we were mourning in his presence on account of her death he observed: "I cannot mourn as you do, expecting to see her soon again." The pious wish he had expressed in a poem composed at the time of his marriage with Eliza, in which he says:

> At the close of life's short journey
> Father! lead us hand in hand
> Through the terrors of Death's valley
> To the promised land.

was almost literally fulfilled. The decline of his bodily strength was apparent to all, though the vigor of his mind remained unimpaired and his eyes retained their brightness to the last moment of his life. This full possession of his mental powers enabled him at times to enter with his friends into conversations on philosophical subjects. Thus he observed once to a friend : "I must tell you something of great importance, which belongs to Pneumatology. It appears to me, that I can discern a twofold nature in myself. a spiritual and a carnal. The spiritual rises above the carnal. Both principles are striving with each other in man, and only by means of a full and complete mortification of every sensual appetite is it possible that the connection between them can be broken. However our own strength is inadequate to the task it requires the assistance of God." Every conversation, which had not God and the measures he had taken for the salvation of man for its subject, or with which it was at least not seasoned, was disagreeable to him; and in reference to this he said : "I have felt no ennui since the commencement of my illness unto the death of my wife, but since she is gone, time passes heavily. For he also longed to be home, to be liberated from every earthly thought and care. For more than six months, previous to his death, he had loathed every kind of solid food, notwithstanding the exertions of the most skilful physicians to restore the tone of the stomach, and as the symptoms of the dropsy in his breast became daily more alarming it was easy to foresee, that we would enjoy his presence among us but a few days longer.

In this situation he one day said to a female friend : "I shall now very soon depart!" and to her observation : "O how happy are you, to be able to say so," he answered, "Well, I am glad that you know and feel this truth."

Learning that his end was approaching, we were determined notwithstanding our grief, to improve every moment of his presence for our edification and for the strengthening of our faith. For if his life and conversation ever exercised this blessed influence, it was particularly the case on his death-bed, while he waited for the moment of his departure with a wonderful presence and peace of mind, and as a faithful christian glorified Christ in the very agonies of death by his filial resignation to the will of God, who visibly strengthened and supported him. The close of his life was an evidence of the truth of the christian religion; for no Deist or Rationalist can depart this life with that peace and serenity of mind with which this advanced christian died, if he is in possession of a similar strength of mind and consciousness, as our departed father preserved to the last moments of his life. To the honor of the cause therefore, which he defended and to the glory of God I feel myself called upon, to give to the world a description of his last days, and to make known the most important declarations, which he made during that time, according to the testimony of his friends and particularly of the attending physician.

Feeling the approach of death he desired once more to see all his children, but was soon after troubled with the idea, that they might neglect some official duty on his account, and therefore observed when he found, that they stayed longer than usual : "I know my departure is delayed longer than you expected, you will neglect your business too much, go attend to your calling." Having obtained satisfaction on this subject, he permitted one of his children to remain with and constantly attend him. For until now he had used a bell, when he wished to call one of the family from an adjoining room, as he was fond of being alone. His frequent inquiry after the hour during the last two days of his life, proves, that he was anxiously desirous of reaching his eternal home. During the night of the 80th of March he spoke a great deal with his youngest son of his approaching death, which he had never done before, and supposing his dissolution was near at hand, desired him towards break of day to call his brothers and sisters. However he once more revived and requested his friends to fill a pipe for him. The nature of his disease—Dropsy in the breast—had created much difficulty in breathing and a distressing cough; but all these symptoms left him the day before his death. He did not speak much and what he said, was in broken sentences; yet always with perfect consciousness : he slept very little, when he did, it was a light slumber from which he awoke at the most trifling noise in the room. To one of his daughters he observed: "I think, I have passed through the agonies of death, for me-thinks, I am in a desert and yet I feel very comfortable." But she supposing he meant, that all his bodily sufferings were over, and expressing herself to that purpose, he corrected her by replying : "No, No, I'll have yet to pass through many sufferings." It appears also from a declaration he made to another of his daughters, who was conversing with him about death, that the true christian doth not face death either with levity or temerity, for he observed: "It is an important thing to die, it is no trifle!" And at another time he said : "Eternity is a strange thing." From this declaration we may observe, that the transit from the present life to that which is to come, and the approaching day of accounts may appear very serious and important to a man, who has spent his strength in the service of God, and who frequently had the brightest prospects of futurity.

It had been customary with him through life, to speak much during his sleep, this he continued during his last illness; and he was afraid lest he should say something unbecoming the christian. Therefore he once said to one of his daughters : "Since Eliza's death I feel no longer at home, and I am afraid, I talk foolish things during my sleep!" When she replied, that this was not so, that on the contrary he said nothing but what was edifying; he remarked : "This is truly a grace from God." The expressions which fell from his lips during his sleep, were generally such, as: "God has led me through life with inexpressible kindness"—The Lord bless you—&c. As his debility increased, he spoke less in his sleep, and even when awake expressed his kindly feelings less by words than by affectionate looks. When he saw, how anxious we all were, to serve him, he often said: "O my dear children! I give you a vast deal of trouble!" or: "O my dear children! your kindness and love to me affect me greatly, for your sake I hope I shall not die in a paroxysm." He had reference to a certain sickness of the stomach, which was occasioned by the accumulation of humors in his breast; and in allusion to this he repeatedly said: "It is a sad thing to die by suffocation, but it must be so! His study from which so many blessings to the christian world came, and which was adorned with pictures, engravings and tokens of remembrance from his friends, was likewise his sick-room ; his bed was encircled with beautiful flowers in pots. He was paticularly fond of them. One day he said to his youngest son, whose business it was to nurse them: "Look my dear son, at those beautiful flowers, and yonder (pointing to some pictures on the opposite wall) those lovely heads of children." During the night of the last of March he spoke a great deal with me of my parents, brothers and sisters at Hidleberg, as also of my ministerial office. Afterwards he desired a glass of fresh water, which he drank with peculiar relish, and spoke of it with rapture the next day to his daughters. Towards break of day he desired his youngest son to fill a pipe for him, which he appeared really to enjoy. On the morning of the first of April having called his children and grand-children, who were in the house, to his bed-side, he exhorted us as follows: "Dear children, seek vital piety; people often imagine, that no more is needed, than to attend church and partake of the communion, but that won't do, you must surrender yourselves wholly to God, submit cheerfully to the dispensations of his Providence, hold unceasing communion with him and be constant in prayer." He then repeated with much feeling the following verse from the Halle Hymn-book : Hymn 11. v. 12.

I'll glory in nothing but only in Jesus,
Who suffered and died from sin to redeem us,
He shall be my refuge, to him I'll cleave ever,
Thus nothing shall ever my soul from him sever.

When he heard one of his daughters inquire of her sister, where this verse could be found, he handed the Halle Hymnbook to his second daughter, bid her mark some of the most beautiful hymns, and let the children in the institution commit them, observing : "Memorize a great many hymns and passages of scripture, you'll find them a consolation in time to come. When afterwards the conversation turned upon certain of his friends, he said : "Tell these dear friends, that I frequently thought of them in my last days, that I love them, and that when we next meet, we will have materials enough for conversation; and to a friend, who had visited him the evening before, he observed: I should like to talk a great deal with you, but I am too weak now ; however the time will soon come when we can converse without weakness." On that day many friends came to see him for the last time with the hope of being edified by his lively faith and perfect resignation in his sufferings. Many hearts were drawn heavenward by his conversation and were ready to exclaim: Let me die the death of the righteous, and let my latter end be like his !

When he saw his friends looking in at the half open door, opposite his bed, he would manifest his love to them by a friendly nod and when he happened to feel sufficiently strong, would say a few words to each. That affectionate, lively disposition, which he had manifested throughout his life, and which had made him many friends, did not forsake him even on his death-bed. For instance, when on the day previous to that of his death he observed a certain female friend look in at the door, he said : "Mrs. R—— looks through the key-hole." Towards noon another female friend having expressed her satisfaction, for having become acquainted with him, spoke of his clear mind, which the Lord had given him, to which he replied : "You ought not to praise me." To the same friend he afterwards said : In my youth I once owned a flute, which dropt out of my hands and broke ; and though its cost exceeded not twelve kreuzers (about one shilling) I wept almost incessantly for two days, but at that time, money was very scarce. To another friend he said : Tell me, what have the reviewers been able to effect with all their severity ? About this time he sent for me and inquired, how the Jubilee of the Reformation would be celebrated ? and when I told him, that I was convinced it would be celebrated with great solemnity, he expressed himself perfectly satisfied. The watches which hung near his bed he had hitherto wound up himself and he likewise daily put in order the drawer of the small table, which stood before his bedside, and this love of order did not forsake him in the last hours of his life. He even took notice of the wilted flowers on his table, and ordered them to be exchanged for fresh ones, and named the kind of flowers he wished them to bring. As his lips and throat were swollen, he asked for a glass-tube, gave direction of what length it ought to be, and wishing to express his satisfaction at this mode of taking his drink, said facetiously : "In using the tube even the douaniers in my throat perceive nothing of my drinking. Towards evening he again frequently slumbered, and once when he awoke, observed to his daughters, "I always think it is morning. Well, on the other side of the grave I hope the sun will rise !" When his second daughter brought him a bou-

quet of flowers which her pupils had collected, and said : "Dear
father, the children send you these flowers:" he replied with un-
affected simplicity : "The dear children ! They too are like the
tender flowers which willingly unfold themselves to the genial influence of the sun."

Towards six o'clock he conversed with his physician on his
situation and about the excellency of the water in a well at
Baden called the Herrenbrunnen. Soon afterwards his oldest
son Jacob arrived from Rastadt. The conversation turning
on the departure of his mother, and her present happiness, my grand-father replied : "On this subject we cannot
say much, she is now past suffering, and I must yet continue to
be active or suffer." Afterwards when I observed, that the li-
lies of the valley, which were in a glass on his table, were very
beautiful flowers, and one of his daughters remarked: Dear father, you will soon behold beauties of a higher order, he replied:
"We cannot know, but feel it." After a while he said :
"Though I love you all dearly, yet a separation does not grieve
me ;" and when his eldest son said : "The reason is because
you love the Lord Jesus more than us, he answered: "Yes, that is
the cause." The same son he afterwards admonished in these
words : Remain steadfast in the faith, for that faith hath never
led me astray, it will likewise guide you to the desired haven,
and to this faith we will cleave to the end!" and added, "Abide
in love, dear angels!" and when one of his daughters observed:
you, dear father, are our angel, he replied: "We will be angels to
each other." During these conversations night came on, and he
slept at intervals, but whenever he awoke, and felt strong enough
for conversation, he cheerfully discoursed with those who happened to be present. Once he said : "It would have been well,
if our Redeemer could have had such drink to refresh him in his
sufferings as I have, but they gave him vinegar, mocked and de-
rided him, and he said : "Father forgive them, for they know
not, what they do." This is the most sublime prayer, that ever
has been uttered." Then he prayed thus : "Father, if it is in
accordance with thy holy will, that I shall still remain here,
give me strength that I may willingly labor and suffer." When
one of his daughters remarked, how uncomfortable you lie ; he

replied : "Do not say so, our Lord's situation was worse than mine." When the night lamp was brought, he said : "I shall not want it, I shall travel all night." Towards morning he told some of his children : "I have been very much engaged in my dream with my departed Eliza, afterwards the grey man appeared and told me, I should not trouble myself about my wife, she was happy, he had led her himself from one step to another, but you must wait." Soon afterwards he expressed himself as follows : "I feel a tranquility of mind, which I cannot describe, and I doubt whether you can observe it in the midst of my bodily sufferings." Sometimes his weakness increased so much, that he was unable to speak coherently, but he again recovered and the tranquility of his mind became visible in his countenance, and in this state he felt sufficient strength to commend his family and friends in a fervent prayer to the Lord, and besought him to preserve all his children in the faith of Christ Jesus, to keep them as branches united to him the vine, that after the lapse of thousands of years he might find them bound up in the bundle of life. On the second of April early in the morning when he felt that his end was approaching, and that he was departing to the Fatner,—feeling himself sufficiently strong for the performance of a last solemn act, he called us all around his bed, and having asked us whether we had aught against his present intention, and having received from us the assurance of our entire acquiescence and satisfaction, he ordered us to kneel down, uncovered his head, folded his hands and prayed thus in the full strength of his mind and faith : O thou! who hast shed thy blood for us on the tree of the cross, who hast conquered death and hell, and who didst pardon thine enemies, thou divine redeemer! pardon us, if we now dare to perform an act in our weakness, which under any other circumstance we would consider presumption !" He then took the plate on which he had broken the bread in pieces, pronounced the words of the institution and added: "And thou O Lord! bless this food likewise." Then he said : "Take and eat, this is his body, who hath tasted death for our sins." Thus we all partook of the sacred feast, deeply affected by the solemnity of this aged christian, who almost in the moment of his departure celebrated with his family the covenant of love. And after having expressed the wish that his children at Hidleberg might also be present, he took his usual drinking cup and said : "Drink ye all of it, it is the cup of the New Testament in his blood, which is shed for you and for many for the remission of sins ; and having drank of it last of all, he stretched forth his hands to bless us and exclaimed : "The Lord be with you!" Having finished this solemn act. according to pure evangelical principles on his death-bed as a christian Patriarch, he lay down to slumber, and the peace of his soul shone bright in the countenance of this hero of faith.

From this time his weakness continually increased, and the spasms became so violent that we feared, every moment would be his last. It was heart-rending to behold the venerable christian in his agony folding his hands and raising his eyes to heaven, supposing that the next moment would deprive him of life. In this situation nothing remained for us, but to pray that God would grant our dear father an easy passage through the dark valley of death. When the paroxysms returned, he prayed: Lord, receive me into thine everlasting habitations ! and again when he found it difficult to regain his breath after a paroxysm, he stretched his arm towards heaven, and exclaimed : "Away ! away !" In the mean time his friends were engaged in moistening his lips and palate with refreshing drinks; and in taking them his love of cleanliness and order was perceptible to the last. In one of his spasmodic paroxysms he prayed : "Grant strength, thou conqueror of death!" His eyes were during all this time resting upon his children and grand-children, who surrounded his bed, either engaged in mental prayer or in active services, and endeavoring to sooth the dying moments of their father by every means in their power, and if one of us left the bed to procure any thing for him, he would cast an anxious glance after him and say : "None of you must leave me." When he had observed, that we were mourning and deeply affected by his sufferings, he exhorted us to patience. To a friend who came in the morning to his bed and said : "He, who suffered on the cross, will aid you in obtaining the victory," he answered : Yes, I have no doubt of it." And when that friend pronounced the verse :

> What happiness, what joy and happiness
> Shall we above possess,
> When we adore him, with angels bow before him
> And see his face—what happiness !

he replied : "Yea and Amen."

But gradually the mournfully solemn moment was approaching. This christian was to drink the cup of trial to the dregs, for a glorious testimony to the world.—It was the middle of the sacred week.* With his Savior he went to meet his death and consummation. In looking at his face beaming with dignity and love, we could truly exclaim : "O death ! where is thy sting, O grave! where is thy victory! but thanks be to God, who has given him the victory, through his Lord Jesus Christ!"

While he was in the agonies of death his solemn but sweet looks were frequently directed towards us and more than once he exclaimed: "Persevere in prayer!" which of course we did not omit.

As long as possible we moistened his parched palate with refreshing drinks, till he said: "Let it alone, I can no more swallow." Frequently during his paroxysms he stammered forth such words of supplication as these to the hearer of prayer: "Lord cut off the thread of life!" and then again: "Father receive my spirit!" and we believed the last moment had come— but his constitution was so strong, that he once more revived, which gave him an opportunity to prepare for the last shock ; he cast one last look upon the picture of the child Jesus in the arms of his mother, which was hanging opposite his bed; his eyes became glazed, he closed them with his whole strength, while we stood breathless around him, persevering in prayer— the cramp dreadfully distorted the traits of the sufferer, once or twice it seemed as if the noble mien of our father would be des-

---

*The week before Easter during which in German churches the sufferings of the Saviour form more particularly than at other seasons the subject of public discourses as well as of pious meditations.

troyed in the agonies of death, but behold—it returned, we again discovered the dignity and serenity of his venerable countenance: about noon his breath ceased, the christian had conquered, his faith was his victory.

His departing soul left her tenement of clay impressed with all its own sweetness, purity and dignity. Christians of all ranks lamented the loss of the departed and prayed to God for a similar consummation of their faith.

On earth there is mourning, deep mourning for the sainted benefactor, adviser, friend and father, but in heaven there is joy among the blessed, and his redeemed soul sings eternal Hallelujahs before the throne of God !

Stilling's Hymn of praise.

O thou, who in the realms of heaven
The fate of all thy creatures weigh'st,
Whom myriads of worlds have given
And give the off'ring, thou deserv'st ;
Surrounded by Seraphic praises
And shining with celestial light,
Amidst the lays, which heaven raises,
Spurn not th' oblations of thy child.

Earth, hear in silence ! listen heaven !
And roaring thunder, cease thy voice !
A song of praise shall now be given
To him, in whom I will rejoice:
Ye Seraphs, in the heav'nly mansion,
O teach me your triumphant lays !
I'll sing my Savior's condescension
To me, a worm, in all my ways.

O God of love and great compassion!
From Thee my soul shall ne'er depart.
Accept, I pray! with satisfaction
The off'rings of a grateful heart.
What was I, when Thy love did call me,
And took me from the miry clay?
A peasant boy—but I obey'd Thee,
And night was turned into day.

Thy mercy chose me an example
Of Thy kind Providence and Grace!
My heart and soul be hence Thy temple
To Thee I dedicate my days!
My life shall hence confess Thee ever,
O grant me strength to keep my vow!
No trials shall from Thee me sever
Where is a friend, as kind as Thou?

Thou source of life and every blessing!
Thine eye beheld my poverty:
In troubles great and soul-distressing
Thou pitied'st and redeemedst me!
Thou heardst the father's supplication,
The mother's sigh escap'd Thee not:
Thou spak'st: I'll answer your petition,
Thy mercy changed my humble lot.

Through trials, all who will obey Thee
Must enter in the realms of light
My burden too Thou didst assign me,
To bear through troubled scenes of night.
Appointing at that early season
The sphere of my activity;
And shewing to astonish'd reason
The rugged path awaiting me.

An angel from the realms of heaven
Receives command concerning me ;
The crown, to blessed Spirits given
He lays aside in mystery ,
He seem'd a stranger to kind pity,
His heart from tender feelings free,
A judgment angel without mercy
He doubtless destin'd was to be.

With angel's faithfulness he led me
Through all the chequered scenes of youth :
I follow'd him with fear—but ready—
To do his stern commands of truth.
Sometimes through thorny tracts he guides me,
I follow him with wounded feet :
Sometimes a stormy sea receives me,
This fate from day to day I meet.

Sometimes a doubtful, distant glimmer
Of hope, with joy inspired me,
That soon the hand of my Redeemer
Would suffer me the goal to see:
But suddenly my guide's direction
Points out another craggy path
And heedless of my supplication
Bids me, push on ! in dread of wrath.

Amidst these trials sore distressing
A heavy load of debt I bore ;
And in my path with grief progressing
The deepest gloom oppress'd me sore.
No Zephyr cheer'd the weary trav'ler
With cooling stream of kindly air ;
No friend in need became my buckler
Against the shafts of dread despair.

Thus I pursu'd in sadness over
My path without a pity'ng friend !
But suddenly Thy Grace and Favor
Brought all my troubles to an end.
My guide, no longer sternly frowning
Reliev'd my shoulders from the load,
He took it, with kind pity smiling,
And rolled it in oblivion's flood.

With lighter steps though faint and weary
I pass'd along my rugged way :
Until at length a ray of glory
Announc'd to me approaching day !
It came, it came, the joyful morning,
I had at length attain'd the goal
No anxious cares my heart were gnawing,
Rejoice in triumph, O my soul !

Ye angels, in the realms of heaven !
Join me in songs of praise on earth !
Until the crown to me is given
To conqu'rors promis'd over death,
When I shall join *your* blessed choir
Before Jehovah's sacred throne,
And strike the strings of heaven's lyre
In tunes to mortal worms unknown !

Till then, may peace from heav'n's fair mansion
Pour strength and comfort in my heart !
To conquer every sinful passion
Arising through corruption's art.
Meanwhile I'll sow, in hopes of reaping
In yonder realms,—the seed of tears,
And on the Savior's word relying
I bid adieu to all my fears.

CPSIA information can be obtained
at www.ICGtesting.com
Printed in the USA
BVOW06s0845111017
497376BV00007B/25/P